Gender Identity in International Law

Gender Identity in International Law:

A Certain Inconvenience

By

Alessandra Asteriti

Cambridge Scholars
Publishing

Gender Identity in International Law: A Certain Inconvenience

By Alessandra Asteriti

This book first published 2024

Cambridge Scholars Publishing

Lady Stephenson Library, Newcastle upon Tyne, NE6 2PA, UK

British Library Cataloguing in Publication Data
A catalogue record for this book is available from the British Library

ISBN (10): 1-0364-0550-8
ISBN (13): 978-1-0364-0550-2

Jerry, just remember. It's not a lie... if you believe it.
'George Costanza,' Seinfeld.

TABLE OF CONTENTS

PREFACE

This book is five years in the making. The day in April 2019 when I dared tweet that women have sex-based rights was a day that was going to change my life, though I did not know it then. I thought I had said something obvious, banal even. But I knew already that for some reason my colleagues had become eerily silent about this obvious fact. What happened next is a matter of public record.[1] The usual litany of online abuse, death threats sent to my university email account, calls for me to be fired, disciplined, silenced. There is nothing special in what happened to me, unfortunately. Many women suffered a worse fate. If there is one thing that I will not countenance is to be told what to think, so that day in April 2019 meant the beginning of five years of research. For five years I have read and researched all aspects of gender identity theory.

Although gender identity and trans rights seem to be everywhere, actually researching them in a scientific manner proved elusive. All the literature I accessed took for granted the existence of gender identity, without any objective evidence of it. Like sand, the more I tried to hold it, the more it escaped my grasp. Used to apply legal logic to propositions, I was faced with a plethora of logical fallacies. At times, I thought I may be losing my mind. Were my colleagues really serious when they said some men are women inside? Had they not thought of the legal, political and social consequences of such a proposition? Had they not realised how sexist it was to claim all women think and feel in a certain "feminine" way and that men can know and mimic this?

At times it felt really lonely work. Debating this issue was almost impossible. The "No debate" injunction silenced academics and made us

[1] And by this I mean that it was played out on social media, where I used my name and that the consequences were the source of some attention from German media, where I lived and worked at the time. The Frankfurter Allgemaine Zeitung published a largely sympathetic article on the phenomenon of cancel culture in academia using my story as an example: Thomas Thiel,"Ende einer Treibjagd," Frankfurter Allgemeine Zeitung, September 28, 2022, https://www.faz.net/aktuell/karriere-hochschule/hoersaal/cancel-culture-rufmord-kampagne-an-der-universitaet-lueneburg-18328668.html.

walk on eggshells on social media, where a pronoun could get you permanently suspended. Fortunately, I found a community of like-minded people, mostly women, with whom to share information, and to laugh and bond over the absurdity of it all. These women made these last five years endurable and enjoyable. They are too many to list, they know who they are and this book is dedicated to them.

The book is not dedicated to my academic colleagues, but it is addressed to them. I counted on them to ask and answer the questions I ask in this book, to engage, to debate, to argue and defend their position, if they had one. As I often quipped, lawyers who debated earnestly whether Jaffa Cakes were biscuit or cake, refused to answer the question "what is a woman." With very few exceptions, academics refused to engage on this issue, though some of them told me privately they agreed with me, but they could not say so publicly. Some wrote to me to tell me to stop talking. I dare say that they did not understand what academic freedom of speech is, and that it does not only grant us more latitude than the general public in expressing our opinion in the academic marketplace of ideas, but it enjoins us to use this freedom. It is not just a right. It is actually our job, for which we get paid, to research, without fear, and go where research takes us, not to lead research to the conclusions we want to reach.

The results of these five years of research are contained in this book. There is so much more that could be said, as gender identity theory is having an effect in almost all areas of public life, from sports, to prisons, to schools, to hospitals, to Lesbian, Gay and Bisexual (LGB) rights. The book focuses on the effect of gender identity theory on international institutions and international law more generally. It is not just a critique, but a plea to reframe this concept and give it its proper place in human rights law as a belief, not shared by all, and not to be imposed either as a form of social control or via legal rules. It seems an immense task, as gender identity has been embedded in international and domestic law and, more troublingly, has generated a whole new area of medicine, dedicated to the disruption of the physical and intellectual development of children on the basis of a presumed disconnect between mind and body, a suspicious distinction in medicine if there ever was one. Children are being reinforced in their delusion that their body is somehow wrong and in need of being fixed through a litany of medication and surgeries. Females are, as always, especially targeted. The female body has always been the locus of exploitation and othering, from Eve born out of the rib of Adam, all the way to the nullification of femaleness in girls barely old enough to know what their body is like, before they know what a female body is capable of doing.

I did not set out to write a book about feminist international law, but simply a book where international law is taken seriously and not bent out of shape to accommodate an ideology. And I speak about ideology not necessarily as a pejorative term, but simply to outline the difference between the claim that "some people" have a gender identity (a belief, or a theory) and the claim that "everyone" has a gender identity, even if they do not know it, or they disagree with the concept of gender identity (an ideology). The moment in which international law accepted as a definition the idea that all human beings have a gender identity, it transformed this theory into an ideology. The push to make this definition mandatory in social interactions and legislative acts risks transforming this concept from an ideological one to a totalitarian one. The fact that I cannot say *I* do not have a gender identity without receiving some form of abuse should make all academics stand up and take notice. Why is my belief in the idea of gender identities necessary for the protection of gender identities? International law does not require that beliefs are universally shared in order to grant individuals the right to hold them. It is a crucial principle, in human rights law, that only the right of people to hold a belief is protected, not the belief itself, and that human rights law does not impose on individuals the duty to respect any particular set of beliefs, but only to respect the right of people to hold them.

I did end up writing a sort of feminist international law book, in the sense that I always centred women in gender identity theory, to investigate the effects on women and girls of the momentous change demanded by gender identity theorists. I found out quite early on in my work that there are two reactions to any criticism of gender identity theory: the first one, that this theory does not affect women; in fact, we benefit from it (though no-one can really point to any such material benefit for women specifically); the second, it does affect women, but the disadvantage to women is worth it, because "transwomen" are the most oppressed women, and we "cis women" have cis privilege. We are supposed to believe that Iranian women killed for refusing to wear a veil, Afghan girls prevented from going to school, even newborn girls killed because of their sex, are privileged compared to Jennifer Pritzker, American billionaire who decided to "become a woman" at the age of 63. This work cannot help being a feminist book, in the sense that it refuses to see international law through the lens of gender identity theory. It refuses to un-see sex in order to elevate gender identity to prominence. I know there are many who will accuse me of not being a feminist because I am not a trans-inclusive feminist. This work is not an activist's work, so I do not have to prove what brand of feminism I support. It is a book about international law and its uneasy relationship with gender identity theory. It is not only about that, it is also a proposal to reframe this relationship on an altogether different basis, more firmly grounded on established principles and rules of international law.

Finally, the subtitle. "A Certain Inconvenience" is how the *Goodwin* Court described what society has to bear in order for transsexual people to enjoy their "rights." I cannot think of any other civil rights movement that is premised on the idea that their rights are an inconvenience for society at large. As it turns out, it is women who have to bear more than a certain inconvenience, as this book will show.

I am not going to name names in acknowledging and thanking people, not least because some of the women are still anonymous for their own safety. So I will thank the deeds. To those who supported me and made me laugh in these five years. To those who helped me in my work and who reassured me I was not going insane for holding on to reality. To all the feminists who rejected "Be kind" as their new slogan and their new command.

LIST OF ABBREVIATIONS

ACHR: African Court of Human Rights
APA: American Psychiatric Association
BIPOC: Black, Indigenous and Other People of Colour
CAHVIO: Committee on Preventing and Combating Violence against Women and Domestic Violence
CAT: Convention against Torture
CCPR: Committee on Civil and Political Rights
CEDAW: Convention on the Elimination of All Forms of Discrimination against Women
CHR: Commission on Human Rights
CJEU: Court of Justice of the European Union
CoE: Council of Europe
CRC: Convention on the Rights of the Child
DSD: Differences of Sexual Development
DSM: Diagnostic and Statistical Manual of Mental Disease
EA: Equality Act
ECHR: European Convention on Human Rights
ECHR: European Court of Human Rights
ECOSOC: Economic and Social Council
ETBB: Equal Treatment Bench Book
FTA: Free Trade Agreement
GIDS: Gender Identity Development Service
GIRES: Gender Identity Research & Education Society
GRA: Gender Recognition Act
GRC: Gender Recognition Certificate
HRC: Human Rights Council
IACHR: Inter-American Court of Human Rights
IACHR: Inter-American Commission on Human Rights
ICC: International Criminal Court
ICCPR: International Covenant on Civil and Political Rights
ICD: International Classification of Diseases
ICERD: International Convention for the Elimination of All Forms of Racial Discrimination
ICESCR: International Covenant on Economic, Social and Cultural Rights
ICJ: International Court of Justice
ICJ: International Commission of Jurists

ICTLEP: International Conference on Transgender Law and Policy
IE on SOGI: Indipendent Expert on Sexual Orientation and Gender Identity
IHBGDA: International Harry Benjamin Gender Dysphoria Association
ILGA: International Lesbian, Gay Association
ILGA World: International Lesbian, Gay, Bisexual, Trans and Intersex Association
ISHR: International Service for Human Rights
LGB: Lesbian, Gay and Bisexual
LGBT: Lesbian, Gay, Bisexual and Trans
LGBTIQ+: Lesbian, Gay, Bisexual, Trans, Intersex, Queer+
MPRG: Multi-Professional Review Group
NGO: Non-Governmental Organisation
NHS: National Health Service
NICE: National Institute for Clinical Excellence
OHCHR: Office of the High Commissioner for Human Rights
ONS: Office for National Statistics
SHAFT: Self-Help Association for Transsexuals
SOGI: Sexual Orientation and Gender Identity
SOGIESC: Sexual Orientation, Gender Identity and Expression and Sex Characteristics
SRS: Sex Reassignment Surgery
STEMM: Science, Technology, Engineering, Math and Medicine
TGEU: Transgender Europe
UDHR: Universal Declaration of Human Rights
UN: United Nations
UNAIDS: United Nations AIDS Programme
UNDP: United Nations Development Programme
UNHCR: United Nations High Commissioner for Refugees
UNICEF: United Nations Children's Fund
UNPF: United Nations Population Fund
WHO: World Health Organization
WPATH: World Professional Association for Transgender Health
YP: Yogyakarta Principles

GENDER IDENTITY: AN INTRODUCTION

Trans women are women at the end of the day. Every woman is a woman. Women are multifaceted, intergenerational, international. They are limitless, formless ... women are the world.
—Aaron Rose Philip, quoted by UN Women,6 March 2020[2]

As gender identity theory continued its march across institutions, I could not help notice how little critical assessment there was on the origin and the history of this concept, its incorporation into international and domestic law and, most urgently, the consequences of its incorporation. After all, gender identity was not even used as a term before the 1960s. How did it manage to become so influential and "inevitable" in such a short time? There are many areas of public life where gender identity theory has pushed all other ideas out of the field, from politics, to sociology, criminology, philosophy, medicine, biology. But my field of expertise is international law, and so I was particularly interested in the way this theory managed to establish itself as the hegemonic theory in the traditionally sceptical world of international lawyers.

Inevitably, the international legal regime most likely to adopt and then disseminate this theory is the international human rights regime. Therefore, this work focuses on the genealogy of gender identity within international human rights institutions and courts, including the European Court of Human Rights (ECHR), the Court of Justice of the European Union (CJEU) and United Nations treaty bodies, especially those whose remit potentially covers gender identity issues.This project is also part legal history, with the proviso that gender identity has no legal pedigree at all. The more one excavates its genealogy, the more one finds there are no roots; gender identity was imported wholesale from the world of sexology in the 1960 and the world of transgender activists, especially from the 1980s, activists who had a legal background and were therefore well

[2] https://x.com/UN_Women/status/1235977079839166464?s=20.

placed to create, through strategic litigation in US courts,[3] the legal grounding this concept sorely lacked.[4]

The thread followed in unraveling this genealogy is the work of the Independent Expert on Sexual Orientation and Gender Identity (IE on SOGI).[5] As noted in their webpage, "the UN Human Rights Council (HRC) created the mandate of Independent Expert on protection against violence and discrimination based on sexual orientation and gender identity through HRC resolution 32/2."[6] It is especially in the work of the IE on SOGI that a narrative is developed, embedding gender identity in human rights law as if it were an inevitable and natural part of the fabric of human rights; the creation of this narrative was crucial, because gender identity has no direct grounding either in any conventional treaty or in customary law. In fact, the HRC resolution establishing the mandate is unusual in that it has no specific legal basis in one of the United Nations human rights treaties, nor a direct reference to a recognised protected category. The mandate was created on the basis to Article 2 of the Universal Declaration of Human Rights,[7] its equality and non-discrimination provision, ensuring that nobody is discriminated against on the basis of the listed grounds and also "other status," making this an open list, where gender identity and sexual orientation can be read into the Article. The Resolution also invokes in its Preamble the 1993 Vienna Declaration and Programme of Action;[8] and finally the UN Resolution

[3] Both the medical and the legal pedigree of this concept are firmly rooted in the United States. For a comprehensive and up-to-date review of US jurisprudence on gender identity issues, see Jillian Weiss and David Cruz, Gender Identity and the Law (Durham: Carolina Academic Press, 2021).

[4] In this entire collection of papers of a Symposium titled "Queering International Law," there is no investigation or reporting on the history of gender identity and its entry in international law materials and debates; see American Journal of International Law, 116 (2022): 1- 37, doi: 10.1017/aju.2021.72.

[5] Notably with the 2021 Report "The Law of Inclusion," A/HRC/47/27, https://www.ohchr.org/en/documents/thematic-reports/ahrc4727-law-inclusion-report-independent-expert-sexual-orientation-and.

[6] Human Rights Council, "Protection against violence and discrimination based on sexual orientation and gender identity," A/HRC/RES/32/2, https://ap.ohchr.org/documents/dpage_e.aspx?si=A/HRC/RES/32/2.

[7] United Nations, Universal Declaration of Human Rights, 1948, https://www.un.org/en/about-us/universal-declaration-of-human-rights.

[8] World Conference on Human Rights in Vienna, Vienna Declaration and Programme of Action, 25 June 1993, https://www.ohchr.org/en/instruments-mechanisms/instruments/vienna-declaration-and-programme-action.

which established the HRC.[9] In other words, there is no direct reference in the supporting resolutions and declaration either to sexual orientation or gender identity. The political rather than legal character of this mandate is reflected in the voting pattern: of the 47 State Members of the HRC, 23 voted in favour, but 18 against, with 6 abstentions, making the favourable votes a minority. For contrast, the resolution for the mandate of the UN Special Rapporteur on Extreme Poverty was adopted by consensus.[10] Inevitably, this voting pattern reflects the rejection of same-sex orientation in many UN Member States. Since this work is exclusively focused on gender identity, any criticism is to be directed only at gender identity theory, and not to be read as a criticism of LGB rights or praise to the countries that oppose them within the United Nations and in any other international organisation.

In this work I do not take issue with the idea that humans have an awareness of their sex and, as they grow up, of how gender expectations built around the sexes affect them and their life chances (and this especially for women), but with the idea that all humans have an innate and internal gender identity which is also fluid and mutable and trumps sex in defining our identity; or even, that sex is as mutable and fluid as gender identity, as much a social construct as gender is;[11] or that is gender identity that determines the sex of our bodies (so that a male sexual organ becomes a female sexual organ if the person expresses a female gender identity) and that sex is nothing but a colonial invention to control our bodies in a capitalistic society.[12] While naturally people are free to ideologise sexual differences, it is another matter when international law transforms these ideological conjectures into legal rules. While international

---

[9] UNGA Resolution "Human Rights Council," A/RES/60/251 of 3 April 2006, https://www2.ohchr.org/english/bodies/hrcouncil/docs/a.res.60.251_en.pdf. The resolution also mentions "other status."

[10] HRC Resolution 8/11 of 18 June 2008, "Human Rights and Extreme Poverty," https://ap.ohchr.org/documents/E/HRC/resolutions/A_HRC_RES_8_11.pdf.

[11] As posited by Judith Butler, Gender Trouble: Feminism and the Subversion of Identity (New York: Routledge 1990).

[12] See Sally Hines, Is Gender Fluid? (London: Thames & Hudson Ltd, 2018); Marìa Lugones, "Heterosexualism and the Colonial/Modern Gender System," Hypatia 22(1) (Winter 2007): 186-209; Lugones, Marìa. "The Coloniality of Gender." In The Palgrave Handbook on Gender and Development, ed. Wendy Harcourt (London: Palgrave Macmillan, 2016), 13-33; Andrèa Gill, "From Binary to Intersectional to Imbricated Approaches: Gender in a Decolonial and Diasporic Perspective," Contexto Internacional 41(2) (May/August 2019): 275-302, doi: https://doi.org/10.1590/S0102-8529.2019410200003.

law has not done so in conventional means, such as treaties, these ideas are being accepted and disseminated in international legal materials, such as court judgments and international organisations documents. This work is a plea to stop and consider the origin and meaning of the concept, and the consequences of incorporating it into the law. There is a small disclaimer that ought to be incorporated into this plea: it is true that gender identity theory is more diverse, and more open to contestation,[13] than its translation into the international law regimes shows, as the analysis of the case law and the legal materials will illustrate. So before gender identity theorists go up in arms about my reconstruction of the genealogy of gender identity in international law, I recognise that the theory is not as rigid, or as simplistic, as it is in legal materials. But this is precisely because gender identity theory is an academic endeavour and not a legal one. And like it or not, law needs stability, predictability, and yes, binary solutions.[14]

It is therefore particularly fruitful to investigate how the exercise of narrative building that underpins the embedding of gender identity theory in international law manages to avoid the strictures of legal logic. This work intends to focus not so much on the why, but on the how. How has gender identity managed to evolve from an obscure idea developed by sexologists in post-war United States, people as John Money, the discredited sexologist responsible for the Reimer twins' experiments[15] or Harry Benjamin,[16] into something that the UN IE on SOGI says all human beings have? What are the effects of the incorporation of gender identity

---

[13] Though these disputes are always endogenous to the theory. There is no challenge to the idea of gender identity *per se*. In this regard, they are comparable to theological differences within a religion. The idea of God (gender identity) is not to be questioned, let alone refuted.

[14] One does not need to be a Luhmann scholar to get the importance of binary distinctions in law, as starkly illustrated by the conduct of criminal trials. Niklas Luhmann, Law as a Social System, Trans. Klaus A Ziegert (Oxford: Oxford University Press, 2004).

[15]A story of the Reimer twins in Gaetano, Phil, "David Reimer and John Money Gender Reassignment Controversy: The John/Joan Case." Embryo Project Encyclopedia (November 15, 2017). ISSN: 1940-5030, https://hdl.handle.net/10776/13009.

[16] Together with Money, Benjamin started the first clinic for sex reassignment surgery at Johns Hopkins Hospital in Baltimore, the Johns Hopkins Gender Identity Clinic; see Charalampos Sotos and Others, "Origins of Gender Affirmation Surgery: The History of the First Gender Identity Clinic in the United States at Johns Hopkins," Annuals of Plastic Surgery, 83(2) (August 2019): 132-136, https://doi:10.1097/SAP.0000000000001684.

theory into human rights law on the rights of women, children and LGB people? One of the goals of this work is to invite a frank, legally grounded, debate on the legal consequences of the momentous change gender identity theorists want to implement in international and domestic law.

Given how obscure gender identity theory was and how small the group affected,[17] a reconstruction of the genealogy of this concept involves investigating the work of single influential individuals, reading magazines that never reached mainstream success, following the proceedings of conferences that were never reported in the media.[18] It is painstaking work, but it is necessary to establish the genealogy of gender identity, a concept that has been accepted in academia, policy making and politics without any attention being paid to its origin and its intellectual background. Gender identity has become a legal artefact shared around different international bodies, seemingly acquiring more legal legitimacy with each reproduction. In reality gender identity has no proper legal or theoretical basis, as we will see the more we consider the assumptions that one needs to make in order to make sense of it.

The legal theorist Ronald Dworkin compared judicial law-making to a "chain novel."[19]According to Dworkin, judges work in a continuous dialogue to create a legal narrative that has to follow its own internal logic and coherence. It is a powerful metaphor, and evocative of the work of judges, especially in common law systems. However, I believe it may have

---

[17] The last UK census is the only official statistic on the number of people who define themselves as transgender: the census 2021 shows that 0.10% of people identified as transmen and 0.10% as transwomen. Giulia Castagnaro, "The Office for National Statistics' Sexual Orientation and Gender Identity Census 2021, GenderGP, January 13, 2023,
https://www.gendergp.com/sexual-orientation-and-gender-identity-census-2021-england-and-wales/#:~:text=The%20Census%202021%20includes%20the,identify%20as%20a%20trans%20man. The number of people with a gender recognition certificate under the Gender Recognition Act 2004 is considerably lower, 5,871 in December 2020, so 0.0089% of the British population; "Gender Recognition Fee Reduced," GovUK, May 4, 2021,
https://www.gov.uk/government/news/gender-recognition-certificate-fee-reduced#:~:text=As%20of%20December%202020%2C%20there,people%20living%20in%20the%20UK.

[18] In this research, the material collected in the Digital Transgender Archive, at https://www.digitaltransgenderarchive.net/, has been invaluable.

[19] Ronald Dworkin, Law's Empire (Cambridge: Cambridge University Press, 1986): 229.

a fatal flaw: once an element is incorporated into the logic of the chain novel, it becomes very difficult to dislodge it. The element acquires legitimacy and status at each new chapter of the novel. Each judicial iteration, and each legislative and administrative recognition, makes the removal of this element more difficult to accomplish.

Gender identity constitutes the perfect case study for this potential flaw. After having entered the case law of the ECHR in *Goodwin v UK*[20] with little or no scientific evidence, it acquired authority and legitimacy, so that each following chapter of the novel just referred back to *Goodwin* in a validation exercise. The *Goodwin* case is fetishised beyond any reasonable judicial approach to previous jurisprudence, on the basis of poor legal reasoning and a very flimsy factual basis.

This book will focus exclusively on how international law understands gender identity and transgender rights and how gender identity was developed as a legal concept. However, my interest in the concept cannot be separated from the reality of my life as a woman and my understanding of feminism and women's place in the world, and how international law accommodates, or fails to accommodate, that place. Much is made in gender identity theory literature of the right not to be discriminated against because of one's gender identity. This work is an attempt to make sense of this narrative and expose its weak points and logical fallacies. One of the most glaring ones is that the reality of discrimination against "transgender" individuals does not prove that gender identity is anything other than a belief. People can be discriminated against because of their religious beliefs. That in itself does not prove the existence of God or of the immortal soul. There is no proof, other than what is affirmed dogmatically, that gender identity is an objectively observable material reality and not a belief.

I think most people would agree that we have some form of identity connected to our sex, though many feminists would prefer to talk about a sex identity, in order not to lose sight of the material reality of our sexed bodies. I think also it is a common understanding that we are not simply and not only, sexed animals. We grow up in societies where rules, norms, ideas and preconceptions about sex are deeply ingrained. We call this "gender." For feminists, these are negative superstructures women should

[20]*Case of Christine Goodwin v the United Kingdom*, 11 July 2002, Application No. 28957/95.
https://hudoc.echr.coe.int/eng#{%22itemid%22:[%22001-60596%22]}.

dismantle to achieve the liberation of women from "patriarchy." For conservatives, these are necessary rules to keep women subservient to men. Both sides acknowledge the reality of sex. Gender identity theory leverages a lot of feminist theory in recognising that sex is accompanied in any society by a plethora of ideological constructs, cultural practices, political understandings, of what it means to be a man or a woman.[21] These gender rules, in most, if not all, societies, are designed to keep women in an inferior position. Additionally, the exploitation of women's reproductive capacity is the oldest axis of oppression. It is superficially attractive for women to be told that they do not have to accept the constraining rules of gender because sex does not matter.

As any woman, I remember acquiring an understanding and awareness of what being born female meant. This awareness went beyond knowing I *was* female. In that sense, I developed an identity *as* a female, first a girl then a woman. And I could see that gender predetermined not so much what my female body allowed me to do, but what gendered rules prevented me from doing. The goal of feminism is not to dispute the reality that humans, being an anisogamous and sexually dimorphic species, are either males or females. Feminism is the intellectual and political project for dismantling the misconception that sexual dimorphism establishes a hierarchy between the sexes, with a dominant male sex and a dominated female sex.Women are not inferior to men, they are simply different from men, and this difference is a strength. If diversity is a worthy political goal, then pretending there is no diversity in one of the most fundamental aspects of our human experience is certainly not wise.[22] As an example, not registering the sex of newborn children, as gender identity theorists propose, is not going to make oppression, discrimination

---

[21] Usually misrepresenting the work of Simone De Beauvoir, The Second Sex, translated by H.M. Parshley (London: Jonathan Cape, 1953). When De Beauvoir wrote that "one is not born, but rather becomes a woman" she was starting from her stated premise that "The division of the sexes is a biological fact, not an event in human history." She simply suggested gender rules constrain the path that a woman can take and usually reduce her to her reproductive function. Not that men can become women by self-declaration.

[22] In Davina Cooper, Robyn Emerton, Emily Grabham, Han Newman, Elizabeth Peel, Flora Renz, and Jessica Smith, Abolishing Legal Sex. Final Report, King's College, London (2022). https://www.kcl.ac.uk/law/research/future-of-legal-gender-abolishing-legal-sex-status-full-report.pdf.) the authors argue the following: "Our research identified benefits to decertification. These included: dismantling a legal system which formally places people, from birth, in unequal social categories of female and male." (Overview, para 5).

and exploitation of females disappear; it is just going to make it impossible to record them and track them. If one followed this approach to its logical conclusions, no difference and diversity should ever be acknowledged. We should deny that there are people of a different colour, because racism exists, so statistics should not be kept. And colour is a superficial, biologically irrelevant, difference in most cases (though ethnic origin, which is not the same as race anyway, can have a role in the incidence of certain diseases). Sex is a fundamental difference, the very distinction that allows our reproduction as individuals and as a species. Every child ever born was born out of a woman, and resulted from the fertilisation of an egg by a sperm. Noticing this is not "reducing" people to their biology, it is acknowledging the essential role biology plays in our existence. Denial and contempt of nature is a facet both of conservative religious movements and extreme capitalism. Religions claim that body and spirit/soul are separate and the soul prevails over the body (and of course, patriarchal religions relegate women to the lowly body). Capitalism claims that humans can control, and monetise, all aspects of nature and has reached the point in which bodies are monetised not just through the exploitation of labour, but also through the monetisation of bodily functions and parts (hence surrogacy) and of body modification (hence transgender surgeries).

As a feminist, I did not think that, in order to escape the gender roles imposed on me by society, I had to reject my sex (a fool's errand, as sex is part of what makes us who we are, just as our date of birth situates us in a specific time, over which we have no control), but that I had to fight the gender roles that were imposed on me and on women in general because of our sex. Gender is the tool of oppression, not sex. Gender identity theorists leverage the work done by feminists specifically on gender stereotypes and roles, to posit that gender identity is a fluid, changeable object, not in order to liberate women from the constraint of gendered norms; instead gender identity is used to deny the reality of sex, as if recognising that sex is real and immutable was equivalent to recognising that sexism is also real and immutable. Gender identity is then presented not simply as the awareness of our sexed body and of the constraints society puts upon it, but as a tool to negate our sexed body and self-determine our gender as the only relevant aspect of our identity. At the same time, it reframes knowledge of science around sex as anti-trans, making it impossible for women to even have a ground over which to argue their rights.[23]

This is a leap that defies logic and reality. It seems that no-one who should have done so, assessed the consequences of this leap. It is quite clear that, within the community that engineered it, negating the relevance of birth sex may have been the point all along, as we shall see in Chapter 3. Whether they originally planned to completely erase the significance of sex, to the point of arguing that if a man says he is a woman, his penis becomes a female organ,[24] is not clear. Certainly some fringes of the transgender movement planned this all along. And again, some fringes of the feminist movement might have been superficially attracted to the idea that sex was completely irrelevant and should be erased from the law, in the mistaken belief that not giving legal recognition to sex would finally accomplish full equality for women.[25] Clearly only women living in the

[23]As illustrated clearly in this quote: "In the United Kingdom, anti-trans rhetoric, arguing that sex is immutable and gender identities not valid, has also been gaining baseless and concerning credibility, at the expense of both trans people's civil liberties and women's and children's rights." EP Committee on Equality and Non-Discrimination, Combating Rising Hate against LGBTI People in Europe, Doc 15121 Ref 4524 (September 2020) 20210921-RisingHateLGBTI-EN.pdf (coe.int). The Report is quoted in the Proceedings of the Roundtable organised by the Office of the Council of Europe Commissioner for Human Rights "Human Rights of LGBTI People in Europe: Current Threats to Equal Rights, Challenges Faced by Defenders, and the Way Forward," CommDH(2021)32, Report of the Round Table with LGBTI HR defenders (coe.int), which in turn is quoted by the Council of Europe "Thematic Report on Legal Gender Recognition in Europe," CM/Rec (2010)5, https://rm.coe.int/thematic-report-on-legal-gender-recognition-in-europe-2022/1680a729b3. Embedding the idea that to consider sex immutable is in itself anti-trans is no different from framing the knowledge that our body is mortal as anti-Christian.

[24] One finds claims such as this one in some areas of trans rights literature and media sources such as this article, Josh Jackman, "Pose Star Indya Moore: Trans Women's Penises are Biologically Male," Pink News, February 19, 2019, https://www.thepinknews.com/2019/02/19/pose-indya-moore-trans-penises-biologically-female/. A more critical treatment in Malcolm Clark "All Rise for the 'Female Penis,'" The Critic, February 8, 2023 https://thecritic.co.uk/all-rise-for-the-female-penis/.

[25] The entirety of transfeminism is predicated upon the fact that "transwomen are women," but with feminists doing all the lifting work of including them in feminism; see for example Talia Mae Bettcher, "Trans Feminism: Recent Philosophical Developments," Philosophy Compass, 12(11) (November 2017): e12438, doi:https://doi.org/10.1111/phc3.12438. I believe transfeminism latched

US, UK or similarly situated countries could ever conceive of this as a possibility, given their experience of growing up in societies that, by and large, allow girls to develop a personality, get an education, make life choices, including the crucial choices about reproduction which shape a woman's life. Millions of women do not have these choices, not because they identify as women, but because they are women.

Gender identity is presented as a universal experience but also as a matter of group belonging. While there is the recognition that group rights depend on an applicable definition, there is no recognition that positive rights should not be granted to people on the basis of self-identification without a material basis. Gender identity theorists have to decide whether gender identity is a universal experience or whether only transgender individuals have a gender identity, if nothing else because if gender identity is a universal experience, "cis women" are discriminated on the basis of it. There is no "cis privilege" for women. Additionally, sex, while being a personal immutable characteristic, is also a relational and social characteristic. The sex of others matter, at species level, because only sexual differentiation allows for the continuation of our species;[26] at social level, because there are norms and rules attached to our sex, and not all of them are the result of discrimination against women (in fact, it is the task of the law to distinguish between rules that discriminate against women and rules that exist either to protect women against discrimination or to guarantee specific rights to women on the basis of their sex); and at individual level, both because we establish relationships on the basis of our sex and because our behaviour and experience of the world are coloured and influenced by our sex.

The gender identity of others does not hold the same significance because it is not perceptible in the same way that sex is. The reason we need to "ask for pronouns" is because gender identity is not evident to the eye.[27]

---

on a certain attitude within feminism to reduce or ignore the reproductive role of women as inherently inferior; see Elaine Tuttle Hansen, Mother Without Child. Contemporary Fiction and the Crisis of Motherhood (Berkeley: University of California Press, 1967),
https://publishing.cdlib.org/ucpressebooks/view?docId=ft1d5nb0ft;brand=ucpress.

[26] This is not a form of biological essentialism, because it does not express an "ought" proposition, but only an "is" proposition. Stating that sex is the mechanism for reproduction does not mean sex ought to be [only] a mechanism for reproduction.

[27] The rules on language imposed by gender identity theory are only intelligible in English, as other languages have different rules on gendered pronouns. The

All one can say is that a "transgender identity" is evident in the sense that there is a disconnect between the perceived sex and the chosen presentation, although of course that brings into place stereotypes of femininity and masculinity embraced by the transgender individual. Gender identity theory forbids us from relying on the cues that our brain gives us about the sex of the individual we are seeing and forces us to transfer to others the power to name what we see. The demand that we use third person pronouns, not in accordance to our perception of reality, but in compliance to a demand made by the person those pronouns refer to, is an unreasonable demand, especially evident when those pronouns are not the familiar ones in one's language, but made up by gender identity theory or even by the transgender individuals themselves (zir, per, and so on). Pronouns are a fundamental part of speech, and one that is selected automatically and naturally in response to cues given by our brain about the sex of the individual we see or hear. From the speaker's perspective, the "correct pronoun" is the one that matches the visual and audio cues given to us by our brain. If we see a man, our brain and our language is primed to refer to him as "he." The demand that we refer to him as "she," "they," "zir," "per," or any other pronoun they come up with, and/or we switch pronouns back and forth on the basis of their demands, puts a considerable onus on the speaker, one not justified by any legal or moral obligation. It goes beyond freedom of speech, because we do not refer to a man as "he" because we are free to do so, but because breaking the link between language and reality makes communication impossible. While we are free to decide what to say, and how to say it, that freedom does not include our right to call things what they are not. Or better, while we are free to call a chair a table, we cannot expect others to understand us and certainly we do not have the right to compel others to call chairs tables. It is true that language evolves, but not by compelling others to ignore the link between reality and words. From a feminist perspective, the power to name reality, which men have always arrogated to themselves, is an especially precious conquest, always fragile, as gender identity demands prove. Forcing a woman who has been raped to refer to her rapist as "she," or seeing him referred to as a woman by others, is a further violation of her

---

adoption of English pronouns by non-English speakers, in their social media profiles for example, is a good illustration of the cultural imperialism of gender identity theory, which needs English as the carrier language for many of its supposedly universal principles.

autonomy and her right to name the violence and the body violation she has suffered.[28]

This book is not just a historical reconstruction of gender identity in international law, but contains a proposal for a reframing of this concept. There is nothing, as I shall be noting in several instances in the course of this work, in international human rights law that requires the State, or any third party, to believe that people have a gender identity, and/or that it is actually possible for people to change their birth sex in any significant way, in order to put in place clear rules to protect the belief in gender identity in international human rights law and domestic equality law and to guarantee the proper mental health care for people whose belief in gender identity becomes a disabling condition.[29] Inevitably, reframing gender identity as a belief (much as having an immortal soul is a belief held by Christians) involves re-assessing how it ought to be protected in human rights law. The proposal will be explored more fully in the Conclusions chapter. For now suffices to say that an important element of belief protection is an assessment of the way in which the belief potentially affects the rights of others.

The book is structured in the following manner. **Chapter 1** outlines the terminology adopted in the work and the methodology followed, namely the focus on primary sources and the close analysis of the jurisprudence. Unusually for a legal monograph that is not strictly about legal history, there is more attention paid to the older jurisprudence, in order to track the entry and the development of the concept of gender identity in international law. With **Chapter 2** the book moves on to an historical narration which focuses on the development of this concept in the United States, on the one hand in the areas of sexology and the medical treatment of transsexuality,

---

[28] This argument is not intended to draw a link between transwomen and sexual violence, but only to reaffirm the right of women to name reality as they see it.

[29] In those cases, we can more properly speak of body integrity dysphoria, akin to anorexia. Just as no-one would suggest gastric band surgery for an anorexic patient, I argue gender dysphoric patients (more accurately body or sex dysphoric patients) should not be cured by surgery but through therapy, in keeping with the most fundamental tenet of gender identity theory, that gender (identity) and sex are not the same thing, and that affirming your gender identity does not require body modification. The link is also made in this publication, though I disagree with the conclusions: Leandro Loriga, "Body Identity Dysphoria and 'Just Amputation:' State of the Art and Beyond," Human Affairs-Postdisciplinary Humanities & Social Sciences Quarterly (Berlin: Walter De Gruyter Gmbh, 2023), doi: 10.1515/humaff-2022-1005.

and on the other within the trans rights movement, again with a focus on primary sources. **Chapter 3** tracks the migration of gender identity in the legal materials produced by international and regional organisations, and **Chapter 4** more specifically the work of the United Nations Treaty Bodies, because of their quasi-judicial function. **Chapter 5** is dedicated to the case law originating from European courts. Europe has provided the longest and richest jurisprudence on gender identity in the judicial work of the European Court of Human Rights and of the Court of Justice of the European Union. The case law of the ECHR is considered chronologically, and divided into three parts: the first, on the case law from *Rees* to *Goodwin*. The second, a close analysis of the seminal *Goodwin* case, and the third, on the post-*Goodwin* case law. **Chapter 6** considers the case law of the Inter-American Court of Human Rights and of the work of the Inter-American Commission for Human Rights, while **Chapter 7** looks at the work of the African Union. There is as of yet no case law from the African Court of Human Rights, but in **Chapter 8**, which contains selected cases from domestic courts, there are some cases from African courts. In fact all the cases in this chapter come from "peripheral" courts in relation to the "centre" of gender identity theory, the developed West. **Chapter 9** considers "the backlash" against gender identity theory, from two perspectives: the first, the effects "on the ground" of gender identity theory, especially on women, children and LGB individuals; the second, the internal backlash in the regime of global health law in the area of transgender care "affirmative approach." Finally, **Chapter 10** offers both conclusions and a proposal for reframing gender identity as a belief.

At the outset of this work, I think a disclaimer on language is necessary, as gender identity theory rests on a revolutionary approach to language use (exemplified by the rules on pronouns) and development. For the first, I avoided using pronouns when these would signal allegiance to gender identity theory. For the second, I always adopt the traditional distinction between sex and gender, using the first to refer to the reality of our sexed bodies, and the second to refer to the social constructs built on that reality. The only exception is when I refer to such commonly used phrases as "gender pay gap." When quoting legal materials, I quote the terms as they are used. For what concerns more specific transgender terminology, I mostly follow the usage of the times when the material was produced. Therefore transsexuals for the older materials, and transgender for the newer ones. I try not to use the terms "transwoman" and "transman," unless called for by the context, as I find them confusing and potentially misleading. As the terms are commonly used in legal materials, I often use MtF man to refer to a man who identifies as a woman (with or without surgical/medical transition) and FtM for a woman who identifies as a man. The condition of being transgender has gone from being referred to as gender identity disorder, to gender dysphoria, to gender incongruence. I follow the nomenclature as it evolves.

CHAPTER 1

TERMINOLOGY AND METHODOLOGY

Agender, Androgyne, Androgynous, Bigender, Cis, Cisgender, Cis Female, Cis Male, Cis Man, Cis Woman, Cisgender Female, Cisgender Male, Cisgender Man, Cisgender Woman, Female to Male, FTM, Gender Fluid, Gender Nonconforming, Gender Questioning, Gender Variant, Genderqueer, Intersex, Male to Female, MTF, Neither, Neutrois, Non-binary, Other, Pangender, Trans, Trans, Trans Female, Trans* Female, Trans Male, Trans* Male, Trans Man, Trans* Man, Trans Person, Trans* Person, Trans Woman, Trans* Woman, Transfeminine, Transgender, Transgender Female, Transgender Male, Transgender Man, Transgender Person, Transgender Woman, Transmasculine, Transsexual, Transsexual Female, Transsexual Male, Transsexual Man, Transsexual Person, Transsexual Woman, Two-Spirit*

—The 58 gender identities offered by Facebook[30]

The issue of definitions makes discussing gender identity as a legal artefact especially fraught, as legal definitions serve to exclude and contain the application of the law. Gender identity theory, being predicated upon self-identification, resists this normative function.[31] It is banal to note

---

[30] Russell Goldman, "Here's a List of 58 Gender Options for Facebook Users," ABC News, February 13, 2014, https://abcnews.go.com/blogs/headlines/2014/02/heres-a-list-of-58-gender-options-for-facebook-users.

[31] The rejection is all encompassing, as gender identity theory constantly refines its jargon, maintaining individuals in a constant state of alarm about acceptable language. Just as an example, Dianne Duffy, "Contested Subjects of Human Rights: Trans- and Gender-variants Subjects of International Human Rights Law," The Modern Law Review, 84(5) (2021): 1041-165, at 1055 notes that the term "transgender" is problematic: "The Anglophone understanding of 'transgender' implies a narrative of passage from one binary gender to another. This implies a boundary, between two genders; a male/female duality and a subject who has transitioned from an identifiable A to an equally identifiable B." Even the term gender identity, or at least its definition, has been criticised: see again Dianne Duffy and Dianne Otto, "Queering Gender [Identity] in International Law," Nordic Journal of Human Rights, 33(4) (2015): 299-318, doi: 10.1080/18918131.2016.1123474. The acronym SOGI, supposedly designed to avoid the pitfalls of transgenderism, has also been criticised as unitary and monolitic (Duffy, ibidem).

that no legal rule conferring positive rights can accept self-identification as the basis for conferral. Simply put (and somewhat simplistically, from a legal theory perspective), positive rights are rights that require positive duties from the State, putting the State under a duty to act, as opposed to negative rights, which enjoin the State from acting, or better, interfering. The right to privacy, or, as Judge Brandeis defined it, the "right to be let alone,"[32] is a classic negative right.[33] The right to education is a classic positive right, because it requires the State to provide resources for schools, teachers etc.

Human rights can be seen through the universal/group lens as well. Certain rights belong to all humans "as humans." They go beyond the traditional rights championed by the revolutions of the Enlightenment era. The era of ideologies of the last century[34] showed that civil rights could not survive the classification of entire groups of people as subhumans and the deprivation of full citizenship[35] (the master key for obtaining rights in society), their exclusion from society, and eventual physical elimination. The real distinguishing characteristic between the Enlightenment rights and post-war human rights is the internationalisation of the latter; human rights are not just guaranteed by domestic constitutions, but contained in international treaties, by which States promise *each other* that they will respect the human rights of the people of their territory. Not, as in constitutions, a social contract with the citizens, but an international promise between States. The second innovation is the possibility for individuals to vindicate their rights directly against the State (once domestic remedies are exhausted) in international courts.

International human rights are either universal or group rights. While the 1948 Declaration of Human Rights can be understood as an instrument of

---

It is a game of infinite regress. There is no escape from the cisgender heteronormative matrix. Unless one is trans, in which case inhabiting the cisgender matrix and demanding no criticism for this choice is absolutely acceptable.

32 Samuel D.Warren and Louis Brandeis, "The Right to Privacy," Harvard Law Review, IV(5) (December 1890)
https://groups.csail.mit.edu/mac/classes/6.805/articles/privacy/Privacy_brand_warr2.html.

33 Interestingly, the ECHR reconceptualises Article 8, the right to a private life, as a positive as well as a negative right, as we shall see in Chapter 5.

34 What Hobsbawn called the short century. Eric J. Hobsbawm, Age of Extremes: The Short Twentieth Century 1914-1991 (London: Penguin Books 1994).

35 The right to have rights, as Hannah Arendt defined it. Hannah Arendt, The Origins of Totalitarianism (New York: Schocken Books, 1951).

the first kind, it was never converted as such into a single treaty. The history of the codification of human rights is too complex to be reported here; suffices to say that all UN-sponsored human rights treaties are not strictly of the universal kind. They either restrict their scope thematically, or in application to groups. In the thematic group we can list, chronologically, the 1951 Convention on the Prevention and Punishment of the Crime of Genocide;[36] the 1966 International Covenant on Civil and Political Rights (ICCPR);[37] the International Covenant on Economic, Social, and Cultural Rights (ICESCR);[38] the 1984 Convention Against Torture (CAT),[39] and the 2010 International Convention for the Protection of All Persons from Enforced Disappearance.[40] In the second group, the 1965 International Convention on the Elimination of All Forms of Racial Discrimination (ICERD);[41] the 1979 Convention on the Elimination of All Forms of Discrimination Against Women (CEDAW);[42] the 1989 Convention on the Rights of the Child (CRC);[43] the 1990 Convention on the Protection of the Rights of All Migrant Workers and Members of their Family;[44] and the 2006 Convention on the Rights of Persons with Disabilities.[45]

The overarching principle of non-discrimination, which applies to all human rights treaties, has to be balanced in two different ways in sectoral treaties: first, because those treaties themselves discriminate between those who are granted the protection of the treaties and those who are not; and second, because, within the protected group, there cannot be discrimination

---

[36] Convention on the Prevention and Punishment of the Crime of Genocide, 9 December 1948, 78 UNTS 277.

[37] International Covenant on Civil and Political Rights, 16 December 1966, 999 UNTS 171.

[38] International Covenant on Economic, Social and Cultural Rights, 16 December 1966, 993 UNTS 3.

[39] Convention against Torture and Other Cruel, Inhuman or Degrading Treeatment or Punishment, 10 December 1984, 1465 UNTS 85.

[40] International Convention for the Protection of All Persons from Enforced Disappearance, 20 December 2006, 2716 UNTS 3.

[41] International Convention on the Elimination of All Forms of Racial Discrimination, 7 March 1966, 660 UNTS 195.

[42] Convention on the Elimination of All Forms of Discrimination against Women, 18 December 1979, 1249 UNTS 13.

[43] Convention on the Rights of the Child, 20 November 1989, 1577 UNTS 3.

[44] International Convention on the Protection of the Rights of All Migrant Workers and Members of Their Family, 18 December 1990, 2220 UNTS 3.

[45] Convention on the Rights of Persons with Disabilities, 13 December 2006, 2515 UNTS 3.

based on any other characteristic (for example, discrimination on the basis of the race or religious belief of women is not allowed under the CEDAW).

It is crucial to uphold these distinctions, because rights that are granted on the basis of group identity have to be subjected to a test of applicability. It is normally the treaty itself that provides, through treaty-specific definitions, the test of applicability of the treaty to individuals. These sectoral treaties can either focus on eliminating discrimination on the basis of the protected characteristic (ICERD and CEDAW) or set up a specific framework for especially vulnerable groups (such as children, migrants or disabled people). All of them are normally a mixture of both, but in the first case, it is more likely that the treaty will define discrimination rather than the protected characteristic itself. So for example Article 1 of ICERD recites as follows:

> 1. In this Convention, the term "racial discrimination" shall mean any distinction, exclusion, restriction or preference based on race, colour, descent, or national or ethnic origin which has the purpose or effect of nullifying or impairing the recognition, enjoyment or exercise, on an equal footing, of human rights and fundamental freedoms in the political, economic, social, cultural or any other field of public life.

And Article 1 of the CEDAW states as follows:

> For the purposes of the present Convention, the term "discrimination against women" shall mean any distinction, exclusion or restriction made *on the basis of sex* [emphasis added] which has the effect or purpose of impairing or nullifying the recognition, enjoyment or exercise by women, irrespective of their marital status, on a basis of equality of men and women, of human rights and fundamental freedoms in the political, economic, social, cultural, civil or any other field.

For the second approach, consider the definition provided in Article 1 of the CRC:

> For the purposes of the present Convention, a child means every human being below the age of eighteen years unless under the law applicable to the child, majority is attained earlier.

Neither in the ICERD nor in the CEDAW the protected characteristic (race or sex) itself is defined, nor does the CEDAW define what a woman is. It is banal to state it, but for millennia women were discriminated against, oppressed and exploited without anyone ever stopping to wonder what exactly a woman was and how to recognise one. Although race in itself is an artificial distinction on the basis of superficial differences, and not a fundamental distinction such as the one between the sexes common to most of the animal and plant world, it is equally evident that skin colour has been used as a discriminating characteristic between human groups. Just as it is impossible to identify out of one's group-based oppression, the law does (or should) prohibit identifying into a protected characteristic when doing so can result in differential treatment or specific rights designed to remedy past and/or present discrimination.

The movement for the advancement of LGB rights historically focused on non-discrimination and equality. This is a goal that finds universal support from anyone who believes that all human beings deserve to be treated equally, and to have their dignity respected, regardless of personal characteristics, including sexual orientation. A similar demand to extend anti-discrimination rules to transgender individuals should receive universal approval. No-one should be prohibited from getting employment, housing or civil rights on the basis of their personal characteristics. What gender identity theory posits though is that individuals can identify into a sex class of their choice, with minimal or no criteria, and be able to access the rights that international human rights law and domestic equality law grant women on the basis of sex.[46] Beyond the obvious negative consequences for women, which will be explored in this book, there is conceptually no need for the law to posit that transgender individuals are the sex of their choice, in order to avoid discriminating against them, nor is it necessary for society to believe that gender identity is a universal characteristic of the human species in order to treat with dignity those who believe in it.[47]

---

[46] Women who identify as men are not granted specific rights. Access to the privileges that male humans receive in all societies is always beyond their grasp. Political representation tells its own story. The list of transgender politicians on Wikipedia lists 133 elections of transwomen (i.e. males who identify as women) and 25 of transmen (i.e. females who identify as men) and non-binary individuals (these will include both females and males). 18% females (probably slightly less) and 82% males.
https://en.wikipedia.org/wiki/List_of_transgender_political_office-holders#cite_note-17.

[47] A consequence of framing trans rights as compliance with gender identity theory and not as non-discrimination rights is that, no matter how much more accepting society becomes, transgender people report higher and higher levels of discrimination: see for example the survey of the European Agency for Fundamental Rights, reporting that 60% of transgender people reported feeling discriminated against in 2019 compared to 43% in 2012. May this be because by 2019 pronouns had

In order to give to definitions the place they deserve in gender identity theory, and assess its feasibility as a theory generating international standards and rules, this book needs to follow the development of the concept of gender identity quite close to the ground. So there will be a lot of analysis of primary materials, a quite close doctrinal analysis of case law, especially the older case law, an historical and "genealogical" examination of the idea of gender identity: how did it enter international law, when did it do so, how did it spread, who championed it, which obstacles did it meet?[48] There will be much less examination of the immense and always positive literature on gender identity,[49] for the simple reason that it fails to answer any of the questions that I posed above, and in

---

become a form of discrimination? European Union Agency for Fundamental Rights, "A Long Way to Go for LGBTI Equality," 2020, A long way to go for LGBTI equality (europa.eu).

[48] There is a dearth of secondary literature on critical approaches to gender identity, especially in international law. The only recent contribution is the necessarily short chapter by Auchmuty, Rosemary and Freedman, Rosa, "Sex and Gender in Law" In Sex and Gender. A Contemporary Reader, eds. Alice Sullivan and Selina Todd (London: Routledge, 2024): 125-138.

[49] A part from the immense output from gender studies academics, there is a considerable amount of literature on gender identity and law. See for example Jillian Weiss and David Cruz, Gender Identity and the Law (Durham: Carolina Academic Press, 2021); Isabel C. Jaramillo and Laura Carlson, Trans Rights and Wrongs. A Comparative Study of Legal Reforms Concerning Trans Persons (New York: Springer International, 2021); Anne Hellum, ed., Human Rights, Sexual Orientation and Gender Identity (New York: Routledge, 2107); Chris Ashford and Alexander Maine, eds., Research Handbook on Gender, Sexuality, and the Law (Cheltenham: Elgar Publishing Ltd, 2020); Holning Lau, Sexual Orientation and Gender Identity Discrimination (Leiden: Brill, 2018); Flora Renz, Gender Recognition and the Law: Troubling Transgender Peoples' Engagement with Legal Regulation (Social Justice) (New York: Routledge, 2024); Ruth Colker, Sexual Orientation, Gender Identity, and the Law in a Nutshell (Eagan: West Academic Publishing, 2023); Laura Palazzini, Gender in Philosophy and Law (Dordrecht: Springer, 2012); Ivana Krstić, Marco Evola and Maria Isabel Ribes Moreno, eds., Legal Issues of International Law from a Gender Perspective (New York: Springer, 2023); Debra DeLaet and Renée Ann Cramer, eds., Gender, Sexuality, and the Law (New York: Routledge, 2019); Andreas von Arnaud, Kerstin von der Decken and Mart Susi, eds., The Cambridge Handbook of New Human Rights: Recognition, Novelty, Rhetoric (Cambridge: Cambridge University Press, 2020); Susan Stryker and Stephen Whittle, eds., The Transgender Studies Reader (New York: Routledge, 2013); Jens Scherpe, ed., The Legal Status of Transsexual and Transgender Persons (Cambridge: Cambridge University Press, 2015); Alex N. Sharpe, Transgender Jurisprudence: Dysphoric Bodies of Law (London: Cavendish, 2002).

fact, it normally asks a different set of questions, answering which would have resulted in an altogether different work.[50]

The 2021 Report by the IE on SOGI, "The Law on Inclusion," includes a substantial part on definitions.[51] In here we see how the inclusion of gender identity as a proxy for sex is accomplished in stages. The Report first defines "gender diverse:"

> [...] the term gender-diverse to refer to persons whose gender identity and/or expression are at odds with what is enforced as a gender norm in a particular context at a particular point in time.[52]

This definition invites questions on the nature of this gender norm and on its establishment, especially in an international setting. In democratic countries, most people will follow some gender norms and break others. Also, depending on national setting, many will follow gender norms even if they do not believe in them, because non-compliance may be dangerous (this of course affects mostly women), so that gender conformity may be socially and even legally imposed, evidencing that gender diversity is not necessarily a matter of identity, but a marker of the relative social freedom in a society. A highly individualistic society such as the US one has a completely different conception of identity compared to one in which identity is always relational and "collective." Speaking about "enforcement" is equally meaningless, unless one specifies the meaning of enforcement. There is a world of difference between the practice that women take on their husband's name upon marriage, which is followed in progressive countries such as the US and the UK, and the prohibition for girls to pursue secondary education. Both are gender norms, but it is much easier for a woman in the UK to break the first one than for a girl in Aghanistan

[50] An example of a question that does not meet the minimum standard set by this work is in this article: Florence Ashley, "What is it like to Have a Gender Identity?," Mind, 132 (October 2023):1053-1073. https://www.florenceashley.com/uploads/1/2/4/4/124439164/ashley_what_is_it_like_to_have_a_gender_identity.pdf. The article signals the absolute incapacity of gender identity theorists to accept that not all people believe in the existence of a changeable gender identity.

[51] "The Law of Inclusion," Report of the Independent Expert on protection against violence and discrimination based on sexual orientation and gender identity, Victor Madrigal-Borloz, 3 June 2021, A/HRC/47/27, https://www.ohchr.org/en/documents/thematic-reports/ahrc4727-law-inclusion-report-independent-expert-sexual-orientation-and.

[52] Ibidem, paras 17-22.

to break the second one. We do not normally define a woman who keeps her own surname after marriage as gender diverse, nor actually the girl who wants to attend school in Afghanistan. Gender diversity seems confined to superficial behaviours such as adopting a style of dress traditionally and stereotypically associated with the opposite sex, maybe while doing nothing to dismantle more fundamental gender roles.[53]As is evident, this definition provides no clarity, which is especially troubling because the report's own definition of "gender norm" is problematic. Gender norms are, according to the report, "roles, forms of expression and behaviours that are considered entitlements or burdens according to their sex assigned at birth."[54] It is common scientific knowledge that sex is determined at conception and can be detected prenatally through testing, from a simple ultrasound to sophisticated genetic testing, and is recorded at birth with a 99.98% accuracy between visual inspection and chromosomal sex.[55] Using the "assigned at birth" terminology greatly exaggerates the incidence of sex ambiguity at birth and dismisses medical and scientific advancement in sex detection testing in the last 70 years.

However, anyone familiar with gender identity theory will recognise "assigned at birth" as one of the signals that one is a follower of the theory. In this context, it renders the definition of gender norms meaningless. The report claims that gender norms inform the discrimination and violence affecting women and girls around the world, "including lesbian, bisexual and trans women."[56] However, if gender norms really did affect people according to their "sex assigned at birth" then "transwomen" would be affected by gender norms regulating male behaviour, as their sex at birth is the male sex. As the report itself recognises, gender norms confer entitlements on the male sex, not burdens.

---

[53] Many cross-dressing men are in very traditional heterosexual marriages.

[54] "The Law of Inclusion," Report of the Independent Expert on protection against violence and discrimination based on sexual orientation and gender identity, Victor Madrigal-Borloz, 3 June 2021, A/HRC/47/27, para 8 https://www.ohchr.org/en/documents/thematic-reports/ahrc4727-law-inclusion-report-independent-expert-sexual-orientation-and,.

[55] On sex differentiation, DSDs and intersex conditions, see Hilton, Emma and Wright, Colin, "Two Sexes." In, Sex and Gender. A Contemporary Reader, eds. Alice Sullivan and Selina Todd, (London: Routledge, 2024): 16-34, 27: "When assessing DSD frequency rationally restricted only to individuals with ambiguous reproductive anatomy or a disparity between their reproductive sex and external genitalia, the frequency drops dramatically to approximately 0.018 percent."

[56] IE Report, A/HRC/47/27, para 3.

The term "trans" is defined as follows in the SOGI IE's Report: "Persons whose gender identity does not correspond to the gender that they were assigned at birth."[57] In order for this definition to be understood, there are three assumptions that one needs to accept. The first one is that sex and gender are both synonymous and distinct. Previously the Report spoke of sex assigned at birth, now this has become gender assigned at birth. If, as gender identity theory posits, gender and sex are not the same, this slippage between sex and gender is unacceptable, unless one uses gender as the polite substitute for sex. Second, one needs to accept that sex is assigned, rather than simply recorded, at birth. Third, and most crucially, that all individuals have a gender identity. The entirety of gender identity theory is predicated on the dogma that gender identity is universal and on the invention of a default "cis" identity for those who are not trans, or, as the Report offers, "persons whose experience of gender is, or is perceived to be, in conformity with the sex assigned at birth." What is an "experience of gender" in the context of a society that rigidly divides roles on the basis of sex, and in one that does not? No data could be produced that divides a population on the basis of an "experience" that there is no way of assessing objectively.

In order to embed gender identity theory in international law, there needs to be a process of embedding terms such as "gender identity" and "trans/cis" across space and time. One way to do so is to reinterpret all historical and global experiences of "gender non conformity" through the lens of gender identity theory. All specific cultural experiences are flattened and reshaped to fit the cis/trans binary.The IE's Report refers to "two-spirit persons (North America), muxes (Mexico), hijra (India), kathoey (Thailand), bakla (Philippines), travestis (Argentina and Brazil), fa'afafine (the Samoan islands) and leiti (Tonga)."[58] Although the report acknowledges that these examples do not necessarily fit the categories devised by gender identity theory, it still brings them up to bolster the claim that gender identity is a universal cultural presence.[59] In reality, all of these names, and

---

[57] IE Report, A/HRC/47/27, para 8.

[58] IE Report, A/HRC/47/27, para 9.

[59] There has been criticism from gender scholars to this approach, although by lumping all non-Western experiences of gender together follows in the same Western hegemonic binarism it is so keen to decry. In his last report, the former IE on SOGI focuses on the "colonialist" dimension of sex and gender; "Protection against Violence and Discrimination Based on Sexual Orientation and Gender Identity, Report of the Independent Expert on protection against violence and discrimination based on sexual orientation n gender identity, 25 July 2023,

more (e.g. the femminielli in Naples), are used to describe effeminate gay males who were accepted in these very traditional societies only to the extent that they made no claim to manhood. Rather than proving that these societies had or have less rigid binary rules on sex roles, they prove precisely the opposite: the rules were/are so strict and so rigid that the only way to accommodate those who did not comply was to exclude them. Nobody thought that effeminate gay men were real women: the point was that they were not "real" men. There is no equivalent gender diversity for women, who were simply not allowed to escape the gender roles assigned to them on the basis of sex. The only example that is sometimes brought up is that of the Albanian "sworn virgins" (*burrnesha*),[60] girls who live as boys if they grow up in families with no male children, to make sure that property is inherited through the male line, as per tradition. This confirms, rather than challenges, the patriarchal nature of Albanian traditional culture.

The history and development of the concept of gender identity is quite precisely situated in a specific time and place, the post-war period in advanced Western countries. But this specificity is inconsistent with the project to naturalise gender identity as an essential and omnipresent facet of the human experience. Therefore gender identity theory lumps together quite distinct traditions affecting a tiny number of gay males in patriarchal societies, and in a move designed to embed gender identity not only in society, but in law, claims that several legal systems recognised genders outside the female/male binary.[61] The proliferation of "post-colonial" studies in universities situated in the former colonial powers or its "white" colonies (so UK, US, Canada, Australia, New Zealand) has resulted in an immense academic production pushing one single narrative, that colonialism and the British empire imposed sex binarism and taught biological sex to "noble natives." It is a narrative that is adopted uncritically in gender identity theory even if it contradicts much of what we know about human culture.[62] Just to give one example, this narrative misinterprets the absence

---

A/78/227, https://documents-dds-ny.un.org/doc/UNDOC/GEN/N23/218/47/PDF/N2321847.pdf?OpenElement.

[60] Marija Brujić and Vladimir Krstić, "Sworn Virgins of the Balkan Highlands," Traditiones 50/3 (2021): 113-130.

[61] As noted, the last report from Victor Madrigal-Borloz as Independent Expert focuses on this topic; see A/78/227 https://www.ohchr.org/en/documents/thematic-reports/a78227-protection-against-violence-and-discrimination-based-sexual.

[62] See Lalor, Kay, "Queer Legacies of Colonialism. " In The Queer Outside the Law, eds. Senthorun Raj and Peter Dunne (London: Palgrave MacMillan, 2021):

of specific laws against male homosexuality in colonial territories (laws that were often imposed by the British Empire) as a sign that pre-colonial societies accepted homosexuality. In the first instance, this narrative flattens the histories of different countries in different continents across time. Additionally, it fails to recognise that not all cultures sanction behaviour by means of legal rules. For example, in Italy homosexuality was never illegal, not even during fascism (and this is one of the reasons why English homosexuals did not fear arrest in Italy).[63] However, a mix of Catholic rules and social mores ensured that homosexuality was condemned and shunned by society. Only an analysis that takes into account the diversity of pre-colonial cultures and the ways in which they regulated social and sexual behaviour can shed light on attitudes on sexual orientation. This narrative also fails to take into account what practices were considered acceptable and what was the rationale of their existence and recognition.[64] Instead we get a very unsophisticated application of the "colonialist" framework, especially in its white Western model, to diverse cultures that are all flattened under the gender identity theory pattern. It goes without saying that normally these societies implemented a strict control of women and their bodies, against which there was no respite in the form of alternative gender roles.

Gender identity theory is predicated on a strict and rigid understanding of gender norms grounded in sex difference, which makes the very existence of a transition possible and "readable." Without accepting that females are recognised by the roles they play, it would be impossible for males to inhabit those roles and make themselves recognisable as women. In fact, most MtF men embrace stereotypes of femininity that are considered with horror by women in progressive societies.[65] How much gender identity

---

23-48. The chapter focuses on the effect of colonialism on UK law, but opens with the usual reference to sodomy laws in former British colonies.

[63] Beccalossi, Chiara, "The Italian Vice: Male Homosexuality and British Tourism in Southern Italy." In Italian Sexualities Uncovered, eds.Valeria P. Babini, Chiara Beccalossi and Lucy Riall (London: Palgrave MacMillan, 2015): 185-206.

[64] In Afghanistan the rape of young boys was and is condoned by social rules, though now it is illegal. See Musa Khan Jalalzai, Child Sex, Bacha Bazi and Prostitution in Afghanistan (Saarbrücken: Lap Lambert Academic Publishing GmbH, 2011).

[65] This interview with a US transsexual from the 1970s is very revealing: "I'm really at odds with the women's movement," announced Beth, a five years postoperative transsexual, married, with four adopted children. "I believe in equal pay for equal jobs, but that's about as far as it goes. I certainly disapprove of the breaking down of the male and female roles. When you start putting women in

theory depends on rigid gender roles is exemplified by this passage by Kerry O'Halloran on the transitioning process:[66]

> It might be added that transitioning cannot be seen as an event: it is a process that may take many years and never be completed; it may also happen that sufficient transitioning will be subjectively achieved by merely changing external appearance – name, clothes, hairstyle, speech etc. – to conform with *social expectations* [emphasis added] of desired gender identity.

Without the social expectations there is no conforming and no desired outcome of "passing" as the preferred sex/gender identity. Liberalising gender norms makes gender roles more fluid and more difficult to pin down to rigid masculine/feminine identities. Without clearly readable gender roles, how would we even recognise transgender persons? FtM women tend to follow even stricter models of masculinity, helped, no doubt, by the stronger effect testosterone has on the female body, making their passing as males easier, though they rarely adopt the model of the effeminate male.

Gender identity theory adopts a "male as default" view of gender diversity. In reality, the majority of women who fight gender norms around the world are not even aware of gender identity theory and do not believe they have a gender identity that they are empowered to change in order to avoid oppression. If it were true that gender identity overrides one's sex, women could easily avoid gendered oppression by identifying out of their sex. This is not open to them, not even to save their own lives, because one cannot identify out of one's sex. One can hide or disguise one's sex, and women have done this in the past sometimes to save their life or to access professions traditionally closed to women. Gender non-conformity is an artificial interpretation of the very nuanced way in which one approaches

---

male roles you destroy the family unit. I certainly don't want to give up rny role as a wife and mother. Men are expected to act in a certain fashion and so are women. I personally enjoy being treated as a woman. I don't even like dressing as a man. I hate, for example, wearing pants. I feel extremely feminine and I always want to look that way, too." The article acknowledges that clinging to femininity stereotypes is both necessary and desirable for transsexuals. Lynda Crawford, "A Charm School for Transsexuals," TVIC Journal, 6(54) (16 April 1977): 2. https://www.digitaltransgenderarchive.net/files/pz50gw148. Gender identity theorists fetishise the history of transsexuality and the courage of "transwomen" of the past. Reading the primary materials paints quite a different picture.

66 Kerry O'Halloran, Sexual Orientation, Gender Identity and International Human Rights Law (London: Routledge, 2020), 26.

the norms regulating one's sex in society. In fact, gender conformity is on a spectrum, and most people are neither fully conforming nor fully rebelling. This is also because some gender norms are not oppressive, but necessary to allow for the different biology of men and women to be recognised when it affects men and women, and especially women, whose biology is more challenging in societies shaped by the male experience of the world. It may very well be that in a society designed taking into account that the human experience is not just the male experience, there would be no need for special rules to remedy the male-as-default model. But we do not live in such a society anywhere in the world. And it may very well be that, if men never sexually assaulted women, in time our need for privacy would reduce and we would feel freer to share spaces and services with males. We clearly are not there yet, nor will we get there sooner if we force women to share spaces with men in the current conditions, when male sexual violence is endemic.

In the attempt to bolster gender identity as a natural human experience, gender identity theory conflates transgender identities with "intersex" people who have their sex "assigned" after tests (in the past sex would be very rarely wrongly assigned if no appropriate testing was available, but the history of intersex conditions is flattened into an ahistoric landscape where what happened 70 years ago still happens). The argument is that intersex conditions prove that sex is not binary, therefore sex can be on a spectrum, therefore transgender people are simply moving along the spectrum.[67] In reality, people with differences of sexual development (DSDs) are still male or female. Sex is not determined by chromosomes, but by gametes. Humans are either "designed" to produce small motile gametes (sperm) or large immotile ones (eggs) and our bodies are always organised around these two reproductive functions,[68] even when they cannot perform them successfully or at all. If genetic conditions affect the chromosomal profile or secondary or primary sex characteristics, these conditions do not change the potential reproductive function of the individual affected by a DSD. These conditions are not identities one can take on or abandon at will and have nothing to do with a gender identity, which, we are told, does not reside in the body.

---

[67] Even if sex were on a spectrum,"transwomen" would be at the very end of the male spectrum.

[68]Although it would seem banal to state it, this does not mean women and men have to perform this reproductive function, but only that they have the in-built capacity to do so.

Only by performing this close textual analysis one can reveal the lack of foundations of the edifice of gender identity theory. The definitions developed through such tools as the Yogyakarta Principles[69] will be relied upon in domestic and international courts as the basis of the reasoning and for conferring rights to transgender individuals. Specifically, the definition of gender identity developed in the Yogyakarta Principles will "migrate" into numerous legal materials produced by international organisations and courts, both international and domestic. A crucial part of the definition is that gender identity is not a facet of the transgender experience, but a universal aspect of the human condition. Another essential element is the construction of a strict trans/cis binarism, whereby the existence of an ineffable "cis" identity is derived from the transformation of a supposed mental health condition (dysphoria) into an "identity." The terms trans and cis are of course central in gender identity theory. It may come as a surprise that the term trans was barely used in the Yogyakarta Principles, and the term cis never used.[70] Neither of them has much of a history in international legal texts, however they are being used more and more and

[69] These Principles, developed in 2006, were drafted by a group of human rights activists and academics, and they will be examined in more detail in Chapter 4, "The Yogyakarta Principles. Principles on the Application of International Human Rights Law in Relation to Sexual Orientation and Gender Identity," March 2007, https://yogyakartaprinciples.org/.

[70] In an interview in 2016 Stephen Whittle clarifies that this was not an oversight, but a deliberate choice. To the question "The language is very particular, there is no mentioning of trans. Why?" Whittle replies: "The use of the language is very deliberate, because the principles are about universal values–rights that every person has a right to. It was important that what we created was absolutely universal; human rights for people whose gender identity was variant in some way, shape or form or whose sexual orientation did not follow a heteronormative pathway. And that we wanted the principles to be an opening of the debate rather than a closing down of the debate. So they had to be open, they had to envisage a legal framework in the world in which people had true liberties and choices to develop autonomously as individuals those aspects of their identity which was best for them; to make personal and political choices that were different from the normative values that were otherwise expected of them." Caroline Ausserer, "Stephen Whittle: 'The Yogyakarta Principles provide guidance and are a constant reference point,' Heinrich Böll Stiftung, 21 July 2016, https://www.boell.de/en/2016/07/20/yogyakarta-principles-provide-guidance-and-are-constant-reference-point. The interview is part of a series on the ten years from the Principles. In the entire series there is no dissenting voice and not a single criticism, except that the Principles do not go far enough. https://www.boell.de/en/focus-human-rights-lgbti-people-ten-years-yogyakarta-principles.

this is evident in the work done by the IE on SOGI. The literature on this binary distinction is considerable, especially in the fields of sociology and gender studies.[71]

A paradigmatic example of how "cis" has started being used in legal texts[72] is in Kerry O'Halloran recent monograph on gender identity in common law jurisdictions. In the Background chapter at the beginning of the work, he describes in the following terms the alienation that can be felt by LGBT individuals:[73]

> While sexual identity usually corresponds to gender as determined at birth (cisgender), for some it does not, and this can lead to profound feelings of alienation: the LGBT community as a whole has long suffered alienation, but because of social rejection rather than a self-perceived disconnect between gender and sexuality

We note the slippage between sexual identity and gender (at birth), knowing full well that sex and gender are not the same thing, and that it is not gender to be determined at birth, but sex. More worryingly, the term cisgender, completely unintelligible to those who do not follow and are conversant in gender identity theory, is introduced without explanation and without any reference to its origin[74] and meaning, as if it were a normal descriptive word, such as sex, or sexual orientation.

Additionally, when the definition of a protected category is changed in law, all the individuals belonging to that protected category are affected. Changing the definition of woman from a definition based on material reality to one based on self-identification modifies the relationship between the protected category and all those who are defined as belonging to it. If the definition of property in law were modified to include those

---

[71] Providing even a pared down literature is an impossible task. The work of Judith Butler is apparently inevitable. Her Gender Trouble has generated a whole field of studies. Gender Trouble: Feminism and the Subversion of Identity (New York: Routledge 1990).

[72] This work does not focus on US practice, but as an example, the New York City Human Rights Commission adopts gender identity terminology in full, see https://www.nyc.gov/site/cchr/law/legal-guidances-gender-identity-expression.page.

[73] Kerry O'Halloran, Sexual Orientation, Gender Identity and International Human Rights Law (London: Routledge, 2020), 14.

[74] The term cissexual (zissexuell in the original German) was first used by German sexologist Volkmar Sigusch in "The NeoSexual Revolution," Archives of Sexual Behaviour 27 (1998): 331-359,doi:10.1023/A:1018715525493

who self-identify as property owners, and not just those who can prove title, all property owners would be affected, not least because there could be competing claims to movable or immovable property, one based on title, the other on self-identification. By analogy this is what is happening to women. Their "title" to certain rights, based on the material reality of being born with a female body, is contested by individuals born with a male body who claim to be women on the basis of some unspecified and unverifiable self-identification. Although race is an artificial distinction based on superficial differences, and it truly is on a spectrum, people who self-define as belonging to one particular racial group without displaying those superficial differences are immediately called out as impostors, as most famously the case of Rachel Dolezal proves.[75] Why does society think that appropriating the history of oppression of African Americans is deplorable, but appropriating the history of oppression of women is not, unless society really is not ready to acknowledge that history of oppression at all?

As already noted, gender identity theory posits that gender and sex are two separate realities, although at times it uses the two terms interchangeably, to engineer the switch from sex to gender (identity) in an underhand manner. Analysis of the legal sources will show that gender and sex sometimes are used interchangeably and, as we shall see, when gender was introduced in legal texts, somewhat controversially, it was used to refer to the rules that restrict and limit the self-determination and autonomy of women in society. Evidently, in order to elevate this term to an identity worthy of protection, it needs to be stripped of these negative connotations. Therefore gender identity theory neutralises the term gender and strips it of the meanings associated with sexism, that is, the feminist use of gender. It is in the slippage between the feminist use of gender and

---

[75] See Doreen St. Phélix, "The Rachel Divide: A Disturbing Portrait of Dolezal's Racial Fraudulence," The New Yorker, April 26, 2018, https://www.newyorker.com/culture/culture-desk/the-rachel-divide-review-a-disturbing-portrait-of-dolezals-racial-fraudulence. Robin Dembroff and Dee Payton argue in this article why the two are not comparable but since the argument basically claims that difference rests on the fact that "transwomen are women," coupled with some ahistorical argument about racial oppression being intergenerational and sex oppression not being so (which clearly conflicts with the previous claim) and therefore totally misses the point of the debate, it really provides no intellectual assistance. "Why We Shouldn't Compare Transracial to Transgender Identity," Boston Review, 18 November 2020, https://www.bostonreview.net/articles/robin-dembroff-dee-payton-breaking-analogy-between-race-and-gender/.

gender as an identity worth of legal protection that gender identity theory is at its weakest. In order to embed gender identity in international human rights law, it needs to be proven that gender always meant something different from sex (which is not true), that it does not necessarily refer only to women, and yet was developed as a concept by feminists in the 1970s who did not accept biological determinism. There is indeed evidence that we live in gendered societies, but this does not mean that those power hierarchies and preconceptions become our identity. Gender identity is described in gender identity theory positively, as a deeply intimate thought process that then may be expressed, or not, as "gender expression." While rejecting biological determinism, gender identity theory embraces "gender determinism," positing that women dress, speak and think in a certain way. How did the deeply negative concept of gender become neutralised by its distillation into a gender identity that is our own subjejctive creation, instead of an exogenous imposition? In the next chapter we will track its history with the post-war obsession with transvestism and transsexualism and the beginnings of trans rights activism.

CHAPTER 2

GENDER IDENTITY IN MEDICAL AND TRANSGENDER RIGHTS ORGANISATIONS LITERATURE

We vow upon our sacred honor to break the bonds of fear, degradation, oppression and bigotry. We come to build bridges of trust, dignity, compassion, and love. Hand in hand, pursuing life, liberty, and happiness, we go out with love in our hearts, care in our eyes and comfort for one another on our lips. Let it be known that we passed through this world for no other purpose than to share our special gifts for the good of all humankind.
Note: At the conclusion of the presentation it is appropriate to exchange greetings and other signs of mutual jubilation which may be enhanced as desirable with displays of fireworks.
—Declaration of Gender Liberty, Last Paragraph, ICTLEP[76]

The concept of gender identity seems to have come into being in international law fully formed, like Athena from the head of Zeus.[77] In the literature produced by the Independent Expert on SOGI the genealogy of this term is not outlined at all, giving an impression of historical permanence. In the words of the IE, "Human experience in relation to gender identity and expression is both complex and rich."[78] There is no reference to the history of this term in the Report or in any of the material

---

[76] Proceedings from the Fifth International Conference on Transgender Law and Employment Policy, July 1996, https://www.digitaltransgenderarchive.net/files/0g354f33w.

[77] Looking for an explanation of the origin of the term in academic literature will not bring any result. Usually its existence is simply affirmed in a dogmatic manner. Sandra Duffy, "Contested Subjects of Human Rights: Trans–and Gender-variant Subjects of International Human Rights Law," Modern Law Review, 84(5) (2019): 1041–1065, doi: 10.1111/1468-2230.12633. At 1043 the author claims not to want to engage in a "deconstruction" of the term gender identity in international law, without giving a reason. It is the only linguistic artefact that scholars who specialise in deconstructing everyting are unwilling to subject to any analysis at all. Gender identity simply "is."

[78] IE on SOGI Report, A/HRC/47/27, para 16.

produced by the Independent Expert since the creation of the mandate, or in any of the secondary literature that I have accessed from gender identity scholars, who all seem singularly uninterested in the origin of this term.

In this chapter I will track the development of gender identity narratives in the work of transgender rights activists and medical institutions. It is useful to track these concurrently, because the two areas, the political/legal and the medical, are tightly interwoven, in a fashion that is unprecedented for any other social rights movement. Disability rights do not constitute an appropriate analogy because gender identity theorists insist that there is no pathological element to transgenderism at all.

One of the earliest uses of gender identity in medical literature is by Robert J Stoller, an American psychiatrist, in a 1964 article titled "The Hermaphrodic Identity of Hermaphrodites."[79] The title gives an idea of the intellectual milieu in which the term was developed. In the article, professor Stoller claims that the infant-parent relationship and children's perception of their own genitalia are determining factors in developing the "ultimate gender identity," as he described it, referencing the work of John Money.

John Money was the psychologist and sexologist responsible for the treatment of David Reimer, a baby who had been left mutilated by a botched circumcision.[80] His parents saw Dr Money in a TV interview and contacted him; Dr Money convinced them to let the doctors perform so-called sex reassignment surgery on the baby and then raise him as a girl, to prove his theory that a child's gender identity was malleable in the first years of life. David Reimer and his twin brother were raised as a girl and as a boy respectively and forced to enact sexual behaviours in front of the doctor. Both twins committed suicide eventually, David Reimer after trying to revert to a male body and identity.

---

[79] Robert J. Stoller, "The Hermaphrodic Identity of Hermaphrodites," Journal of Nervous and Mental Disease, 139(5) (1964):53-57. John Money and Claude Migeon opened the Johns Hopkins Gender Identity Clinic in Boston in 1965 https://studentaffairs.jhu.edu/lgbtq/education/lgbtq-history-at-jhu/#:~:text=1965%3A%20John%20Money%20and%20Claude,student%20organization%20at%20JHU%20Homewood.

[80] The National Library of New Zealand includes in its collection several papers from Dr Money. https://natlib.govt.nz/records/22819054. The history of the Reimer twins can be found here https://embryo.asu.edu/taxonomy/term/148752.

What is crucial for the development of gender identity theory is the intersection between the work done by sexologists and psychiatrists, such as Stoller, Money and Benjamin in the 1960s, and the movement for the rights of transvestites and transsexuals (as they were then called) also coming into prominence in the 1960s. In 1963, a New York transvestite, Fred Shaw/Siobhan Fredericks, started publishing a magazine titled "Turnabout." From this blog[81] we learn that the magazine was more open to transsexuality and of activities that Victoria Prince, a well-known transvestite in the US at the time, regarded as fetishistic.[82] Turnabout was published off and on, from 1963 to 1968. In it, Fredericks wrote a section titled "Kaleidoscope" with news of interest to the transvestite/transsexual community. In Issue number 2, from October 1963, we find this report in the Kaleidoscope section of the magazine.[83]

> Early in the Summer, the Schering Corporation published a precis of its Third International Simposium on the potential of women, held at the University of California Medical Center in San Francisco. Among the participants was Dr. John Money, associate professor of medical psychology and pediatrics at John Hopkins University, Baltimore, and a leader in the fast-growing field of genetics. Dr. Money, speaking about hermaphrodites in particular and about human beings in general, pointed out that the evidence he has collected "shows that it is possible for psychosexual differentiation to be contradictory to chromosomal sex, gonadal sex, hormonal sex, external genital sex, internal genital sex, and to agree instead with the assigned sex." Dr. Money went on to say, "One is confronted with the conclusion that there is no primary genetic or other innate mechanism to preordain the masculinity or femminility of psychosexual differentiation." No matter what an individual's various sexual components are, Dr. Money seems to find that his gender role and identity become "imprinted" through environmental influences in early childhood and then become, usually, irreversible. "The die is cast, pretty well, by the age of six," he noted, although he does not hold that environmental influences are the sole components in this complex process.

---

[81] A Gender Variance Who's Who, https://zagria.blogspot.com/2012/10/siobhan-fredericks-193-scientist.html#.Y_DOfnbMLwY.

[82] Victoria Prince was another New York transvestite and publisher of the magazine "Transvestia" which had a much longer run, into the 1980s. The first issue was published in 1960. Revealingly, it starts with a quote from the Gospel According to Thomas, an extra-canonical gospel; Virginia Prince, Transvestia, Vol. 01 No. 01, January 1960, https://www.digitaltransgenderarchive.net/files/9k41zd73v.

[83] Siobhan Fredericks, "Kaleidoscope," Turnabout, Vol 1 No. 2 (October 1963): 28-30, https://www.digitaltransgenderarchive.net/files/tx31qh944.

This article illustrates the theory Dr Money supported, that you could raise a child in the "correct" psychosexual sex even if sex had been "assigned" wrongly, generalising from the tiny number of infants born with DSDs to the general population. This is at the basis of his above-mentioned experiment with David Reimer. Money's conclusion was that "there is no primary genetic or other innate mechanism to preordain the masculinity or femininity of psycho-sexual differentiation." He believed that "gender identity can be taught" and to this extent modern gender theory, positing an innate gender identity, diverges significantly from one of its founding fathers. The early post-war era also saw several well publicised surgeries, such as George/Catherine Jorgensen in the 1950s,[84]and Reed/Rita Erickson and George Jamieson/April Ashley in the 1960s.[85] The stereotypical image of the transsexual at the time was the attractive, very feminine individual with a public persona and always post-operative. In reality, the primary sources of the time give us the image of heterosexual males, often middle aged, very often married, with a secret transvestism fetish.

In 1969, the Albany Trust and the Erickson Educational Foundation[86] organised the "First International Symposium on Gender Identity."[87] The Symposium was chaired by Prof C.J. Dewhurst, who was professor of obstetrics at Queen Charlotte's Hospital in London. In his opening remarks, Prof Dewhurst notes that it would be "presumptuous" of him to attempt to define gender identity, noting all one can say is that it signals "a doubt in the mind of an individual about their true sex."[88] Gender identity (or better, the disconnect between the mind and the body about sex) is presented as a medical condition for which there ought to be a cure, at least in childhood, the question being whether in adulthood it ought instead to be accepted and affirmed through surgery and legal recognition.

---

[84] Christine Jorgensen, A Personal Autobiography (Minneapolis: Cleis Press, 2000).

[85] Reed Erickson is the founder of the Erickson Educational Foundation (see below); April Ashley became famous for the *Corbett v Corbett* case, [1970] 2 AER 33 concerning the validity of their marriage in the English courts.

[86] The Albany Trust was founded in 1958 and describes itself as a specialist counselling and psychoterapy charity, with a focus on sexuality (https://www.albanytrust.org/); the Erickson Educational Foundation was founded in 1964 by Reed Erickson, a woman FtM individual and millionaire. Erickson was a patient of Harry Benjamin (https://www.nyclgbtsites.org/site/erickson-educational-foundation-new-york-office/).

[87] There were in total 4 symposia: the first one in London in 1969; the last one in California in 1980.

[88] https://www.wpath.org/media/cms/Documents/History/Symposium/1969/Prof%20Dewhurst%20Opening%20Remarks.pdf.

From the medical world[89] the concept of gender identity migrates into the writings of transgender and transsexual rights activists in the United States, as evident from the documentation contained in the Digital Transgender Archive.[90]A lot gets lost in this "translation" and a lot of misinformation starts getting spread in the media, to make transsexuality acceptable, and its surgical affirmation a routine medical treatment. A 1964 article from the US tabloid "The National Insider" contains all the prejudices of the era, and the building of the narrative of normalisation of what is preposterously called "the fourth sex" (the other three being male, female and homosexual).[91] The article contains an interview with Dr Benjamin, which provides a veneer of legitimacy to these claims, but also reveals how fundamental the sexual aspect of transsexuality was considered at the time (strictly male sexuality), and how this was frankly discussed.

When the above-mentioned First International Symposium on Gender Identity took place in London in 1969, the Erickson Educational Foundation had already established its pivotal role in the promotion of transgender rights in the US and internationally; Reed Erickson, who had built a fortune through oil investments, donated millions in support of transgender causes in the US. From the very beginning, "trans rights" were supported by wealthy donations, making them qualitatively different from classic civil rights causes. An important player in the development of gender identity theory and trans rights specifically was the International Conference on Transgender Law and Policy (ICTLEP), founded in 1992 by Phyllis Randolph Frye, the first transsexual judge in the United States.[92] The conference took place between 1992 and 1997 in Texas.[93] Frye is a crucial source for the history of the inclusion of the "T" (transgender/transsexual)

---

[89] The history of the medicalisation of transgender individuals will be considered in Chapter 10.
[90] https://www.digitaltransgenderarchive.net/.
[91]Arnold Wells, "The Fourth Sex!," The National Insider, July 19, 1964, 4-5, https://www.digitaltransgenderarchive.net/files/hm50tr91d.
[92] https://www.digitaltransgenderarchive.net/news/2016-07-the-international-conference-on-transgender-law-and-employment-policy.
[93]As Frye recounts in "The International Bill of Gender Rights vs. The Cider House Rules: Transgenders Struggle with the Courts Over What Clothing They Are Allowed to Wear on the Job, Which Restroom They are Allowed to Use on the Job, Their Right to Marry, and the Very Definition of Their Sex," William&Mary Journal of Women&Law, 7(1) (2000): 133-212. https://scholarship.law.wm.edu/wmjowl/vol7/iss1/6, the term transgenderist was coined by Virginia Prince (formerly Charles Prince) in the 1970s.

in the LGB rights movement. The alliance between the "LGB" and the "T" is one of the founding myths of gender identity theory. The consistent narrative about the communion of interests in the LGBT community, going back to time immemorial, or at least to the 1969 Stonewall riots, is obsessively repeated by gender identity theorists.[94] This is not what Frye reports in this 2000 article:[95]

> At the beginning of the struggle for transgender inclusion in ENDA [Employment Non Discrimination Act] (1994), many gay and lesbian detractors argued with us that we were simply trying to catch onto the coat tails of a twenty year old gay and lesbian political movement. It was akin to saying that we had not paid our dues: that we were trying to add on. On the airplane flight back from a heated discussion with the Human Rights Campaign (HRC) on September 17, 1995, Tere Prasse, Sarah DePalma and I were decompressing and rehashing what had been argued and discussed. Tere asserted that we needed to change our stance from being wanted in for the first time to being reintegrated into a community of which we originally belonged and only during the past two decades has been excluded.

At the Second ICTLEP in 1993, an "International Bill of Gender Rights" was discussed. From the recorded history we see that Stephen Whittle, a regular contributor to the Conference and in the advisory committee for the Yogyakarta Principles (as well as being involved in the drafting of the Gender Recognition Act 2004) is one of the people linking all these initiatives together.

The 1993 Conference also allows us an insider's perspective on developing gender identity theory, which did not come into mainstream consciousness until the late 2010s, engendering the impression that its most extreme demands, such as the claim that sex is subordinated to gender identity, or that it is a colonial invention, were a new phenomenon, quite separate

---

[94] Stonewall UK takes its name from the famous 1969 New York riots. Stonewall was an LGB rights organisation until 2015, when it added the T. Since then there has been a campaign of rewriting of history establishing the transgender credentials of the Stonewall riots and of the political association between LGB and trans rights. https://www.stonewall.org.uk/our-work/campaigns/2015-stonewall-extends-remit-become-lgbt-charity-and-begins-journey-trans.

[95] Phyllis Randolph Frye, The International Bill of Gender Rights vs. The Cider House Rules: Transgenders Struggle with the Courts Over What Clothing They Are Allowed to Wear on the Job, Which Restroom They are Allowed to Use on the Job, Their Right to Marry, and the Very Definition of Their Sex," William&Mary Journal of Women&Law, 7(1) (2000): 133-212, note 65.

from the reasonable demands of equality and non discrimination of “traditional” transsexuals. On the contrary, contributions to the conference evidence quite developed thinking along those lines already. For example, Laura Skaer[96] recalls how arguments about the anatomy of transsexuals were advanced, to the effect that “there were women who just happened where the clitoris is a little big. Our vagina didn’t quite open and ovaries formed in the wrong place.” We see here the narrative of the “female penis” or the wrong body narrative that acquired so much currency in the new millennium. The proceedings also report the speech by Phyllis Frye at the famous 1993 March on Washington for Gay, Lesbian and Bi Rights and Liberation:

> The transgendered community includes crossdressers and transvestites, passing women and female impersonators, drag queens and male impersonators, and pre-, non-, and post-operative transsexuals. We definitely include female-to-males as in Joan of Arc, George Sand, Leslie Feinberg and the transgendered women who fought bravely as soldiers of our colonial and civil wars. Knowing this, why is it that with two rally stages, all day long, there are no no female-to-male transgendered speakers? We embrace all races, sexual orientations, creeds, religions, ethnicities, nationalities, ages and physical impediment. Why is it then, that with two rally stages, all day long, there is only one transgendered political speaker? Our history reveals that the majority of those people who died at the beginning of the Nazi Holocaust while wearing pink triangles were the transgendered of all sexual orientations. Our history reveals that the real heroes in the Stonewall uprising were the transgendered, the leather cultists, and the street hustlers who stood up to the bully cops and presented in-your-face resistance to being pushed around further. Why then, are the transgendered being omitted and snubbed from the focus of the upcoming Stonewall 25? Sadly, the reward to the transgendered, the leather cultists and the street hustlers of Stonewall is condescension and stereotyping.

In the speech a trans identity is attributed to female figures from the past who did not conform to the gender stereotypes of their times (in an extremely regressive move, instead of recognising their courage as women, the narrative implies that if they wanted to write books, or go to battle, they could not possibly have been “real women”). The speech went on to say:

---

[96]A MtF transsexual man who talks about transition in this interview https://thecrossingchurch.com/Resource/Listen/im-trans-and-i-love-jesus.

> In order for us to resist this bigots' ploy, this division, we must today embrace each others stereotypes. We must embrace each other's labels with pride; we must unite. We must go into Congress and into the state houses speaking for lesbian and gay and bisexual AND TRANSGENDER–AND TRANSGENDER–say it–AND TRANSGENDER–and transgender rights. We must seek legal language that protects us on the basis of both "sexual orientation AND GENDER IDENTIFICATION." When you speak to your Member of Congress, tell them House Bill 431[97] needs to be amended to add "and gender identification"–"sexual orientation and gender identification."

The extensive excerpts give us a glimpse of the genealogy of these political claims. The language evidences their shaky intellectual foundations: "embrace each others [sic] stereotypes." From a theoretical point of view, the most revealing contribution to the 1993 ICTLEP is by Ronald Garet, Professor of Law and Religion at the University of Southern California Law Center. It is an attempt to ground in history gender identity theory, and provide it with a quasi-religious foundation. The entire contribution is worth reading, especially for those who have already noticed how gender identity theory leverages religious thinking to embed its tenets into policy (including the repetition of creeds such as "transwomen are women"),[98] for its attempt to ground the tenets of gender identity theory in Christian thinking and in the Bible.

---

[97] H.R. 431–Civil Rights Act of 1993, Outlawing discrimination on the basis of sexual orientation.
https://www.congress.gov/bill/103rd-congress/house-bill/431/text?s=1&r=33.

[98] The ubiquitous nature of this statement rests on an unspoken agreement never to question its intellectual basis. An example in Peter Dunne's article, "(Trans)Forming Single-Gender Services and Communal Accommodations," Social & Legal Studies, 26(5) (March 2017): 1-25, doi:
https://doi.org/10.1177/0964663917692027. At page 6 Dunne quotes Wodda and Panfil to the effect that "unequivocally 'trans women are women.'" One would expect the article cited would contain further information on this apodictic statement. In the article, Aimee Wodda and Vanessa Panfil, "Don't Talk to me about Deception: the Necessary Erosion of the Trans* Panic Defense," Albany Law Review 78(3) (2015): 927-971, page 952, cited by Dunne, simply state, "As mentioned earlier in this article, trans women are women," quoting an article on the Guardian by Jessica Valenti, an interview to a transwoman with no theoretical grounding to the statement; Jessica Valenti, "Transgender people want to exist without having to prove they are 'real'," The Guardian, June 20, 2014, https://www.theguardian.com/commentisfree/2014/jun/20/transgender-janet-mock-passing-realness. It is just a game of infinite regress. It is "turtles all the way down."

In the Proceedings of the Conference, the news is given that the International Bill of Gender Rights was slated to be presented at "some Committee with the United Nations" and the news is confirmed by one of the drafters of the Bill, Sharon Stuart, an attorney expert in military law. There seems to be no evidence in the UN's documents repository of any meeting at which the International Bill of Gender Rights was presented, though one can see certain similarities with the Yogyakarta Principles, and, as noted, Professor Stephen Whittle was a participant to ICTLEP at the time, and also involved in the drafting of the Principles. Professor Whittle also attended the 2004 meeting of the Human Rights Commission in Geneva as a member of the International Service for Human Rights.[99] This NGO was founded in 1984. One of their goals was to liberalise attendance by human rights NGOs to the proceedings of the Sub-Commission on Human Rights, as its founder recounts.[100] By the mid-2000s they were heavily involved in pushing gender identity in international law and they were involved in the Yogyakarta Principles' drafting. Several of the rights that we now associate with the Yogyakarta Principles, including the idea that gender is a universal aspect of the human condition,[101] the right to self-define one's gender identity, the right to affirmative medical care,[102] the right to access female only spaces on the

---

[99] Commission of Human Rights, Sixtieth Session, List of Attendance, E/CN.4/2004/INF.1, https://documents-dds-ny.un.org/doc/UNDOC/GEN/G04/139/58/pdf/G0413958.pdf?OpenElement.

[100] International Service for Human Rights, "Adrien-Claude Zoller: ISHR Founder" https://ishr.ch/defender-stories/adrien-claude-zoller-ishr-founder/.

[101] "All human beings carry within themselves an ever-unfolding idea of who they are and what they are capable of achieving. The individual's sense of self is not determined by chromosomal sex, genitalia, assigned birth sex, or initial gender role. Thus, the individual's identity and capabilities cannot be circumscribed by what society deems to be masculine or feminine behavior. It is fundamental that individuals have the right to define, and to redefine as their lives unfold, their own gender identities, without regard to chromosomal sex, genitalia, assigned birth sex, or initial gender role."

[102] The Right To Control And Change One's Own Body
All human beings have the right to control their bodies, which includes the right to change their bodies cosmetically, chemically, or surgically, so as to express a self-defined gender identity. Therefore, individuals shall not be denied the right to change their bodies as a means of expressing a self-defined gender identity; and further, individuals shall not be denied Human or Civil Rights on the basis that they have changed their bodies cosmetically, chemically, or surgically, or desire to do so as a means of expressing a self-defined gender identity.

basis of gender identity and not sex,[103] are already contained in the International Bill of Gender Rights.

In 1986, Tel Aviv hosted the Second Symposium on Psycholegal Aspects of Sexual Problems.[104] Funding was provided by the Schering Corporation, a company involved in financing research into transsexuality and one of the main producers of hormones for the pharmaceutical market, which we already saw mentioned as financing the "Third International Simposium on the Potential of Women," at the University of California Medical Center in San Francisco. This evidences another characteristic of the gender rights movement, the connection with pharmaceutical companies, a further distinguishing characteristic from other civil rights movements.[105] The programme of the symposium was relying on scholars from the United Kingdom, as noted in the introduction:

> A group of internationally known writers and researchers in this area were recruited from the United Kingdom; five speakers, whose papers are presented in the following pages attended, formed the basis of the seminar. Dr Haslam as author of "Sexual Disorders," and a researcher in this area and clinician for many years chaired the meeting. Professor DJ West from Cambridge spoke on the "Legal Aspects of Homosexuality," Mary Lorrigan from Newcastle spoke on the theme of the "Law, and Female Sexuality" and Dr Roy Mottram spoke on the "Legal Aspects of Transsexualism." Dr Willmott and Harry Brierley (both clinical psychologists working in the field in Great Britain) presented a paper on

[103] "The Right Of Access To Gendered Space And Participation In Gendered Activity.
Given the right to define one's own gender identity and the corresponding right to free expression of a self-defined gender identity, no individual should be denied access to a space or denied participation in an activity by virtue of a self-defined gender identity which is not in accord with chromosomal sex, genitalia, assigned birth sex, or initial gender role. Therefore, no individual shall be denied access to a space or denied participation in an activity by virtue of a self-defined gender identity which is not in accord with chromosomal sex, genitalia, assigned birth sex, or initial gender role."

[104] Second International Congress on Psychiatry, Law and Ethics, "Symposium on Psycholegal Aspects of Sexual Problems" Israel February 12th–16th 1986, https://www.digitaltransgenderarchive.net/downloads/cc08hf820.

[105] The medical dimension of this movement distinguishes it from all the civil rights movements of the past, including the LGB rights movement. The "right" to hormones and surgery, both genital and feminising surgery, is prevalent from the very beginning of this movement and recurs insistently in the ICTLEP proceedings and transgender and transsexuals publications, which are peppered with advertisements from plastic surgeons and endocrinologists.

> "Sex Change, the Dilemma," and Dr Richard Ekins, a sociologist in Northern Ireland involved with cases before the Court of Human Rights spoke on "Transsexualism and the Court of Human Rights."

Unfortunately the paper by Dr. Mottram, which could have shed some light on early legal strategies, is not available in the Archive. But he is the subject of an article published in 1984 in "The Listener," a magazine published by the BBC from 1929 to 1991. The article describes Dr. Mottram as a former naval officer and university lecturer, and a transvestite. The description of Mottram's background reveals all the usual elements: covert transvestism since childhood, a marriage, children and then a divorce by a non-accepting wife. Mottram also reveals ties with the Beaumont Society,[106] described as an organisation for heterosexual transvestites. The article's description of Dr. Mottram is highly revealing:

> Dressed as Rosemary, Dr Mottram sews his own clothes, gardens and goes shopping. He has two bikes, one for Rosemary, the other for Roy. "I cannot conceive of Rosemary standing up in front of 150 medical students and holding that audience" he says. "Similarly, when I'm working at home, if circumstances are right, then it's Rosemary that works on, say, bookwriting, essay-marking or lecture-preparing."

The people who were arguing for transgender rights in the 1980s and 1990s thought women were not authoritative enough to hold students' attention. Time and again the primary materials reveal sexist attitudes towards women, combined with a desire to inhabit those stereotypical roles, and therefore a hostile attitude towards women's liberation and the accompanying freedom to dress, act and speak without having to submit to stereotypes of femininity.

Sociologist Richard Ekins had no legal background, but his paper is the only one made available in the Transgender Archive and it is of considerable interest as it analyses the cases of *Corbett v Corbett*[107] and *M.T. v J.T.*[108] These two cases, the first from 1970 and decided in the High

---

[106] https://www.beaumontsociety.org.uk/. The Beaumont Society was founded in 1966 as a UK chapter of the US' Full Personality Expression secret society, established by Victoria Prince in 1962.
https://oac.cdlib.org/findaid/ark:/13030/c8dz0bfv/admin/. The unmistakable roots of gender identity theory in male cross-dressing and transvestite behaviour are all the more evident the more one researches its history.

[107] *Corbett v Corbett* [1970] 2 All ER 33.

[108] *M.T. v J.T.*, Superior Court of New Jersey, Appellate Division, United States (22 March 1976).

Court in the UK and the second in the Appellate Division of the Superior Court in New Jersey and from 1976, came to opposite conclusions as to what determined sex in the law and therefore whether transsexuals had the right to marry. According to the Judge in *Corbett v Corbett*, "biological" sex is what matters in law:

> I must now deal with the anatomical and physiological anomalies of the sex organs, although I think that this part of the evidence is of marginal significance only in the present case. In other cases, it may be of cardinal importance. All the medical witnesses accept that there are, at least, four criteria for assessing the sexual condition of an individual. These are-
>
> (i) Chromosomal factors.
> (ii) Gonadal factors (ie presence or absence of testes or ovaries).
> (iii) Genital factors (including internal sex organs).
> (iv) Psychological factors.
>
> [...] the biological sexual constitution of an individual is fixed at birth (at the latest), and cannot be changed, either by the natural development of organs of the opposite sex, or by medical or surgical means. The respondent's operation, therefore, cannot affect her true sex.

A considerable section of the judgment is dedicated to the question whether it is possible to consummate a marriage between a post-op MtF man and another man, given that in English law a marriage that had not been consummated could be declared null and invalid. This aspect is not necessarily relevant here, though it is quite revealing of the prejudices of the time. In contrast, the Judge in *M.T. v J.T.* took a different approach, ushering the era of gender identity as the true signifier of sex in US case law. In his reasoning, he explains it as follows:

> We cannot join the reasoning of the Corbett case. The evidence before this court teaches that there are several criteria or standards which may be relevant in determining the sex of an individual. It is true that the anatomical test, the genitalia of an individual, is unquestionably significant and probably in most instances indispensable. For example, sex classification of an individual at birth may as a practical matter rely upon this test. For other purposes, however, where sex differentiation is required or accepted, such as for public records, service in the branches of the armed forces, participation in certain regulated sports activities, eligibility for types of employment and the like, other tests in addition to genitalia may also be important.

According to Dr. Ekins, in a revealing summary of these two cases, following *M.T. v J.T.* "A psychological essentialism has replaced the biological essentialism of *Corbett v Corbett*." We know that international law did not take the road pointed by Judge Ormond in *Corbett v Corbett*, though Judge Ormond had practised as a medical doctor before he entered the legal profession and therefore was better qualified to understand the medical implications of the case; Judge Handler, the judge in *M.T. v J.T.* had no such background so he relied more heavily on the expert opinions, which included the Plaintiff's own doctor, and a specialist from Johns Hopkins Gender Clinic. The Plaintiff's doctor, Dr. Ihlenfeld, testified that:

> There was, however, "very little disagreement" on the fact that gender identity generally is established "very, very firmly, almost immediately, by the age of 3 to 4 years." He defined gender identity as "a sense, a total sense of self as being masculine or female;" it "pervades one's entire concept of one's place in life, of one's place in society and in point of fact the actual facts of the anatomy are really secondary."

Charles Ihlenfeld had worked with Dr. Harry Benjamin. In 2006 a group of human rights practitioners and academics drafted a set of principles, which came to be known as the Yogyakarta Principles, for the protection of the rights of homosexual, bisexual and transgender individuals. A second set of principles specifically dedicated to transgender rights was drafted in 2017.[109] The Principles define gender identity for the first time, in the following terms:

> Gender identity is understood to refer to each person's deeply felt internal and individual experience of gender, which may or may not correspond with the sex assigned at birth, including the personal sense of the body (which may involve, if freely chosen, modification of bodily appearance or function by medical, surgical or other means) and other expressions of gender, including dress, speech and mannerisms.

Just as in the International Bill of Gender Rights, gender identity is conceptualised as a universal human experience. It relies on stereotypes of masculinity and femininity (dress, speech and mannerisms) which are culturally, geographically and chronologically contingent, making them an unreliable marker of any sort of identity. It decouples gender identity from sex (may or may not correspond), additionally decoupling gender expression from gender identity, making the latter impossible to ascertain without information from the individual concerned, creating the need for self-identification. The gender identity of infants and disabled people remains

---

[109] The Yogyakarta Principles. Principles on the Application of International Human Rights Law in Relationn to Sexual Orientation and Gender Identity, March 2007, https://yogyakartaprinciples.org/principles-en/yp10/.

unexplored, pointing to the creation of a class of people capable of having and expressing a gender identity, and a class of people deprived of this allegedly fundamental aspect of our humanity. Michael O'Flaherty was selected as rapporteur for this self-selected group of human rights experts and practitioners for the drafting of the Principles. O'Flaherty insists on the universal nature of gender identity and sexual orientation.[110] We could describe this as an example of forced teaming, whereby the legitimacy of a contested concept, gender identity, is increased by reference to an established and understood one (sexual orientation). It is common-sensical to accept the idea that human beings express a sexual orientation towards the opposite sex (heterosexual), the same sex (homosexual) or both sexes (bisexual). However, a gender identity that may or may not correspond to our sex and may or may not correspond to our gender expression is not grounded in material reality and is not objectively verifiable. According to the Yogyakarta Principles'definition, a person could be born a female, have a male gender identity and a female gender expression.

The Yogyakarta Principles stand at the intersection of the work done by transgender rights organisations and international organisations, especially the UN. We have already seen that the people involved in drafting the International Bill of Gender Rights targeted the UN internationally (as much as they targeted Congress for their domestic lobbying). The people involved in drafting the Principles were brought together by two NGOs, the International Commission of Jurists and the International Service for Human Rights.[111] The Yogyakarta Principles are now quoted by international organisations[112] and courts as having legal authority. They are in reality only Principles written down by a group of self-selected experts in relation to sexual orientation and gender identity, ostensibly

---

[110] Michael O'Flaherty, "The Yogyakarta Principles at Ten," Nordic Journal of Human Rights,33(4) (2015): 280-298, at 284. doi: 10.1080/18918131.2015. 1127009. On January 2024, O'Flaherty was elected Council of Europe Commissioner for Human Rights:
https://www.coe.int/en/web/portal/-/michael-o-flaherty-elected-council-of-europe-commissioner-for-human-rights.

[111] International Commission of Jurists, "The Yogyakarta Principles," March 1, 2007, https://www.icj.org/yogyakarta-principles/. The ICJ though does not mention the Principles in its history page https://www.icj.org/history/part-three-from-the-1990s-into-the-21st-century/.

[112] Most recently a Report by the Council of Europe's European Committee for the Prevention of Torture and Inhuman or Degrading Treatment or Punishment, "Prison Standard", 33rd General Report CPT/Inf (2024) 16 – part, 1680af7216 (coe.int).

applicable to all human beings, though the rationale for their necessity is the discrimination and violence suffered by LGBT individuals. Critiquing their cogency and their intellectual underpinning is not to be read as an endorsement of violence or discrimination against LGBT people.This work demonstrates that it is not necessary to believe that all human beings have a gender identity as defined in the Principles, in order to support the notion that no individual should suffer discrimination on the basis of their belief in gender identities. Professor Wintemute, who participated in drafting the first set of Principles in 2006, has recently expressed reservations on their scope, admitting that no attention was paid at the time to the possible consequences for women of allowing males to self-identify into women's spaces, services and rights.[113] He argues, as does this work, that sex remains an important variable to be considered in such diverse areas as statistics, criminology, women's rights, prisons, hospitals, health matters, education and sports.[114]

2006 was a pivotal year for gender identity theory. In addition to the Yogyakarta Principles, the International Conference on LGBT Human Rights in Montreal issued the "Declaration of Montreal," drafted by Joke Swiebel and Robert Wintemute and adopted by its International Scientific Committee.[115] A noticeable difference between the Principles and the Declaration is the absence in the Declaration of definitions (apart from a generic reference to a person's identity as a male or female or neither not necessarily being determined by their body). However the usual demands for affirmative medical care and recognition of gender identity in identity documents are there.

Finally, the Yogyakarta Plus Ten Principles, issued in 2017, focus on gender identity and sex characteristics (these latter still absent in the original Principles), advocating, at Principle 31, for the right to have identity documents without having to disclose one's sex, gender identity, gender expression or sex characteristic (and sexual orientation, but since identity document never contain such information it is not quite clear what

---

[113] Julie Bindel and Melanie Newman, "The trans rights that trump all," The Critic, April 2021, https://thecritic.co.uk/issues/april-2021/the-trans-rights-that-trump-all/.

[114] For detailed arguments on the continued relevance of sex in all these areas, and more, see Alice Sullivan and Selina Todd, Sex and Gender. A Contemporary Reader (London: Routledge, 2024).

[115] As we have seen, Professor Wintemute also contributed the drafting of the Yogyakarta Principles. The text of the declaration is here, https://www.declarationofmontreal.org/DeclarationofMontreal.pdf.

this refers to). The Principle is evidently designed to eliminate any reference to sex in identity documents,[116] but, as long as sex is registered, to allow people to have their gender identity recorded in place of sex with no criteria, including, ominously, the absence of a criminal record.

Principle 35 seeks to eliminate the right of women to single sex services such as toilets, by appealing to a "right to sanitation." The right of women to have safety, privacy and dignity in circumstances relating to their bodily functions which are different from males' and specific to them only, is completely ignored–the proviso that the sanitation facilities have to be provided in circumstances that are "consistent with human dignity" is not a sufficient guarantee, as sex is not even mentioned in the Principle, although the open list ("without discrimination, including on the basis of sexual orientation, gender identity, gender expression or sex characteristics") might allow for its incorporation.

Outside of the listed additional Principles, but with reference to the original 2007 Principles, the 2017 Principles list the right of people to participate in sports in the category of their choice, and to be housed in the prison estate of their choice, or at least to participate in the decision about their placement, therefore swiftly dispensing with female sports and female prisons. The right to gender affirmative health care is expanded to include the right to affirmative material on SOGIESC[117] in medical curricula. Family rights must include the right of parents to include only their self-selected gender identity in the birth certificate of their child and to access surrogacy, where this is legal, without discrimination.

In the 2017 Principles we see even more starkly that, regardless of protestations that the Principles simply reflect the status of public international law, they instead promote an extreme set of demands designed to completely erase sex from the law, and replace it with self-selected gender identity, gender expression or sex characteristics, that may or may not overlap in each individual. This replacement is at odds with

---

[116] "States shall ensure that official identity documents only include personal information that is relevant, reasonable and necessary as required by the law for a legitimate purpose, and thereby end the registration of the sex and gender of the person in identity documents such as birth certificates, identification cards, passports and driver licences, and as part of their legal personality." This statement begs the question of how one reaches the conclusion that sex is never relevant, reasonable and necessary information in identity documents.

[117] The new acronym, covering sexual orientation, gender identity, gender expression, and sex characteristics.

established rights in international law, including the rights contained in the CEDAW and the non-discrimination right on the basis of sex in most human rights treaties.

CHAPTER 3

GENDER IDENTITY IN THE WORK OF INTERNATIONAL INSTITUTIONS

Every year, transphobia kills hundreds of trans women worldwide. A reminder from the @un that ALL women have a right to be safe and live free from violence and discrimination - #transwomen included! #StandUp4HumanRights #TranswomenAreWomen[118]

—UN Free & Equal Twitter Account, 19 December 2022

International law develops along parallel lines, with treaties and customary law, the main sources of binding obligations in international law, interacting in complex ways. It is clearly beyond the scope of this work to explore their interactions and distinctions, but suffice it to say that they are, by universal agreement, the two principal sources of international legal obligations. It is easy to ascertain that there are no treaties, universal, bilateral or multilateral, recognising and protecting gender identity. Customary law develops through the practice of States (including treaty-making) as a separate and discrete set of obligations for States. The

---

[118] Sensationalising the abuse and violence that some transgender individuals undoubtedly are subjected to is an unfortunate habit of gender identity theorists and activists. In his report "The Law of Inclusion" the IE Victor Madrigal-Borloz recounts the appalling story that the majority of "trans men" he met in Georgia were missing their middle finger, as the authorities requested that their middle finger be amputated to provide biological material for "prosthetic" penis if they wanted to be recognised as transgender. The report quotes, at footnote 75, the Report of his country visit to Georgia in 2019, "Visit to Georgia," Report of the Independent Expert on protection against violence and discrimination based on sexual orientation and gender identity, 15 May 2019, A/HRC/41/45/Add 1. https://documents-dds-ny.un.org/doc/UNDOC/GEN/G19/139/35/PDF/G1913935.pdf?OpenElement. This report does not contain any evidence of this story, and in fact, an internet search in English does not bring up any other reference to this practice, fortunately. It does bring up an article from 2002, originally in Russian, titled "Finger Transplant in the Creation and Reconstruction of the Penis" seemingly with no reference to SRS; https://pubmed.ncbi.nlm.nih.gov/12449578/ (and a lot of links that are better left unopened).

practice has to be general, protracted over time and overall consistent.[119] There is as of yet no evidence from State practice that gender identity is a recognised category in customary international law, nor that the majority of States are acting out of a legal obligation in this regard. In short, international law does not recognise gender identity as a conventional or customary source of legal obligations for States. Gender identity theorists who have a legal background in international law must know this. Arguing that gender identity *should be* protected in international law is patently not the same as arguing that gender identity *is* protected in international law.

At the more extreme end of gender identity theorists working in international organisations, a way to avoid the qualifying criterion for a rule to be binding is to question the legitimacy or continued relevance of the status of treaty and customary law as the main sources of binding obligations in the international legal regime. When former IE on SOGI Victor Madrigal-Borloz gave advice to Scottish Parliament on the amendment of the Gender Recognition Act,[120] he accompanied the advice with a letter,[121] in which he opined that, "recognition of an instrument by the United Nations is not a matter of a binary classification of binding/not binding on the sole basis of whether the instrument is a treaty." This is a misrepresentation of the status of international law, as customary rules are also binding. In any event, it is not for individuals to decide what international law considers binding. Specifically, the Yogyakarta Principles do not become binding because someone wishes them to be. The Principles are not "cherished" around the world, as he claims,[122] and even

[119] The most detailed explanation of the functioning of customary law and its interplay with conventional (treaty law) in *North Sea Continental Shelf,* Judgment, I.C.J. Reports 1969, p. 3, https://www.icj-cij.org/sites/default/files/case-related/52/052-19690220-JUD-01-00-EN.pdf.

[120] Equalities, Human Rights and Civil Justice Committee, Official Report of Monday 19 December 2022, https://www.parliament.scot/chamber-and-committees/official-report/search-what-was-said-in-parliament/EHRCJ-19-12-2022?meeting=14062&iob=127362.

[121] Mandate of the Independent Expert on protection against violence and discrimination based on sexual orientation and gender identity, Ref.: OL GBR 15/2022, https://spcommreports.ohchr.org/TMResultsBase/DownLoadPublicCommunicationFile?gId=27757.

[122] "The Yogyakarta Principles are justly cherished around the world as a major achievement of activism in the field of sexual orientation and gender identity. As proven by the reference made to them by global and regional bodies, they hold a singular value as a doctrinal source that has done great service to the furtherance of

if they were, that would not make them binding on States. Binarism is as relevant to law as it is to sex differentiation. Law is either binding or it is not, and this is unaffected by whatever social mores or moral duties impose as the appropriate behaviour. Fuller's principles of legality are as relevant in international law as they are in domestic law, and clarity, in this case on the binding nature of rules, is one of the principles.[123]

In order to promote the incorporation of gender identity in international law, there are two avenues: the first one, and safest from a theoretical perspective, is to argue that gender identity is included in the "other status" language present in the non-discrimination clauses in many human rights treaties.[124] Though the position advanced in this work is that gender identity and transgenderism could be protected as beliefs (and disability if appropriate), the argument to include gender identity under "other status" has legal plausibility and feasibility. A disadvantage, from the point of view of most gender theorists and trans rights activistis, is that this interpretation restricts protection of gender identity and transgenderism to non-discrimination, with no logical connection to their claim that gender identity trumps sex for all legal purposes.

The second avenue is to "retrofit" gender identity where international law refers to sex. This is attempted by the IE on SOGI in his work but we see also specific attempts outside of this work, especially for what concerns the CEDAW.[125] This avenue is eminently problematic, as there is no

the human rights of lesbian, gay, bisexual, trans, non-binary and other gender diverse persons." Page 8, note 46 of the cited letter.

[123] Lon Fuller, The Morality of Law (New Haven and London: Yale University Press, 1964).

[124] For example Article 14 of the ECHR, https://www.echr.coe.int/documents/d/echr/Guide_Art_14_Art_1_Protocol_12_ENG at 36. See also *Identoba and Others v Georgia*, Application No 73235/12, Judgment of 12 May 2015.

[125] A clear example of this in Rikki Holtmaat and Paul Post, "Enhancing LGBTI Rights by Changing the Interpretation of the Convention on the Elimination of All Forms of Discrimination Against Women," Nordic Journal of Human Rights, 33(4) (2015): 319-336, doi:10.1080/18918131.2016.1123502. It is not quite clear why a Convention for Women should be used to protect the rights of LGBTI people, including homosexual males. Is that because they are not "real men"? The argument that the Convention should protect "all kinds of sexes" (at 323) hopelessly muddles the distinction between sex and gender, over which the entirety of gender identity theory supposedly rests (this is evident by the inclusion of transgender, intersex and differently sexed and transgendered people in the category sex). Clearly there are no more than two sexes, as no-one has ever been

textual or legal basis for this interpretation of the word sex in the intention of the drafters, and reading gender identity where the text mentions sex deprives of meaning or renders inapplicable legal texts, where these refer specifically to the constraints put on women on the basis of their sexed body. From the point of view of gender identity theorists, this approach guarantees that positive rights are available on the basis of one's gender identity, not just non-discrimination rights.

For those who oppose the substitution of sex with gender identity, the first and most obvious problem is that this project deprives individuals of the right to interact with reality without the mediating tool of gender identity ideology.[126] Unless one accepts that gender identity replaces sex, one cannot help apprehending reality on its terms and recognising sex with incredible speed and accuracy.[127] This mediating imposition is clearly more troubling for women, who have never historically been considered reliable sources for describing and witnessing reality. Historically, women were not allowed to describe or research reality, and were not considered reliable witnesses of reality (and in some societies still are not).[128] One can study the entirety of human history until very recently without ever hearing a woman's voice. They are so rare that a considerable effort needs to be made to uncover them and listen to them. Another more pointed criticism is that if gender identity is read in place of sex, in such legal texts as the CEDAW, women who identify as men lose the protection of the Convention, which is directed to women exclusively, while still being

able to clarify what the names of the other sexes are, what is their functional role and how we recognise them objectively.

[126] I use the word ideology here instead of the more neutral term of theory because, to the extent that one is compelled to adopt gender identity as a mediating tool between one's experience and the world, one can speak of an ideological project.

[127] Women are even better at this skill, which all humans deploy from a very early age with considerable accuracy. See Alessandro Cellerino, Davide Borghetti and Ferdinando Sartucci, "Sex Differences in Face Gender Recognition in Humans," Brain Research Bullettin 63(6) (July 2004): 443-449.

[128] In Saudi Arabia a woman's testimony in court is usually valued as half a man's testimony: Maryam Khalil, "Is the testimony of a man equal to that of two women", Al Islam, January-March 2017, https://www.alislam.org/articles/is-testimony-of-man-equal-to-two-women/. But if in Western countries a woman testifies as being raped by a man and the court records the crime as being committed as a woman, effectively her testimony does not count at all.

subjected to sexist oppression on the basis of their sex, or needing special protection for their sex-based rights.[129]

In the 1993 Vienna Declaration and Programme of Action,[130] and the Programme of Action of the International Conference of Population and Development[131] we find the first instances of the use of the word gender.[132] In both documents gender can be read as a synonym of sex (as in gender-specific data or gender-based violence). A similar use is in the 1994 Cairo Declaration on Population and Development and the 1995 Bejing Platform for Action of the Fourth World Conference on Women.[133] This latter document also reveals that a debate was taking place within the UN around a "feminist" understanding of gender, and the use of gender as a polite substitute of sex, so much so that a separate Annex (Annex IV) was appended to the document to reflect the agreed understanding of the term. The Annex states as follows:

> 2. Having considered the issue thoroughly, the contact group noted that: (1) the word "gender" had been commonly used and understood in its ordinary, generally accepted usage in numerous other United Nations forums and conferences; (2) there was no indication that any new meaning or connotation of the term, different from accepted prior usage, was intended in the Platform for Action.

---

[129]A little discussed issue is that women identifying as men are more likely to pass as men after surgery and hormone treatment, as testosterone has a more disruptive effect on the female body than oestrogen on the male body. To that extent, they may be able to leave behind the oppression and discrimination women are subjected to from birth, and also the risks inherent in moving in society with a recognisibly female body.

[130] World Conference on Human Rights, "Vienna Declaration and Programme of Action, 25 June 1993, https://www.ohchr.org/en/instruments-mechanisms/ instruments /vienna-declaration-and-programme-action.

[131] Department of Economic and Social Affairs, "Population and Development. Programme of Action adopted at the International Conference on Population and Development," Cairo, 5-13 September 1994, ST/ESA/SER.A/149, https://www.un.org/development/desa/pd/sites/www.un.org.development.desa.pd/files/files/documents/2020/Jan/un_1995_programme_of_action_adopted_at_the_international_conference_on_population_and_development_cairo_5-13_sept._1994.pdf.

[132] The term is used once in the introduction of the CEDAW, talking about the "impact of cultural factors on gender relations" but never in the body of the treaty text or even its Preamble.

[133] UN Women, "Bejing Declaration and Platform for Action," 2015, https://www.un.org/womenwatch/daw/beijing/pdf/BDPfA%20E.pdf.

> 3. Accordingly, the contact group reaffirmed that the word "gender" as used in the Platform for Action was intended to be interpreted and understood as it was in ordinary, generally accepted usage. The contact group also agreed that the present report should be read by the President of the Conference as a president's statement and that the statement should be part of the final report of the Conference.

The Statement is reflective of the need to compromise, so much so that it avoids clarifying the "ordinary [...] accepted usage of the term gender" and signals the battle that was taking place between those who promoted the feminist use of the word gender and those who resisted this usage. The trans turn in international law signified a shift from the feminist understanding of gender to the adoption of gender identity alongside sex, with the opposition to "feminist gender" now joined by the opposition to gender identity. "Gender critical" voices tend to get lost in the political battle at the international level.[134] I am not interested here in following debates within feminism on the multiple meanings of gender, but only to track its usage and to understand how much critical feminists reflections on gender, i.e. the social constructs around sex, have been reinterpreted as a signifier for sex and eventually a replacement of sex as the significant legal category.[135]

The inclusion of the word "gender" in the documents of the United Nations is a case of cultural imperialism. The word gender is capable of being interpreted in different ways only in English. Other languages either have no word that maps even partially on the multiple meanings of the English "gender" or use this word only for grammatical gender (one of the

---

[134] ILGA Europe 2023 Annual Review of the Human Rights Situation of Lesbian, Gay, Trans and Intersex People in Europe and Central Asia talks about anti-trans rethoric and anti-trans groups n the UK, failing to acknowledge that the majority of "gender critical" women in the UK are left wing, feminists, lesbians. https://www.ilga-europe.org/files/uploads/2023/02/annual-review-2023.pdf. The Report of the IE on SOGI Madrigal-Borloz titled "Practices of Exclusion," A/76/152, interprets all criticism of gender theory as informed by "ultraconservative political leaders and religious groups using their platforms to promote bigotry, dehumanize persons on the basis of sexual orientation, gender identity, and gender expression, and foster stigma and intolerance among their constituencies."

[135] For a history of feminism in international law, from a gender identity theorist's perspective, see Otto Dianne. "International Human Rights Law: Towards Rethinking Sex/Gender Dualism." In The Ashgate Research Companion to Feminist Legal Theory, eds. Margaret Davies and Vanessa E Munro (Burlington: Ashgate Publishng Company, 2013), 197-215.

four possible meanings of the word gender in English, the other ones being a euphemism for sex, the feminist meaning of gender, and as part of the term "gender identity"). The creative ambiguity that is characteristic of treaty drafting, and which allows Contracting Parties to reach an agreement around the final text while leaving interpretative ambiguity to the application and interpretation of the treaty to political and/or judicial settings, is also a hallmark of the negotiating around other legal materials produced by the United Nations, such as General Assembly Resolutions and documents produced by treaty bodies. In all those circumstances, the imposition of the term "gender" in the English version of the documents, supposedly as a replacement for sex and/or sexism, makes subsequent different interpretations of the word possible.

In the 2007 Convention on the Rights of Persons with Disabilities, gender is used as a synonym of sex, to define the gender norms imposed mainly on women, and in "gender perspective," i.e. a policy approach informed by the differences between men and women (this is part of the gender mainstreaming policy adopted by the UN).[136] In the 2007 International Convention for the Protection of All Persons from Enforced Disappearance the word gender is used only once, as a synonym of sex ("balanced gender representation"). As a significant category, together with race, religion, nationality etc, the Convention always uses the term "sex."

Up until 2000 at least, gender was never used to express an identity or in reference to transgender individuals.The first mention of the term "gender identity" following a search in the repository of UN documents[137] is in a 2001 Interim Report by Sir Nigel Rodley, Special Rapporteur of the Commission on Human Rights.[138] In the report, Sir Nigel reports instances

[136] United Nations, Gender Mainstreaming: An Overview (New York: United Nations Publications, 2002).

[137] The search of the term "gender identity" returned 500+ entries. Only six of them precede 2010 (and this is a full text search from all United Nations documents since its foundation). This is not surprising, the term sexual orientation does not appear before 1994 either. The real difference though is between the term sex (first appearing in a 1952 document) and gender (first appearance in 1994). The UN Social and Economic Council established a Sub-Commission on the Status of Women in 1946 which was turned into a Commission in June 1946; see "Short History of the Commission on the Status of Women," https://www.un.org/womenwatch/daw/CSW60YRS/CSWbriefhistory.pdf.

[138] Question of torture and other cruel, inhuman or degrading treatment or punishment, A/56/156, https://documents-dds-ny.un.org/doc/UNDOC/GEN/N01/445/79/pdf/N0144579.pdf?OpenElement.

of abuse and torture on the basis of sexual orientation and gender identity. Gender identity is not defined in the report, which relies on the definition provided by Amnesty International.[139]

The establishment of the Human Rights Council (HRC) in 2006[140] was seen as a chance, by the NGOs working in the area of sexual orientation and gender identity, to mainstream SOGI in the work of the HRC. This is not simply a hypothesis. In June 2006, less than three months after the establishment of the HRC, seven organisations with consultative status at the UN[141] issued a statement, "Implementation of General Assembly Resolution 60/251 of 15 March 2006 entitled 'Human Rights Council'" with the subtitle "The Promise of the Human Rights Council: Marginalised Groups, Sexual Orientation and Gender Identity."[142] This is an extended excerpt of the statement:

---

[139] Amnesty International, "Crimes of hate, conspiracy of silence: Torture and ill-treatment based on sexual identity" (ACT 40/016/2001), https://www.amnesty.org/en/documents/act40/016/2001/en/. The definition is as follows: "Gender identity refers to a person's experience of self-expression in relation to social constructions of masculinity or femininity (gender). A person may have a male or female gender identity, with the physiological characteristics of the opposite sex."

[140] By UN General Assembly Resolution 60/251 of 15 March 2006, A/RES/60/ 251, https://www2.ohchr.org/english/bodies/hrcouncil/docs/a.res.60.251_en.pdf.
As noted, 2006 was already a pivotal year for trans rights activists, with the Yogyakarta Principles and the Montreal Declaration being produced in that year.

[141] Action Canada for Population and Development (now Action Canada for Sexual Health and Rights); Canadian HIV/AIDS Legal Network (now HIV Legal Network); Centre for Women's Global Leadership; Global Rights; International Service for Human Rights; International Women's Health Coalition (now International Alliance for Sexual and Reproductive Health, Rights, and Justice; New Ways: Women for Women's Human Rights (now Women for Women's Human Rights). Two things are noticeable: Canadian NGOs are overrepresented; and most of these NGOs have since shifted their focus from women or LGB rights to gender identity, LGBT+ rights (most noticeably the Health Coalition, which focused on female health, now with a focus on women and gender diverse people). These NGOs were joined by 40 others with no consultative status, LGBT rights NGOs, including ILGA Europe.

[142]Joint written statement submitted by Action Canada for Population and Development (ACPD), Canadian HIV/AIDS Legal Network, Centre for Women's Global Leadership (Global Center, CWGL), Global Rights, International Service for Human Rights (ISHR), International Women's Health Coalition (IWHC) and New Ways: Women for Women's Human Rights [The promise of the Human

We, the undersigned NGOs from all regions of the world, join with other members of the international community in welcoming the Human Rights Council, and engaging in its inaugural session in a spirit of optimism and constructive dialogue. The increased weight and status attached by members of the international community to human rights within the UN system, the increased time that will be dedicated to addressing these issues throughout the year, the affirmation of the valuable role of UN Special Procedures and NGOs, the willingness of States to voluntarily submit their human rights records for international consideration through the Universal Period[ic] Review – all these signal a new beginning, new hope, and new promise. To what extent will this promise be realized? That is up to States themselves. As UN High Commissioner for Human Rights Louise Arbour has stated:

"Fulfilling the promise of the Council will require a change of culture as much as institutional transformation. Countries must demonstrate the political will to put the defence of human rights above narrow interests. Human rights are neither a weapon nor a shield. They are the birthright of all people everywhere. If we lose sight of this fundamental fact, all the work to create the council and reaffirm the central role of human rights will have been wasted."

Building on this affirmation, the Council will have important work to do in the area of standard-setting, and will need to rise beyond political and regional tensions to address emerging issues, particularly in areas such as sexual orientation and gender identity that have gone unaddressed or not yet received due consideration. As Canada noted during its high level statement to last year's Commission:

"What do we expect from a multilateral system for promotion and protection of human rights? ... This system should be flexible, so that we can make progress in new areas, such as fighting discrimination based on sexual orientation and gender identity".

Numerous UN Special Procedures have expressed concern about violations of the human rights of lesbians, gays, bisexuals and transgender people, including arbitrary arrests, deprivation of food and water, beatings, rape and murder. The Human Rights Council's success in addressing persistent human rights violations against marginalized groups will be a litmus test of the credibility and effectiveness of the reform process and the United Nations as a whole.

[…]

Rights Council: Marginalised groups, sexual orientation and gender identity], A/HRC/1/NGO/47 of 28 June 2006.

> Regrettably, the voices of lesbians, gays, bisexuals and transgender people have often been silenced or marginalized within the international system. As recently as last month, the ECOSOC NGO Committee rejected every application for consultative status by NGOs representing lesbians, gays, bisexuals and transgender people, thus denying these groups the ability to even speak with their own voice before this inaugural meeting of the Council. Ultimately, however, these voices will not be silenced, and the message we bring to this Council is one of hope. In ever-increasing numbers, lesbians, gays, bisexuals, transgender people, their friends, supporters and allies are raising their voices, and just as NGOs are speaking out, so too we are encouraged at the increasing numbers of States recognizing that these persistent rights violations must be urgently addressed.
>
> [...]
>
> This Human Rights Council will work if we, the international community, want it to work; if we, NGOs and States alike, join together to make it work. We look to States to be proactive in raising issues of sexual orientation and gender identity. We look to States to safeguard the principle of universality, and ensure that all persons are truly treated as free and equal in dignity and rights. We look to States to cooperate with and support the work of the Special Procedures, and respond in a timely, meaningful and substantive way to address the human rights concerns they identify. We look to States to reflect forthrightly on how each can improve its own human rights record, and engage in the Universal Periodic Review in a spirit of openness and a commitment to genuine reform. And we look to States to welcome, indeed embrace, the role of NGOs as we support your efforts to meet these commitments. In this way, the Human Rights Council can be successful in fulfilling its potential. We look forward to working with you towards a world in which all people can be treated with equal freedom, dignity and respect.

The stage is set; even before the Yogyakarta Principles had been finalised (work was being done in 2006), the HRC was being pressured to include SOGI issues in its work. The Commission on Human Rights had folded amongst accusations of inefficacy and corruption,[143] and the HRC was keen to prove it could protect human rights efficiently and fairly: what better occasion than a brand new marginalised group to protect and a set of NGOs and individuals ready to help, even providing the definition and a catalogue of rights. Shortly thereafter, in December 2006, the co-founder

[143] For a history of the CHR, see John P. Pace, The United Nations Commission on Human Rights. A Very Great Enterprise (Oxford: Oxford University Press, 2020).

of Arc International,[144] John Fisher, addressed the 3rd Session of the HRC, commending a Statement made by Norway in support of sexual orientation and gender identity rights.[145] The demand that no-one should be persecuted, tortured or killed because of their sexual orientation or gender identity is of course, as Fisher said, impossible to disagree with.[146]

In December 2008, 66 States sent a letter to the President of the General Assembly;[147] in the letter, they reaffirmed that the principle of non-discrimination includes sexual orientation and gender identity, and requested that the Human Rights Council properly investigate human rights violations against sexual orientation and gender identity, finally demanding that States protect individuals against violations and investigate them. In response Syria, together with other 58 States, issued a *note verbale* consisting of a Declaration in response to the letter of the day before, lamenting the absence of legal grounds for sexual orientation and gender identity, and more seriously, claiming that behind sexual orientation the normalisations of behaviours such as paedophilia could take place, and that gender identity "is often suggested to attribute particular sexual interests or behaviours to genetic factors, a matter that has been scientifically rebuffed repeatedly." Just as much as one abhors the claim that protecting homosexuals inevitably results in promoting paedophilia, one cannot help but agree that there is no scientific basis to gender identity. The Declaration deplores the creation of these new rights outside the scope of the UDHR and calls upon other States to focus on the enumerated categories in human rights law. Finally, in March 2009 the

---

[144] Arc International is an advocacy organisation for the advancement of LGBT rights, especially active in Geneva to lobby about LGBT issues at the HRC. Their domain name seems to have expired so their website is not accessible anymore. Fisher is currently Deputy Director for Global Advocacy at Human Rights Watch https://www.hrw.org/about/people/john-fisher.

[145] This statement is also mentioned in this piece, https://www.indybay.org/newsitems/2006/12/05/18335263.php, but I could not find any record of it in the written Proceedings of the 3rd Session for 1 December, when the Statement was allegedly made. The content can be gleaned by the comments.

[146] UN Human Rights Council. Third Regular Session, Compilation of Statements by Amnesty International, https://www.amnesty.org/fr/wp-content/uploads/2021/08/ior410342006en.pdf.

[147] Letter dated 18 December 2008 from the Permanent Representatives of Argentina, Brazil, Croatia, France, Gabon, Japan, the Netherlands and Norway to the United Nations addressed to the President of the General Assembly, A/63/635, https://digitallibrary.un.org/record/644995?ln=en.

United States issued its own letter to the Secretary General of the UN,[148] simply stating that "The United States wishes to associate itself with the statement on human rights, sexual orientation and gender identity contained in the annex to the letter dated 18 December 2008." It is useful to remember that all these pronouncements were made before the Yogyakarta Principles were released, so there was no agreed definition in international law, not even a non-binding one, for the concept of gender identity. There is no analogy with the concept of sexual orientation, since homosexuality was a well known legal term (could not have been made illegal otherwise), though sexual orientation is the more neutral and general presentation of it.

This "forced teaming" of gender identity with sexual orientation is part of the strategy to introduce and legitimise a new term, gender identity, by pairing it with another one that is already well known and understood, sexual orientation.[149] In the second decade of the new millennium, gender identity, without or without a reference to the Yogyakarta Principles, became more common in UN materials.[150] In HRC Resolution 17/19, of 17 June 2011, we see that the following language is used:

---

[148] Letter of 18 March 2009 to the Secretary General of the UN, A/63/778, https://digitallibrary.un.org/record/650295?ln=en.

[149] We have seen this forced teaming in the demands of the ICTLEP (chapter 3).

[150] Human Rights Council Resolution 17/19, "Human rights, sexual orientation and gender identity," 14 July 2011, https://ap.ohchr.org/documents/dpage_e.aspx?si=A%2FHRC%2FRES%2F17%2F19; Human Rights Council Resolution 27/32, "Human rights, sexual orientation and gender identity," 2 October 2014, https://ap.ohchr.org/documents/dpage_e.aspx?si=A/HRC/RES/27/32; Human Rights Council, "Discrimination and violence against individuals based on their sexual orientation and gender identity," Report of the Office of the United Nations High Commissioner for Human Rights, 4 May 2015, A/HRC/29/23, paras. 21, 78 and 79, https://documents.un.org/doc/undoc/gen/g15/088/42/pdf/g1508842.pdf?token=Y1aJxyaz6sIOZ48cQ8&fe=true; Report of the Special Rapporteur on the right of everyone to the enjoyment of the highest attainable standard of physical and mental health Dainius Puras–Addendum–Visi to Malaysia (19 November–2 December 2014, 30 Aprill 2015, A/HRC/29/33/Add.1, paras. 86, 88 and 111 (q), https://ap.ohchr.org/documents/dpage_e.aspx?si=A/HRC/29/33/Add.1; General Assembly Resolution 69/182, "Extrajudicial, summary or arbitrary executions," 30 January 2015, https://documents.un.org/doc/undoc/gen/n14/708/34/pdf/n1470834.pdf?token=ZbFMpwdtAeIuoytC3r&fe=true; Committee on Economic, Social and Cultural Rights,

Expressing grave concern at acts of violence and discrimination, in all regions of the world, committed against individuals because of their sexual orientation and gender identity,

1. Requests the United Nations High Commissioner for Human Rights to commission a study, to be finalized by December 2011, documenting discriminatory laws and practices and acts of violence against individuals based on their sexual orientation and gender identity, in all regions of the world, and how international human rights law can be used to end violence and related human rights violations based on sexual orientation and gender identity;

2. Decides to convene a panel discussion during the nineteenth session of the Human Rights Council, informed by the facts contained in the study commissioned by the High Commissioner and to have constructive, informed and transparent dialogue on the issue of discriminatory laws and practices and acts of violence against individuals based on their sexual orientation and gender identity.

General Comment No. 20, "Non-discrimination in economic, social and cultural rights," 2 July 2009, para. 27, https://www.refworld.org/legal/general/cescr/2009/en/68520; Committee on Economic, Social and Cultural Rights, general comment No. 22, "On the right to sexual and reproductive health," 2 May, 2016, paras. 23 and 40, https://docstore.ohchr.org/SelfServices/FilesHandler.ashx?enc=4slQ6QSmlBEDzFEovLCuW1a0Szab0oXTdImnsJZZVQfQejF41Tob4CvIjeTiAP6sGFQktiae1vlbbOAekmaOwDOWsUe7N8TLm%2BP3HJPzxjHySkUoHMavD%2Fpyfcp3Ylzg; Committee on the Rights of the Child, General Comment No. 15, "On the right of the child to the enjoyment of the highest attainable standard of health," 17 April, 2013, para. 8, https://www.refworld.org/legal/general/crc/2013/en/96127; Committee on the Rights of the Child, General Comment No. 20, "On the implementation of the rights of the child during adolescence," 6 December, 2016, paras. 33 and 34, https://www.ohchr.org/en/documents/general-comments-and-recommendations/general-comment-no-20-2016-implementation-rights; Committee against Torture, General Comment No. 2, "On the implementation of article 2 by States parties." 24 January 2008, para. 21, https://www.ohchr.org/en/documents/general-comments-and-recommendations/catcgc2-general-comment-no-2-2007-implementation; Human Rights Committee, "Concluding observations on the third periodic report of Kuwait," 11 August 2016, CCPR/C/KWT/CO/3, paras. 12 and 13, https://tbinternet.ohchr.org/_layouts/15/TreatyBodyExternal/Download.aspx?symbolno=CCPR%2FC%2FKWT%2FCO%2F3&Lang=en and Human Rights Committee, "Concluding observations on the seventh periodic report of the Russian Federation," 28 Appril 2015, CCPR/C/RUS/CO/7, para. 10, https://tbinternet.ohchr.org/_layouts/15/TreatyBodyExternal/Download.aspx?symbolno=CCPR/C/RUS/CO/7&Lang=En.

In the late 2000s the Yogyakarta Principles started to be mentioned in UN documents regularly. All in all, the exclusively feminist use of gender, before the "trans turn" and the introduction of gender identity, lasted barely more than ten years. The UN was openly targeted by the drafters of the Principles to guarantee the incorporation of the definition of gender identity in its legal materials.[151] While the chances of a specific convention on SOGI rights were very slim indeed (for some unfortunate reasons as well, including the openly hostile attitude to homosexuality displayed by most religions and many Member States of the UN), the possibility to influence human rights agencies and UN representatives, even of countries hostile to LGBT rights, enjoyed a much higher chance of success, especially from the drafters of the Yogyakarta Principles, human rights experts with well established connections within the UN.

The 2008 Guidance Note on Refugee Claims Relating to Sexual Orientation and Gender Identity, published by the United Nations High Commissioner for Refugees (UNHCR), is the first UN document to mention the Principles.[152] At page five the Guidance claims that the Principles reflect "binding international legal standards."

Binding standards can only be contained in a treaty or a recognised customary rule, and neither is presented in support of this assertion. In any event it seems the UNCHR is not ready to extend recognition specifically to gender identity, at least for what concerns the claim to binding status. More problematically, while transgender status is arguably a legitimate ground for conferring asylum, there simply is not sufficient precision on the definition of gender identity in order for an application for asylum to be made. Again we are faced with the tension between the necessity to protect people who are identified as transgender for the purpose of discrimination/persecution, which should receive some form of legal

---

[151] Michael O'Flaherty, "The Yogyakarta Principles at Ten," Nordic Journal of Human Rights,33(4) (2015): 280-298, 284, doi: 10.1080/18918131.2015.1127009. See also Andrew Park, "Yogyakarta Plus 10: A Demand for Recognition of SOGIESC," North Carolina Journal of International Law, 44 (2019): 223-271, 229: "[...] the Yogyakarta Principles were the result of an opportunity structure, or a series of circumstances and trends present in the mid-2000s, each of which helped propel the first Principles from a document aimed at the elite circle of United Nations human rights mechanisms located in Geneva, to a document that has shaped how LGBTI issues are viewed globally and in many countries."

[152] UN High Commissioner for Refugees (UNHCR), UNHCR Guidance Note on Refugee Claims Relating to Sexual Orientation and Gender Identity, 21 November 2008, http://www.refworld.org/docid/48abd5660.html.

recognition, and the claim that gender identity is a universal experience. If that were the case, the victims of discrimination on the basis of their female 'cis' gender identity would greatly outnumber transgender victims.

We also find the Yogyakarta Principles in General Comment No. 20 by the UN Committee on Economic, Social and Cultural Rights of 2009.[153] At para. 32, the documents recites as follows:

> 32. "Other status" as recognized in article 2, paragraph 2, includes sexual orientation. States parties should ensure that a person's sexual orientation is not a barrier to realizing Covenant rights, for example, in accessing survivor's pension rights. In addition, gender identity is recognized as among the prohibited grounds of discrimination; for example, persons who are transgender, transsexual or intersex often face serious human rights violations, such as harassment in schools or in the workplace.

The Committee is using the more legally legitimate means of introducing gender identity in the Covenant, as "other status" ground of discrimination. But what is more important, is the reference to the definition of the Principles, and the grouping of transgender, transsexual and intersex under gender identity, as if they were a cohesive group.

We see that treaty monitoring bodies are preferred entry points for the Yogyakarta Principles into the work of the United Nations. The launch of the Principles in Geneva was scheduled to coincide with a session of the HRC.[154] The HRC and its Rapporteurs have referred to the Principles in their work. They do so especially through the Universal Periodic Review, the main innovation of the HRC. It is through this review that the HRC assesses the human rights performance of UN Member States.[155]

In 2009 the Principles are mentioned in the Report of the Special Rapporteur on the Promotion and Protection of Human Rights and Fundamental Freedoms while Countering Terrorism.[156] It is worth quoting in full the

---

[153] UN Committee on Economic, Social and Cultural Rights, General Comment No. 20, "Non-discrimination in economic, social and cultural rights, 2 July 2009, E/C.12/GC/20, https://www.refworld.org/docid/4a60961f2.html.

[154] Michael O'Flaherty, "The Yogyakarta Principles at Ten," Nordic Journal of Human Rights, 33(4) (2015): 280-298, 286.

[155] United Nations Human Rights Council, "Universal Periodic Review," https://www.ohchr.org/en/hr-bodies/upr/upr-home.

[156] United Nations General Assembly, "Report of the Special Rapporteur on the promotion and protection of human rights and fundamental freedoms while countering terrorism," 3 August 2009, A/64/211,

paragraph in which the Principles are referenced, as it puts them in context, and they are not simply footnoted as the source of the definition of gender identity:

> Gender is not synonymous with women[157] but rather encompasses the social constructions that underlie how women's and men's roles, functions and responsibilities, including in relation to sexual orientation and gender identity, are defined and understood.This report will therefore identify the gendered impact of counter-terrorism measures both on women and men, as well as the rights of persons of diverse sexual orientations and gender identities. As a social construct, gender is also informed by, and intersects with, various other means by which roles, functions and responsibilities are perceived and practiced, such as race, ethnicity, culture, religion and class. Consequently, gender is not static; it is changeable over time and across contexts. *Understanding gender as a social and shifting construct rather than as a biological and fixed category* [emphasis added] is important because it helps to identify the complex and inter-related gender-based human rights violations caused by counterterrorism measures; to understand the underlying causes of these violations; and to design strategies for countering terrorism that are truly non-discriminatory and inclusive of all actors. International human rights law, including the Convention on the Elimination of All Forms of Discrimination against Women, the International Covenant on Civil and Political Rights, and the International Covenant on Economic, Social and Cultural Rights, requires States to ensure non-discrimination and equality (de jure and de facto) on the basis of gender, sex, sexual orientation and gender identity, as well as to address instances where gender inequality intersects with other prohibited grounds of discrimination, such as race, colour and religion.

The passage is revealing for the usual slippage between gender as sex-based oppression, gender as sex and then gender as a substitute of sex. The paragraph starts with a reasonable analysis of how gender is used to oppress and limit the life chances of women; then the paragraph moves on to the claim that gender is a social construct rather than a biological fact. Of course gender is a social construct, it is sex that is biological and fixed. Then gender is reconceptualised as a positive concept, as expressed in gender identity (and here the reference to the Yogyakarta Principles in a footnote). Only this level of close reading allows us to see how gender identity is engineered into human rights standards, using two legitimate

---

https://www2.ohchr.org/english/issues/terrorism/rapporteur/docs/a-64-211.pdf. The topic of the report seems singularly inappropriate to shoehorn gender identity in.

[157] As noted, barely ten years and already feminist analysis is out the door, but this time, in the name of "progress."

tools, with a longer history and a recognised pedigree, feminist rights and LGB rights. It is not surprising to find this detailed treatment of gender identity in this document, which by topic does not seem the most appropriate place for it, when we see that the Special Rapporteur on Terrorism was Professor Martin Scheinin, one of the signatories of the Yogyakarta Principles.[158]

In his 2010 Report,[159] the Special Rapporteur on the right of everyone the enjoyment of the highest attainable standard of physical and mental health refers to the Principles' definitions of sexual orientation and gender identity, though the focus in the Report is more clearly on sexual orientation than on gender identity. In the 2016 Report of the Special Rapporteur on the human right to safe drinking water and sanitation,[160] the focus is on gender equality, yet, as this includes inequalities between men and women, and on the basis of gender identity, it is not clear how females can be guaranteed female only toilets, a recognised need to minimise the risk of sexual assaults, unless there is a separate provision for transgender individuals (a reasonable solution), something that the report does not seem to promote. The very fact that sex is mentioned only 4 times in the report (and only 2 times to refer specifically to female needs) but gender 110 times, is a stark illustration of the balance of interests.

In 2010, the first three years of the Yogyakarta Principles were assessed by two human rights lawyers, with a view of embedding them firmly within the corpus of international human rights law.[161] The study is interesting to review the appearance of the Principles in UN documents and can be used as a reference to their early years. The legal analysis leaves something to be desired. This is how they introduce the topic: "Simply put, the Yogyakarta Principles are a statement of the status of current international human rights law as it applies to sexual orientation and gender identity." Simply put, this statement is incorrect. The

---

[158] https://yogyakartaprinciples.org/annex/.

[159] Report of the Special Rapporteur on the Right of Everyone to the Enjoyment of the Highest Attainable Standard of Physical and Mental Health (27 April 2010) A/HRC/14/20, https://www2.ohchr.org/english/bodies/hrcouncil/docs/14session/a.hrc.14.20.pdf.

[160] Of 27 July 2016, A/HRC/33/49, https://documents-dds-ny.un.org/doc/UNDOC/GEN/G16/166/97/PDF/G1616697.pdf?OpenElement.

[161] Paula L. Ettelbrick and Alia Trabucco Zeràn, The Impact of the Yogyakarta Principles on International Human Rights Law Development, https://yogyakartaprinciples.org/wp-content/uploads/2016/10/Yogyakarta_Principles_Impact_Tracking_Report.pdf.

Yogyakarta Principles do not reflect the status of the law, as it is not for individuals to make the law, but for States. They are at best *lex ferenda*, not *lex lata*. If indeed it was true that they reflect international law, there should be proof of binding international law rules that reflect the Yogyakarta Principles. There is no rule of international law for the removal of sex from birth certificates (Yogyakarta Principle 3), nor any human rights rationale to do so. The only possibly legitimate claim, as already noted, is that sexual orientation and gender identity may be covered by "other status" in non-discrimination provisions such as Article 14 ECHR, not that international law confers any positive rights on the basis of sexual orientation and gender identity. It is easy to demonstrate that the claim that the Principles reflect international law is incorrect, as the authors themselves mention the failed Brazilian resolution on LGB rights at the 2003 meeting of the Commission of Human Rights (now HRC) and the strategising that went on from 2004 to advance LGB rights. It is impossible that concepts that were rejected in 2003 and were struggling for UN visibility in 2004 are settled law in 2007. International law never moves so fast, especially in the absence of any written basis. As they acknowleged:

> At an International Dialogue hosted by ARC International in Geneva in December 2004, activists recognized that no one resolution could overcome the significant obstacles to progress in this area, and that advancing LGBT rights internationally would be *a long-term, incremental process* [emphasis added].

The influence and inprint of international NGOs and other organisations, such as the International Commission of Jurists, the International Service for Human Rights led by Chris Sidoti, ARC International, and other, more LGBT-specific NGOs, is equally evident. All this lobbying work was done apparently with little or no coordination with women's rights NGOs (none is listed in the study or mentioned in the summary of the events leading up to the drafting of the Principles), somewhat counter to the common narrative that women were the natural allies of trans rights organisations.

In 2010 the European Parliament's Committee on Civil Liberties, Justice and Home Affairs commissioned a comprehensive report "Transgender Persons' Rights in EU Member States,"[162] which adopted the Yogyakarta

---

[162] Directorate General for Internal Policies, Cristina Castagnoli, "Transgender Persons' Rights in the EU Member States," 2010, https://www.europarl.europa.eu/RegData/etudes/note/join/2010/425621/IPOL-LIBE_NT%282010%29425621_EN.pdf.

Principles Definition for gender identity. The EU had already passed the so called Recast Directive,[163] in which for the first time gender reassignment was mentioned as a separate ground of discrimination, in Recital 3:

> The Court of Justice has held that the scope of the principle of equal treatment for men and women cannot be confined to the prohibition of discrimination based on the fact that a person is of one or other sex. In view of its purpose and the nature of the rights which it seeks to safeguard, it also applies to discrimination arising from the gender reassignment of a person.

The European Agency of Fundamental Rights in 2009 had adopted an even more extreme position, suggesting that:

> [T]here is no reason not to extend the protection from discrimination beyond these persons, to cover "cross dressers," and transvestites, people who live permanently in the gender "opposite" to that on their birth certificate without any medical intervention and all those people who simply wish to present their gender differently.[164]

Transvestic disorder is listed as a paraphilia in DSM-5;[165] and cross-dressing is one of the most common paraphilias amongst sex offenders.[166] There is no human rights rationale for suggesting cross-dressers should be a protected category together with young girls with gender dysphoria. The source of the proposal is given as a report commissioned by the Equalities Review and co-authored by Stephen Whittle.[167]

---

163 Directive 2006/54/EC of the European Parliament and of the Council of 5 July 2006 on the implementation of the principle of equal opportunities and equal treatment of men and women in matters of employment and occupation (recast) OJ L 204, 26.7.2006, p. 23–36.

164 European Union Agency for Fundamental Rights, Homophobia and Discrimination on the Grounds of Sexual Orientation in the EU Member States: Part I – Legal Analysis'(2009) https://fra.europa.eu/sites/default/files/fra_uploads/192-FRA_hdgso_report_Part%201_en.pdf.

165 American Psychiatric Association, Diagnostic and Statistical Manual of Mental Disorders, Fifth Edition (Arlington, VA: American Psychiatric Association, 2013).

166 UK Parliament, Dr. Nicola Williams, "Written Evidence from Fair Play for Women," PPP0011, December 2017, https://committees.parliament.uk/writtenevidence/84415/html/ with references to several recent studies.

167 Stephen Whittle, Lewis Turner and Maryam Al-Alami, "Engendered Penalties: Transgender and Transsexual People's Experiences of Inequality and Discrimination,"

As noted, from the second decade of the 2000s the references to gender identity become more frequent in primary materials, most notably in the work of the HRC.We see that in its work, including the Universal Periodic Review, gender identity is increasingly mentioned, always in conjunction with sexual orientation, in resolutions of the HRC of the human rights situations for groups sharing these characteristics.

The most recent (at the time of writing) statement issued from the UN including language about gender identity is a resolution of the Third Committee of the General Assembly in charge of social, humanitarian and cultural issues (including human rights) on the criteria for elections.[168] It is the standard non-discrimination provision contained in the Preamble and gender identity is included in the list of prohibited grounds. It does not reference the Yogyakarta Principles.

To find references both to gender identity and transgender rights, raised independently from the Yogyakarta Principles, we have to move to Europe and look at the jurisprudence of the European Court of Human Rights. In doing so, we will see how tight the connection was between gender identity and transgender or transsexual status, a connection that is all but invisible in the documents that we have seen so far at UN level, where in fact the focus is on gender identity as a universal experience.

The Council of Europe has long been at the forefront of embedding gender identity theory in its human rights work. The Committee of Ministers of the Council of Europe is the "executive" branch of the Council of Europe. It is the first international body to use the language of gender identity theory in its materials, which is not surprising when we consider that the ECHR is the first international court to consider this matter as well, up to the seminal judgment of *Goodwin v UK*. The first use of the term gender identity is in two documents from the 1990s, where it refers to the

(2007): 74, https://www.ilga-europe.org/sites/default/files/trans_ country_report_-_engenderedpenalties.pdf. This Report provides an interesting overview of the tactics used by trans rights activists, including seeking corporate sponsors and lobbying local politicians, 8 ff.

[168] United Nations General Assembly Third Committee, "Strengthening the role of the United Nations in the promotion of democratization and enhancing periodic and genuine elections," A/C.3/78/L.51, 31 October 2023, https://digitallibrary.un.org/record/4026084?ln=en#record-files-collapse-header.

development of a gender identity in children, produced by the Steering Committee for Equality between Men and Women:[169]

> What is the impact on children of experiencing abuse and of witnessing abuse (e.g. of the mother) in the home? How do boys, in particular, interpret, cope with and react to such experiences in developing their gender identity, their perceptions of gender relations and of women? How do they use or avoid violence?.

The first document in which gender identity is used with reference to gender identity theory, and transgenderism more specifically, is a Meeting of Ministers' Deputies in which recent cases in the ECHR are discussed, including cases on what was then defined as transsexualism[170] and specifically the *Van Kück* case.[171]

It bears restating that the Council of Europe was at the forefront of debates around what was then called transsexualism. In 1993, the Council of Europe, in cooperation with the Free University of Amsterdam, organised a colloquium.[172] The Dutch were the first to develop a medical pathway for "gender affirmative" care in children, including the protocol for giving puberty blockers and cross-sex hormones.[173] It is not surprising to see them hosting this international conference on the topic. The proceedings are a very interesting document to reconstruct the genealogy of gender identity and of the "trans turn" in human rights law in Europe. A very relevant strand is the creation of the concept of "legal sex"[174] as a discrete

---

[169] Council of Europe Steering Committee for Equality between Men and Women, 18th Meeting, Strasbourg, 21-23 April 1999, CM/99/82. https://rm.coe.int/16804dc09c.

[170] Ministers' Deputies Decisions, 863rd (DH) Meeting 2 and 3 December 2003, CM/Del/Dec(2003)863, https://rm.coe.int/16805dde1e.

[171] See Chapter 6.

[172] XXXIII Colloquy on European Law on the topic "Transsexualism, Medicine and Law" (Strasbourg: Council of Europe, 1995) https://search.worldcat.org/title/transsexualism-medicine-and-law-proceedings-xxiiird-colloquy-on-european-law-vrije-universiteit-amsterdam-netherlands-14-16-april-1993/oclc/1126345517?referer=di&ht=edition.

[173] Michael Biggs, "The Dutch Protocol for Juvenile Transsexuals: Origins and Evidence," Journal of Sex and Material Therapy, 49(4) (2023): 348-368, doi: https://doi.org/10.1080/0092623X.2022.2121238. See also Chapter 10.

[174] The idea of legal sex has acquired especial significance in the UK as a consequence of a series of judgments that interpreted the relationship between the Gender Recognition Act 2004 and the Equality Act 2010 as being built upon a distinction between biological sex, i.e. the sex of women born female, and legal

category from birth sex and not necessarily mapping on it, and concurrently, the move to eliminate sex as a relevant legal category altogether. This is how Frans van der Reijt of the Dutch Gender Foundation introduces these ideas at the opening of the colloquium:

> The mention of sex on the birth certificate serves no purpose; if you [...] think it over, you will realise that nowdays your armies, for example are filled with males and females alike. Would then Napoleon, should he live today, have the mention of sex included in that document? During these three days our learned medical friends will, undoubtedly, show evidence that the mention of sex is the most dubious information figuring on the certificate. Could we, lawyers, not do better than avoid such ambiguities from the start by simply not mentioning it at all?

About thirty years later, the UK Economic Social and Research Council funded a project to put forward the same proposal as an innovative project, The Future of Legal Gender.[175] Transforming legal sex into a signifier for gender identity, and not biological sex, is a necessary step towards this goal. Once legal sex refers to a changeable feature of one's identity, it becomes irrelevant to record it. One cannot help noting that, if sex is not recorded anymore, gender identity vanishes as a significant category as well, notwithstanding the fact that the validation of one's gender identity is one of the tenets of gender identity theory. The only validation remains the social one, on the basis of gender stereotypes of femininity and masculinity.

---

sex, i.e. the sex of males in possession of a Gender Recognition Certificate. There is no textual support for this distinction in the EA 2010. There is considerable case law now being created on this point. The two cases, respectively FSW1 and FWS2 where this distinction was upheld both originate in Scottish courts and therefore are not binding on the rest of the UK: *Opinion of Lady Haldane in Petition of For Women Scotland Limited for Judicial Review of the Revised Statutory Guidance Produced by the Scottish Ministers under S7 of the Gender Representation on Public Boards (Scotland) Act 2018*, [2022] CSOH 90, appealed [2023] CSIH37; and *Opinion of the Court delivered by Lady Dorrian, in the Reclaiming Motion by For Women Scotland Limited, against the Lord Advocate, the Scottish Ministers* [2022] CSIH 4. FWS was given permission to appeal to the UK Supreme Court on 16 February 2024, https://forwomen.scot/16/02/2024/appeal-to-the-uk-supreme-court/.

[175] Davina Cooper, Robyn Emerton, Emily Grabham, Han Newman, Elizabeth Peel, Flora Renz, and Jessica Smith, Abolishing Legal Sex. Final Report,King's College, London (2022). https://www.kcl.ac.uk/law/research/future-of-legal-gender-abolishing-legal-sex-status-full-report.pdf.

This focus on birth certificates is one of the first phenomena I noticed and that got me to reflect on the significance of this trans turn in human rights. We all know that birth certificates do not list the gender of the newborn child, but his or her sex. In 99.98% of cases, the sex can be correctly recorded through visual inspection alone. In a tiny percentage of cases, sex cannot be ascertained through a visual inspection and further testing will be necessary. In all cases, a baby will be either a male or a female, with a very small percentage of babies affected by severe DSDs that make sex ambiguous (some DSDs do not do that, to the point that some people are not aware of being affected by them at all). So in the first instance, the argument that transsexual people had to have the right to have their gender updated on a birth certificate seemed to me simply misguided. You cannot change what is not there.

The United Nations recognises that every child should be registered at birth. Article 7 of the Convention of the Rights of the Child contains this specific right. In the Background Note on Sex Discrimination in Child Registration,[176] the UNHCR and UNICEF focus on sex discrimination against women in their ability to register the birth of their own child. However, the UN also defined the legal identity of human beings in the following terms:

> Legal identity is defined as the basic characteristics of an individual's identity, e.g., name, sex, place and date of birth conferred through registration and the issuance of a certificate by an authorized civil registration authority following the occurrence of birth.[177]

The Second Report of the Independent Expert Review Group on information and accountability for women's and children's health, published in 2013, addresses the specific challenges that girls and women face, including the need to improve civil registration.[178] Amongst the issues affecting girls that may be hidden by failing to register girls at birth or failing to register

---

[176] UNHCR and UNICEF, "Background Note on Sex Discrimination and Birth Registration," 6 July 2021, https://www.refworld.org/docid/60e2d0554.html.

[177] Economic and Social Council, "Introduction of the United Nations Legal Identity Agenda: a holistic approach to civil registration, vital statistics and identity management: report of the Secretary General," 18 December 2019, E/CN.3/ 2020/15,
https://digitallibrary.un.org/record/3841896?ln=en#record-files-collapse-header.

[178] World Health Organization, "Every woman, every child: strenghtening equity and dignity through health," 1 January 2013,
https://www.who.int/publications/i/item/9789241505949.

their sex, are the loss of data on female infanticide and the phenomenon of child marriages.

All the same, the entire 1993 Colloquium ignored the potential effects on women of the project of elimination of (biological) sex as a legally significant category, focussing instead on how efficiently modern medicine approximated the "acquired sex" in transsexuals. This focus alone dates this conference quite accurately, as more contemporary understandings of gender identities decouple the recognition of one's gender identity from any medical intervention, which is now seen as an unlawful interference with one's right to bodily integrity.

Stefano Rodotà, an Italian constitutionalist, also intervened at the Colloquium with a paper titled "General Presentation of Problems Related to Transsexualism." It is a paper very much of its times, the post-1989 naïve spirit that the world was at the cusp of a new era of peace and individual freedoms, guaranteed by technological innovation. Here is Professor Rodotà:

> The problem is one of recording not only natural features, but the results of a process of self identification by the persons actually concerned, for whom changing civil status is the final step and represent formal approval. Before that, however, comes a process based on a freely made decision and the acknowledgement that it is for the person concerned to define themselves independently. This is the result of a cultural change and even of scientific progress. Much has been said – in relation to this and other fields, particularly with regards to procreative genetics – about the "technologies of freedom", that is, technologies which enable individuals to make a choice, whereas in the past they had to make do with natural processes.

He goes as far as to claim that transsexualism breaks the boundaries of sex in the same way that the French revolution broke the feudal system. One wonders why only transsexuals are capable of overcoming the "feudal" limitations of sex, and whether it did not occur to Professor Rodotà that the limitations imposed on women by society are absolutely unaffected by any right granted to male, or even female, transsexuals.

In August 1989, Rodotà was the Rapporteur to the Committee on Legal Affairs and Human Rights of the Parliamentary Assembly of the Council of Europe and he authored a Report to the Committee titled "Conditions of transsexuals."[179] This report was the basis for the 29 September 1989 Recommendation 1117 by the Parliamentary Assembly, here reported in full:[180]

> The Assembly,
>
> 1. Considering that transsexualism is a syndrome characterised by a dual personality, one physical, the other psychological, together with such a profound conviction of belonging to the other sex that the transsexual person is prompted to ask for the corresponding bodily ''correction"' to be made;
>
> 2. Considering that modern medical progress, and in particular recourse to sexual conversion surgery, enable transsexuals to be given the appearance and, to a great extent, the characteristics of the sex opposite to that which appears on their birth certificate;
>
> 3. Observing that this treatment is of a nature to bring the physical sex and the psychological sex into harmony with one another, and so give such persons a sexual identity which, moreover, constitutes a decisive feature of their personality;
>
> 4. Believing that account of the changes brought about should be taken in the transsexual's civil status records by adding such details to the original record so as to update the data concerning sex in the birth certificate and identity papers, and by authorising a subsequent change of forename;

---

179 Council of Europe Committee on Legal Affairs and Human Rights, "Condition of Transsexuals," 16 August 1989, https://assembly.coe.int/nw/xml/XRef/Xref-XML2HTML-EN.asp?fileid=6256&lang=en. In it Rodotà refers to the reasoning of the *Rees* judgment: "What must be done therefore is to define with precision the aims of a law governing at least the principal aspects of transsexualism. It should be clear from what has been said above that the point is to specify the essential conditions under which a private frame of reference can be correctly built up in transsexuals and made fully consistent with the public image.

This, firstly, entails legitimising the various treatments for realising the true sexual identity, as well as legal recognition of this "new" identity. Hence the "psychological" sex prevails, as it were, over the "genetic" one. A more analytical distinction is drawn in paragraph 16 of the *Rees* judgment, between psychological sex and chromosomal, gonadal and apparent sex (as revealed by examination of the external genitalia and body form)."

180 Council of Europe Parliamentary Assembly, Recommendation 1117 (1989), "Condition of Transsexuals," 29 September 1989, https://assembly.coe.int/nw/xml/XRef/Xref-XML2HTML-en.asp?fileid=15151&lang=en.

> 5. Considering that a refusal of such amendment of the civil status papers exposes persons in this situation to the risk of being obliged to reveal to numerous people the reasons for the discrepancy between their physical appearance and legal status;
>
> 6. Noting that transsexualism raises relatively new and complex questions to which states are called upon to find answers compatible with respect for human rights;
>
> 7. Observing that, in the absence of specific rules, transsexuals are often the victims of discrimination and violation of their private life;
>
> 8. Considering, furthermore, that the legislation of many member states is seriously deficient in this area and does not permit transsexuals, particularly those who have undergone an operation, to have civil status amendments made to take account of their appearance, external morphology, psychology and social behaviour;
>
> 9. Considering the case-law of the European Commission and Court of Human Rights;
>
> 10. Referring to the resolution which the European Parliament adopted on 12 September 1989, in which, among other things, it called on the Council of Europe to enact a convention for the protection of transsexuals,
>
> 11. Recommends that the Committee of Ministers draw up a recommendation inviting member states to introduce legislation whereby, in the case of irreversible transsexualism:
>
> a. the reference to the sex of the person concerned is to be rectified in the register of births and in the identity papers;
> b. a change of forename is to be authorised;
> c. the person's private life is to be protected;
> d. all discrimination in the enjoyment of fundamental rights and freedoms is prohibited in accordance with Article 14 of the European Convention on Human Rights.

By the late 2000s both the UN and regional European organisations have reframed gender identity, decoupling it from any sort of medical and surgical intervention, which is left to the initiative and demand of individuals. A similar reframing takes place in the jurisprudence of the ECHR.[181] In 2009, in the paper Human Rights and Gender Identity,[182] the Commissioner for Human Rights of the Council of Europe stated that:

---

[181] See Chapter X.

> It should be stressed that the eligibility conditions for the change of sex in documents vary widely across Europe. It is possible to roughly distinguish three categories of countries. In the first category, no provision at all is made for official recognition. As pointed out above, this is in clear breach of established jurisprudence of the ECtHR. In the second and smaller category of countries, there is no requirement to undergo hormonal treatment or surgery of any kind in order to obtain official recognition of the preferred gender. Legal gender recognition is possible by bringing evidence of gender dysphoria before a competent authority, such as experts from the Ministry of Health (in Hungary), the Gender Reassignment Panel (in the UK) or a doctor or clinical psychologist. In the third category of countries, comprising most Council of Europe member states, the individual has to demonstrate:
>
> 1. that (s)he has followed a medically supervised process of gender reassignment–often restricted to certain state appointed doctors or institutions;
>
> 2. that (s)he has been rendered surgically irreversibly infertile (sterilisation), and/or
>
> 3. that (s)he has undergone other medical procedures, such as hormonal treatment.
>
> *Such requirements clearly run counter to the respect for the physical integrity of the person.* [emphasis added]

In Resolution 1728 of 2010,[183] The Parliamentary Assembly of the Council of Europe recommends that Member States ensure the right of transgender persons to obtain official documents without any obligation to undergo sterilisation, SRS or hormonal treatment.

In 2011, the term gender identity was used for the first time in a treaty text, the Council of Europe Istanbul Convention Preventing and Combating Violence Against Women and Domestic Violence.[184] This is the first international, or better regional, treaty where gender identity is

---

[182] Council of Europe Commissioner for Human Rights, "Human Rights and Gender Identity," 2009 CommDH/IssuePaper(2009)2, https://rm.coe.int/human-rights-and-gender-identity-issue-paper-commissioned-and-publishe/16806da753.

[183] Council of Europe Parliamentary Assembly, Resolution 1728 (2010), "Discrimination on the basis of sexual orientation and gender identity," 29 April 2010,
https://assembly.coe.int/nw/xml/XRef/Xref-XML2HTML-en.asp?fileid=17853.

[184] Council of Europe Convention on Preventing and Combating Violence against Women and Domestic Violence, 11 May 2011, 3010 UNTS 52313.

specifically mentioned. Article 4(3) (Fundamental Rights, Equality and No-Discrimination) of the Convention recites as follows:

> Article 4 – Fundamental rights, equality and non-discrimination
>
> 3. The implementation of the provisions of this Convention by the Parties, in particular measures to protect the rights of victims, shall be secured without discrimination on any ground such as sex, gender, race, colour, language, religion, political or other opinion, national or social origin, association with a national minority, property, birth, sexual orientation, gender identity, age, state of health, disability, marital status, migrant or refugee status, or other status.

The explanatory report provides the following text to justify the inclusion of gender identity in the protected categories:

> Certain groups of individuals may also experience discrimination on the basis of their gender identity, which in simple terms means that the gender they identify with is not in conformity with the sex assigned to them at birth. This includes categories of individuals such as transgender or transsexual persons, cross-dressers, transvestites and other groups of persons that do not correspond to what society has established as belonging to "male" or "female" categories.

The familiar language of gender identity theory is making an appearance (e.g. sex assigned at birth). Although the convention is ostensibly for violence against women, the reference to sex, gender and gender identity reduces the effectiveness of the protection. While it is true that both men and women can be victims of domestic violence, there is a clear gendered aspect to this sort of violence, that the Convention dilutes at the same time as for the first time it seeks to recognise and make visible. Additionally, it is not clear what is the basis for including male cross-dressers in a convention for combating violence against women. This is an incomprehensible extension of the class of females to include any male who does not conform to male stereotypes, but conforms to female stereotypes, while excluding women who embrace male gender stereotypes. It is also quite unclear why not conforming to male stereotypes transforms a male into a woman entitled to the protection of the Istanbul Convention. Notice also that in this convention there is no claim that having a gender identity is a universal experience. Gender identity is apparently relevant only for those whose gender identity does not match their sex at birth. There follows the list, clearly not a closed list (see "such as") of individuals whose gender identities grants them special protection under the convention. The perverse effect is that a woman who submits to the rigid gender norms imposed on her sex is not a visible subject of the Convention. And yet, for a woman to submit to gender norms without rebellion may mean giving up on further education, accepting to marry a man considerably older than herself when she is still legally a child, accepting to be beaten by her husband without reporting him to the authorities, having sex with him even when not wanting to, not taking contraception because her husband does not approve of it, resigning from her work upon marriage… The list is endless. But all these violations of women's rights are invisible because without rebellion, there is no gender identity discrimination and without reporting, the sex based discrimination can be ignored (and will be ignored). The only criticism of the introduction of gender identity in the Convention that is reported and noted is the criticism coming from conservatives and religious groups.[185] Any concern raised by feminists is ignored and dismissed, or reframed as conservative, funded by right wing groups, bigoted, uninformed etc. This can be said for the Istanbul Convention but more widely for any critical voice arising from the women who are sometimes defined as "gender critical."

The inclusion of gender identity created resistance during the negotiation of the text, as we can glean from the *traveaux préparatoires*. In the Report of the 3rd meeting of the Ad Hoc Committee for preventing and combating violence against women and domestic violence (CAHVIO) composed of governmental representatives of Council of Europe Member States, it was reported that:[186]

> Concerning the equality and non-discrimination clause contained in article 3, several delegations commented on the grounds of discrimination as currently listed. While some preferred an extensive list, others questioned

---

[185] Valentine Berthet "Norm under Fire: Support for and Opposition to the European Union's Ratification of the Istanbul Convention in the European Parliament," International Feminist Journal of Politics, 24(5) (2022): 675-698 https://doi.org/10.1080/14616742.2022.2034510; Turkey withdrew from the Convention, see Başak Çali and Laurence Helfer, "The Gender of Treaty Withdrawal: Lessons from the Istanbul Convention," EJIL Talk!, November 28, 2022, https://www.ejiltalk.org/the-gender-of-treaty-withdrawal-lessons-from-the-istanbul-convention/.

[186] Council of Europe Ad Hoc Committee on Preventing and Combating Violence against Women and Domestic Violence, "Report of the 3rd Meeting," CAHVIO (2009) 34 Rev, 16 April 2010, https://rm.coe.int/CoERMPublicCommonSearchServices/DisplayDCTMContent?documentId=0900001680593859.

> the inclusion of grounds such as "gender identity" and "sexual orientation". In particular, the Russian Federation stressed its view that the scope of the future convention should not extend to same-sex relationships and that the grounds for discrimination should not include "sexual orientation".

Russia did not change its reservations and we can also see that Lithuania expressed more pointed reservations specifically to gender identity in the 8thmeeting. Russia never did sign the Convention. Lithuania has signed it but not ratified it. Ukraine has entered the following declaration:

> Ukraine notes that in accordance with the Constitution of Ukraine, no ideology is recognized by the State as mandatory and is not subject to introduction. Ukraine declares that it will apply the Convention in accordance with the values, principles and norms within the limits determined by the Constitution of Ukraine, in particular with regard to the protection of human rights and fundamental freedoms, equality of the rights and opportunities of women and men, gender identity, the formation of responsible motherhood and fatherhood, the support of family and the protection of childhood.

At the opposite end of the spectrum, in September 2009 ILGA Europe presented a report on the inclusion of lesbian, bisexual and transgender women in the Istanbul Convention.[187]As previously noted, the inclusion of "transwomen" (who are males) but not of "transmen" (who are female) ignores the transgender population more likely to be affected by sex-based discrimination, leaving them unprotected by the Convention. ILGA strongly supports the idea of an innate and universal gender identity, even more so than the Yogyakarta definition that undoubtedly constitutes the inspiration for their own definition, disregarding the fact that entire groups of individuals are left out from this supposedlly universal characteristic of humans, that prevails over observed sex:

> The notion of "gender identity" offers the opportunity to understand that the sex assigned to an infant at birth might not correspond with the innate gender identity the child develops when he or she grows up. It refers to each person's deeply felt internal and individual experience of gender, which may or may not correspond with the sex assigned at birth, and includes the personal sense of the body and other expressions of gender (i.e. "gender expression") such as dress, speech and mannerisms.

---

[187] https://rm.coe.int/CoERMPublicCommonSearchServices/DisplayDCTMContent?documentId=0900001680594272.

In 2018 the Council of Europe issued a "Questions and Answers" document on the Istanbul Convention, because of the continuing debates and criticisms about the language of the Convention and the use of the word "gender."[188] As usual, the document is directed at "religious and ultra conservative groups" and their position with respect to the feminist reading of gender. The fact that the Convention includes "transwomen" in the sex class of women[189] does not receive any attention in the document.

In the 2011 Report "Discriminatory Laws and Practice and Acts of Violence Against Individuals Based on their Sexual Orientation and Gender Identity,"[190] the High Commissioner for Human Rights recommends that States:

> Facilitate legal recognition of the preferred gender of transgender persons and establish arrangements to permit relevant identity documents to be reissued reflecting preferred gender and name, without infringements of other human rights.[191]

In 2013 the Parliamentary Assembly of the Council of Europe adopted Resolution 1945,[192] significantly titled "Putting an End to Coerced Sterilisations and Castrations," in which it recommended that no-one

---

[188] Council of Europe, Ending misconceptions about the Convention on Preventing and Combating Violence against Women and Domestic Violence, News 2018, 22 November 2018, https://www.coe.int/cs/web/portal/news-2018/-/asset_publisher/n3Yff4uZZo3L/content/ending-misconceptions-about-the-convention-on-preventing-and-combating-violence-against-women-and-domestic-violence?_101_INSTANCE_n3Yff4uZZo3L_languageId=fr_FR.

[189] As said at page 10 of the document: "[...] all women, including lesbian, bisexual and transgender women have access to domestic violence shelters, for example, and the right to live a life free from violence. This may also include gay men who are confronted with domestic violence."

[190] "Discriminatory laws and practices and acts of violence against individuals based on their sexual orientation and gender identity", Report of the United Nations High Commissioner for Human Rights, 17 November 2011, A/HRC/19/41, https://www.ohchr.org/sites/default/files/Documents/Issues/Discrimination/A.HRC.19.41_English.pdf.

[191] At paragraph 72 the High Commissioner mentions that the requirement of sterilisation in order to obtain gender recognition is a practice to be abandoned.

[192] Council of Europe's Parliamentary Assemby, "Putting an end to coerced sterilisations and castrations," Resolution 1945 (2013) https://assembly.coe.int/nw/xml/XRef/Xref-XML2HTML-en.asp?fileid=19984&lang=en#:~:text=Text%20adopted%20by%20the%20Assembly,Council%20of%20Europe%20member%20States.

should be coerced into sterilisation or castration "for any reason."Also in 2013 the Special Rapporteur on Torture in his Report[193] reported forced sterilisation as a practice of concern inviting States:

> [...] to repeal any law allowing intrusive and irreversible treatments, including forced genital-normalizing surgery, involuntary sterilization, unethical experimentation, medical display, "reparative therapies" or "conversion therapies," when enforced or administered without the free and informed consent of the person concerned. He also calls upon them to outlaw forced or coerced sterilization in all circumstances and provide special protection to individuals belonging to marginalized groups.

At UN level, the World Health Organisation (WHO), United Nations Children's Fund (UNICEF), Office of the High Commissioner for Human Rights (OHCHR), UN Women, UNAIDS, United Nations Development Programme (UNDP) and United Nations Population Fund in 2014 issued a multiagency statement titled "Eliminating Forced, Coercive and Otherwise Involuntary Sterilization"[194]in which they recommend that States ensure that sterilisation is not a prerequisite for the legal change of gender.

In 2015, the Council of Europe's Parliamentary Assembly passed the seminal Resolution, 2048,[195] titled "Discrimination Against Transgender People in Europe," which is not just about preventing discrrimination, but about granting considerable positive rights to transgender people and singling them out for preferential treatment. This approach is evident by the inclusion of specific sections on legal gender recognition, gender reassignment treatment and health care, information, awareness raising and training, on top of the section dedicated to non-discrimination provisions.

In fact the mid-2010s signal the comprehensive mainstreaming of gender identity in all major international organisations, to the point that it becomes difficult to track and keep up with the production of legal materials ostensibly dedicated to SOGI but more and more focusing on

---

[193] Report of the Special Rapporteur on torture and other cruel, inhuman and degrading treatment or punishment, 1 February 2013, A/HRC/22/53, https://documents-dds-ny.un.org/doc/UNDOC/GEN/G13/105/77/PDF/G1310577.pdf?OpenElement.

[194] "Eliminating forced, coercive and otherwise involuntary sterilization," World Health Organization, 2014, https://www.unaids.org/sites/default/files/media_asset/201405_sterilization_en.pdf.

[195] Council of Europe's Parliamentary Assembly, "Discrimination against transgender people in Europe," Resolution 2048 (2015), https://assembly.coe.int/nw/xml/xref/xref-xml2html-en.asp?fileid=21736.

gender identity issues. By the mid 2010s, the mainstreaming also reached the general public, by way of items in the news and in social media. By then the narrative had been set, but one of the elements, typical only of the approach to the general public, is that all these matters are not up for debate. It is not possible to question, critique and investigate anything relating to gender identity, lest being accused of transphobia.[196] Interestingly, UN agencies such as UN Women[197] position themselves at the intersection of these two phenomena.[198] UN Women uses social media incessantly[199] to push gender identity theory, adopting the same language used by trans activists, with slogans such as "Trans Rights Are Human Rights," "Women's Rights=Trans Rights=Human Rights," and "Trans Lesbians Are Lesbians." This last one is especially provocative for many lesbians, as many "transwomen" do not undergo any surgery, and, while calling themselves lesbians they are very likely to still have male genitalia, and the assumption that lesbians should have sexual intercourse with individuals with male genitalia because those individuals call themselves lesbians seems to bring us back to the 1970s with their homophobic jokes about lesbians needing to experience heterosexual sex to be "converted."

In its 2020 Report on Legal Gender Recognition, the EU Commission goes as far as to promote the use of "correct pronouns."[200] The Report includes interviews with "transgender individuals," whose stories are reported throughout the text; they are invariably stories of children not

---

[196] The definition of transphobia from Stonewall, for example, includes denying the gender identity of trans people, making it impossible to argue that one does not believe gender identity trumps sex without being accused of transphobia. https://www.stonewall.org.uk/list-lgbtq-terms.

[197] https://www.unwomen.org/en, created by the General Assembly in 2010 https://www.unwomen.org/en/news/stories/2010/7/un-creates-new-structure-for-empowerment-of-women-

[198] In their official role, they maintain a much more "conservative" profile. All the same, in their Strategic Plan 2022-20225 (UNW/2021/6) they simply refer, as one of the multiple grounds of discriminations women suffer) their gender identity. The confusion engendered by gender identity theory means it is not clear if this includes women who are transgender (i.e., transmen) or not. If one follows the theory, they are not included because they are in fact men. https://documents-dds-ny.un.org/doc/UNDOC/GEN/N21/186/22/PDF/N2118622.pdf?OpenElement.

[199] https://twitter.com/search?q=trans%20(from%3AUN_Women)&src=typed_query.

[200] European Commission, "Legal gender recognition in the EU," 2020, https://op.europa.eu/en/publication-detail/-/publication/7341d588-ddd8-11ea-adf7-01aa75ed71a1/language-en.

fitting the stereotypes associated with their sex. Instead of fighting those stereotypes, gender identity theory posits that these children must therefore be the opposite sex. Because real boys do not play with dolls, and real girls want their hair long.

> "As a child [growing up in Nigeria] … I [asked] my mum why she didn't give birth to me as a girl and she beat the living daylights out of me […] I didn't feel comfortable at all and it was very confusing […] When I tried to cook with my grandma, or play with girls' toys or play with the girls, they would beat me up and tell me not to do that […] Between three and five years' old, as soon as I started talking, I discovered my innate sense of self, that I was a girl."

> "Looking back at photos of myself as a five or six-year old, I see how obvious it was that I was a boy…I tried to accept my sex [assigned at birth] during my teenage years by growing my hair out and wearing female clothes but this didn't work out."

> "My mother told me that in Finland there is this culture that boys don't cry…then she said … "You can cry at home after school" … This meant I started bottling up my emotions and I prayed every night that I would magically turn into a girl."

> "Now that I am a man, people listen to me when I talk. In particular, when they do not know that I am trans. It is a very sexist thing […] I am not harassed anymore in the street; I can get angry without being told that I am hysterical […]"

Amongst the production by international organisations, it is also useful to list the work done by the Office of the High Commissioner for Human Rights.[201] The OHCHR initiated a campaign, Free and Equal,[202] involving the LGBTIQ+ community (signaling the first time the UN is involved in a specific campaign for an undefined group, the + group).[203] Amongst the

---

[201] The OHCHR had been asked in 2011 to investigate SOGI human rights issues (Resolution 17/19 on Human rights, sexual orientation and gender identity; A/HRC/RES/17/19, https://ap.ohchr.org/documents/dpage_e.aspx?si=A/HRC/RES/17/19. The Report is from 2015: OHCHR, "Update of Report A/HRC/19/41 (on Discriminatory Laws and Practices and Acts of Violence against Individuals Based on Their Sexual Orientation and Gender Identity)."

[202] Free and Equal, https://www.unfe.org/.

[203] On the website of the Free and Equal initiative, the following definition is provided for the +: "other people with sexual orientations, gender identities and expressions and sex characteristics that are perceived not to conform to social

result of this campaign effort is the production of two major reports, Born Free and Equal[204] and Living Free and Equal.[205] In 2016 the SOGI Mandate is established,[206] creating a dedicated venue for all SOGI issues, although SOGI mainstreaming into all UN agencies and bodies continues.

The 2020 EU Commission's document, "Union of Equality: LGBTIQ Equality Strategy 2020-2025" illustrates how comprehensively gender identity theory has been embedded in the work of the EU.[207] The documents adopts the acronym LGBTIQ and defines it as follows:

> LGBTIQ people are people:
>
> - who are attracted to others of their own gender (lesbian, gay) or any gender (bisexual);
> - whose gender identity and/or expression does not correspond to the sex they were assigned at birth (trans, non-binary);
> - who are born with sex characteristics that do not fit the typical definition of male or female (intersex); and
> - whose identity does not fit into a binary classification of sexuality and/or gender (queer).

The EU Commission defines homosexuality and bisexuality not as same sex attraction, or attraction to both sexes, but as "same gender" attraction. Sex is "assigned at birth," rather than simply recorded at birth (if not earlier). Babies with DSDs are described as individuals with a special identity, and not with medical conditions sometimes accompanied by serious symptoms, including cardiac problems or developmental delays,

---

norms." This "monstering" of social norms is a disturbing development, especially from a safeguarding perspective. Social norms are not always negative. They can be a powerful and effective tool in safeguarding women and children against abusive male sexual behaviours.

204 In 2011; the second edition was issued in 2019, HR/PUB/12/06/Rev.1. https://www.ohchr.org/sites/default/files/Documents/Publications/Born_Free_and_Equal_WEB.pdf.

205 HR/PUB/16/3, https://www.ohchr.org/sites/default/files/Documents/Publications/LivingFreeAndEqual.pdf.

206 https://www.ohchr.org/en/special-procedures/ie-sexual-orientation-and-gender-identity. The current holder is Graeme Reid, the second one after Victor Madrigal-Borloz.

207 Communication from the Commission to the European Parliament, the Council, the European Economic and Social Committee and the Committees of the Regions, "Union of Equality: LGBTIQ Equality Strategy 2020-2025," COM 2020/698 final, https://eur-lex.europa.eu/legal-content/EN/TXT/?uri=CELEX%3A52020DC0698.

and almost always resulting in sterility. The word queer, an insult that in the past often accompanied mental and physical abuse of homosexuals, is reclaimed, not by homosexuals, but by straight academics and policy makers. One struggles to think of another insult reclaimed in law and policy by people who were never affected by it. Possibly the most problematic development is the inclusion of children in LGBTIQ rights:

> Discrimination affects LGBTIQ people at every stage in life. From an early age, LGBTIQ children and young people, and children of LGBTIQ or rainbow families, where one of the members is LGBTIQ, are often stigmatised, making them targets of discrimination and bullying that affects their educational performance and employment prospects, their daily lives and their personal and family well-being.

While clearly teenagers who start interrogating their sexual orientation should not be victims of discrimination, it is highly contested that children can be transgender or "queer" at an early age (undefined but clearly potentially including children well below the age of puberty, who, the document claims, already have a sexuality). There is growing critical literature and social activism around the capture of educational and paediatric health care organisations and the creation of the "trans child."[208] The European Union goes one step further with the creation of the "queer child."

The Commission document recasts language so as to minimise the role of sex and embed the concept of gender identity in EU law, until it becomes evident one can be used for the other, hence gender identity is none other than a sex based identity. This is no coincidence, or oversight. To give just an example, we can look at the work of the Women's Rights and Gender Equality Committee of the European Parliament. In its Report of 17 March 2022 on the proposed Directive of the European Parliament and Council to strengthen the application of the principle of equal pay for equal work or work of equal value between men and women through pay transparency and enforcement mechanisms, the Committee suggests several amendments for the introduction of gender identity as a protected category.[209] The first relevant amendment is the addition of a new recital in the Directive, stating as follows:

---

[208] The medicalisation of transgender, especially of minors, will be the topic of Chapter 10.

[209] Legislative Train Schedule, Binding Pay Transparency Measures, https://www.europarl.europa.eu/legislative-train/theme-a-new-push-for-european-democracy/file-binding-pay-transparency-measures.

> (3a) The terminology used in Article 157 TFEU dates from 1957. Since then, social and legal changes, as well as research in the medical and biological fields have led to the recognition, in the definition of "sex," of diversity in addition to women and men. For example, in some Member States it is currently possible for persons to legally register themselves as having a third, often neutral, gender. The Court of Justice of the European Union (the "Court") has also held that the principle of equal treatment for men and women cannot be limited to the prohibition of discrimination based on the fact that a person is of one or other sex. In view of the purpose and the nature of the rights which the principle of equal treatment seeks to safeguard, it also applies to discrimination arising from the person's gender identity.[210]

No serious scientist believes there are more than two sexes, male and female. It is indeed worrying that such pseudo-scientific language is being proposed in an official document of the EU. There is no medical test to ascertain any of these other sexes and DSDs are not other sexes, but differences of sexual development, affecting males and females differently. There is no logical or necessary connection between the false premise (sex is not binary) and the reasonable demand (people who believe they have a gender identity should not be discriminated against on the basis of this belief). As already noted, this work seeks to prove that it is not necessary to accept the false premise in order to accede to the reasonable demand. The following relevant amendment is another newly drafted recital:

> (3b) This Directive applies a human rights oriented approach that seeks to protect persons from pay discrimination irrespective of their sex, gender, gender identity, gender expression or sex characteristics and therefore interprets its legal basis, namely discrimination on the grounds of sex, in the broadest and most inclusive way, in order to foster gender equality and encompass people in all their diversity. Employers should take into account workers that do not identify as either female or male in their pay reporting obligations and should mention them in a category separate from female and male workers. When calculating the gender pay gap, those workers' pay should be compared to the average level of pay of male workers. An employer should only mention workers who do not identify as either female or male in their pay reporting obligations where those workers are legally registered as not identifying as female or male or where that information has been proactively and voluntarily disclosed to the employer.

[210] In its jurisprudence, the ECJ/CJEU refers to gender reassignment, not gender identity (the case law is analysed in Chapter 6).

This insistence on eliminating sex as a protected, recognisable category, does not sit well with the language necessary to describe the predicament of female workers in issues such as pay and working conditions. For example, if sex is replaced with gender identity, as proposed by the Committee, dealing with comparator issues, which are crucial in a discrimination claim, becomes a great deal more difficult. Would a FtM woman constitute a valid male comparator in a discrimination claim brought by a female worker? How would a woman defend herself from discrimination based on her femaleness if the "valid" comparator is a MtF man who has to face none of the challenges affecting women? It is evident that allowing people to move across sex categories at will makes assessing a sex discrimination claim an exercise in futility.

These examples are sufficient to illustrate the concerted move at EU level to dilute or eliminate the language regarding sex and reinforcing the language related to gender identity and expression. As for the proposed directive, the final text was agreed on 25 January 2023. The proposed amendments, and specifically the new recitals, 3 and 3b, and the replacement of sex with gender in the comparator recital, were not accepted. Instead, there is a reference to gender reassignment as a further ground of discrimination, in line with previous EU law and case law. It is not surprising that such extreme language as that proposed by the Committee was rejected. It is equally evident that gender identity theory has made considerable inroads in the EU Commission, as the strategy document evidences. The document promotes the inclusion of LGBTIQ-specific funding in all EU-wide funding programmes, such as on education and health and specific training in employment environments, with little or no evidence that this targeting is necessary at all (where is the hard data that "queer" students underperform in schools, or that "intersex" people are discriminated in employment, as some DSDs are not even detected).

The Commission paper also covers the prohibition on conversion practices and unnecessary medical intervention for transgender individuals, by analogy with gay conversion and intersex surgery, neither of which provide an apt analogy for dysphoria treatment and surgical intervention in "transgender" minors. Promoting the narrative that being attracted to the same sex may be a symptom one is transgender is in itself a form of conversion therapy, as comments about eliminating gay youth at the

Tavistock evidence.[211] Surgical interventions affecting healthy organs on minors that could not possibly consent to them (especially young girls already affected by puberty blockers, which delay or stop the intellectual development associated with puberty that would make it possible for them to take reasoned decisions about irreversible surgery) cannot be compared to surgery on newborns with severe DSDs. In the conclusions, the paper significantly omits sex as a protected characteristic against discrimination, in line with contemporary gender theory linguistic preferences, referring instead to sex characteristics.[212]

The work done by international organisations is influenced by, and its turn influences, regional human rights courts. The ECHR especially was instrumental in developing a jurisprudence on transsexual rights, slowly building the four-pillar structure that props up gender identity recognition: human dignity, body integrity, self-determination, and private life. The 2022 ECHR Guide to Article 14 contains a specific section on gender identity, which is included in the "other status" category,[213] complemented by the jurisprudence of the ECHR on gender identity-related issues. The analysis of this case law evidences the development of the concept of (trans)gender identity by the Court, from a name to give to a distressing condition and its surgical treatment to a self-selected identity with no connection to any material or medical reality and in fact, to be shielded from any requirement of a diagnosis or treatment.

The work of international courts is also potentially affected by gender identity theory, more so if they deal with cases concerning natural persons, and not only inter-State cases. The International Court of Justice is rarely involved in cases concerning human rights issues,[214] and in fact there is no

---

[211] "It Feels Like Conversation Therapy for Gay Children", The Times 8 April 2019, https://www.thetimes.co.uk/article/it-feels-like-conversion-therapy-for-gay-children-say-clinicians-pvsckdvq2.

[212] As evidenced for example in the language adopted in the Yogyakarta Principles plus 10 of 2017, starting from title: Additional Principles and State Obligations on the Application of International Human Rights Law in Relation to Sexual Orientation, Gender Identity, Gender Expression and Sex Characteristics to Complement the Yogyakarta Principles.

[213] See *Ratzenböck and Seydl v Austria*, Application No 28475/12, Judgment of 26 October 2017, https://hudoc.echr.coe.int/eng#{%22itemid%22:[%22001-177916%22]} (sexual orientation covered under other status in Article 14).

[214] Although ICERD has been at the basis of one case recently, see Application of the International Convention on the Elimination of All Forms of Racial Discrimination (Qatar v United Arab Emirates),

evidence of the Court ever dealing with gender identity-related issues. The International Criminal Court deals with international crimes as defined by the Rome Statute,[215] which include war crimes and crimes against humanity. These can include practices such as rape, sexual slavery, enforced prostitution, forced pregnancy, enforced sterilization, or persecution on the basis of "gender."[216] In 2016 for the first time the Court convicted an individual on the basis of having used rape as an instrument of war.[217] So it is not surprising that they are more receptive to gender identity theory. In 2022 they produced a policy document titled "Policy on the Crime of Gender Persecution." Gender is defined very narrowly in Article 7(3) as referring solely to the distinction between male and female, "within the context of society," surely to appease those countries that were against the feminist interpretation of gender as a social construct to oppress women (the Rome Statute was finalised in 1998, to contextualise chronologically those debates). This is the definition of gender in the 2022 document:

> Under article 7(3) of the Rome Statute ("Statute"), "gender" is understood as the two sexes, male and female, within the context of society. Gender refers to sex characteristics and social constructs and criteria used to define maleness and femaleness, including roles, behaviours, activities and attributes. As a social construct, gender varies within societies and from society to society and can change over time. This understanding of gender is in accordance with article 21 of the Statute.

Article 21(3) of the Statute, Applicable Law, recites:

> The application and interpretation of law pursuant to this article must be consistent with internationally recognized human rights, and be without any adverse distinction founded on grounds such as gender as defined in article 7, paragraph 3, age, race, colour, language, religion or belief, political or other opinion, national, ethnic or social origin, wealth, birth or other status.

---

https://www.icj-cij.org/index.php/case/172.

[215] Rome Statute of the International Criminal Court, https://www.icc-cpi.int/sites/default/files/RS-Eng.pdf.

[216] Article 7 of the Statute (Crimes Against Humanity) includes at paragraph 3 the following language: "For the purpose of this Statute, it is understood that the term 'gender' refers to the two sexes, male and female, within the context of society. The term 'gender' does not indicate any meaning different from the above."

[217] *The Prosecutor v Jean-Pierre Bemba Gombo and Others*, ICC-01/05-01/13. Bemba was acquitted on appeal, *The Prosecutor v Jean-Pierre Bemba Gombo*, ICC-01/05-01/08.

Notice the *renvoi* to Article 7(3) for the definition of gender. The "constructive ambiguity" of the drafting of the Rome Statute has been noted before.[218] It is designed, as it often is in treaty texts, to allow an agreement to be reached on the treaty text and displace the disputes at the moment of application and interpretation of the treaties in a judicial setting, where different interpretative approaches, of which the "living instrument" doctrine is one, will determine the outcome of the case.[219]

"Male and female" on one side, and "in the context of society" on the other, allow for both interpretations of gender (one as a synonym of sex, the other, the "feminist" meaning of gender). And in fact the policy document uses the "in the context of society" proviso to retrofit the definition of gender as the social constructs associated with sex, stating that this definition is in accordance with Article 21, therefore making it part of the applicable law.[220] The policy document also replaces the word sex with the term sex characteristics, as done in the Yogyakarta Principles +10 (in the definition of gender and of gender persecution), though it refers to WHO documents. The definition of gender-based crimes is especially invidious:

> At their core, gender-based crimes are used by perpetrators to regulate or punish those who are perceived to transgress gender criteria that define "accepted" forms of gender expression manifest in, for example, roles, behaviors, activities, or attributes. These criteria often regulate every aspect of life, determining the extent of individuals' freedom of movement, their reproductive options, who they can marry, where they can work, how they can dress and whether they are simply allowed to exist.

[218] David Hunt, "The International Criminal Court: High Hopes, 'Creative Ambiguity' and an Unfortunate Mistrust in International Judges, " Journal of International Criminal Justice 2 (2004): 56-70, doi:https://doi.org/10.1093/jicj/2.1. The term "gender" has been singled out as an example of constructive ambiguity: Valerie Oosterveld, "The Definition of 'Gender' in the Rome Statute of the International Criminal Court: A Step Forward or Back for International Criminal Justice?," Harvard Human Rights Journal, 18 (2005): 55-84.

[219] See also, Caroline Davidson, "How to Read International Criminal Law: Strict Construction and the Rome Statute of the International Criminal Court," St John's Law Review, 91(1) (Spring 2017): 37-103.

[220] The *traveaux préparatoires* reveal that the interpretative note on the meaning of gender was added to the draft text, see Preparatory Committee on the Establishment of an International Criminal Court, Report of the Inter-sessional Meeting from 19 to 30 January 1998 in Zutphen, The Netherlands, A/AC.249/1998/L.13, 33 https://digitallibrary.un.org/record/250636?ln=en.

Rape, one of the gravest gender-based crime, is not committed against women who do not conform to the accepted forms of gender expression; all women and girls are potential victims, regardless of how they behave. Girls only a few months old get raped, as well as 90 year old women. The definition seems to imply that some women bring rape upon themselves because they do not dress appropriately, or because they drink too much or in some other way do not conform to the gender norms applicable to them. To attribute rape somehow to women's behaviour is such an extremely regressive and sexist framing that it is hard to believe it is contained in a document of the International Criminal Court. The Court states that "people of all genders" can be victims of gender-based violence, erasing the significance of sex in the statistics. Sexual offences disproportionately affect women, and are committed almost exclusively by men, against women and against other men. The policy paper was drafted by The Office of the Prosecutor's Special Adviser on Gender Persecution, Prof Lisa Davis,[221] who argued for sexual orientation and gender identity being protected in international law in the *Atala v Chile* case.[222] It is clear that the only approved brand of feminism in international organisations currently is "trans inclusive" feminism. The fact that the word "sex" is used only in conjunction with "characteristics"[223] indicates that the policy document has effectively erased sex as a discrete category and replaced it on the one hand with gender, using this word not only as a polite synonym of sex, but also to refer to the assumptions made on the basis of it, on the other with sex characteristics, which are not necessarily limited by sex. The definitions adopted, as others we have seen, are built on a basic misunderstanding about the nature of gender. Gender is not something that we do, but something that is done to us. Women do not innately want to play a subordinate role, they are forced into one. This essentialisation of gender is necessary to the development of gender identity as an innate, or in any case internal, aspect of the human condition, as opposed to a social construct that is internalised to various degrees, from complete compliance to chosen adoption (some women choose to be mothers and home-makers, some women are forced into that role). At the same time in which the document speaks of gender roles, it attributes what is sex based violence to

---

[221] https://www.icc-cpi.int/sites/default/files/itemsDocuments/otp/bios/Bio-Lisa-Davis-(IOP).pdf.

[222] *Case of Atala Riffo and Daughters v Chile*, Judgment of 24 February 2012, Inter-American Court of Human Rights https://www.corteidh.or.cr/docs/casos/articulos/seriec_239_ing.pdf. The case concerned discrimination based on sexual orientation, not gender identity.

[223] And once to refer to "women sex workers."

those gender roles only. While it is superficially true that modest women run a lower risk in certain countries to be raped by strangers, for the simple fact that they never leave the house unaccompanied, the point is that women are raped by their own husbands, fathers and relatives too, and modesty is no protection in that case. The fact that the document is concerned with "gender violence" in the context of war makes this characterisation doubly inaccurate. Rape is a well known instrument of war, and it is not provoked by lack of compliance with gender roles.

International organisations with no specific remit on SOGI, such as the World Trade Organisation, are not immune from the influence of gender identity theory. In the 2023 Report "Gender Mainstreaming in Gender Agreements,"[224] the duty to incorporate gender in trade agreements is said to be subjected to an "intersectional" and "multidimensional" interpretation, i.e. to include MtF men in the definition of woman. In the Report of the 2022 World Trade Congress on Gender, "Making Trade Work for Women,"[225] the word woman is given the same interpretation, so when the Report notes that "there are more than 300 provisions across 100 FTAs [Free Trade Agreements] that refer explicitly to women's interests or gender equality," the word woman is not to be interpreted as to refer to females, but to females and males who identify as females. Gender is being mainstreamed in many economic agreements. The proviso that gender has an "intersectional" meaning deprives of significance the promises made in the context of these "gender mainstreaming" declarations.[226]

---

[224] Katrin Kuhlmann and Amrita Bahri, Gender Mainstreaming in Trade Agreements: A Potemkin Façade? https://www.wto.org/english/res_e/booksp_e/making_trade_work_for_women_ch12_e.pdf.

[225] https://www.wto.org/english/res_e/booksp_e/making_trade_work_for_women_e.pdf.

[226] Canada is spearheading the initiative on gender mainstreaming in international economic agreements; see "Trade and Gender in Free Trade Agreements: The Canadian Approach," https://www.international.gc.ca/trade-commerce/gender_equality-egalite_genres/trade_gender_fta-ale-commerce_genre.aspx?lang=eng.

CHAPTER 4

GENDER IDENTITY IN THE WORK OF TREATY BODIES

LGBTI stands for lesbian, gay, bisexual, transgender and intersex. It is commonly used to refer to people who are attracted to people of the same gender, people with gender identities that differ from the sex assigned to them at birth, people with nonbinary identities and people whose sex characteristics do not fit typical definitions of female or male. While this acronym has universal recognition, different people in different contexts identify with other terms including hijra, meti, lala, skesana, motsoalle, mithli, kuchu, kawein, travesty, muxé, fa'afafine, fakaleiti, hamjensgara and Two-Spirit.

—Office of the High Commissioner for Human Rights

United Nations' Treaty Bodies are tasked with monitoring the compliance of State Parties with the human rights treaties of the United Nations, from the two main Covenants, ICCPR and ICESCR, to thematic treaties such as CEDAW and CAT. In particular, they receive individual complaints on treaty violations, issue general comments/recommendations aiding in the interpretation and application of the treaty and comment on country reports.[227] Since there is not currently a treaty on SOGI, we can only track whether gender identity issues are raised in individual complaints and general comments arising in the work of the treaty bodies for the existing UN human rights treaties. The table collects all the materials produced by the treaty bodies where the terms "transgender" or "gender identity" are mentioned, and is followed by an examination of the most significant contexts in which these terms are used.

A reference to gender identity is not always relevant to the facts of the case. In fact the first case in which it appears, the *Lourdes da Silva Pimentel v Brasil*, concerns a case of maternal death. Gender identity is mentioned by the Committee in general terms as one of the grounds of discrimination under the CEDAW, which seems particularly inappropriate

---

[227] https://www.ohchr.org/en/treaty-bodies/what-treaty-bodies-do. They also can nominate special rapporteurs on specific rights in the treaty of their competence.

as no “transwoman” will ever risk maternal death though “transmen” might, not because of their gender identity, but because of their sex.

A review of the cases shows that most do not concern the rights of transgender individuals or issues of gender identity, except the ones noted. There are some that involve the right to political expressions (almost all cases from Russia, including one about having a demonstration for “Trans Day of Remembrance”); however most of them simply refer to gender identity or transgender rights in the context of the protected grounds in the relevant treaty.

The general comments, not contained in the table and examined separately, may provide a better context to the terms which in the individual communications are often just included in the list of grounds of prohibited discrimination. In the general comments, the treaty bodies tend to expand more on those terms, and include them more organically in the topic of the general comment.

	2011	2012	2013	2015	2016	2017	2018	2019	2020	2021	2022
ICCPR[228]	SE[229]	RU[230]	SE[231]		DK[232]	AU[233] DK[234] AU[235]	RU[236]	DK[237]	CA[238] SE[239] RU[240]	SE[241] DK[242] RU[243]	RU[244] RU[245]

[228] I am using the two letters country acronym: AU (Australia); BR (Brazil); CA (Canada); CH (Switzerland); DK Denmark); FI (Finland); HU (Hungary); LK (Sri Lanka); MK (North Macedonia); RU (Russia); SE (Sweden).
[229] *X. v Afghanistan, Sweden*, CCPR/C/103/D/1833/2008 https://juris.ohchr.org/casedetails/1390/en-US.
[230] *Fedotova v Russian Fed.*, CCPR/C/106/D/1932/2010 https://juris.ohchr.org/casedetails/1272/en-US.
[231] *M.I. v Sweden*, CCPR/C/108/D/2149/2012 https://juris.ohchr.org/casedetails/1675/en-US. (inadmissible)
[232] *M.K.H. v Denmark*, CCPR/C/107/D/2462/2014 https://juris.ohchr.org/casedetails/2169/en-US.
[233] *G. v Australia*, CCPR/C/119/D/2172/2012 https://juris.ohchr.org/casedetails/2220/en-US.
[234] *M.Z.B.M. v Denmark*, CCPR/C/119/D/2593/2015 https://juris.ohchr.org/casedetails/2240/en-US. (no violation)
[235] *C. v Australia*, CCPR/C/119/D/221672012 https://juris.ohchr.org/casedetails/2375/en-US.
[236] *Kirill Nepomnyashchiy v Russian Fed.*, CCPR/C/123/D/2318/2013 https://juris.ohchr.org/casedetails/2546/en-US.
[237] *R.M. and F.M. v Denmark*, CCPR/C/126/D/2685/2015 https://juris.ohchr.org/casedetails/2792/en-US.
[238] *M.B. v Canada*, CCPR/C/128/D/2957/2017 https://juris.ohchr.org/casedetails/2835/en-US.
[239] *M.I. v Sweden*, CCPR/C/108/D/2149/2012 https://juris.ohchr.org/casedetails/1675/en-US.
[240] *Alekseev v Russian Fed.,* CCPR/C/130/D/2757/2016 https://juris.ohchr.org/casedetails/3273/en-US and https://juris.ohchr.org/casedetails/3297/en-US. .
[241] *H.G. v Sweden*, CCPR/C/132/D/3266/2018 https://juris.ohchr.org/casedetails/3178/en-US.
[242] *J.R.R, L.A.A. v Denmark*, CCPR/C/132/D/2787/2016 https://juris.ohchr.org/casedetails/3183/en-US.
[243] *Ivanov v Russian Fed.*, CCPR/C/131/D/2635/2015 https://juris.ohchr.org/casedetails/3244/en-US.
[244] *Mikhailova et al. v Russian Fed.*, CCPR/C/134/D/2943/2017 https://juris.ohchr.org/casedetails/3211/en-US.
[245] *Savolaynen v Russian Fed.*, CCPR/C/135/D/2830/2016 https://juris.ohchr.org/casedetails/3605/en-US.

CAT	SE[246]			CA[247]		SE[248]	CA[249] CH[250]			SE[251] DK[252]	
CEDAW	BR[253]						DK[254] DK[255]	RU[256]	HU[257] MK[258]		LK[259]
CRC										FI[260]	

246 *Uttam Mondal v Sweden*, CAT/C/46/D/338/2008, https://juris.ohchr.org/casedetails/52/en-US.
247 *J.K. v Canada*, CCPR/C/56/D/562/2013 https://juris.ohchr.org/casedetails/2064/en-US.
248 *E.A. v Sweden*, CCPR/C/61/D/690/2015 https://juris.ohchr.org/casedetails/2285/en-US.
249 *Joyce Nakato Nakawunde v Canada*, CCPR/C/64/D/615/2014 https://juris.ohchr.org/casedetails/2445/en-US.
250 *H.R.E.S v Switzerland*, CAT/C/64/D/783/2016 https://juris.ohchr.org/casedetails/2466/en-US.
251 *P.S. v Canada*, CATC/72/D/1000/2020 https://juris.ohchr.org/casedetails/3343/en-US.
252 *H.S. v Denmark*, CAT/C/71/D/792/2016 https://juris.ohchr.org/casedetails/3369/en-US.
253 *Lourdes da Silva Pimentel v Brazil*, CEDAW/C/49/D/17/2008 https://juris.ohchr.org/casedetails/1701/en-US.
254 *A.S. v Denmark*, CEDAW/C/69/D/80/2015 https://juris.ohchr.org/casedetails/2636/en-US.
255 *S.A.O. v Denmark*, CEDAW/C/71/D/101/2016 https://juris.ohchr.org/casedetails/2458/en-US.
256 *K.K. v Russian Fed.*, CEDAW/C/721/D/98/2016 https://juris.ohchr.org/casedetails/2653/en-US.
257 *G.H. v Hungary*, CEDAW/C/76/D/114/2017 https://juris.ohchr.org/casedetails/3037/en-US.
258 *S.B. and M.B. v North Macedonia*, CEDAW/C/77/D/143/2019 https://juris.ohchr.org/casedetails/3118/en-US.
259 *Flamer Caldera v Sri Lanka*, CEDAW/C/81/D/134/2018 https://juris.ohchr.org/casedetails/3047/en-US.
260 *A.B. v Finland*, CRC/C/86/D/51/2018 https://juris.ohchr.org/casedetails/2946/en-US.

The first case at the CCPR concerning a "transgender" individual, *G. v Australia*, was initially submitted in 2011 and the Committee issued its Views in 2017. The author of the communication was a MtF man. The Committee reported that in Australia sex is not necessarily a biological matter, following a decision on appeal from the Family Court of Australia regarding the right of a FtM woman to marry a woman.[261] "G." had undergone SRS but not amended the birth certificate, as the law prevented married individuals from doing so,[262] and "G." did not intend to divorce. The applicable law protected "G." from discrimination based on transgender identity, and contrary to the claim made by "G.," this was the case even without an amended birth certificate for the purpose of women-only services or jobs.[263] The Australian Human Right Commission supported "G."'s argument that "Marital status should not be a relevant consideration as to whether or not a person can request a change in legal sex." The complaint to the Committee claimed a violation of Article 17 ICCPR (Right to Privacy), relying, amongst other things, on Principle 3 of the Yogyakarta Principles[264] and the 2011 Report of the OHCHR.[265] Even at this relatively early stage of embedding of gender identity into domestic and international law, the complainant could already leverage domestic

---

[261] *Attorney-General for the Commonwealth v Kevin and Jennifer*, [2003] FamCA 94 (21 February 2003). https://www.icj.org/sogicasebook/in-re-kevin-validity-of-marriage-of-transsexual-family-court-of-australia-12-october-2001/ with link to appeal decision.

[262] The provision, Art. 3(B)(1)(c) of the NSW Births, Deaths and Marriage Registration Act 1995, has since been repealed.

[263] From the State's observations: in circumstances where a relevant job is only available to women, refusal of employment may constitute discrimination on transgender grounds under section 38B (1) (a) of the New South Wales Anti-Discrimination Act 1977 and would therefore breach section 38C of the said Act. The same provisions apply with regard to refusal of access to female-only gyms.

[264] Everyone has the right to recognition everywhere as a person before the law. Persons of diverse sexual orientations and gender identities shall enjoy legal capacity in all aspects of life. Each person's self-defined sexual orientation and gender identity is integral to their personality and is one of the most basic aspects of self-determination, dignity and freedom. No one shall be forced to undergo medical procedures, including sex reassignment surgery, sterilisation or hormonal therapy, as a requirement for legal recognition of their gender identity. No status, such as marriage or parenthood, may be invoked as such to prevent the legal recognition of a person's gender identity. No one shall be subjected to pressure to conceal, suppress or deny their sexual orientation or gender identity.

[265] Discriminatory Laws and Practices and Acts of Violence against Individuals Based on their Sexual Orientation and Gender Identity, A/HRC/19/41, at para 84 https://ap.ohchr.org/documents/dpage_e.aspx?si=A/HRC/19/41.

law and case law, and international organisations' legal materials, in support of the complaint.

The Committee found for the complainant, establishing that the differential treatment of unmarried and married transgender individuals was not "necessary and proportionate to a legitimate interest" (the test under Article 17) and was therefore unreasonable and a breach of the Convention. As often, the entire case rests on the claim that preventing the applicant from having the birth certificate amended is a breach of privacy as it reveals transgender status. This claim makes sense only if one accepts that it is the birth certificate to reveal transgender status, and not simply the evidence of one's own eyes, *a fortiori* when medical and surgical transition are not required or sought by the individual.

The *M.I. v Sweden* case was found inadmissible by the CCPR but it is interesting because the complainant, an asylum seeker who had had his application rejected and was slated to be deported back to Afghanistan, claimed a breach of Article 7 (torture) in relation to his sexual orientation and his gender identity, which he described as identifying as between male and female, volunteering pictures of himself expressing himself in "gender non conforming ways." The Committee was unconvinced by the very late claim to the asylum authorities and the quality of the photographic evidence.

We have already seen that one of the first mentions of the Yogyakarta Principles, and so of gender identity, is in the General Comment No 20 of the ICESCR Committee.[266] In 2016 the ICESCR Committee issued Comment 22[267] on sexual and reproductive health.[268] The comment includes a recommendation to States not to compel treatment for transgender or intersex individuals[269] and to combat homophobia and transphobia as a ground of discrimination potentially affecting the right to sexual health. In the Violations section, the Committee singles out:

---

[266] E/C.12/GC/20 2 July 2009, https://www.refworld.org/docid/4a60961f2.html.

[267] General comment No. 22 (2016) on the right to sexual and reproductive health (article 12 of the International Covenant on Economic, Social and Cultural Rights), E/C.12/GC/22,
https://tbinternet.ohchr.org/_layouts/15/treatybodyexternal/Download.aspx?symbolno=E%2FC.12%2FGC%2F22&Lang=en.

[268] Included in the right to the highest attainable standard of physical and mental health protected in article 12 of the Convention.

[269] Para. 23.

> Laws and policies that indirectly perpetuate coercive medical practices, including incentive- or quota-based contraceptive policies and hormonal therapy, as well as surgery or sterilization requirements for legal recognition of one's gender identity, constitute additional violations of the obligation to respect. Further violations include state practices and policies that censor or withhold information, or present inaccurate, misrepresentative or discriminatory information, related to sexual and reproductive health.

The CEDAW Committee in 2010 issued a General Comment on the Core Obligations of the State Parties to the Convention.[270] The Committee was then still not influenced by gender identity theory, and it is very clear on the source of the discrimination women are subjected to, and that gender is the "tool" of sex-based oppression, not a positive aspect of one's identity, deserving of protection in human rights law:

> 4. The objective of the Convention is the elimination of all forms of discrimination against women on the basis of sex. It guarantees women the equal recognition, enjoyment and exercise of all human rights and fundamental freedoms in the political, economic, social, cultural, civil, domestic or any other field, irrespective of their marital status, and on a basis of equality with men.
>
> 5. Although the Convention only refers to sex-based discrimination, interpreting article 1 together with articles 2 (f) and 5 (a) indicates that the Convention covers gender-based discrimination against women. The term "sex" here refers to biological differences between men and women. The term "gender" refers to socially constructed identities, attributes and roles for women and men and society's social and cultural meaning for these biological differences resulting in hierarchical relationships between women and men and in the distribution of power and rights favouring men and disadvantaging women. This social positioning of women and men is affected by political, economic, cultural, social, religious, ideological and environmental factors and can be changed by culture, society and community. The application of the Convention to gender-based discrimination is made clear by the definition of discrimination contained in article 1. This definition points out that any distinction, exclusion or restriction which has the effect or purpose of impairing or nullifying the recognition, enjoyment or exercise by women of human rights and fundamental freedoms is discrimination, even where discrimination was not intended. This would mean that identical or neutral treatment of

[270] General recommendation No. 28 on the core obligations of States parties under article 2 of the Convention on the Elimination of All Forms of Discrimination against Women, CEDAW/C/GC/28, https://documents-dds-ny.un.org/doc/UNDOC/GEN/G10/472/60/PDF/G1047260.pdf?OpenElement.

> women and men might constitute discrimination against women if such treatment resulted in or had the effect of women being denied the exercise of a right because there was no recognition of the pre-existing gender-based disadvantage and inequality that women face. The views of the Committee on this matter are evidenced by its consideration of reports, its general recommendations, decisions, suggestions and statements, its consideration of individual communications and its conduct of inquiries under the Optional Protocol.

By 2017, when the Committee issues "General Recommendation 35 on Gender Violence," updating General Recommendation 19,[271] factors influencing violence against women include being transgender or intersex, without any textual or legal support in previous work of the Committee.

Transgender students are mentioned specifically in General Recommendation 36[272] on the Right to Education. There is never any clarification as to what remedy young "transboys" (i.e. girls who identify as boys) have under CEDAW. Their female body exposes them to sex based violence and discrimination, apparently without a remedy, as their male gender identity excludes them from the group of "transgirls" and equally from the original group covered by the protection of the Convention, girls and women. This apparent gap in the protection of CEDAW is not picked up by the Committee.

The CAT Committee only issued four General Comments in its history. General Comment No. 2 is especially relevant, as it clarifies the extent of the obligations of the State Parties with respect to the implementation of

---

[271] General recommendation No. 35 on gender-based violence against women, updating general recommendation No. 19, CEDAW/C/GC/35, https://tbinternet.ohchr.org/_layouts/15/treatybodyexternal/Download.aspx?symbolno=CEDAW%2FC%2FGC%2F35&Lang=en.

[272] General recommendation No. 36 (2017) on the right of girls and women to education, CEDAW/C/GC/36, https://tbinternet.ohchr.org/_layouts/15/treatybodyexternal/Download.aspx?symbolno=CEDAW%2FC%2FGC%2F36&Lang=en. "Transgender women and girls" (males) are also a group of particular concern in General Recommendation No. 37 (2018) on the gender-related dimensions of disaster risk reduction in the context of climate change, CEDAW/C/GC/37, https://tbinternet.ohchr.org/_layouts/15/treatybodyexternal/Download.aspx?symbolno=CEDAW%2FC%2FGC%2F37&Lang=e; and General recommendation No. 39 (2022) on the rights of Indigenous women and girls, CEDAW/C/GC/39, https://tbinternet.ohchr.org/_layouts/15/treatybodyexternal/Download.aspx?symbolno=CEDAW%2FC%2FGC%2F39&Lang=en.

Article 2 CAT.[273] Amongst the characteristics of especially marginalised groups, we find listed sex, gender and transgender identity (presumably the difference between sex and gender is to be interpreted according to the CEDAW Committee's General Recommendation No. 28).

Transgender status is seen as constituting a special form of vulnerability also for violence against children, as outlined in General Comment No. 13 of 2011 of the Committee on the Convention on the Rights of the Child.[274] General Comment No. 20, on the Rights of Adolescents, singles out transgender adolescents (as part of the LGBTI group):[275]

---

[273] General Comment No. 2, Implementation of Article 2 by State Parties, CAT/C/GC/2 (2008) https://tbinternet.ohchr.org/_layouts/15/treatybodyexternal/Download.aspx?symbolno=CAT%2FC%2FGC%2F2&Lang=en.

[274] The right of the child to freedom from all forms of violence, CRC/C/GC/13, https://tbinternet.ohchr.org/_layouts/15/treatybodyexternal/Download.aspx?symbolno=CRC%2FC%2FGC%2F13&Lang=en. On the rights of "LGBTI children" specifically in the work of UN treaty bodies, and especially the CRC Committee, see: Kirsten Sandberg,"The Rights of LGBTI Children under the Convention on the Rights of the Child," Nordic Journal of Human Rights, 33(4) (2015): 337-352, doi: 10.1080/18918131.2015.1128701.

[275] General comment No. 20 (2016) on the implementation of the rights of the child during adolescence, CRC/C/GC/20, https://tbinternet.ohchr.org/_layouts/15/treatybodyexternal/Download.aspx?symbolno=CRC%2FC%2FGC%2F20&Lang=en. Transgender children are also singled out for especial vulnerability in General comment No. 21 (2017) on children in street situations, CRC/C/GC/21, https://tbinternet.ohchr.org/_layouts/15/treatybodyexternal/Download.aspx?symbolno=CRC%2FC%2FGC%2F21&Lang=en; in Joint general comment No. 4 (2017) of the Committee on the Protection of the Rights of All Migrant Workers and Members of Their Families and No. 23 (2017) of the Committee on the Rights of the Child on State obligations regarding the human rights of children in the context of international migration in countries of origin, transit, destination and return, CMW/C/GC/4-CRC/C/GC/23, https://tbinternet.ohchr.org/_layouts/15/treatybodyexternal/Download.aspx?symbolno=CRC%2FC%2FGC%2F23&Lang=en; Joint general comment No. 3 (2017) of the Committee on the Protection of the Rights of All Migrant Workers and Members of Their Families and No. 22 (2017) of the Committee on the Rights of the Child on the general principles regarding the human rights of children in the context of international migration, CMW/C/GC/3-CRC/C/GC/22, https://tbinternet.ohchr.org/_layouts/15/treatybodyexternal/Download.aspx?symbolno=CRC%2FC%2FGC%2F22&Lang=en; General comment No. 25 (2021) on children's rights in relation to the digital environment, CRC/C/GC/25,

> Adolescents who are lesbian, gay, bisexual, transgender and intersex commonly face persecution, including abuse and violence, stigmatization, discrimination, bullying, exclusion from education and training, as well as a lack of family and social support, or access to sexual and reproductive health services and information. In extreme cases, they face sexual assault, rape and even death. These experiences have been linked to low selfesteem, higher rates of depression, suicide and homelessness.
>
> The Committee emphasizes the rights of all adolescents to freedom of expression and respect for their physical and psychological integrity, gender identity and emerging autonomy. It condemns the imposition of so-called "treatments" to try to change sexual orientation and forced surgeries or treatments on intersex adolescents. It urges States to eliminate such practices, repeal all laws criminalizing or otherwise discriminating against individuals on the basis of their sexual orientation, gender identity or intersex status and adopt laws prohibiting discrimination on those grounds. States should also take effective action to protect all lesbian, gay, bisexual, transgender and intersex adolescents from all forms of violence, discrimination or bullying by raising public awareness and implementing safety and support measures.

It is noteworthy that in Joint General Comment No. 13 (2017) the Committee divides children in two groups, the first girls and transgender children, and the second one of boys. Once again the tension between the insistence that a transgender person is the sex he or she wants to be, and the fact that transgender status does not map seamlessly on sex is brought to the fore. One also wonders whether postulating the existence of the transgender child (or of the LGB child) is appropriate, as child covers any age from 0 to 18.

The work of the treaty bodies evidences a focus on the category of "transgender" (as then applied in the context of the specific treaty i.e. people who express a gender identity which is not congruent with their sex) as opposed to the concept of gender identity, which is almost unmentioned; the progressive embedding of the language of gender identity theory in the general comments and the "judicial" work of the Committees; and the conflictual relationship with the concept of gender that one can read between the lines in the CEDAW Committee, with the eventual adoption of gender identity theory language somewhat abruptly in 2017.

---

https://tbinternet.ohchr.org/_layouts/15/treatybodyexternal/Download.aspx?symbolno=CRC%2FC%2FGC%2F25&Lang=en .

CHAPTER 5

REGIONAL COURTS IN EUROPE

No concrete or substantial hardship or detriment to the public interest has indeed been demonstrated as likely to flow from any change to the status of transsexuals and, as regards other possible consequences, the Court considers that society may reasonably be expected to tolerate a certain inconvenience to enable individuals to live in dignity and worth in accordance with the sexual identity chosen by them at great personal cost.
—*Christine Goodwin v UK*, ECHR 2002

The Council of Europe and the European Union

The absence of a conventional instrument for the recognition of gender identity in international law, and the difficulty of introducing one at global level, has resulted in a two-pronged tactic from gender identity theorists and trans rights activists, with the strategic goal to embed this concept in international law. On the one hand, lobbying international and regional organisations with the goal of making them adopt gender identity language in their materials and apply it in their work (for example UN treaty bodies and the Council of Europe). On the other, litigation at the international, regional and domestic level. These tactics have been very successful, and all the more so the tactic of strategic litigation. The richest international jurisprudence on the topic comes from the court of the Council of Europe, the European Court of Human Rights (ECHR).[276] In the following sections there will be a very close analysis of the early cases in which the topic of transsexualism (as it was then) was tackled by the Court, up to the seminal *Goodwin* case; then a close analysis of *Goodwin*, and finally a short overview of the case law since Goodwin, to assess how far the court has come since that judgment.[277]

---

[276] This acronym can also refer to the European Convention for Human Rights: Convention for the Protection of Human Rights and Fundamental Freedoms, 3 September 1953, 213 UNTS 221.

[277] A non-legal analysis of the jurisprudence of the ECHR on transgender cases in Anna van der Vleuten, "Contestations of Transgender Rigths and/in the Strasbourg

It is a salutary reminder that international law has no rule of precedent and that the Court is not bound by its own jurisprudence, though it is very cautious in departing from it. Additionally, only the parties to the case (meaning the State party to the case) are bound by the judgment,[278] though clearly the other State Parties (to the Convention) are put on notice that a similar case may be decided in the same manner. However, it is incorrect to say that *Goodwin* is "international law." It is settled jurisprudence, with no binding value outside of the UK (the State party to the case). Finally, even for the UK, *Goodwin* has no direct effect on its domestic law. While the UK had an international obligation to abide by the judgment, it remained within its sovereign powers to decide how to do so, and failure to implement the judgment had no consequences in its domestic law. On an international plane, going "against *Goodwin*" now (for example by repealing the Gender Recognition Act) would not force the UK to leave the Council of Europe and *a fortiori* would not necessarily result in the UK being expelled from it. Failure to implement or abide by a judgment of the Court does not result in expulsion from the Council of Europe. The only country ever to be expelled was Russia, following its illegal invasion of Ukraine.[279]

Although one tactic adopted by trans rights activists is to argue for retrofitting the term gender (identity) whenever a treaty refers to sex, from a legal point of view, it is much safer, as already noted, to argue that gender identity is covered by the "other status" provision in human rights treaties' non-discrimination duty (for example, article 14 of the ECHR). In his 2021 Report the IE on SOGI IE states:[280]

Court" Politics and Governance, 8(3) (2020): 278-289, doi: 10.17645/pag.v8i3 .2876. As is customary, there is no engagement with the basis of transgender rights and the usual reduction of any criticism to a toxic mix of "radical right populism, conservative nationalism and religious fundamentalism." That much of the criticism from women in the UK (one of the least religious countries in Europe) is coming from women who describe themselves as left or centre left is ignored. It is also to be expected that an academic piece would engage with the criticisms on the merits, not on the basis of political or religious positions. The review does not bear out the preconception that judges from less gender theory-friendly countries tend to decide cases on that basis.

[278] Article 46 ofthe ECHR.

[279] Council of Europe Newsroom, "The Russian Federation is excluded from the Council of Europe," March 16, 2022, https://www.coe.int/en/web/portal/-/the-russian-federation-is-excluded-from-the-council-of-europe.

[280] "The Law of Inclusion," 3 June 2021, A/HRC/47/27, para 18,

> [...] the jurisprudence of the European Court of Human Rights on article 14 of the Convention for the Protection of Human Rights and Fundamental Freedoms (European Convention on Human Rights) adopts an expansive conception of the notion, which extends protections to individuals on the grounds of sexual orientation and gender identity, and under the sex discrimination test of article 14, the Court has built up a fairly expansive understanding of gender theory.

Quite apart from whether it is appropriate to read gender identity into sex as a protected category, the important issue, in any case about discrimination, and this matters for equality as well as human rights law, is determining the correct comparator. Issues of comparators are sometimes wrongly decided in lower domestic courts or inaccurately described in academic literature. In the UK case *Shamoon v Chief Constable of the RUC*,[281] Lord Scott of Forscote described the function and operation of comparators in the following manner:

> [...] the comparator required for the purpose of the statutory definition of discrimination must be a comparator *in the same position in all material respects as the victim save only that he, or she, is not a member of the protected class.* [emphasis added]

Consequently, in cases involving a MtF man or FtM woman, it is crucial to determine if the correct comparator is a female or male (respectively) who is not transexual, as supporters of gender identity theory aver, or the other way around (i.e. a male who is not transsexual for a MtF man and a female who is not transsexual for the FtM woman), in my opinion the correct interpretation, which avoids two fundamental problems with the first option: the first one is that effectively one lets the person claiming discrimination select their own comparator (all the more so if the identification as the opposite sex does not have any legal basis); additionally, that the issue of comparator may work differently in discrimination or victimisation cases, as opposed to the legitimate exclusion from a single or separate sex service on the basis of a sex exception in the applicable legislation.[282]

---

https://documents.un.org/doc/undoc/gen/g21/123/16/pdf/g2112316.pdf?token=ZkQzioJDfSr5coESUx&fe=true. .

[281] *Shamoon v Chief Constable of the Royal Ulster Constabulary*, Judgment of 27 February 2003, [2003] ICR 337 HL.

[282] I am basing the argument on the application of the UK Equality Act 2010, which prohibits discrimination on the basis of gender reassignment but allows, on the basis of the sex exceptions contained in Schedule 3, to discriminate against

The Court of Justice of the European Union (CJEU) clarified that in Council Directive 76/207/EEC, the comparator for a male with the characteristic of gender reassignment is a male without the characteristic of gender reassignment.[283]

> ... [w]here a person is dismissed on the ground that he or she intends to undergo or has undergone gender reassignment, he or she is treated unfavourably by comparison with persons of *the sex to which he or she was deemed to belong before undergoing gender reassignment* [emphasis added]. To tolerate such discrimination would be tantamount, as regards such a person, to a failure to respect the dignity and freedom to which he or she is entitled and which the Court has a duty to safeguard." (paragraphs 21-22).

The jurisprudence of the ECHR has been crucial in embedding gender identity in human rights law and so it is an inevitable step in reconstructing the genealogy of this concept.[284] *Goodwin v UK* was a seminal case, but

---

males in the provision of single and separate sex services for women, including against males with the protected characteristic of gender reassignment. The operation of these exceptions and the interpretation of the word sex in the Act, and its relationship with the Gender Recognition Act 2004, has generated contrasting case law in relation to another piece of legislation, the Gender Representation on Public Boards (Scotland) Act 2018: *For Women Scotland Ltd v The Lord Advocate*, Opinion of 18 February 2022 delivered by Lady Dorrian, [2022] CSIH 4; *Opinion of Lady Haldane in Petition for For Women Scotland Limited*, Opinion delivered on 13 December 2022, [2022] CSOH 90; *For Women Scotland v The Scottish Ministers,* Opinion of the Court delivered on 1 November 2023, [2023] CSIH 37. See Michael Foran, "Scottish Feminists Lose Appeal on Definition of 'Woman,'" UnHerd, November 1, 2023,
https://unherd.com/thepost/scottish-feminists-lose-appeal-on-definition-of-woman/.

[283] *P. v S. and Cornwall County Council*, Judgment of 30 April 1996, C-13/94. The Report submitted to the EU Parliament, Cristina Castagnoli, "Transgender Persons' Rights in the EU Member States," 2010, claims this is not the case, "The Recast Directive has taken into account the Court of Justice of the European Union's jurisprudence on gender identity. The Court affirmed that equal treatment legislation in matters of employment and occupation, on equal pay and social security benefits, is applicable to transgender people. In addition, theory [sic] Court pronounced that equal treatment for transgender people has to be applied on the basis of the acquired gender after a gender reassignment and not the sex given at birth." This interpretation does not seem to respect the plain language of the *P. v S. and Cornwall County Council* case.

[284] A review of the jurisprudence of the Court in Lena Holzer, "Legal Gender Recognition in Times of Change at the European Court of Human Rights,"

we would not have gotten there without the cases that preceded it. The series of cases involving the rights of transsexual people and the development of the concept of "gender identity" normally involve alleged breaches of Article 8, which recites as follows:

> ARTICLE 8 - Right to respect for private and family life
>
> 1. Everyone has the right to respect for his private and family life, his home and his correspondence.
>
> 2. There shall be no interference by a public authority with the exercise of this right except such as is in accordance with the law and is necessary in a democratic society in the interests of national security, public safety or the economic well-being of the country, for the prevention of disorder or crime, for the protection of health or morals, or for the protection of the rights and freedoms of others.

Article 8 is a qualified, not absolute, right. This means that even if the Court finds that the State has interfered with someone's private and family life, it still needs to determine whether, on the basis of the content of paragraph two, the State had a legitimate reason to do so. In determining whether this is the case, the Court will perform a proportionality analysis, that is, determine whether the interference is proportionate to the interest being defended.[285] The most important part of this analysis is the fourth step, i.e. the assessment of the importance of the interest being defended: the more important the interest, the higher the allowed interference. For example, security of the State at a time of war allows quite a considerable interference with private life or with freedom of expression (another qualified right). It is important to remember that, amongst the conflicting interests that the State could invoke as a defence for an interference with a qualified right, are the rights of others, and quite a few cases in the ECHR involve conflicting rights, for example freedom of expression v freedom of religion.

ERAForum, 23 (2022): 165-182; Damian A Gonzalez-Salzberg, Sexuality and Transsexuality Under the European Convention of Human Rights. A Queer Reading of Human Rights Law (London: Bloomsbury, 2019). See also Henriette Jakobien Liesker, "Caught in a Balancing Act. The European Court of Human Rights and the Road to Recognition for Sexual Minorities," Oslo Law Review, 4(3) (2017): 172-194, doi: https://doi.org/10.18261/issn.2387-3299-2017-03-04.

[285] The literature on the concept of proportionality and its use by the court is immense. A primer here.
https://hrcak.srce.hr/ojs/index.php/eclic/article/view/11899.

The quite considerable quasi-political power that the Court has to assess the legality of States' policies or acts against their obligations under the Convention is tempered by the doctrine of the margin of appreciation,[286] i.e. the idea that the Court, in determining whether the State is in breach of the Convention, needs to take into account that, in the words of the Court (*Handyside v UK*)[287]:

> By reason of their direct and continuous contact with the vital forces of their countries, State authorities are in principle in a better position than the international judge to give an opinion on the exact content of these requirements as well as on the "necessity" of a "restriction" or "penalty" intended to meet them.

Both concepts, proportionality and margin of appreciation, need to be kept in mind when looking at the jurisprudence of the ECHR in the area of gender identity.[288]

The Jurisprudence of the ECHR: From Rees to Goodwin

Rees v UK

The *Rees v United Kingdom* case[289] was decided in 1986 by the Plenary Court. The applicant was born in 1942 as Brenda Margaret Rees and registered female. Starting in 1971, the applicant began a medical, surgical and legal process to "transition" to the male sex.[290] While Rees was able to obtain identity documents as "Mark" Rees, amending the birth certificate proved impossible. Rees made a formal request in 1980 to the Registrar General under Section 29(3) of the Births and Deaths Registration Act

---

[286]Another fundamental concept; see here https://www.coe.int/t/dghl/cooperation/lisbonnetwork/themis/echr/paper2_en.asp.

[287]*Handyside v United Kingdom*, Application No 5493/72, Judgment of 7 December 1976.

[288] A list of the cases issued in January 2023 is available here https://www.echr.coe.int/documents/d/echr/FS_Gender_identity_eng.

[289] *Rees v the United Kingdom*, Application No 9532/81, Judgment of 17 October 1986. https://hudoc.echr.coe.int/eng#{%22dmdocnumber%22:[%22695441%22],%22itemid%22:[%22001-57564%22]}.

[290] We are told Rees started exhibiting masculine behaviour and had "ambiguous appearance." Since no DSD condition is reported, and given Rees' date of birth (1942) one can infer that Rees was judged against the very sexist and stereotypical gender norms of the time.

1953, on the ground that there had been "a mistake in completing the Register." The request was supported by a medical report attesting that, of the four criteria of sex–chromosomal sex, gonadal sex, apparent sex (external genitalia and body form) and psychological sex–the last was the most important and it was pre-determined at birth, though not evident until later in life.

The Registrar General refused the application, not accepting that, in the absence of a medical report, psychological sex (what now we would call gender identity), was a determining factor (the law allowed to correct birth records in the case of individuals who had been recorded in the incorrect sex at birth, because of medical conditions affecting the appearance of the genitals, especially in the past, when genetic testing was not available).

The Court noted that at the time transsexuals were allowed to amend their identity documents to reflect their current perceived identity, to obtain medical care through the NHS (up and including sex reassignement surgery) but not to amend a birth certificate, which is an historical document not reflecting current identity, nor to marry a person of the same sex but a different psychological sex/gender identity.[291]

The Court also argued that, as there was no consistent practice amongst the Contracting Parties on the recognition of transsexuality (gender/gender identity/transgenderism are still not used by either the claimant or the defendant State, or the Court for that matter) the States enjoyed a wide margin of appreciation. This is a general rule adopted by the Court in such cases: the more the States develop a consistent practice in one area, the smaller the margin of appreciation granted to the States that diverge from that practice.

The Court also noticed, and this is also important in light of future developments, that technically the State could not be accused of "interfering" with the applicant's Article 8 rights; on the contrary, the applicant was demanding a positive act from the State, i.e. amending the Register of Births, with all the administrative and legal consequences that follow, including imposing duties on third parties. This comment is to be read in the context of how the law distinguishes between positive rights and negative rights, where the right to privacy is quite clearly only a negative right, requiring no interference from the State, rather than

---

[291] *Corbett v Corbett* [1971] P. 83, [1970] 2 All E.R. 33.

positive steps.[292]Accusing the State of breaching privacy rights because the State is demanding proof of a document that the State itself issued seems *prima facie* not to engage any Article 8 issues. As the Court noted, showing a birth certificate in the UK is normally not legally required, not even for the purpose of marriage, though it is normally requested proof of identity the first time one applies for a passport (and in that case usually the birth certificate is shown to the State that issued it). The applicant argued a violation of article 8 rights as follows:

> In particular, he complained of the practice of issuing him with a birth certificate on which his sex continued to be recorded as "female." Such a certificate, he alleged, was effectively an irrebuttable description of his sex, wherever sex was a relevant issue and, revealing as it did the discrepancy between his apparent and his legal sex, it caused him embarrassment and humiliation whenever social practices required its production. The Government contested the applicant's claim;

What is lost in the argument is the obvious fact that normally it is the State to request the individual to produce a birth certificate. It is not information that would not be available to the State if the individual refused to produce it (as, for example, sexual orientation, which is a private matter). It is hard to understand how the right to a private life is engaged by such a request, where at most issues of confidentiality are involved, not privacy. In any event, as admitted by the applicant, producing a birth certificate is not a legal requirement but a "social practice" and again, it is difficult to argue that a social practice is a breach of a legal right. Outside the specific facts of the case (and making allowance for the fact that sometimes FtM women "pass" quite successfully, i.e. at a superficial glance a woman who identifies as a man and has taken hormonal and surgical steps can be 'read' as a man) it is a vanishingly rare event that sex is not immediately apparent to humans, normally just from facial features. It may be an acceptable social practice to pretend one does not see sex, but surely this practice cannot be transformed into a legal obligation, requiring the State to amend a birth certificate, production of which is confidential between the State and the individual, in order to avoid the potential embarrassment of the individual knowing that the civil servant will see on paper what is immediately perceptible in real life. The reliance on the quality of the hormonal and surgical transition, presumed to make birth sex undetectable, which is evidenced in the parties' submissions and the judges' discussion (and from such documents already shown in this work),

[292] Guide on Article 8 of the European Convention of Human Rights https://www.echr.coe.int/documents/d/echr/guide_art_8_eng.

is baffling. One wonders whether judges convinced themselves this was the case on the basis of indirect experience, or insisted this must be the case in order to make the demand to change sex plausible and reasonable.

It is also important to understand under what definition of transsexuality the Court interpreted the facts of the case, how UK law applied to them and whether the application of the domestic law to the case may constitute a breach of Article 8 all things considered. This is how the Court described transsexualism:

> 38. Transsexualism is not a new condition, but its particular features have been identified and examined only fairly recently. The developments that have taken place in consequence of these studies have been largely promoted by experts in the medical and scientific fields who have drawn attention to the considerable problems experienced by the individuals concerned and found it possible to alleviate them by means of medical and surgical treatment. The term "transsexual" is usually applied to those who, whilst belonging physically to one sex, feel convinced that they belong to the other; they often seek to achieve a more integrated, unambiguous identity by undergoing medical treatment and surgical operations to adapt their physical characteristics to their psychological nature. Transsexuals who have been operated upon thus form a *fairly well-defined and identifiable group*. [emphasis added]

In line with its assessment of the margin of appreciation doctrine, the Court concluded that there was no breach of Article 8 by the UK, on the basis that allowing an amendment to the birth certificate to reflect psychological sex, "would have important administrative consequences and would impose new duties on the rest of the population." It is important to keep this comment in mind, as ignoring duties imposed on third parties will allow the Court to eventually reach a new consensus in *Goodwin*. The Court added however that the distress suffered by transsexuals was real and changes may be expected in the Contracting Parties' legislation to mitigate it:

> [...] the Court is conscious of the seriousness of the problems affecting these persons and the distress they suffer. The Convention has always to be interpreted and applied in the light of current circumstances [...]. The need for appropriate legal measures should therefore be kept under review having regard particularly to scientific and societal developments.

Three judges dissented with the Court, and, as it is often the case, it is interesting to see what they have to say, as dissenting judges often point in their dissent to future developments of the law. The dissenting judges, who regularly refer to the claimant's "sexual identity" to describe what we would now call gender identity, argued that the UK could have granted the change of birth record to minimise the distress of transsexual individuals in having conflicting identity information, or act in another manner in order to obtain the same result. The dissenting judges acknowledged that the right to privacy and secrecy of the relevant information cannot be guaranteed, as there is a public interest in that the Register of Births be a public record and that it ought to remain so. They also add an important proviso to this effect:

> There is obviously no question of correcting the registers by concealing the historical truth or of claiming that Mr. Rees has changed sex in the biological sense of the term. The idea is merely (as already happens in the United Kingdom in other cases–for example, with adoption) to mention a development in the person's status due to changes in his apparent sex–what we have called his sexual identity–and to give him the opportunity to obtain a short certificate which does not disclose his previous status. This would better reflect the real situation and to that extent would even be in the public interest.

This is a recognition that, even when the public record can be partially amended, clearly it does not mean that sex is changed in any way other than as a legal fiction. In the *Rees* case we notice several elements that will evolve: the relevance of "psychological sex;" the absence of gender identity as a descriptor of this supposed psychological sex (this is important, as gender identity was already a known concept in medicine and psychology); the fact that from the beginning the Court faced cases involving FtM transsexuals, though at the time they were a distinct minority in the transsexual community.

What happened to Mark Rees? Rees had wanted to become a Minister of the Church of England, which at the time did not accept women. Following the passage of the Gender Recognition Act in 2004 Rees could have obtained a GRC, but this would have meant losing the pension to which Rees was entitled as a woman but was too young to collect as a man. Rees eventually applied for a GRC. In a book published in 1987 Rees describes the transition process in these terms:

> Sometimes I think that I should know all about cars, now that I'm supposed to be a man, but many of my male friends don't understand mechanical things. I don't feel that it is essential at all. I see myself as an ideal person in the middle. Having been a woman, and having grown up, albeit reluctantly, in a woman's world, I find that my sympathies are with women. I find many men boring and pompous. I prefer to listen to women,

> and feel I know all about them, having been one. Everybody knows about me and I don't try to hide my background as many female-to-male transsexuals do.

This comment does not seem to chime with the claim in the submissions to the ECHR that it was humiliating and embarrassing to produce a birth certificate in circumstances guaranteeing a much higher level of privacy and confidentiality than those obtaining in social life.

In August 1984, solicitor David Burgess, of Winstanley-Burgess Solicitors in London (who was solicitor for the applicant in the *Rees* case), and Richard Ekins, a sociologist who specialised in transgender issues, presented the legal opinion they submitted in the *Rees* case to the European Commission of Human Rights, as an addendum to their presentation at the Symposium on Psycho-Legal Aspects of Sexual Problems, 2nd International Congress on Psychiatry, Law and Ethics, Tel Aviv, Israel, February, 1986. It is reproduced in full here.

> Following discussions of proposals for a friendly settlement with Mark Rees and with other transsexuals, the proposals agreed are as follows: The United Kingdom Parliament should enact legislation:
>
> 1. Transsexuals should, subject to their having received sex/ gender reassignment surgery, be treated in all respects as of their assumed sex/gender.
>
> 2. Sex/gender reassignment surgery shall be that which in the opinion of prevailing medical opinion from time to time constitutes surgery sufficient to reassign the individuals sex/gender.
>
> 3. The legislation should incorporate non-discrimination provisions in favour of transsexuals including provisions preventing discrimination towards transsexuals in obtaining and retaining employment.
>
> 4. It should also include provisions for amending the birth registration system.
>
> 5. There should be an amendment to the Nullity Act to make clear that transsexuals shall not be treated as being incapable of consummating any marriages they enter into by reason only of their sex/gender reassignment surgery.

The most notable element in the opinion is the proposal of the requirement of surgery in order to amend one's sex/gender, though the medical details are left to the medical opinion prevailing from time to time, so do not necessarily require SRS.

Cossey v UK

The next case to come up to the court after Rees, *Cossey v UK*,[293] was decided by the ECHR in 1990. On the facts it is very similar to the *Rees* case, with the important differences that this is a case involving a MtF man and that the change of birth certificate was necessary for the purpose of marriage.

The applicant was born in 1954 and registered as male. With the onset of puberty, Cossey started to develop what we would probably refer to as gender dysphoria, though the Court refers to a female "psychological sex." It is noticeable that both in this case and in *Rees* the Court always uses pronouns matching the current identity of the applicants, in a way that sometimes introduces some ambiguity in the language.

The applicant changed name to Caroline at the age of 18 and by the age of 20 had completed the hormonal and surgical transition as well (which the Court, for the first time calls "gender reassignment" at para 15). Displaying a sexual attraction towards males, absent the surgical transition, we would describe Cossey as a homosexual or gay male. Instead the Court reports that "A medical report dated 8 February 1984 describes Miss Cossey as a pleasant young woman [...] able to have sexual intercourse with a man." The Court does not seem to be able to countenance the idea of a pleasant young man being able to have sexual intercourse with a man.

Cossey worked as a successful fashion model. The description of Cossey's early life evidences no severe hardship or discrimination: Cossey obtained medical and surgical treatment on the NHS, was issued an amended passport and enjoyed a sex life without the discrimination and condemnation often suffered by young gay males in the 1970s/1980s. In an article from 2017 written on the occasion of the death of Hugh Hefner,[294] Cossey claimed that being outed as transgender by the News of

---

[293] *Cossey v the United Kingdom*, Application No. 10843/84, Judgment of 27 September 1990.

[294] André Naquian-Wheeler, "The first openly trans playboy cover star remembers Hugh Hefner," i.-d.vice,com, October 2, 2017, https://i-d.vice.com/en/article/3ka48y/the-first-openly-trans-playboy-cover-star-remembers-hugh-hefner. An older version of the story, in an article on Cossey published by 19 Magazine in 1981-82,

the World[295] destroyed a burgeoning movie career.[296] This career thus far had included an uncredited non-speaking role in the 1981 Bond movie "For Your Eyes Only."[297] Cossey wrote two autobiographies, one in 1982 and one in 1991. In 1992 Cossey married a Canadian man.

The problems leading to the Court case started in 1983 when Cossey applied to marry an Italian man. The Registrar General rejected the request for a marriage licence on the basis that, as a matter of English law, Cossey was a male and same-sex marriage was not allowed, and that birth certificates could only be amended to record a change of anatomical sex to the extent allowed by medical science. The legal situation had not changed, as we know, from the *Rees* case decided four years before. In 1989 Cossey claimed to have married another man at a London synagogue, but the marriage lasted less than a month. That marriage was declared void by the High Court, with the decree nisi finalised in 1990. The application to the Commission was made under Article 8 and Article 12 (Right to Marry) of the Convention.[298]

As the application was similar to the one made in the *Rees* case, the Court first was interested in determining whether this case could be distinguished from the *Rees* case on its facts. While the Court was not bound to follow its own previous case law, it is also true that the Court rarely departs from its own previous judgments without a reason, especially when the cases are quite close in time, in which case the Court departs from its previous

---

https://www.digitaltransgenderarchive.net/files/v405s9425. The article is the usual collection of stereotypes on womanhood.

[295] In 1983 the News of the World published an interview with Tula (Cossey's name as a model): Rosalie Shann, "Sex-swap Tula changes her life," News of the World, October 30, 1983
https://www.digitaltransgenderarchive.net/files/ms35t871z.

[296] https://i-d.vice.com/en/article/3ka48y/the-first-openly-trans-playboy-cover-star-remebers-hugh-hefner.

[297] https://www.imdb.com/title/tt0082398/fullcredits/?ref_=tt_cl_sm.

[298] The applicant was supported financially by the Self Help Association for Transsexuals (SHAFT), an organisation founded by MtF transsexual Judy Cousins, who transitioned at the age of 53.
https://www.digitaltransgenderarchive.net/files/bg257f21v. This article on the Times of 7 February 1985 on Judy Cousins repeats the narrative that has become widespread in literature and news articles about transsexual individuals. It is titled "I had the wrong soul in the wrong body. "
https://www.digitaltransgenderarchive.net/files/bg257f20k. Shaft then became the Gender Dysphoria Trust International, which operated as a charity between 1993 and 2000.

judgment only if the cases are distinguishable on the facts or if a new consensus developes. The Court decided the two cases were not distinguishable, because the fact Rees was a FtM woman and Cossey a MtF man, and the second wished to marry while the first one did not was irrelevant. What mattered is that they both were transsexuals who sought to have their birth certificate amended.

So the first reason why Cossey could have hoped for the Court reaching a different decision was shut down by the Court. Another reason why the Court may depart from a previous judgment is because of its "living instrument" doctrine of interpretation of the Convention. This was not an easy claim, as only four years had passed since the *Rees* judgment. In fact at the end of the consideration of the claim on the basis of what previously decided four years previous, the Court stated:

> The Court has been informed of no significant scientific developments that have occurred in the meantime; in particular, it remains the case - as was not contested by the applicant - that gender reassignment surgery does not result in the acquisition of all the biological characteristics of the other sex. There have been certain developments since 1986 in the law of some of the member States of the Council of Europe. However, the reports [...] reveal [...] the same diversity of practice as obtained at the time of the Rees judgment. Accordingly this is still, having regard to the existence of little common ground between the Contracting States, an area in which they enjoy a wide margin of appreciation. In particular, it cannot at present be said that a departure from the Court's earlier decision is warranted in order to ensure that the interpretation of Article 8 on the point at issue remains in line with present-day conditions.
>
> [....]
>
> The Court accordingly concludes that there is no violation of Article 8 (art. 8).
>
> The Court would, however, reiterate the observations it made in the Rees judgment [...]. It is conscious of the seriousness of the problems facing transsexuals and the distress they suffer. Since the Convention always has to be interpreted and applied in the light of current circumstances, it is important that the need for appropriate legal measures in this area should be kept under review.

The Court rejected the claim of violation of Article 12 as well, as British law at the time did not allow same-sex marriage. Cossey had argued that the law effecitvely made it impossible for any form of marriage to take place. The Court did not accept this argument, as there was nothing in the law preventing Cossey, who was legally and biologically a male, from marrying a woman. Of course the unspoken element in this case is Cossey's sexual orientation, the only element that prevented marriage with a woman, or better, from wanting to marry a woman. Once again, the Court appealed to inconsistent practice between the Member States to grant the UK a wide margin of appreciation on how to guarantee Article 12 rights in its domestic law.

On a superficial reading, nothing new happened between the *Rees* and the *Cossey* cases. But the dissenting opinions tell a different story. In *Rees*, there were three dissenting judges. In *Cossey*, there is the partly dissenting joint opinion of two judges; a different partly dissenting joint opinion of another two judges; the dissenting opinion of another three judges; and, most importantly, a lenghty dissenting opinion of the highly respected Judge Martens from the Netherlands. Martens' dissenting opinions are legendary.[299] Judge Martens approached the dissenting opinion as a chance to theorise on transsexualism as an issue with important human rights consequences. He started with a specific section on "General Remarks on Transsexualism as a Problem of Human Rights." In his opinion, two conditions had to be necessarily fulfilled in order to guarantee transsexuals' human rights:

> 1. by means of hormone treatment and gender reassignment surgery his (outward) physical sex must be brought into harmony with his psychological sex;
>
> 2. the new sexual identity which he has thus acquired must be recognised not only socially but also legally.

It is clear how far gender identity theory has travelled from this statement. Now the Court would consider imposing a surgical change as a violation of the indvidual's human right to body integrity. But in other aspects, Martens' dissenting opinion treads familiar ground. The discrimination that they suffer is seen as caused by the "deeply rooted taboo" by society about sex change, as opposed by the recognition that it is biologically impossible to do so; transsexuals are seen as "tragic human beings who have suffered so much" and therefore deserve full legal recognition. Martens also, as an international judge is likely to do, considered the state of development of the law in several jurisdictions, to see if one could glean

[299] See Sibrand Karel Martens, W.E. Haak, G.J.M. Corstens and M.I. Veldt, Martens Dissenting: The Separate Opinions of a European Human Rights Judge (Deventer: W.E.J. Tjeenk Willink, 2000).

a common approach. In this he singled out the laws in Sweden, Germany and Italy allowing for the legal recognition of surgical sex changes. On the basis of this assessment of foreign developments, Judge Martens concluded that:

> The principle which is basic in human rights and which underlies the various specific rights spelled out in the Convention is respect for human dignity and human freedom. Human dignity and human freedom imply that a man should be free to shape himself and his fate in the way that he deems best fits his personality. A transsexual does use those very fundamental rights. He is prepared to shape himself and his fate. In doing so he goes through long, dangerous and painful medical treatment to have his sexual organs, as far as is humanly feasible, adapted to the sex he is convinced he belongs to. After these ordeals, as a post-operative transsexual, he turns to the law and asks it to recognise the fait accompli he has created. He demands to be recognised and to be treated by the law as a member of the sex he has won; he demands to be treated without discrimination, on the same footing as all other females or, as the case may be, males. This is a request which the law should refuse to grant only if it truly has compelling reasons, for in the light of what has been said in paragraphs 2.2 and 2.4 above such a refusal can only be qualified as cruel. But there are no such reasons.

One cannot underestimate the importance of this passage. Judge Martens stressed self-determination as the crucial element. This is now often referred to as self-identification, with the decoupling between body modification, which Judge Martens still considered the *conditio sine qua non* for legal recognition, and legal change of sex. One cannot fail to notice that Judge Martens seems simply incapable to understand that allowing a male to change his “legal sex” to female has consequences for third parties, especially females, so that there are legitimate reasons to refuse such recognition or at the very least to interrogate the motives and put in place reasonable criteria for allowing a sex change. He simply does not see women as being potentially affected by reconceptualising “woman” in law from meaning a human (adult) female into a male that has surgically modified himself to resemble a female body and who “lives as a woman,” with all the sexist implications that this had in the late 1970s/early 1980s.

As a matter of legal analysis, Judge Martens disagreed with the Court about the assessment that the application was not about the potential interfence with Article 8 rights, but a demand for positive rights. In Martens’ opinion, the law preventing transsexuals to change their legal sex on the Register of Births constituted an interference with their Article 8 rights. It is worth quoting the passage, as the privacy arguments will be picked up in the development of the jurisprudence of the Court and the legislative history of the UK, all the way to the drafting of the Gender Recognition Act 2004. Martens said:

> Sexual identity is not only a fundamental aspect of everyone's personality but, through the ubiquity of the sexual dichotomy, also an important societal fact. For post-operative transsexuals sexual identity has, understandably, a very special and sensitive importance because they acquired theirs deliberately, at a high cost in mental and bodily suffering. To be condemned to live, as far as that identity is concerned, in opposition to and thus "outlawed" by their country's legal system must therefore cause permanent and acute personal distress to post-operative transsexuals in the United Kingdom. That is to say nothing of the lifelong dread to which the BSD-system [recognising bírth sex as the only legal sex] condemns them, by obliging them, every time that their sex is legally relevant, to make the painful choice between either hiding what legally is "the truth" - with all the legal consequences of such untruthfulness, such as making themselves liable to a criminal charge, dismissal or a demand for nullification of the legal act in question - or revealing that legal "truth" and facing at least the possibility of very humiliating or even hostile reactions.

In summary, Judge Martens considers that societal developments, as evidenced in legislative changes in several countries, should suffice for demanding that the Court depart from its own previous judgment in *Rees*. In Judge Martens' words:

> There is an ever-growing awareness of the essential importance of everyone's identity and of recognising the manifold differences between individuals that flow therefrom. With that goes a growing tolerance for, and even comprehension of, modes of human existence which differ from what is considered "normal". With that also goes a markedly increased recognition of the importance of privacy, in the sense of being left alone and having the possibility of living one's own life as one chooses. These tendencies are certainly not new, but I have a feeling that they have come more into the open especially in recent years.

This case, which on the face of it departs little from the previous decision of the Court, contains, in the dissenting opinions, many of the arguments that will be developed in the following ten years, culminating in *Goodwin v UK*.

In this case also for the first time the transgender body takes centre stage, at least in the dissenting opinions. We have moved away from the clear recognition that transsexual people have a disconnect between biological and psychological sex, to questioning the very idea that sex at birth is a fixed entity. The ground is laid for introducing gender identity.

B. v France

In this case from 1992, the Court for the first time departed from its previous jurisprudence to accept a violation of Article 8 had taken place.[300] One of the consequences is that the dissenting opinions now came from the judges who wished to maintain the standard set by the *Rees* and *Cossey* cases. The case does not now involve the UK and this is relevant to the decision reached by the Court.

The applicant was a French national born in Algeria in 1935 and registered as a male with the name Norbert Antoine. "B." displayed feminine behaviour from a very young age and was described as "noticeably homosexual" during military service. In 1963, "B." moved to France and started work as an entartainer. Following a nervous breakdown, a doctor noted "under-developed genitals" (though no explanation is given for this) and prescribed hormones. Since at the time homosexuality was considered a disorder, it cannot be excluded that the treatment was supposed to deal with "B."'s homosexuality rather than any anatomical issues or potential DSD, and least of all with a presumed "transgenderism."[301] In 1972, the applicant had sex reassigment surgery in Morocco. On several occasions the Court noted that the applicant was still noticeably male in appearance, which is to be expected in individuals who go through male puberty (the applicant would have been 37 years old at the time of the operation).

The legal history of the case started with an attempt by the applicant to be recognised as a female by the French State in order to be able to marry. The application failed in the local court, the court of appeal and the Cassation Court, the highest court in France. At the time it was possible in France to undergo sex reassignment surgery (after the appropriate medical evaluation) and to have one's document changed, though a French law dating back to the Revolution did not allow to change one's name from the one registered on the birth certificate; however the Cassation Court had allowed this in several cases and, since it was not possible to change from

---

[300] *B. v France, Merits*, Application No. 13343/87, A/232-C, Judgment of 25 March 1992,
https://hudoc.echr.coe.int/eng#{%22itemid%22:[%22001-57770%22]}

[301] Chiara Beccalossi, "Italian Sexology. Nicola Pende's Biotypology and Hormone Treatment in the 1920s," Médicalisation de la Sexualité, 12 (2017): 73-97.

a male to a female name or vice-versa, there was a range of "neutral" names available for those wishing to change name officially, and there was considerable case law allowing transsexuals to amend their name on official documents to reflect their "new sex." It is also important to consider that, contrary to the legal situation obtaining in the UK, in France civil status as proven by official identity documents is an important aspect of the State's relationship with its citizens. Conversely, while in the UK birth certificates were considered historical documents, French birth registries were commonly amended to add information as to new civil status (adoption, marriage etc.). The considerably different administrative status of identity and birth documents in the two countries is reflected in the decision of the Court.

A quote from the Court of Cassation's judgment illustrates two aspects that were considered relevant in deciding the case against the applicant:

> On the grounds that if, notwithstanding the principle of the inalienability of the status of individuals, an amendment can be made where "irreversible necessity, independent of the individual, compels this,"which may be the case with real transsexuals, such amendment can be approved only after a long period of observation and reflection prior to the operation stage, during which a qualified medical team can "gradually reach the conclusion that the situation is genuine and irreversible;" that in this case ... "no form of psychological or psychiatric treatment was tried;" that "the first doctor who prescribed hormone treatment did not carry out any protracted observation, no guarantee of such observation was given before the surgical operation carried out abroad;" that "the apparent change of sex was brought about solely by Mr [B.'s] intention and it is clear that even after the hormone treatment and surgical operation he still shows the characteristics of a person of male sex whose external appearance has been altered thanks to cosmetic plastic surgery;" that, therefore, far from having led to the "disclosure of his hidden true sex," the treatment undergone by him indicates a "deliberate intention on his part without any other treatment having been tried and without the operations having been necessitated by Mr [B.'s] biological development"

The Court mentions "real transsexuals;" this concept was clearly still quite prevalent also at the ECHR. The dangers or risks of false or fraudulent transsexuals were still openly debated, as is clear by the discussion on the Merits by the Court. The second element is that if the decision to change sex is exclusively of the individual concerned, the State will not recognise it and will not allow a change of documents and civil status.

The application relied heavily, as Cossey had done, on distinguishing the application from the previous cases, on the one hand, and on the changed social and scientific circumstances, on the other. Two arguments not easy to accept, on the face of it, as "B."s case is almost identical to Cossey's (what changes is the legal framework on identity documents and birth certificates between the two countries, and this in the end is dispositive) and fewer than two years have passed since the Court was last asked to consider a possible Article 8 violation.

The Court had to dispense first with jurisdictional and admissibility challenges from the French government, which are dismissed (but will cause some of the dissenting opinions with which this judgment was received). On the merits, in order to accept that the behaviour of the French government constituted a breach of Article 8, the Court needed to accept as noted, that this case could be distinguished on the facts from the cases previously decided, and/or that changed social and scientific conditions restricted the margin of appreciation that States had in dealing with these requests to amend birth certificates/identity documents.

The applicant also claimed that "by failing to allow the indication of her sex to be corrected in the civil status register and on her official identity documents, the French authorities forced her to disclose intimate personal information to third parties." This claim seems inconsistent with the acknowledgement that the applicant remained recognisably male. Disclosure of male birth sex cannot possibly be seen as a breach of privacy when the person is evidently male. If anything, a female legal identity inconsistent with perceived sex would bring with it the inevitable conclusion that the individual has legally transitioned sex. This logic inconsistency is neither picked up nor solved by the Court. On scientific developments, the Court decides not refer directly to the evidence brought by the applicant in the course of the proceedings, but quotes them approvingly at para. 46:

> According to the applicant, science appears to have contributed two new elements to the debate on the contrast between appearance (changed somatic sex and constructed gonadal sex) and reality (unchanged chromosomal sex but contrary psycho-social sex) as regards the sex of transsexuals. Firstly, the chromosomal criterion was not infallible (cases of persons with intra-abdominal testicles, so-called testicular feminisation, or with XY chromosomes despite their feminine appearance); secondly, current research suggested that the ingestion of certain substances at a given stage of pregnancy, or during the first few days of life, determined transsexual behaviour, and that transsexualism might result from a chromosome anomaly. There might thus be a physical, not merely psychological

> explanation of the phenomenon, which would mean that there could be no excuse for refusing to take it into account in law.

The Court apparently accepted that DSDs may prove that chromosomal sex is not dispositive of sex determination in transsexuals (we know that these are different conditions with no necessary connection with transsexualism) or that certain unspecified substances ingested by the mother during pregnancy may cause "transsexual behaviour." It is noteworthy that the Court did not seem interested in establishing a logical connection between a biological element in transsexuality[302] and an actual change of sex in individuals. This oversight will have serious consequences in subsequent case law. In this as in other cases, oversights and minimisation of the effective consequences of legalising the fiction of a sex change are ignored by those promoting gender identity theory and by the Courts accepting it in its reasoning.

As for the changed social and legal conditions, the Court seems to be swayed by the pronouncements of the Assembly of the Council of Europe and the European Parliament in these matters.The Council of Europe, in its already quoted Recommendation 1117 (1989) had stated that:[303]

> Recommends that the Committee of Ministers draw up a recommendation inviting member states to introduce legislation whereby, in the case of irreversible transsexualism :
>
> a. the reference to the sex of the person concerned is to be rectified in the register of births and in the identity papers;
> b. a change of forename is to be authorised;
> c. the person's private life is to be protected;
> d. all discrimination in the enjoyment of fundamental rights and freedoms is prohibited in accordance with Article 14 of the European Convention on Human Rights.

---

[302] There is no mention of dysphoria or gender, although gender identity disorder was first included as a diagnosis in childhood by the American Psychiatric Association in DSM-III in 1980 and extended to adulthood in DSM-III-R in 1987, both of them preceding this case; https://www.psychiatry.org/psychiatrists/practice/dsm/about-dsm/history-of-the-dsm; the WHO maintained transsexualism as a mental health disorder in its International Classification of Diseases and Related Health Problems until 2018 https://icd.who.int/en.

[303] Council of Europe Parliamentary Assembly, "Condition of Transsexuals" 29 September 1989 https://assembly.coe.int/nw/xml/XRef/Xref-XML2HTML-en.asp?fileid=15151&lang=en.

The Assembly had referred to a resolution passed by the European Parliament in September 1989 calling for States to legislate for the protection of transsexual persons against discrimination.[304] Both these documents were already available when the Court decided on the *Cossey* case and had indeed been quoted by Judge Martens in his Dissenting Opinion.

Overall, the Court does not seem convinced that the changes in the social, legal and scientific framework justify departing from its previous jurisprudence. Instead, it stressed the differences between the English and the French systems as a reason to justify its finding. In short the Court considered that the factual differences, in the rectification of civil status documents (including birth certificates), change of name and issue of documents warranted a different treatment between the previous cases and the present case.

For the first time there is a finding of breach of Article 8, and this time the six dissenting opinions are on the other side of the argument, and, rather than pointing to the development of the law, they assess the rigour and legal quality of the reasoning of the Court. Did the Court reach this opinion in a legally consistent manner and with a proper grounding in the Convention, albeit interpreted as a "living instrument"?

The dissenting judges certainly did not think so. Judge Matscher did not consider the judgment to be sufficiently clear in establishing how exactly the State is in breach of Article 8. Judge Pinheiro Farinha was even more scathing. His criticism is multifaceted. Firstly, he averred that the judgment risked trivialising irreversible surgical operations undertaken without suitable psychiatric evaluation (the applicant had had the operation abroad though it would have been available in France, but subject to a medical evaluation). Secondly, and most importantly from a legal point of view, Judge Pinheiro considered that the Court had acted *ultra vires*; though the Court can interpret the Convention as a living instrument, it cannot read into the Convention rights that are not there, and for him "The Convention does not guarantee the right to change sex, nor the right to amendment of civil status documents, nor, unlike the

---

304 Resolution on Discrimination Against Transsexuals, Doc. A 3-16/89, OJ C 256, 9.10.1989, p. 33https://eur-lex.europa.eu/legal-content/EN/TXT/?uri=CELEX%3A51989IP0016%2802%29.

International Covenant on Civil and Political Rights (Article 24), that of a public civil status register."

The Judge also properly engaged with the issue of the unintended consequences of legalising sex changes, mentioning two that he considered important: an illegitimate child seeking recognition of paternity when the father has legally changed sex; and the possibility for a person who has changed legal sex to marry a person of their same biological sex. Clearly there is a bias against same-sex relationship, not unusual for the times. But what is important is that the Judge engaged with the possibility of consequences for third parties from a legal change of sex. This is more than the Court is prepared to do in a considered manner.

Judge Pettiti was also critical of the reasoning of the Court. He considered that the *B. v France* case did not seem to warrant, on the facts of the case, the treatment it received by the Court. Pointedly, he noted that:

> From the point of view of jurists who favour a broad interpretation of the status of transsexuals, the B. judgment would be easier to appreciate if cases of true transsexuals (operated on in public hospitals with medical supervision and documentation) had been systematically refused by the French courts. This is not the case.

The case of "B." did not involve a proper medical evaluation and a course of treatment by the French health care system (as French law would have allowed). The Judge wondered why the Court decided to choose a case in which the facts did not indicate that a legal change of sex would have been the appropriate course of action in accordance with French law. He added that

> The theory that any person who has the irrepressible will to live under a sex other than that of origin, and is convinced that this is his true destiny, must be able to obtain rectification of his civil status, is a highly debatable one, even if it is motivated by legitimate concern for social integration and private life. For where hormone treatment alone has taken place, that may be reversible. Many cases of true or false transsexual applicants correspond to psychiatric states which should be treated by psychiatry only, so as not to risk disaster, and for this reason a medical report is essential. Furthermore, cases of double personality and schizophrenia are known to medicine. If one were to be guided solely by the wish to make the individual will of the patient coincide with his social life, one would then have to accept change of civil status even in such deviant cases.

The language may be too strong for our modern sensibilities, but it is important that the law may be able to operate distinctions between those suffering from a condition from which the only possible solution seems to be a medical intervention recognised by the State through a legal change of sex, and those who could either take advantage of this or undergo irreversible treatment unnecessarily. Judge Pettiti was equally alive to the issue of unintended consequences:

> There is another aspect of considerable importance. For States like France whose civil status law is highly precise and compulsory, a consequence of rectification is that there is no obstacle to the marriage of a transsexual with a person of the same sex as his original sex. There is also the problem of adoption being available to the new couple. Let us also bear in mind the legal confusion which results from certain rectifications where the person obtaining rectification was previously married, with or without children. Let us not ignore the possibility of artificial insemination after rectification or after an operation. The whole of civil law and inheritance law could be thrown into confusion.

Judges Valticos, Loizou and Morenilla also all dissented from the judgment on similar grounds. Judge Morenillo added that the applicant, whose domestic court cases concerned the right to be married, then presented a case to the Court exclusively on the basis of a breach of Article 8, and that the request made to the French court may be more properly be described as a correction of the register, from incorrect male to correct female, rather than as a recognition of transsexual identity. It is finally worth noting the Concurring Opinion of Judge Walsh because a certain term makes its first appearance in the jurisprudence of the Court:

> The applicant is psychologically self-identified with the female sex and apparently that condition has existed since childhood and has grown more pronounced with age. It ultimately led the applicant to undergo "sex-change" surgery necessitated by psychological imperatives rather than medical ones. In the result the applicant adopted a new "gender identity" in that the new identity is to all outward appearances a female identity.

X., Y., and Z. v UK

The *X.,Y., and Z.* case[305] is from 1997 and once again it involves the United Kingdom. We are going back to a FtM woman, and this time with a new element that will acquire relevance in future cases and policy: the

[305] *X., Y., and Z. v the United Kingdom*, Judgment of 22 April 1997, Application No. 21830/93, https://hudoc.echr.coe.int/fre#{%22tabview%22:[%22document%22],%22itemid%22:[%22001-58032%22]}.

rights of a child born of the union involving a transgender person. The anonymous applicants were British citizens living in Manchester. "X." was a FtM woman, in a stable relationship with "Y.,"a female, and "Z."was their child, born through artificial insemination thanks to donor sperm (AID). From the summary of the facts provided by the Court we evince the usual narrative about the "masculine girl." The Court recounts mental illness and depression. Whether this was brought about by the distress of experiencing homosexuality in 1960s England is not mentioned, although we now know that lesbians are over-represented in the adolescent girls cohort experiencing dysphoria (as data from the Tavistock clinic in London evidences).[306]

"X." had undergone both hormonal treatment and sex reassignment surgery. When the couple wished to start a family, they had recourse to artificial insemination for "Y.," which they did for both their children ("Z.," and a child who was born subsequently). In the process of getting permission for AID, which was initially refused, the couple had to declare that, for the purpose of going ahead with the procedure, "X." was the father of the child within the meaning of the Human Fertility and Embryology Act 1990. As a matter of English law applicable at the time, "X." and "Y." could not have gotten married, as the law did not recognise "X." as a man for the purpose of marriage (*Corbett v Corbett*). "X." could not legally register as the father either. Although now the GRA and the Marriage (Same Sex Couples) Act[307] would allow "X." and "Y." to get married either as a man and a woman or as two women, the law still does not allow a female to register as the father of a child, even a female who has obtained a Gender Recognition Certificate. This is shown by the recent case of Freddie McConnell, the FtM woman who sought to be legally registered as a father.[308] However, English law allowed for a residence

---

[306] "The Surge in Referral Rates of Girls to the Tavistock Continues to Rise," Transgender Trend Blog, July 1, 2019 https://www.transgendertrend.com/surge-referral-rates-girls-tavistock-continues-rise/.

[307] Marriage (Same Sex Couples) Act 2013, https://www.legislation.gov.uk/ukpga/2013/30/contents/enacted.

[308] Though the fact of this case are different since McConnell is the biological mother of the child who wishes to be recorded as the father. https://www.theguardian.com/society/2020/nov/16/trans-man-loses-uk-legal-battle-to-register-as-his-childs-father. The case is being appealed to the UKSC. For the case history, see *R. (On the Application of T.T. v The Registrar General for England and Wales and Others*, Judgment of 25 September 2019[2019] EWHC 2384 (Fam); and *The Queen (on the application of (1) Alfred McConnell, (2) Y.Y. (by his litigation friend Claire Brooks)) and The Registrar General for England*

order to be made, in accordance with Section 8 of the 1989 Children Act, granting parental responsability to an individual other than the biological or adoptive parent (in this case, "X.") as long as the residence order remained in place. "X." and "Y." had not applied for a residence order with respect to "Z." and the younger sibling.

"X." argued that the jurisprudence of the Court indicated that the Court interpreted family life in a social sense, rather than formal legal status. The Government countered that, in the absence of a residency order, two women living together with the child of one of them did not constitute a family. It is easy to condemn the approach taken by the Government, but again, one ought to remember that at the time this was the state of the law. The interpretation of family life was a threshold issue, because if the Court did not accept that the living arrangement of "X.," "Y.," and "Z." constituted "family life" for the purpose of the Convention, the application would be declared inadmissible.[309] In the event, the Court did determine the case to be admissible, stating:

> In the present case, the Court notes that X is a transsexual who has undergone gender reassignment surgery. He has lived with Y, to all appearances as her male partner, since 1979. The couple applied jointly for, and were granted, treatment by AID to allow Y to have a child. X was involved throughout that process and has acted as Z's "father" in every respect since the birth (see paragraphs 14-16 above). In these circumstances, the Court considers that de facto family ties link the three applicants.It follows that Article 8 is applicable.

As in previous cases, the question turned on how wide a margin should be granted to States dealing with claims of breaches of Article 8 rights to

---

and Wales and (1) Secretary of State for Health and Social Care; (2) Minister for Women and Equalities; (3) Secretary of State for the Home Department and The Aire Centre, Judgment of 29 April 2020, [2020] EWCA Civ 559.

[309] It may help to note here how issues of jurisdiction and admissibilty can affect a case and how they differ. In short, jurisdiction relates to the role of the Court or the tribunal, while admissibility relates to the case itself. To illustrate, if the Court determines that it is not the correct Court to hear the case (for example because the complaint relates to another instrument, and not the ECHR) it would be an issue of jurisdiction. If the Court determines that the applicant has not exhausted domestic remedies, it would be an issue of admissibility. As it is self-evident, issues of jurisdiction are final and cannot be "cured." Either the Court is competent to hear the case or it is not (and it is for the Court, and the Court only, to determine this); issues of admissibility can be solved (for example, by exhausting domestic remedies), therefore they are not necessarily final.

private or, in this case, family life involving transsexual individuals. In the first instance the applicants needed to argue that the case was sufficiently different from previous cases on the facts, so that the Court may feel entitled to depart from its previous jurisprudence. The applicants argued that there had been developments in the legal framework, adding the recently decided case by the ECJ (*P. v and S. and Cornwall County Council*). The applicants also quoted several scientific publications, which, in the applicants' view, supported the position that transsexuals possess the "sexual identity" (still so defined) of the opposite sex to their sex at birth. A perusal of the literature presented in support reveals that scientists hypothesised that transsexualism may have a biological basis, not that transsexuals are 'literally' the opposite sex. The applicants also claimed that their case differed on the facts from previous cases (such as *Rees*) because it did not concern the right of transsexual individuals to amend their own birth certificate, but the right of transsexual parents to get their child's birth certificate amended, and since this involved the best interest of the child, the State should enjoy a smaller margin of appreciation than usual.

This argument evidences, in my view, a misunderstanding of what the margin is and how it operates. The margin of appreciation is not there to affect the proportionality analysis performed by the Court to determine how the balance between the interference with the Convention right and the conflicting public interest ought to be drawn, but how the Court should take into account the state of the law in the State parties to determine how much margin *they* ought to have been given in making that decision about interference. In other words, the margin is the leeway granted to the State in all cases involving that particular right, not a criterion to assess the particular case on the facts. It is true the facts of the case may affect how much margin a State is given, especially in relation to how these are treated in other CoE countries: but this is precisely the reason why the margin ought to have been especially wide in this case, as at the time, no CoE country allowed women to be recorded as the father of a child.

And in fact the UK Government argued that precisely because cases concerning parental rights in AID cases are regulated differently in different States, and *a fortiori* when these cases concern transsexual parents, the States should be granted a wide margin in regulating this new and complex area of law. The Court accepted that this case could be distinguished from the previous ones on the facts, as averred by the applicants. However, it went on to add:

> Since the issues in the case, therefore, touch on areas where there is little common ground amongst the member States of the Council of Europe and, generally speaking, the law appears to be in a transitional stage, the respondent State must be afforded a wide margin of appreciation.

As for whether the balance between the interference with Article 8 rights and the public interest was struck properly, the Court was willing to engage with the possible unforeseen consequences of any legal change sought by the applicant, which it had never properly done for the unforeseen consequences on women of allowing males to register as women. In fact the Court said:

> First, the Court observes that the community as a whole has an interest in maintaining a coherent system of family law which places the best interests of the child at the forefront. In this respect, the Court notes that, whilst it has not been suggested that the amendment to the law sought by the applicants would be harmful to the interests of Z or of children conceived by AID in general, it is not clear that it would necessarily be to the advantage of such children. In these circumstances, the Court considers that the State may justifiably be cautious in changing the law, since it is possible that the amendment sought might have undesirable or unforeseen ramifications for children in Z's position. Furthermore, such an amendment might have implications in other areas of family law. For example, the law might be open to criticism on the ground of inconsistency if a female-to-male transsexual were granted the possibility of becoming a "father" in law while still being treated for other legal purposes as female and capable of contracting marriage to a man.

The Court also considered that the possible disadvantages to the child can either be easily remedied or are not severe. It was then inevitable that the Court would conclude as follows:

> In conclusion, given that transsexuality raises complex scientific, legal, moral and social issues, in respect of which there is no generally shared approach among the Contracting States, the Court is of the opinion that Article 8 cannot, in this context, be taken to imply an obligation for the respondent State formally to recognise as the father of a child a person who is not the biological father. That being so, the fact that the law of the United Kingdom does not allow special legal recognition of the relationship between X and Z does not amount to a failure to respect family life within the meaning of that provision (art. 8). It follows that there has been no violation of Article 8 of the Convention.

However, once again the decision attracted considerable dissent (14 votes to six). The dissenting opinion of Judges Casadevall, Russo and Makarczyk argued that, since the State approves and even finances sex change operations, it then should accept all consequences that flow fom it, including allowing a FtM woman to be registered as the father of the child. This does not seem to me a good argument. To the extent that hormonal and surgical treatment is sought and granted to alleviate a debilitating mental health condition (and this was very much the consensus at the time) it does not follow logically that it should also affect the rights of third parties, especially vulnerable parties such as children. Judges Thór Vilhjálmsson, Foighel and Gotchev also dissented, arguing, in Foighel's case that, if the non biological parent had been a man (for example the partner of a woman undergoing AID because of infertility of her partner) he would have been allowed to register as the father and that 'X.' was not because of her transsexual status. This argument, in my opinion, wrongly deals with the comparator. The correct comparator is not a male who is not transsexual, but a female who is not transsexual. No non-transsexual female would be allowed to register as the father of a child, so there is no discrimination in not allowing "X." to do so.

Sheffield and Horsham v UK

Only one year after the *X., Y., and Z. v UK* case, we are back in the Court with another British case;[310] the two applicants were referred separately by the Commission but are being considered together by the Court. Both applicants were born male in 1946 in the UK (Horsham was also a naturalised Dutch national). Sheffield lived as a male until the age of 40, got married and fathered a child, living the life of an heterosexual male. In 1986, Sheffield started medical treatment, including surgery, changed name by deed poll and applied for documents to be reissued with a female name. Sheffield also underwent surgery well into middle age, in 1993, though making the usual claim of having known about being a transsexual already as a child. Both applicants complained about the instances in which they were required to disclose their birth sex, including in the context of police records. Sheffield's application included the matrimonial history, and specifically the fact that medical professionals required proof of divorce in order to have access to surgery and that all contact with the daughter was severed, following the judge's decision that contact with her was not conducive to her welfare. In the absence of specific information on the divorce, it is not possible to ascertain whether this was justified.

---

[310] *Sheffield and Horsham v the United Kingdom*, Judgment of 30 July 1998, Application No. 31–32/1997/815–816/1018–1019, https://hudoc.echr.coe.int/fre#{%22itemid%22:[%22001-58212%22]}.

Horsham complained specifically that the same sex marriage contracted in the Netherlands was not recognised in the UK. The applications then evidence that these two individuals shared some similarities (both transitioned in middle age) and some important differences. Sheffield had been in a heterosexual marriage, while Horsham was married with a man in the Netherlands.

The applicants, supported by the civil rights organisation Liberty, claimed, as in previous cases, that recent scientific developments justified the Court taking a different approach and depart from its previous jurisprudence, and that the margin of appreciation granted to States in these matters ought to be narrowed, now that only four member States of the Council of Europe explicitly prohibited amending birth certificates. The applicants also relied on the case decided in 1996 by the ECJ, *P. v S. and Cornwall County Council*. This case, which we have already considered, concerned the dismissal from employment of a transsexual and properly dealt with the issue of he comparator, stating that the proper comparator for a person with the characteristic of gender reassignment is a person of their same sex without the protected characteristic of gender reassignment.[311]

The applications were presented to the Commission in 1993 and in both cases the Commission determined that there had been a violation of Article 8 of the applicants. Now the case was to be heard by the Court. The decision of the Court is quite short, and it is clear that the Court had no intention to depart from its previous judgments though there is a sense that the UK would not continue to be granted the current margin of appreciation much longer. No breach of Article 8 was found, and the individual opinions of the judges dissenting or distinguishing themselves from the decision cover a good half of the total judgment.

There are no major surprises in the reasoning of the Court but one cannot help but notice how slippery and imprecise the language around gender is becoming.There is continuous slippage between gender and sex, to the point of complete unintelligibility. This is just one example:

> The continued insistence in English law on the use of purely biological criteria for the determination of gender meant that they were unable to have the register of births amended to record their post-operative gender. The applicants challenged the official view that it was impossible to amend or update the facts contained in the register save for cases of clerical or

[311] *P. v S. and Cornwall County Council*, Judgment of 30 April 1996, Case C-13/94, para 21.

> factual error. They pointed to instances where the register had been amended to take account of a person's change of sex and reasoned that if it were possible to update the register in cases of adoption it should also be feasible to do so in respect of gender reassignment. (paragraph 44).

It is impossible to understand if the Court is using gender as a synonym for biological sex, or as meaning psychological sex or any other of the meanings that gender identity theory attributes to this word. Certainly the birth certificate does not list gender, so it is impossible to amend it, nor does surgery change the gender of a person as the Court seems to imply. A most unfortunate confusion. The Court was not persuaded that the inconvenience experienced by the applicants rose to the level of an interference with their Article 8 rights. Nor was it persuaded that developments in the science surrounding gender identity issues warranted a different approach.

Nine judges either partially or completely dissented with the judgment. The seven judges who penned the partially dissenting opinion argued that changes in the legislation of other Council of Europe's Member States narrowed the margin of appreciation granted to the UK, and that interpreting the Convention as a living instrument should result in a violation of Article 8. There is the almost ritualistic invocation of the complex legal, scientific and social issues raised by transsexualism, without any actual engagement with the issues themselves nor with the consequences of any legislative change. Complexity is invoked and then waived away in order to defend the right to privacy and dignity of people who wish to change sex. Gender identity theory has almost completed its work. The only obstacle standing in its way is the view that transsexualism requires for its recognition in law an actual transition, medical and surgical. As an example, this is how the partially dissenting opinion considers the issue:

> We accept, as the Court observes in paragraph 58 of its judgment, that transsexualism raises complex scientific, legal, moral and social issues, in respect of which there is no generally shared approach among the Contracting States. However, what this means is that the legal recognition of a change of sex–or its repercussions in areas of law such as marriage, filiation, privacy, adoption, etc–takes diverse forms in the different countries. But how can we expect uniformity in such a complex area where legal change will necessarily take place against the background of the States' traditions and culture? However, the essential point is that in these countries, unlike in the United Kingdom, change has taken place–whatever its precise form is–in an attempt to alleviate the distress and suffering of the post-operative transsexual and that there exists in Europe a general

> trend which seeks in differing ways to confer recognition on the altered sexual identity.

The Dutch judge penned his own dissenting opinion. He is the most forceful in his dissent with the Court and the one who gets the closest to more contemporary understandings of "gender identity" (though he does not name it so):

> Personally, I would not characterise the issue of the legal status of postoperative transsexuals as one of minorities, but rather as one of privacy: everyone's right to live one's life as one chooses without interference, and everyone's right to act and be treated according to the identity that corresponds best to one's innermost feelings, provided that by doing so one does not interfere with public interests or the interests of others. Even if there were only one post-operative transsexual in the United Kingdom claiming legal recognition of the reassignment of his or her sex, that would not make the claim any weaker.

Though he added the "interests of others" proviso, it is clear he had not considered what these may be, especially for what concerns women, who are the most affected by a MtF transsexual man claiming a new female identity which is necessarily relational. It is never just an issue of privacy. Transsexuality/transgenderism is a public matter. It is not at all comparable with sexual orientation, which is indeed a private life issue. Transsexual individuals demand public recognition of their chosen gender identity. They demand public records to be changed, names to be amended, questions that might be asked not be asked anymore. And it is obvious that Judge Van Dijk has not considered this in the least. The privacy framing completely misses the relational and public aspect of gender identity and of sex. Further, Judge Van Dijk claimed that, on top of being a privacy issue, this also was a matter of self-determination and human dignity, just as Judge Martens had done:

> [...] most importantly, what is at stake here is the fundamental right to self-determination: if a person feels that he belongs to a sex other than the one originally registered and has undergone treatment to obtain the features of that other sex to the extent medically possible, he is entitled to legal recognition of the sex that in his conviction best responds to his identity. The right to self-determination has not been separately and expressly included in the Convention, but is at the basis of several of the rights laid down therein, especially the right to liberty under Article 5 and the right to respect for private life under Article 8. Moreover, it is a vital element of the "inherent dignity" which, according to the Preamble to the Universal Declaration of Human Rights, constitutes the foundation of freedom, justice and peace in the world.

When human rights practitioners dial up the rhetoric, it is because there is no legal basis to their claims, and this is a perfect example. Nobody is entitled to the legal recognition of their innermost feelings, and peace in the world is quite irrelevant to the topic. Finally, there is one section of the dissenting opinion that will be making its appearance in the reasoning of the Court in Goodwin:

> [...] society and individual third parties may be required to accept a certain inconvenience to enable their fellow citizens to live in dignity and worth in the same society in accordance with the sexual identity chosen by them at great personal cost.

"A certain inconvenience." This is the price society, for which we can read women, will have to pay.

The Jurisprudence of the ECHR: Goodwin

This seminal case[312] brought about the introduction of the Gender Recognition Act 2004 in the UK[313] and ushered in the era of "trans rights" in human rights law and more widely in culture and politics.[314] The *Goodwin* case treads some familiar ground. The facts are very similar to previous cases. Christine Goodwin was born in 1937, so already middle age at the time of the proceedings. The summary of Goodwin's early life reveals a straight male with a cross-dressing habit, rather than a young gay male. As we have seen, both categories already presented in previous cases, and the Court makes no distinction, although clearly there is. We are told Goodwin liked to dress as a woman from early childhood, with the usual connection being made between womanhood and clothing habits. No judge is apparently progressive enough to stop at this point and wonder what validity a claim of womanhood based on the kind of clothes one likes to wear can possibly have. Coming of age in the 1950s-1960s, Goodwin was subjected to "aversion therapy" and officially diagnosed as a

---

[312] *Christine Goodwin v The United Kingdom*, Application No. 28957/95, Judgment of 11 July 2002.
https://hudoc.echr.coe.int/fre#{%22itemid%22:[%22001-60596%22]}.

[313] Gender Recognition Act 2004,
https://www.legislation.gov.uk/ukpga/2004/7/contents.

[314] This case has attracted a lot of commentary, none of it, to my knowledge, critical of it on the basis of the conflict with women's rights. An example Rhona KM Smith, "Goodwin v. United Kingdom App. No. 28957/95 and I. v. United Kingdom App. No. 25680/94," The American Journal of International Law, 97(3) (July, 2003): 659-664.

transsexual. Goodwin got married and had four children, and yet the Court reports the usual diagnosis of "brain sex" not matching body sex. In 1985 Goodwin started medical treatment, including sex reassignment surgery in 1991.

In the application to the Court, Goodwin noted incidents of employment discrimination, and breaches of privacy resulting from the employer being able to check Goodwin's employment history; an allegation of having lost out on a chance to apply for car insurance as this would have meant having to disclose the male birth certificate. In the application, Goodwin claimed transsexuality enjoyed a much higher level of social acceptance than it did in the past, bringing this as an example:

> The applicant also pointed to increasing social acceptance of transsexuals and interest in issues of concern to them reflected by coverage in the press, radio and television, including sympathetic dramatisation of transsexual characters in mainstream programming.

For the non-British readers, this is a reference to the character of Hayley Cropper in the popular UK soap Coronation Street, the first "transgender" character in a mainstream programme.[315] The irony is that this transsexual character was played by a female actress, Julie Hesmondhalgh, who became a patron for Press for Change.[316] The public were softened to the idea of a man being a woman by having a woman playing a transsexual. Clearly this looked eminently plausible as the actress was really a woman. The irony is clearly lost on the Court.

As we have seen, transsexual individuals had over time acquired quite a considerable number of rights, either via a lax application of the law, or specific exceptions. They also had access to medical care, free of charge. One need not spend too much time to consider how difficult it was for women at the time to be granted the choice of an hysterectomy, if they were of child-bearing age, even if they expressed no intention to have children, because they may change their mind ("la donna è mobile" after

---

[315] "Coronation Street–Hayley comes out as transgender," https://player.bfi.org.uk/rentals/film/watch-coronation-street-hayley-comes-out-as-transgender-1998-online.

[316] Rachel Bosenterfer, "Haley Cropper–Coronation Street's Trojan Horse," Material Humanism, June 25, 2020, https://uncommongroundmedia.com/hayley-cropper-coronation-streets-trojan-horse/.

all). It still is almost impossible,[317] unless, of course, one declares a trans identity.[318]

The one thing transsexuals had not gained yet was the right to have their birth certificate amended to reflect their "psychosocial sex." In 1999 the Home Department had instituted a Working Group to examine the conditions of transsexuals in the UK, with specific reference to the issue of birth certificates. The movement to eliminate sex on birth certificates, could not have started without first dislodging the fixity and reliability of birth registration. In the UK birth certificates are considered historical documents,[319] so the sex of the child at birth is not affected by any subsequent changes to the gender of the individual concerned. Lobbying to allow the recognition of one's gender provided a veneer of legitimacy and reasonableness to a demand that had no basis in logic and in law. In logic because one cannot "update" one's gender in a birth certificate as gender is not listed in the birth certificate to begin with; and in law because, if gender and sex are different, changing the second to match the first the integrity of the historical record is affected by a legal change that may have taken places 50 years or more after the birth.

The transgender rights group Press for Change started lobbying in the 1990s and was consulted in drafting such documents as the Employment Regulations 1999, the above-mentioned Report of the Working Group, and the Gender Recognition Act 2004. For what concerns birth certificates, the Working Group came to this conclusion:

> 5.1. Transsexual people deal with their condition in different ways. Some live in the opposite sex without any treatment to acquire its physical attributes. Others take hormones so as to obtain some of the secondary characteristics of their chosen sex. A smaller number will undergo surgical procedures to make their bodies resemble, so far as possible, those of their acquired gender. The extent of treatment may be determined by individual

---

[317] Melissa Davey, "'Why is it such a scandalous thing?' the women who have to fight for their right to be child-free," The Guardian, June 8, 2021, https://www.theguardian.com/society/2021/jan/08/why-is-it-such-a-scandalous-thing-the-women-who-have-to-fight-for-their-right-to-be-child-free.

[318] Some European countries allow sex reassignment surgery from the age of 16. European Union Agency for Fundamental Rights, Access to sex reassignment surgery, October 19, 2018, https://fra.europa.eu/en/publication/2017/mapping-minimum-age-requirements-concerning-rights-child-eu/access-sex-reassignment-surgery

[319] Births and Deaths Registration Act 1953, https://www.legislation.gov.uk/ukpga/Eliz2/1-2/20.

choice, or by other factors such as health or financial resources. Many people revert to their biological sex after living for some time in the opposite sex, and some alternate between the two sexes throughout their lives. Consideration of the way forward must therefore take into account the needs of people at these different stages of change.

5.2. Measures have already been taken in a number of areas to assist transsexual people. For example, discrimination in employment against people on the basis of their transsexuality has been prohibited by the Sex Discrimination (Gender Reassignment) Regulations 1999 which, with few exceptions, provide that a transsexual person (whether pre- or post-operative) should not be treated less favourably because they are transsexual. The criminal justice system (i.e. the police, prisons, courts, etc.) try to accommodate the needs of transsexual people so far as is possible within operational constraints. A transsexual offender will normally be charged in their acquired gender, and a post-operative prisoner will usually be sent to a prison appropriate to their new status. Transsexual victims and witnesses will, in most circumstances, similarly be treated as belonging to their acquired gender.

5.3. In addition, official documents will often be issued in the acquired gender where the issue is identifying the individual rather than legal status. Thus, a transsexual person may obtain a passport, driving licence, medical card etc, in their new gender. We understand that many non-governmental bodies, such as examination authorities, will often re-issue examination certificates etc. (or otherwise provide evidence of qualifications) showing the required gender. We also found that at least one insurance company will issue policies to transsexual people in their acquired gender.

5.4. Notwithstanding such provisions, transsexual people are conscious of certain problems which do not have to be faced by the majority of the population. Submissions to the Group suggested that the principal areas where the transsexual community is seeking change are birth certificates, the right to marry and full recognition of their new gender for all legal purposes.

5.5. We have identified three options for the future;

– to leave the current situation unchanged;
– to issue birth certificates showing the new name and, possibly, the new gender;
– to grant full legal recognition of the new gender subject to certain criteria and procedures.

We suggest that before taking a view on these options the Government may wish to put the issues out to public consultation.

The long quote is presented to exemplify the status of transsexual people at the time the Report was drafted. As noted, the main issue presented is one of legal status (including birth certificates) and the right to marry. Far from spearheading the campaign for equal marriage, transgender people simply wanted special treatment for their relationships, with no consideration at all for the rights of homosexual persons to marry their same sex partner. The Working Group rightly notes that this is an issue better left to democratic decision-making.

It is clear by the comprehensive review of the legislative framework in the UK done by the *Goodwin* judges that the Court was laying the ground for overturning its previous jurisprudence. On the face of it, this seems puzzling, as their own summary of the legal situation for transsexual persons in the UK, evidences quite favourable legal rights. The Court approached its reasoning in the spirit of the "living instrument" doctrine, therefore assessing the facts "in the light of present-day conditions." It is unfortunate that these conditions are not based on reality, but on the self-identification of Christine Goodwin, who is said to be living as a female. Goodwin underwent surgery in middle age, therefore went through puberty, got married, had children, and had an easily identifiable male body.[320] If the Court had assessed the facts realistically it would have noted that Christine Goodwin was a male who underwent plastic surgery to approximate the genitalia and secondary sex characteristics of the female sex and preferred to wear traditional feminine clothing. From there it would have moved to consider whether a man should be discriminated against because of the belief that he is a woman, and the assessment would have considered the proportionality of the exercise, on the basis that a belief is legitimate to the extent that it does not affect the rights of others. Instead, the Court framed the issue in the following manner:

> The Court observes that the applicant, registered at birth as male, has undergone gender re-assignment surgery and lives in society as a female. Nonetheless, the applicant remains, for legal purposes, a male. This has had, and continues to have, effects on the applicant's life where sex is of legal relevance and distinctions are made between men and women, as, inter alia, in the area of pensions and retirement age.

---

[320] There are 1000s of differences between male and female bodies, but for the purpose of social recognition the more obvious are height, gait, body shape, voice, adam's apple, skin texture, hair patterns; a few of these can be modified, but usually the results are mediocre at best. Hilton Emma and Wright Colin, "Two Sexes." In Sex and Gender. A Contemporary Reader, eds. Alice Sullivan and Selina Todd (London: Routledge, 2024): 16-34.

There are legitimate reasons why sometimes sex is of legal relevance. Women benefit from becoming "visible" in law, as we all know that in the past the default human was a male, and no account was taken of females who are full humans in their own right, but fundamentally different from males in some respects that have to do with their bodies. Instead, the Court only considered what nugatory negative effect this distinction may have on the tiny percentage of humans who do not accept the reality of their sex and wish to live without acknowledging that reality to themselves and others. The entirety of the Court's summary of the facts of the case takes for granted that Goodwin's reality = social reality. That if it were not for the prohibition to amend one's birth certificate, birth sex would not be intelligible to others. That the humiliation suffered by Goodwin is due to having to disclose a male birth certificate to an unsuspecting employer. That the fact that the NHS pays for sex reassignment surgery to ameliorate a mental health condition imposes a duty on society to accept the results as if the treatment was, instead of a way to deal with a mental health condition through drastic surgery, a way to force all third parties, even those with no knowledge or personal interest in the transsexual individual, to validate their choice of treatment even against their own convictions.

In the paragraph on medical and scientific considerations, the Court runs through the familiar theories of biological differences in the brain of transsexuals (as if, even if this were the case, this proved some way that they are actually the opposite sex) and references to the DSM-IV, which had removed transsexualism from the list of conditions, referring instead to "gender identity disorder." This paragraph from the judgment shows how the Court engages with scientific evidence:

> While it also remains the case that a transsexual cannot acquire all the biological characteristics of the assigned sex, the Court notes that with increasingly sophisticated surgery and types of hormonal treatments, the principal unchanging biological aspect of gender identity is the chromosomal element. It is known however that chromosomal anomalies may arise naturally (for example, in cases of intersex conditions where the biological criteria at birth are not congruent) and in those cases, some persons have to be assigned to one sex or the other as seems most appropriate in the circumstances of the individual case. It is not apparent to the Court that the chromosomal element, amongst all the others, must inevitably take on decisive significance for the purposes of legal attribution of gender identity for transsexuals.

The Court does not make any reference to the function of sex and the significance of sexual differentiation in humans (and in much of the animal and plant world),[321] claiming that only chromosomes are the unchangeable biological characteristic of sex between a woman and a MtF man. This is scientifically inaccurate. Chromosomes are markers of difference, not the difference itself, which is functional. Their argument ignores the fact that reproduction is the essential functional distinction behind sexual differentiation, and remains a defining distinction between men and women. Not because of some sort of biological essentialism, whereby pointing out that women are responsible for the reproduction of our species automatically means that women should be responsible only for the reproduction of our species. There is no is-ought automatism, only the recognition that women are functionally different from men. From this difference arise specific vulnerabilities and strenghts that do not map seamlessly on men's vulnerabilities and strenghts, that our cultures have for millennia limited women's lives on the basis of their reproductive role, and 100 years of feminism have only scratched the surface of these limiting structures. And then, with a final flourish, the Court concluded that chromosomes cannot be decisive for the attribution of gender identity for transsexuals, because a minuscule percentage of humans have chromosomal conditions affecting their sexual development. Whoever thought so? Until now, the Court referred to chromosomes as signifiers of sex, not gender identity. It is a clumsy sleigh of hand, and yet, this is another crucial stepping stone on dismantling sex as the significant difference between men and women. Sophisticated surgery can, the Court confidently asserted, transform a male into a female except chromosomes. Nonetheless, the Court concluded that scientific evidence is not determinative of the issue. Equally, while still according States a wide margin of appreciation, it was willing to look with favour at the emerging international trend in favour of recognition of transsexuals' right to self-determine their sex. In paras 90-91 the Court sets out the reasoning behind its decision to find a breach of Article 8; it is worth quoting in full:

> 90. Nonetheless, the very essence of the Convention is respect for human dignity and human freedom. Under Article 8 of the Convention in particular, where the notion of personal autonomy is an important principle underlying the interpretation of its guarantees, protection is given to the personal sphere of each individual, including the right to establish details of their identity as individual human beings [...]. In the twenty first century the right of transsexuals to personal development and to physical and moral security in the full sense enjoyed by others in society cannot be regarded as a matter of controversy requiring the lapse of time to cast clearer light on the issues involved. In short, the unsatisfactory situation in

[321] Ibidem.

> which post-operative transsexuals live in an intermediate zone as not quite one gender or the other is no longer sustainable. Domestic recognition of this evaluation may be found in the report of the Interdepartmental Working Group and the Court of Appeal's judgment of Bellinger v. Bellinger […].
>
> 91. The Court does not underestimate the difficulties posed or the important repercussions which any major change in the system will inevitably have, not only in the field of birth registration, but also in the areas of access to records, family law, affiliation, inheritance, criminal justice, employment, social security and insurance. However, as is made clear by the report of the Interdepartmental Working Group, these problems are far from insuperable, to the extent that the Working Group felt able to propose as one of the options full legal recognition of the new gender, subject to certain criteria and procedures. As Lord Justice Thorpe observed in the Bellinger case, any "spectral difficulties", particularly in the field of family law, are both manageable and acceptable if confined to the case of fully achieved and post-operative transsexuals. Nor is the Court convinced by arguments that allowing the applicant to fall under the rules applicable to women, which would also change the date of eligibility for her state pension, would cause any injustice to others in the national insurance and state pension systems as alleged by the Government. No concrete or substantial hardship or detriment to the public interest has indeed been demonstrated as likely to flow from any change to the status of transsexuals and, as regards other possible consequences, the Court considers that society may reasonably be expected to tolerate a certain inconvenience to enable individuals to live in dignity and worth in accordance with the sexual identity chosen by them at great personal cost.

"A certain inconvenience." The Court does not seem to have even considered how allowing a male to change his legal sex to female may affect women, who are the female sex by default. It is sometimes facile to resort to claims of structural sexism, to explain the absolute blind spot that institutions have as regards to the effects of their decisions and actions on women. But little else explains the absolute silence of the Court on the inevitable effects of allowing males to redefine womanhood to suit their wants.

The crucial proviso "if confined to the case of fully achieved and post-operative transsexuals" is completely ignored by the legislation passed by the UK to respond to the judgment, the Gender Recognition Act 2004, which does not require any medical or surgical modification to be granted a Gender Recognition Certificate (GRC). This is not simply the UK going above the minimum standard required by the *Goodwin* judgment, but openly going against the qualifying criteria imposed by it.[322] The Gender Recognition Bill was introduced somewhat unusually in the House of Lords by Lord Falconer on 27 November 2003[323] and was debated in the House of Lords on 18 December 2003[324] and 8 January 2004.[325] It was also scrutinised at Committee Stage by a Lords Committee, with the proposed amendments on the 13 and 14 of January 2004. The debate on the amendments, still in the Lords, went on from 21 January to 10 February, for a total of four days. Finally on 23 February, the Bill reached the Commons, for the Second Reading, introduced by the Parliamentary Under-Secretary of State for Constitutional Affairs David Lammy as "[…] part of the Government's commitment to reforming the constitution so that it better meets the needs of all people."[326] Clearly the governmennt did not consider this a bill of major constitutional importance, as those are conventionally always started in the Commons.[327] The Bill passed the Commons vote on 25 May 2004 and received Royal Assent on 1 July 2004. The impression that the Government tried to bury the Bill and pass it without drawing attention to it was noted at the time in the House of

---

322 Gender identity theorists are of course critical of any medical or surgical criterion for legal gender recognition. Alex Sharpe refers to it as "genitocentrism," intended as the focus on genitalia for gender recognition. Alex Sharpe, Transgender Jurisprudence: Dysphoric Bodies of Law (London: Cavendish, 2002): 9. One wishes they would extend this opprobrium for requiring adults to undergo genital surgery to offering genital surgery to older adolescents, such as the child of former CEO of the charity Mermaids, who underwent SRS as a 16 year old. Maya Forstater, "Secrets and Lies," The Critic, August 7, 2023, https://thecritic.co.uk/secrets-and-lies/.

323 Gender Recognition Bill HL, Volume 655: debated on Thursday 27 November 2003, https://hansard.parliament.uk/Lords/2003-11-27/debates/ee89865f-bdce-438f-a6ad-424ee6109ff2/GenderRecognitionBillHl.

324 Gender Recognition Bill HL, Volume 655: debated on Thursday 18 December 2003, https://hansard.parliament.uk/Lords/2003-12-18/debates/1bacc5de-e32f-4556-8cb3-0ca85c51fc63/GenderRecognitionBillHl

325 Gender Recognition Bill HL, Volume 655: debated on Thursday 8 January 2004, https://hansard.parliament.uk/Lords/2004-01-08/debates/52552f71-c05c-48af-940d-74dba6190e06/GenderRecognitionBillHl?highlight=gender%20recognition%20bill#contribution-faf874df-1f35-42a8-835f-656afc2c8539.

326 Gender Recognition Bill, Volume 418: debated on Monday 23 February 2004, https://hansard.parliament.uk/Commons/2004-02-23/debates/7fa2c35f-8043-4516-af9c-b12e02e672ec/GenderRecognitionBill?highlight=gender%20recognition%20bill#contribution-fd79d657-8cb6-4580-b267-aad20edf95e3.

327 Cabinet Office, "Legislative process: taking a bill through Parliament," February 20, 2013, https://www.gov.uk/guidance/legislative-process-taking-a-bill-through-parliament.

Lords' debate.[328]A good portion of the parliamentary debates concerns the effect of the Bill on marriage law as it was at the time and is therefore now irrelevant. The fact that the law was drawn much more widely than *Goodwin* required was noted in the debate.[329] By and large reading the debates, especially in the House of Lords, evidences a keen understanding of the possible repercussions of the Bill were it to become law, especially for women. As Baroness O'Cathain said:[330]

> We must not allow our natural sympathy for those who struggle with a serious psychological problem to blind us to the problems that the Bill will create for other people. If the Government persist in pushing through the Bill, they must make radical amendments to protect the freedom of conscience of those who simply do not believe that the law can declare a man to be a woman or a woman to be a man. It is only common sense and a basic human right for individuals to be free to believe fact rather than fiction, otherwise we are entering a dark future of coerced totalitarian-style law making.

With considerable foresight Lord Chan noted, "There will doubtless be more reports of outrage by women protesting against the use of their

---

[328] Baroness Buscombe on 18 December 2003 debate, column 1291: "I am, however, concerned that the Government may be attempting to play down the Bill and to give it a low profile. Why did the Government choose to exclude it from the gracious Speech, despite the fact that it was clearly part of the immediate legislative agenda? The day before State Opening, I was asked for diary availability for Second Reading before Christmas Recess, yet the following day there was no mention of it in the gracious Speech. What was the reason for that?" Baroness Buscombe was also alive to the effects of the Bill on women. Gender Recognition Bill HL, Volume 655: debated on Thursday 18 December 2003, https://hansard.parliament.uk/Lords/2003-12-18/debates/1bacc5de-e32f-4556-8cb3-0ca85c51fc63/GenderRecognitionBillHl.

[329] See debate on 8 December in the House of Lords, Column 1297, intervention by the Lord Bishop of Winchester, Gender Recognition Bill HL, Volume 655: debated on Thursday 18 December 2003, https://hansard.parliament.uk/Lords/2003-12-18/debates/1bacc5de-e32f-4556-8cb3-0ca85c51fc63/GenderRecognitionBillHl.

[330] Baroness O'Cathain, debate of 18 December 2003, column 1313, Gender Recognition Bill HL, Volume 655: debated on Thursday 18 December 2003, https://hansard.parliament.uk/Lords/2003-12-18/debates/1bacc5de-e32f-4556-8cb3-0ca85c51fc63/GenderRecognitionBillHl.

toilets by people possessing gender recognition certificates as women who have male genitalia."[331]

Christine Goodwin had also raised a claim with regards to Article 12, the right to marry. The Court found a breach of this right as well. They are content to consider that, if a man undergoes surgery, he becomes a woman, conceptualising the sexes as the one who penetrates and the one who is penetrated. This is not said explicitly but significantly, the section opens with the statement, by Christine Goodwin about "enjoy[ing] a full physical relationship with a man," I do not think I am saying something controversial in saying that a man can enjoy a full physical relationship with a man without turning into a woman. However for the Court this is sufficient to consider that since Goodwin felt like a woman, and was penetrated like a woman, Goodwin could marry a man. Meanwhile, men or women who defied traditional sex roles and entered same sex relationships were not granted the basic right to marriage that the Court was sure Christine Goodwin so richly deserved.

The Jurisprudence of the ECHR Post-Goodwin

Since the *Goodwin* case, a steady stream of cases has reached the court dealing with "gender identity" issues.[332] The next case that reached the Court is the *Van Kück v Germany* case from 2003,[333] only a year after the *Goodwin* judgment. The case concerned a German male, who underwent sex reassignment surgery. In Germany as in Italy, the law on transsexuality required an application to the Court to change name and sex in official documents. The applicant had been granted the application, but the issue arose in respect to medical treatment. As the applicant was a civil servant, the customary 50% discount in accessing private medical insurance applied, however the private insurance provider had refused to cover the medical expenses incurred by the applicant for the sex reassignment surgery. The regional court to which the applicant appealed the decision agreed with the insurance provider that surgery was not "necessary

[331] What he could not predict was that males without a GRC would demand access to female toilets, Gender Recognition Bill HL, Volume 655, column 1308: debated on Thursday 18 December 2003, https://hansard.parliament.uk/Lords/2003-12-18/debates/1bacc5de-e32f-4556-8cb3-0ca85c51fc63/GenderRecognitionBillHl.

[332] ECHR, "Gender identity issues," Factsheet January 2023, https://www.echr.coe.int/documents/d/echr/fs_gender_identity_eng.

[333] *Van Kück v Germany*, Application No. 35968/97, Judgment of 18 October 2001.

medical treatment" for the diagnosed mental health condition and that other treatments, such as psychotherapy, were available. Van Kück appealed the judgment and lost again. It is important to note that the applicant's condition being described as a "disease" was not in dispute between the parties (clearly as it would not have been possible for the applicant to make an insurance claim without proving the diagnosis of a disease requiring extensive medical treatment including major surgery). Therefore the only element in dispute was over which treatment was "necessary" for the reimbursement of medical expenses.

The expert for the applicant claimed that psychotherapy would not have sufficed because of the applicant's "chronic narcissistic character structure." The expert also suggested the source of the applicant's transsexuality was infertility (the applicant was also married). The applicant also compared in the submission to the Court the condition of womanhood to one of failed manhood because of infertility. Van Kück claimed a breach of Article 6 (fair hearing) and Article 8 (privacy and family life).

The Court's reasoning with respect to Article 6 against the German courts' decision on the necessity of medical treatment was not straightforward. After arguing that the courts should have sought more expert opinions on medical treatment, they concluded that "gender identity is one of the most intimate areas of a person's private life" and "the burden placed on a person in such a situation to prove the medical necessity of treatment, including irreversible surgery, appears therefore disproportionate." By definition then any request to prove the medical necessity of treatment is disproportionate. This is an impossible test to meet and opens the door to "self-ID" of transsexuality/transgenderism.

In its discussion of the Article 8 claim, the Court claimed that self-determination (by now presented as an element of private life) includes the freedom of defining one's sex. Self-determination is a concept that has a long pedigree in international law, especially in the context of the right of States to determine their own economic and political model, and of their people to self-govern without outside interference, as an expression of sovereignty.[334] What it does not mean is the freedom to impose on others

[334] The bibliography on sovereignty is justifiably immense and difficult to reproduce here. The concept is incorporated in the Charter of the United Nations, as "sovereign equality" (Article 2.1 and Article 78). Sovereignty and self-determination are two sides of the same coin, though self-determination has a

one's self-perception. No amount of repetition can transform this falsehood in a principle of international law or a right in human rights law. There is no normative basis for this interpretation of the concept of self-determination, only the accretion of small falsehoods forming the narrative of gender identity as an indispensable element of our human identity that culminated in *Goodwin* and is now being refined and "polished" by the Court.

The Court averred that under Article 8 the applicant had a "right to gender identity and personal development." The obvious incongruence of presenting transsexualism as a matter of self-determination but also as a "disease" to be cured does not seem to concern the Court, even if it was the applicant to argue that the private insurance ought to pay for the treatment of the disease of transsexualism. The Court waived this all away in this paragraph:

> The Court of Appeal also reproached the applicant with having deliberately caused her transsexuality. In evaluating her sexual identity and development, the Court of Appeal analysed her past prior to the taking of female hormones and found that she had only shown male behaviour and was thus genuinely male orientated. In doing so, the Court of Appeal, on the basis of general assumptions as to male and female behaviour, substituted its views on the most intimate feelings and experiences for those of the applicant, and this without any medical competence. It thereby required the applicant not only to prove that this orientation existed and amounted to a disease necessitating hormone treatment and gender reassignment surgery, but also to show the 'genuine nature' of her transsexuality although, as stated above (see paragraph 75 above), the essential nature and cause of transsexualism are uncertain. (Para. 81).

In summary, since doctors do not know enough about the nature of transsexualism, any claim of transsexualism has to be taken at face value and cannot be questioned. In fact the Court also made assumptions as to what constitutes male and female behaviour, otherwise it could not make any determination as to the transsexuality of the applicant.

---

collective meaning that is lacking from sovereignty, an attribute of States and not of peoples. Self-determination (of peoples) is contained in Article 2.2 of the Charter. Autonomy is the individual equivalent of self-determination, as well as bodily integrity. None of these concepts justifies compelling third parties to accept one's self-defined identity based on internal beliefs. Self-identification is the triumph of unchecked individualism and therefore functionally and genealogically different from the collective and inter-subjective character of self-determination.

The next case decided by the Court is *Grant v UK*.[335] The Court was facing its first post-*Goodwin* case from the UK, a case that concerned pension rights and where the applicant asked the Court to consider, even in the absence of any legislative step yet taken by the UK, the effect of the *Goodwin* judgment on the facts, and to find a violation of Article 8. On its face not a particularly important case, especially because the GRA 2004, passed by parliament before this judgment, made the claim a moot one (Grant could get the pension at the legal female age as a consequence of the GRA), but one that acquires significance because between it and the GRA the House of Lord had the chance to reconsider the same issue that it had faced in *Corbett v Corbett*, i.e. the validity of a marriage involving a transsexual person.[336] Such was the importance placed on this case that the ECHR adjourned the *Grant* case by agreement in order to await the outcome of the *Bellinger* case.[337] The facts were similar to *Corbett v Corbett*, a petitioner born male who had had SRS and then entered a marriage with a man, though in this case the issue was not the divorce, but the validity of the marriage itself.[338] There is much to be commended in this case, not least the correct framing of the issue: the point is not whether sex is or isn't a fixed biological fact (it clearly is) but how much society should accommodate people who do not accept this biological fact about themselves and (importantly) do the outmost, through hormones and surgery, to approximate the outward appearance of the other sex. There is no leeway given to self-identification at all,[339] and this is interesting,

---

[335] *Grant v the United Kingdom*, Application No. 32570/03, Judgment of 23 May 2006..

[336] The case is *Bellinger v Bellinger* [2003] UKHL 21.

[337] This also because in the HoL appeal, a declaration was sought that section 11(3) of the Matrimonial Causes Act 1973, restricting marriage as between men and women was incompatible with Articles 8 and 12 of the ECHR. Because of legal developments since *Goodwin*, the Lord Chancellor accepted in the *Bellinger* proceedings that UK law on marriage was incompatible with Articles 8 and 12 of the ECHR facilitating, the passage of the Gender Recognition Act 2004, which was already in the works of the government at the time.

[338]The case reviews the state of the law in other common law jurisdictions, finding that at the time, marriage was recognised when one of the spouses was transgender in New Zealand (*Attorney-General v Otahuhu Family Court*, [1995] 1 NZLR 603); and Australia, *Australia Re Kevin* (validity of marriage of transsexual) [2001] Fam CA 1074); while courts followed the precedent set by *Corbett v Corbett* in South Africa (*W. v W.* (1976) (2) SALR 308) and Canada (*M. v M.* (A) (1984) 42 RFL (2d) 267).

[339]This paragraph (28) could not be clearer: "The distinction between male and female exists throughout the animal world. It corresponds to the different roles

because the GRA 2004 (less than a year away) effectively provides for a sort of controlled self-identification, as it dispenses completely with the need for "any" medical or surgical intervention in order for recognition of one's desire to be accepted as the opposite sex for the purpose of the law. The Law Lords held that:

> [...] your Lordships' House, sitting in its judicial capacity, ought not to accede to the submissions made on behalf of Mrs Bellinger. Recognition of Mrs Bellinger as female for the purposes of section 11(c) of the Matrimonial Causes Act 1973 would necessitate giving the expressions "male" and "female" in that Act a novel, extended meaning: that a person may be born with one sex but later become, or become regarded as, a person of the opposite sex. This would represent a major change in the law, having far reaching ramifications. It raises issues whose solution calls for extensive enquiry and the widest public consultation and discussion. Questions of social policy and administrative feasibility arise at several points, and their interaction has to be evaluated and balanced. The issues are altogether ill-suited for determination by courts and court procedures. They are pre-eminently a matter for Parliament, the more especially when the government, in unequivocal terms, has already announced its intention to introduce comprehensive primary legislation on this difficult and sensitive subject..

So no change from the *Corbett v Corbett* approach and the reasonable comment that these matters are better left to Parliament where they can be properly debated. As we now know, the UK got new legislation, the GRA 2004, but with minimal public consultation and discussion. On the facts of the *Grant* case, the applicant had beeen allowed to pay lower pension contributions, at the female rate, from 1963 to 1975,[340] though this is not likely to have given rise to a legitimate expectation under administrative

---

played in the reproductive process. A male produces sperm which fertilise the females' eggs. In this country, as elsewhere, classification of a person as male or female has long conferred a legal status. It confers a legal status, in that legal as well as practical consequences follow from the recognition of a person as male or female. The legal consequences affect many areas of life, from marriage and family law to gender-specific crime and competitive sport. It is not surprising, therefore, that society through its laws decides what objective biological criteria should be applied when categorising a person as male or female. Individuals cannot choose for themselves whether they wish to be known or treated as male or female. Self-definition is not acceptable. That would make nonsense of the underlying biological basis of the distinction."

[340] Paragraph 21 of the Judgment.

law, as not meeting the standard of clear, unambiguous and unqualified.[341] Although the Court noted this inconsistency, it was not up to the Court to remedy it.

The only matter of interest to the Court, since the government had in the meanwhile passed the GRA 2004 Act, was from which point in time the applicant could claim a violation of ECHR rights: from the time the application for pension rights was made, as the applicant requested, or from the time the Court issued its *Goodwin* Judgment; the Court decided that the violation would only subsist from the time of the *Goodwin* Judgment.

Passage of the GRA 2004 signals an important shift in the jurisprudence of the Court, as there are no UK cases in the ECHR after it. Arguably this is because the GRA went much further than required by the Court in *Goodwin*, by dispensing with the need of medical or surgical modification in order to have one's reassigned gender recognised for the purpose of marriage and pension rights. In a way we can interpret the case law of the ECHR post-*Goodwin* as a way for the Court to catch up with the GRA. In fact, of the 21 cases decided between 2007 and 2019, 11 directly concern circumstances around sex reassignment surgery.[342] The cases often concern the refusal of the State to grant transsexual status or to allow the legal change of sex without the requirement of sterilisation or sex reassignment surgery having been met. From a theoretical point of view, it is with the GRA 2004 that the category mistake of gender identity theory is finally crystallised in law. That is, the idea that the law can be an instrument for the validation of delusional self-perceptions. Gender identity theorists often analogise gender reassignment in the GRA with the institution of adoption. The mechanism of adoption creates a legal fiction whereby the adoptive parent is given the same rights as a biological

---

[341] Robert E. Riggs, "Legitimate Expectation and Procedural Fairness in English Law," The American Journal of Comparative Law 36(3) (Summer 1988): 395-436, doi: https://doi.org/10.2307/840342;

[342] *L. v Lithuania*, Application No. 27527/03, Decision on Admissibility of 6 July 2006; *Schlumpf v Switzerland*, Application No.29002/06, Judgment of 8 January 2009; *P. v Portugal* (strike out decision); *Y.Y. v Turkey*, Application No. 14793/08, Judgment of 10 March 2015; *D.C. v Turkey* [inadmissible, non-exhaustion of domestic remedies]; *S.V. v Italy*, Application No. 55216/08, Judgment of 11 Octoberr 2018; *X. and Y. v Romania*, Application Nos. 2145/16 and 20607/16, Judgment of 19 January 2021; *M. v France*, Application No. 42821/18, Decision of 26 April 2022; *A.D. and Others v Georgia*, Application Nos. 57864/17, 79087/17 and 55353/19. Judgement of 1 December 2022.

parent. The law creates a "relational" legal fiction, between adoptive parent and child.[343] What the law does not do is create a pretence that the adoptive parent is equivalent for all purposes to the biological parent; for example, it does not compel a doctor to perform genetic testing to see whether the adoptive parent's genes have been passed on to the child, because the legal fiction does not make the adoptive parent literally a biological parent. It does not compel the State to treat as a parent someone who pretends to be one without having a child. Gender identity theorists want us to believe gender reassignment transforms a male literally into a woman, often bordering on the ridiculous (arguing for example that transwomen can have periods, or female penises). It is a category mistake to think that the function of the law allowing a legal fiction in a relational matter (adoption, but also property law, or legal personality of companies) is analogous with the law reifing a fiction into a reality. i.e. transforming the self-perception of a male that he is a female[344] into something the law is required to treat as fact. It is not the function of the law to transform beliefs into facts, no matter how sincerely held they happen to be. The ultimate goal of gender identity theory is to decouple gender reassignment, which in fact becomes a legal sex change, from any need for medical treatment and even of a diagnosis. No other fact about our lives is open to self-definition in this manner. The law can create legal fictions when required in the public interest or in the interest of vulnerable third parties (parentless children) not to validate a narcissistic exercise of self-definition outside the bounds of material reality, and then force third parties to participate in this exercise of delusional self-definition, in which not only third parties may not have an interest, but where they could actually suffer a detriment.

---

[343] Adoption and Children Act 2002, https://www.legislation.gov.uk/ukpga/2002/38/contents.

[344] Or viceversa, but females identifying as males do not *ipso facto* access sex based rights, as men only have sex based extra-legal priviliges, and those remain unattainable to women, no matter how the identify. Probably the only advantage a woman who identitfies as a man can access is reducing the risk of rape and sexual assault, but this only provided a full medical and surgical transition is performed. In fact "transmen" are much more likely to undergo medical and surgical transition than "transwomen" and you never see a feminine woman arguing she is a male, as you see men with a beard and intact male genitalia (about which they are quite graphicly specific) arguing they are women. See https://twitter.com/LilyLilyMaynard/status/841807616212893696/photo/1.

The *L. v Lithuania* case concerned a FtM woman who brought an application for a breach of Article 3 (quickly dismissed by the Court)[345] and Article 8, as the law in Lithuania did not provide a straightforward path to SRS and without it, it was impossible to change all IDs, including the personal code which is coded differently for males and females. In the submission the applicant makes a revealing comment, actually quite common in gender identity case law. This is the claim:

> The applicant further emphasised that, although he had been able to change his name to a gender-neutral form, the law did not provide for a change in the personal code of preoperative transsexuals (see paragraph 28 above). As a result he had forgone numerous opportunities in many areas, such as, employment, health care, social security, freedom of movement, business transactions, socialising and personal development in order to avoid hostility and taunts. He had thus been condemned to legal and social ostracism because he looked male but his personal documents identified him as a woman.

The solution for victimisation and harassment on the basis of gender reassignment is not to change the law so that one's "psychological sex" is recognised. To the extent that one still looks like their birth sex, the hostility and taunts may persist. Clearly it is the belief and/or its expression that require proper protection. Not embedding the belief in the law as if it was a material reality, compelling others to maintain the misrepresentation of one's sex. Nonetheless by now the Court is not even addressing the arguments on the merits, and applies the *Goodwin* standard (so still post-operative transsexuals, the GRA has not started to bite yet), finding a breach of Article 8 because of a delay in the approval of the law that would have allowed the applicant to have the final surgery in Lithuania (a mastectomy had already been performed) and therefore apply for a male personal code. The fact that Lithuania was willing to cover the cost of the surgery abroad was not enough.

In the 2009 *Schlumpf v Switzerland* case, the applicant, a MtF man, argued the two year waiting period between a diagnosis of transsexualism and SRS, a mandatory clause in health insurance policies, was a breach of Article 6 (Right to a Fair Hearing) and Article 8. The applicant had

---

[345] Matteo Bassetti, "Human Rights Bodies' Adjudication of Trans People's Rights: Shifting the Narrative from the Right to Private Life to Cruel and Inhuman or Degrading Treatment," European Journal of Legal Studies, 12(2) (2022): 291-325 argues that trans rights cases should be brought and considered under Article 3 ECHR.

appealed the decision of the insurer but the Federal Court had found in favour of the insurers and denied the right to a public hearing. On this more technical point the Court unanimously found in favour of the applicant. On the Article 8 claim the Court also found for the applicant, as the specific circumstances of the case (the relatively advanced age, 67 of the applicant specifically) and a non-defined set of "medical advances that had been made in identifying 'genuine' transsexualism" should have resulted in a finding in favour of the applicant by the domestic court. We can see the Court here slightly shifting its position with respect to surgery, which basically becomes a matter about "the most intimate aspects of private life" in which the Court has to err always in favour of the applicants and their self-selected medical experts.

Refusal to grant pernission to obtain SRS was also the issue in *Y.Y. v Turkey*, though the applicant was a FtM. Usual claim of breach of Article 8. The background evidences a homophobic family and a young lesbian who in the past would have been described as a tomboy:

> The applicant's mother stated that as a child her daughter had played mainly with boys and as an adolescent had told her mother that she felt more like a boy and wanted to be one. The applicant's mother had therefore consulted psychologists, who had expressed the view that her daughter would be happier if she could live as a man, a view which the applicant's mother shared. The applicant's older brother also said that his sister had played with boys when she was a child, had started to behave like a boy during adolescence and *had had girlfriends* [emphasis added], and that she had been determined to undergo gender reassignment by means of surgery.

The main interest of this case is the changing attitude towards sterilisation and/or SRS: whether it is legitimate for States to impose it as a condition to change sex on the civil register, and whether it is legitimate to impose conditions on obtaining SRS permission. On the face of it these are contrasting and opposite issues. And from the facts and the law applicable to the case, the issue was with the conditions imposed to obtain SRS, as the applicant was refused permission to have surgery for more than five years. The applicable law is Article 40 of the Turkish Civil Code:[346] The language of the article seems

[346] Turkish Civil Code Article 40, https://av-saimincekas.com/en/tmk/turk-medeni-kanunu-madde-40/. Gender Reassignment Article 40–Anyone who wants to change their gender can request permission from the court to change their gender by applying personally. However, in order for the permission to be granted, the

ambiguous enough to warrant both interpretations: either that being sterile is a condition to obtain permission for surgery, or that having undergone surgery and therefore being sterile is a condition for obtaining the change of legal gender, which is obtained only through permission being granted by the Court. In actual fact, the law in Turkey does impose the requirement of sterility in order to access SRS, opening up a space to argue that this form of forced sterility was unacceptable as a requirement to access the right of medical and legal gender reassignment. The rationale for the requirement is offered by the Turkish government itself in the course of the proceedings:

> In view of the seriousness and the irreversible nature of gender reassignment surgery, the uncertainty that remained as to the necessity of such operations in treating gender identity disorders, and the risk of such operations becoming commonplace, with the associated dangers, the State should be allowed a wide margin of appreciation in regulating gender reassignment and determining the criteria which individuals must meet before undergoing gender reassignment surgery.
>
> In order to determine whether the statutory requirements for gender reassignment were fully satisfied, the Mersin District Court had sought to verify that all the prior conditions for the authorisation of gender reassignment had been met, and in particular the condition of being permanently unable to procreate. It had based its conclusions on specialist knowledge and findings.

It is worth reporting the Court assessment extensively to witness how the shift towards self-identification is endorsed, dispensing of the requirement to undergo surgery, even if the Court still ostensibly refers to the right of gender recognition for "post-operative" transsexuals:

> 105. [...] In that regard the Court observes that the possibility for transgender persons to undergo gender reassignment treatment exists in many European countries, as does legal recognition of their new gender identity. It further notes that the regulations or practice applicable in a

---

applicant must be over the age of eighteen and not married; In addition, he is a transsexual and must document the necessity of gender reassignment in terms of mental health and his permanent deprivation of reproductive ability with an official health board report to be obtained from a training and research hospital. If it is confirmed by the official health board report that a gender reassignment surgery has been performed in accordance with the purpose and medical methods, depending on the permission given, the court decides to make the necessary correction in the population registry.

> number of countries that recognise gender reassignment make legal recognition of the new preferred gender contingent, either implicitly or explicitly, on gender reassignment surgery and/or on the inability to procreate ...
>
> In that connection it emphasises that, in the Appendix to Recommendation CM/Rec(2010)5 on measures to combat discrimination on grounds of sexual orientation or gender identity, the Committee of Ministers of the Council of Europe stated that prior requirements, including changes of a physical nature, for legal recognition of a gender reassignment, should be regularly reviewed in order to remove abusive requirements [..] Furthermore, in Resolution 1728 (2010) on discrimination on the basis of sexual orientation and gender identity, the Parliamentary Assembly of the Council of Europe called on the member States to address the specific discrimination and human rights violations faced by transgender persons and, in particular, to ensure in legislation and in practice their right to official documents that reflected the individual's preferred gender identity, without any prior obligation to undergo sterilisation or other medical procedures such as gender reassignment surgery or hormone therapy [...]
>
> 111. The Court also observes that some member States have recently amended their legislation or practice regarding access to gender reassignment treatment and the legal recognition of gender reassignment by abolishing the infertility/sterility requirement ...

The Court also noted that it is arbitrary for the law to require a person to prove sterility in order to access SRS which results in sterility anyway. However, what the argument of the Court accomplishes is to inch further towards the position that is not legitimate for the State to require "any" medical intervention in order to change one's gender:

> 119. In any event, the Court does not deem it necessary to rule on the question of possible access by the applicant to medical treatment that would have enabled him to satisfy this requirement [sterility], since it considers that due respect for his physical integrity precluded any obligation for him to undergo this type of treatment.

The right to physical integrity now provides the fourth pillar, after the right to a private life, the right to self-determination, and the right to human dignity, for granting individuals the right to choose one's gender and have it recognised by the State as the same as one's sex without any hormonal or surgical modification, at the complete discretion of the individual. The edifice of gender theory is almost complete.[347] A crucial element was to decouple sterility from SRS which is in effect impossible unless fertility is preserved through removal of sperm or ova before the surgical procedure and the use of surrogate women in order to undergo the pregnancy and birth.

It is a salutary reminder that the main rationale for allowing transsexuals to change their sex legally was the pain and suffering they went through to approximate the opposite sex. One struggles to understand why the demand to "change" their sex should be accepted when the rationale not only does not apply anymore, but is conceptualised as a human right violation in itself. In fact now the goal of the Council of Europe is the "full depathologisation of the transgender person."[348] This goal sets up a false binarism, between those who want to normalise being transgender and those who want to consider them ill. This binarism is replete with contradictions. The first one of course is that if it is not a pathology, why should any of them undergo surgery not as a form of plastic elective surgery, but as a "life-saving procedure"? Why are parents told that unless they agree to give their child puberty blockers, they will have a dead child?[349] The second one is that it creates a motive for presenting any critique of gender theory as being anti-trans without ever having to engage with the criticism on the merits. Those who disagree that gender identity exists do not *ipso facto* think that anyone who believes that is ill, or crazy,

---

347 See Peter Dunne, "YY v Turkey: Infertility as a Pre-condition for Gender Confirmation Surgery," Medical Law Review 23 (4) (2015): 646-658 at 650: "in recent years, there has been a growing realisation that transgender persons, like all others in society, do have a right to 'physical and moral security.'" The author quotes Art. 3 (1) (d) of Malta's Gender Identity, Gender Expression and Sex Characteristics Act 2015 which specifically guarantees the right to "bodily integrity and physical autonomy," https://legislation.mt/eli/cap/540/eng/pdf.

348 Council of Europe Steering Committee on Anti-discrimination, Diversity and Inclusion, "Thematic Report on Legal Gender Recognition," CM/Rec (2010) 5, 16, https://rm.coe.int/thematic-report-on-legal-gender-recognition-in-europe-2022/1680a729b3.

349 The narrative of the "better a live daughter than a dead son" has been shamefully peddled by trans rights organisations and their representatives. In this piece the claim is reported as made by Susie Green, former CEO of Mermaids, a charity for transgender children and their parents. As already noted, Susie Green took her 16 years old child to Thailand to have sex reassignment surgery. "Suicide by trans-identified children in England and Wales," Transgender Trend Blog, October 9, 2018, https://www.transgendertrend.com/suicide-by-trans-identified-children-in-england-and-wales/.

or mentally defective. Only and simply that this person holds a belief they do not, in good conscience, share. The issue is not with a male holding the belief of having a female brain, but with the law imposing this belief as a reality and forcing all third parties to replace reality with this belief. And as I have noted repeatedly, women are more affected by this demand, as they would by any demand made by a male not to use their own brain, but to trust a male instead (a person that they cannot help perceiving as a male).

A.P., Garçon and Nicot v France[350] concerns three MtF men whose gender identity was not recognised by the French State for different reasons ("A.P." had had surgery abroad and refused to submit to a health assessment as required by French law; Garçon could not substantiate the claim of suffering from gender dysphoria and Picot refused to have surgery, as required by law to have a female gender recognised by law). In the presentation of the facts there are the usual claims of "behaved like a girl and his physical appearance had always been very feminine," "been aware from a very young age of belonging to the female gender," "dressed as a woman and was perceived by others as a woman" [before medical and hormonal treatment], "once his daughter was grown up he had adapted his appearance and social conduct to match his female gender identity." Especially noteworthy is that Nicot, the third applicant who refused to have any surgery or medical treatment, was said to have claimed that:

> While most of the documents he used in everyday life reflected his gender identity, this was not the case of his civil-status documents, passport, driving licence, vehicle registration papers or entry in the national identity register. As a result, he was constantly obliged to refer to his transgender identity, to the detriment of his private life.[351]

It defies belief that the applicant thought that it was the male identity documents to give away the transgender status, as opposed to the male physical appearance. Also noteworthy that transgender status is presented as a detriment to private life. Privacy rights serve to protect information not otherwise available, not to force individuals to modify their perception of reality. If a protected characteristic, such as sex, age, race, is easily perceptible, the task of human rights law is to prevent discrimination on

[350] *A.P., Garçon and Nicot v France*, Application Nos. 79885/12, 52471/12, and 52596/13, Judgment of 6 April 2017.

[351] Although Nicot was a MtF man, unusually the Court uses male pronouns, and not the female ones in accordance with the acquired gender, as it had done since the 1980s.

the basis of that protected characteristic, and nothing else. It is also noteworthy that by now the link between gender and sex has been completely severed, to the extent that individuals can request the sex in their documents, including birth certificates, be amended because of a claim based on their gender identity. In order to accept this claim, one needs to accept that gender identity and sex are both different and interchangeable.

As *Goodwin* signalled the recognition of post-operative transsexuals, this case signals the recognition of the much more open category of transgender people, i.e. people who request the recognition of their gender without any body modification or medical diagnosis. The Court reviewed, as it is wont to do when it intends to change its previous jurisprudence, the state of international and domestic laws on the matter, namely in Council of Europe countries.[352]

---

[352] It emerges from a document entitled "Trans Rights Europe Map 2016," published on 22 April 2016 by the non-governmental organisation Transgender Europe (unfortunately the website does not seem to be active anymore). See also Council of Europe Commissioner of Human Rights, "Discrimination on grounds of sexual orientation and gender identity in Europe," Council of Europe Publishing, June 2011, https://rm.coe.int/discrimination-on-grounds-of-sexual-orientation-and-gender-identity-in/16809079e2; and the comparative-law materials referred to in the judgment in *Y.Y. v Turkey,* that at that time legal recognition of the gender identity of transgender persons was not possible in seven Council of Europe member States (Albania, Andorra, Cyprus, Liechtenstein, Monaco, San Marino and the former Yugoslav Republic of Macedonia).
The document also makes clear that such recognition was subject to a legal requirement to undergo sterilisation in twenty-four Council of Europe member States (Armenia, Azerbaijan, Belgium, Bosnia and Herzegovina, Bulgaria, Croatia, Czech Republic, Finland, France, Georgia, Greece, Latvia, Lithuania, Luxembourg, Montenegro, Norway, Romania, the Russian Federation, Serbia, Slovakia, Slovenia, Switzerland, Turkey and Ukraine). It was possible in sixteen member States without a legal requirement to undergo sterilisation (Austria, Denmark, Estonia, Germany, Hungary, Iceland, Ireland, Italy, Malta, Moldova, the Netherlands, Poland, Portugal, Spain, Sweden and the United Kingdom). France and Norway (following a Law of 17 June 2016) have since joined the second category. The number of member States in which recognition is not subject to a legal requirement to undergo sterilisation has thus risen to eighteen (nineteen in Europe, counting Belarus), compared with twenty-two countries in which it is. In several of the countries concerned, the abolition of this requirement is the result of recent legal developments (an Administrative Court judgment of 27 February 2009 in Austria; a Law of 15 March 2010 in Portugal; a Federal Constitutional Court judgment of

The Court is clear that to impose any requirement as to medical, hormonal or surgical modification is a potential violation of the applicants' Article 8 rights, which, far from being negative rights of non interference, are now fully reconceptualised as a positive duty on States to facilitate gender reassignment on a "on demand" basis. The entire rationale of the early jurisprudence of the Court, "the great personal cost" mentioned by the *Goodwin* Court, which justified demanding that society bear "a certain inconvenience," falls away completely. If the transgender individual is bearing no cost at all, on which basis should society bear a certain inconvenience?

The *S. V. v Italy* case[353] concerned a MtF man who claimed a breach of Article 8 because Italian law 164 of 1982 required surgery in order to apply for a change of sex in court and that, following a Presidential Decree in 2000, first names always had to reflect the sex of the bearer, so that the applicant had to wait for surgery and court authorisation before the change of first name. The case did not concern a requirement of sterilisation, as the previous one, but simply a challenge to the legal process one had to follow to obtain a sex change. It is true that to require SRS is a restrictive reading of Law 164, which refers only to medical OR surgical treatment; however, since the applicant intended to have surgery, the restrictive reading did not affect the merits of the application. The Court found a violation of Article 8 on account of the delay in the judicial proceedings for the approval of the gender reassignment post-surgery. The Court found violations of Article 8 in all subsequent cases raising similar issues, except *Y. v Poland*,[354] where a request to have birth sex amended in the long form birth certificate, which is a confidential document in Poland, was within

11 January 2011 in Germany; a Law of 22 May 2013 in Sweden; a Law of 18 December 2013 in the Netherlands; a Law of 11 June 2014 in Denmark; a Law of 1 April 2015 in Malta; a Law of 15 July 2015 in Ireland; a Court of Cassation judgment of 21 July 2015 in Italy; a Law of 17 June 2016 in Norway; and a Law of 12 October 2016 in France). It appears also that a number of member States are currently reviewing or intend to review the conditions for legal recognition of the identity of transgender persons in order to remove any that appear unreasonable; Council of Europe Steering Committee for Human Rights: Report on the implementation of Recommendation CM/Rec(2010)5 of the Committee of Ministers to member States on measures to combat discrimination on grounds of sexual orientation or gender identity – CDDH(2013)R77 Addendum VI, 21 March 2013, https://www.coe.int/en/web/sogi/rec-2010-5.

[353] *S.V. v Italy*, Application No. 55216/08,Judgment of 11 October 2018.

[354] *Y. v Poland*, Application No. 74131/14, Judgment of 17 May, 2022.

the margin of appreciation for Poland to reject, since the short form birth certificate was amended upon request of the applicant, a FtM woman.

The last goal for gender identity theorists and trans rights activists was to get the ECHR to completely dispose of the requirement of a diagnosis of gender dysphoria or gender identity disorder and to restrict legal gender change to an administrative procedure, without the need for the involvement of a court or a tribunal.[355]

This the Court accomplished in *X. and Y. v Romania*.[356] The two applicants, the first of whom resided in the UK, were FtM women. The first applicant argued that to request a transgender individual to undergo SRS before obtaining a change in the civil record, as required by the Romanian court, "discriminated in favour of 'cisgender' persons and was against Article 14 and Protocol 12of the ECHR."[357] The applicant obtained a GRC in the UK, therefore part of the application concerned the issues arising from having ID documents reporting conflicting information, female sex for Romania and male sex for the UK.[358] The second applicant,

---

[355] As quoted by the Court, "Chapter V of the World Health Organisation's International Classification of Diseases" (ICD-10, no. F64.0) titled "Mental and behavioural disorders," under the category "Disorders of adult personality and behaviour," sub-category "Gender identity disorders." See also Recommendation of the Committee of Ministers to member states on measures to combat discrimination on grounds of sexual orientation or gender identity, CM/Rec (2010)5, 15, https://www.coe.int/en/web/sogi/rec-2010-5. In *X. and Y. v Romania*, the Court cites a report and index by the NGO Transgender Europe listing the countries where one can obtain a legal change of gender without any medical intervention, i.e. Denmark, Ireland, Iceland, Luxemburg, Malta and Norway (para 88 of the judgment). In his 2018 Report "Protection against Violence and Discriminaton Based on Sexual Orientation and Gender Identity," A/73/52, https://digitallibrary.un.org/record/1639754?ln=en, the IE on SOGI recommends that gender recognition should: "Be based solely on the free and informed consent of the applicant without requirements such as medical and/or psychological or other certifications that could be unreasonable or pathologizing."

[356] *X. and Y. v Romania,* Application Nos. 2145/16 and 20607/16, Judgment of 19 January 2021. Full judgment available in French.

[357] Para. 22, own translation.

[358] The case could have raised issues of EU law. A EU Parliament Report from 2010 reports as of yet no case law on transgender individuals' freedom of movement and mutual recognition of gender reassignment: see Transgender Persons' Rights in EU Member States, 12, https://www.europarl.europa.eu/RegData/etudes/note/join/2010/425621/IPOL-LIBE_NT%282010%29425621_EN.pdf. In a more recent report, there is no

who had also challenged the requirement of SRS, eventually underwent the surgical procedure and obtained new ID documents with a male marker, and an amendment of the birth certificate. Submission from the parties evidenced that Romanian jurisprudence on the requirement to undergo SRS was inconsistent.[359] The applicants argued that, not only there should be no requirement of SRS in order to obtain a legal change of gender, but there should be no requirement of medical treatment at all. Clearly if one argues for no treatment, the need for a diagnosis becomes less relevant, to the point of losing its raison d'être. Additionally, the applicants argued that even the requirement to a court application to obtain a legal change of gender constituted a violation of their Article 8 rights. The presence of the Office of the High Commissioner for Human Rights, Transgender Europe, ILGA Europe and Accept[360] as interveners, evidences that this case had been chosen as another test case to push the demands of gender identity theory (in this case the demand for self-ID with no qualifying criteria at all, as recommended by the IE on SOGI in 2018, which are repeated verbatim by the OHCHR), as *Goodwin* had been for gender recognition for post-operative transsexuals and *A.P., Garçon and Nicot* had been for dispensing with the requirement for surgery. In the end the Court does not engage fully with these arguments, simply noting that the applicants had been forced by the Romanian courts to choose between their bodily integrity and their gender identity, and that Romania had not justified through a proper balancing exercise the rights of the applicants against the public interest.

The only topic on which for now the Court has been strict in its interpretation of the law, keeping in due account both the scientific consensus and the rights of third parties (specifically, children) is on the demand by transgender individuals to register parentage in accordance with their gender identity and not their sex and therefore their reproductive

---

indication that the issue of mutual recognition of change of gender within the EU, given the different requirements in different EU countries, can be litigated unless there is an effect on social rights such as pension, or entry into a country. The issue of documents showing different sexes is not raised: European Commission, Legal Gender Recognition in the EU: The Journeys of Trans People Towards Full Equality, 204 https://igualtat.gencat.cat/web/.content/Ambits/LGBTI/normativaLGBTI/Document-EU-autodeterminacio-de-genere-2020.pdf. For an upcoming case in the CJEU where this issue will be debated, see next section.

[359] Para. 78.

[360] Accept is a Romanian LGBT rights NGO that represent Romania at ILGA Europe https://acceptromania.ro/.

roles as mothers or fathers. This line of development of gender identity theory clarifies that the ultimate goal of the theory is to deprive the category of sex of any significance and eliminate any criterion for the recognition of one's gender identity, not to protect the rights of transgender people. Clearly, having a male gender identity is incompatible with the fact of conceiving and giving birth to a child, unless one deprives these acts and these reproductive roles of any significance. The key case in this regard is *O.H. and G.H. v Germany* from July 2023.[361] "O.H." was a FtM woman who had a child after the legal change of gender and demanded to be recorded as the father in the register of births and in the birth certificate, and also that the child's birth certificate did not indicate the sex of the child nor the name of the sperm donor. The Federal Court rejected the request, and motivated its compliance with the Convention by stating that it was within their margin of appreciation to register "O.H." as the mother because at issue was not the sex of the applicant but the reproductive function being exercised. Therefore the State could register "O.H."as the mother because a person registered as a male could give birth and therefore be legally a mother. Underlying this argumentation is the acceptance that biological sex and legal sex are not equivalent. This is a compromise that is not acceptable to gender theorists and trans rights activists (as the very existence of this case, and others, such as the Freddie McConnell one, prove).

The Parliamentary Assembly of the Council of Europe passed a resolution in 2018 on "rainbow families" (there is something quite distasteful about this infantilising language).[362] The resolution recites in paragraph 4.6:

> In addition to the recommendations already adopted by the Assembly in *Resolution 2048 (2015)* and *Resolution 2191 (2017)* regarding the effects of legal gender recognition of transgender and intersex people on their access to or the continuity of their civil partnership or marriage, and regarding the rights of spouses and children, provide for transgender parents' gender identity to be correctly recorded on their children's birth certificates, and ensure that persons who use legal gender markers other than male or female are able to have their partnerships and their relationships with their children recognised without discrimination;

---

[361] *O.H. and G.H. v Germany*, Application Nos. 53568/18 and 54741/18, Judgment of 4 April 2023.

[362] Council of Europe Parliamentary Assembly, "Private and Family Life: Achieving Equality Regardless of Sexual Orientation," Resolution 2239 (2018) https://assembly.coe.int/nw/xml/XRef/Xref-XML2HTML-en.asp?fileid=25166&lang=en .

The Court cites this resolution as the applicable law, together with the CRC and the 2020 Report of the Special Rapporteur on the Right to Privacy.[363] The right to privacy report also recommends self-ID of the parents' gender identity on birth certificates.[364]As mother and father are not gender identities, it is to be presumed that this recommendation does not necessarily affect the correct recording of parentage on birth registries and birth certificates.[365] The "O.H." case also saw interveners in the proceedings, namely TGEU, ILGA,[366] Bundesvereinigung Trans and Professor Sally Hines for the applicants;[367] this time they are joined by several interveners for the Government.[368]

Sometimes it is proper to provide a feminist reading of a case, and this is one such example. Reproductive rights were, after women got their basic civil rights, the feminist battle of the 1900s. Giving women the right to decide on their own body was for women, the *sine qua non conditio* for acquiring full autonomy as human beings. This battle could be fought because women could organise together as a political class on the basis of their sex, and did not have to provide a platform to males whose idea of womanhood is submission and who would never be at risk of an unwanted

---

363 Human Rights Council, "Report of the Special Rapporteur on the Right to Privacy, 24 March 2020, A/HRC/43/52 https://documents-dds-ny.un.org/doc/UNDOC/GEN/G20/071/66/PDF/G2007166.pdf?OpenElement.

364 If both parents identify as neutrois how will the integrity of records be maintained?

365 The Court reports a French case where a child conceived through surrogate pregnancy had their MtF male parent described as the mother on the birth certificate. The French court appealed to the self-determination right under Articles 8 14 of the ECHR, *Madame C. v Madame N.*, Cour d'Appel de Toulouse, 9 February 2022, Case No. 16/04/2022, No. RG 20/03128,
https://www.law.cornell.edu/women-and-justice/resource/toulouse_cour_d%E2%80%99appel_9_fevrier_2022_no._20/03128#.

366 The case summary by ILGA is especially biased: "O.H. and G.H. against Germany," ILGA Europe, June 25, 2019, https://ilga-europe.org/case-law/o-h-and-g-h-against-germany/.

367 The usual interveners with the usual addition of the local NGO, "Bundesverainigung Trans* e.V."
https://www.queer-refugees.de/5812-2/2309/bundesvereinigung-trans-e-v/.

368 European Centre for Law and Justice https://eclj.org/ and Ordo Juris
https://en.ordoiuris.pl/ and other national NGOs.

pregnancy, no matter how many men they had sex with, before or after SRS.[369]

Only recognising women as a sex class with the right to organise politically around that defining characteristic gave women the power to coalesce around certain battles for basic rights. It is true that not all women wanted those rights, for religious or political reasons. It is also true that some women did not need those rights. But no-one ever argued that reproductive rights were not women's rights because some women are against abortions, or they are celibate, or they are lesbians, or they are infertile, or they underwent hysterectomy, or they are post-menopausal. In those more enlightened times, as it turns out, women were at least guaranteed the basic right to organise and fight for their rights, without men telling them they did not exist as a sex class, so what they wanted were "people's rights."[370]

In more general terms, the reproductive work that women do was the basis for the oldest form of labour exploitation, if one wants to adopt a Marxist analysis.[371] This also means that discrimination on the basis of women's reproductive function is one of the most common forms of discrimination. Practices such asking female job applicants whether they are married or intend to have children,[372] making female workers sign blank resignation letters to be used if they get pregnant,[373] firing women while they are pregnant or after giving birth,[374] even forcing workers to undergo

---

[369] Andrea Long Chu, a male who identifies as trans, wrote "Getting f*cked makes you female because f*cked is what a female is." Andrea Long Chu, Females (London: Verso Books, 2019).

[370] In the campaign to legalise abortion in Ireland, Amnesty International claimed that to refer to pregnant people was more inclusive because not all those who can get pregnant are women. https://www.amnesty.ie/itstime/.

[371] Frederick Engels, The Origin of the Family, Private Property and the State, Translated by Alick West, Dona Torr (London: Lawrence and Wishart, 1941).

[372] Jon Heuvel, "Employers must stop asking women whether they plan to have children,"The Times, 22 February 2018, https://www.thetimes.co.uk/article/employers-must-stop-asking-women-whether-they-plan-to-have-children-0j7m29vpz.

[373] This is still a practice in Italy for example. Here is an article about female agricultural workers forced to sign blanked resignation letters, to be used if they become pregnant. https://bari.corriere.it/notizie/economia/21_luglio_08/cgil-donne-campi-costrette-firmare-dimissioni-bianco-3c7528a6-dfe4-11eb-bcd1-476f2dc377d1.shtml.

[374] According to World Bank data in 38 countries it is still legal to fire women for getting pregnant: Olena Mykhlalchenko and Isabel Santagostino Recavarren, "In

hysterectomies to guarantee no loss of work because of pregnancy/birth.[375] All these practices affect only women because of their sex.

The fact that some women wish to present as their stereotypical idea of how a man should look like, while retaining the ability to conceive and birth a child, does not mean that all those rights lose their status as women's rights. In fact the demand that abortion must not be called a women's right anymore because not all people who need an abortion are women illustrates perfectly how gender identity theory affects all women and it is not just about a tiny minority of people, whose demands can be accommodated without any effect on women. Because of a statistically invisible percentage of females[376] who reject their womanhood, we are told that we cannot use the terms women and mothers to describe those who give birth, or that abortion is not a women's right. In fact the Abortion Legislation Reform Bill 2023 in the Parliament of Western Australia never mentions the word woman.[377] And if women complain that these language choices affect their rights they are told they are transphobic, at the very least evidencing that there is a clash of rights, or a clash of political demands. In fact, it seems that we are not allowed to call these rights women's rights not because not all those who get pregnant are women, but because "transwomen" do not want the word woman to be used to define only females.

Decoupling the status of womanhood from the reproductive function of motherhood also allows advancing the demand to use women (and here

---

38 countries, women can still be fired for being pregnant" World Bank Blogs, 31 May 2021, https://blogs.worldbank.org/developmenttalk/38-countries-women-can-still-be-fired-being-pregnant#:~:text=Yet%20in%2020%25%20of%20economies, pregnant%20workers%20in%20their%20laws.

375 Still a practice in certain parts of the world, Abhijit Mulye, "Over 13,000 female sugarcane workers in Beed have undergone uterus removal surgery, says probe panel," The New Indian Express, August 29, 2019, https://www.newindianexpress.com/nation/2019/Aug/29/over-13000-female-sugarcane-labourers-in-beed-have-undergone-uterus-removal-surgery-says-probe-pan-2026166.html#:~:text=%22Information%20on%2082%2C309%20women%20in,25%20too%20has%20undergone%20hysterectomy.

376 Worldwide surely so low as being impossible to calculate, maybe a thousand "transmen" who have a child, if that many, over circa 3.8 billion women, giving a percentage of 0.00002%.

377 Abortion Legislation Reform Bill 2023, Parliament of Western Australia, https://www.parliament.wa.gov.au/parliament/bills.nsf/BillProgressPopup?openForm&ParentUNID=9D7ECED888BE9ED3482589D4001FA98A.

everybody is clear what is intended by women) merely as reproductive means for another couple through the misleadingly named surrogacy. Healthy young women (never "transmen," strangely), who have already given birth are paid or otherwise engaged to provide a child for rich couples or individuals who either cannot or don't want to undergo a pregnancy. We already know that the contracts of surrogacy effectively deprive the expectant woman of the right to terminate the pregnancy (the penalties imposed against this breach of contract make it unlikely the woman is capable of making this choice) and, conversely, compel her to abort some or all of the embryos if the clients decide so. Effectively surrogacy contracts deprive women of their reproductive rights for the duration of the contract (up and including dictating whether she can have sexual intercourse with her husband, as most contracts insist she is an heterosexual married woman, and provide for the husband to sign the contract as well, as if the woman did not have full legal personality).[378] If reproductive rights were properly described as rights that are specific to women as the sex who does all the reproductive work, it would be more difficult to allow men to over-rule a right that he, as a man, should have no power to control or limit, and this was the rationale of all laws on pregnancy termination. It was, by law, only and always the woman's choice. Reframing it as a person's choice may not have consequences for women, but women are not even allowed to raise the issue of consequences. In this as in all matters concerning gender identity, debating what consequences such a momentous change in the way we look at the human experience has become society's strongest taboo.

The Court is for now not willing to cross this last frontier of gender identity theory, appealing to the margin of appreciation to be granted of Germany, in a stance familiar to us from the early jurisprudence, pre-*Goodwin*. For how long?

The Jurisprudence of the ECJ/CJEU

The case law of the ECJ/CJEU is more limited, given the jurisdictional limitations imposed by the subject matter and the applicable law. There are

---

[378] This is a sample surrogacy contract from the State of Oregon, https://media.npr.org/documents/2015/july/Surrogacy_contract_sample_070215.pdf. Oregon allows surrogacy contracts with no restriction as to the identity of the intended parents. The cost of surrogacy in Oregon is between $130,000 and §180,000. https://samelovesurrogacy.com/. Surrogacy is probably the only area in which clarity around sex has not been affected by gender identity theory.

some interesting judgments concerning employment relations. We have already considered the case *P. v S. and Cornwall County Council* of 1996, on the interpretation of Council Directive 76/207/EEC.[379] "P." was a MtF man who had been dismissed from Cornwall County Council. The claim was sex discrimination. The question was referred to the ECJ as the Industrial Tribunal was unsure whether the Directive applied to transsexual individuals on the basis of their status as people seeking or having completed gender reassignment. While the Court confirmed that discrimination on the basis of gender reassignment is covered by the Directive, it also confirmed, as we have already seen, that the proper comparator is an individual of the sex the complainant without the characteristic of gender reassignment.[380] From the point of view of gender identity theory, this case belongs to prehistory; suffice it to say that the reference point in the jurisrpudence of the ECHR is the *Rees* case.

K.B. v National Health Service Pensions Agency,[381] from 2004, concerned the pension rights for transsexual partners (specifically, the FtM female partner of "K.B.," who was a woman). The UK court referred to the ECJ the question for a prelimary ruling whether "the exclusion of the female-to-male transsexual partner of a female member of the National Health Service Pension Scheme, which limits the material dependant's benefit to her widower, constitute sex discrimination in contravention of Article 141 EC and Directive 75/117 [sex equality]."[382]

---

379 Council Directive of 9 February 1976 on the implementation of the principle of equal treatment for men and women as regards access to employment, vocational training and promotion, and working conditions, O.J. 1976 L 39, p. 40, https://eur-lex.europa.eu/legal-content/EN/TXT/PDF/?uri=CELEX:61994CJ0013&from=HU.

380Following this case, the UK passed the Sex Discrimination (Gender Reassignment) Regulations 1999, https://www.legislation.gov.uk/uksi/1999/1102/contents/made. The resolution followed a debate on 21 September 2018 by Jonas Gunnarsson of the Swedish Socialists, Democrats and Greens Group https://pace.coe.int/pdf/325180443987ee44cca30f867d40fbffdf368f9bcd902af518765efee56f07b1/doc.%2014620.pdf.

381 *K.B. v National Health Service Pensions Agency and Secretary of State for Health*, Judgment of 7 January 2004, C-117/01, https://curia.europa.eu/juris/liste.jsf?language=en&num=C-117/01

382 The case is discussed also in Mark Bell, "Gender Identity and Sexual Orientation: Alternative Pathways to EU's Equality Law?," The American Journal of Comparative Law, 60 (2012): 127-147. As the author states: "Queer theory reminds us that any categorization carries the risk of being a straightjacket, which ultimately produces insiders and outsiders, marginalizing those who deviate far

The ECHR had just issued the *Goodwin* judgment, which had found the UK legislation preventing transsexuals from amending their documents and marrying, in breach of article 8 and article 12. The ECJ found a breach on the basis that:

> Article 141 EC, in principle, precludes legislation, such as that at issue before the national court, which, in breach of the ECHR, prevents a couple such as K.B. and R. from fulfilling the marriage requirement which must be met for one of them to be able to benefit from part of the pay of the other. It is for the national court to determine whether in a case such as that in the main proceedings a person in K.B.'s situation can rely on Article 141 EC in order to gain recognition of her right to nominate her partner as the beneficiary of a survivor's pension.

The *Sarah Margaret Richards v Secretary of State for Work and Pensions*[383] case, from 2006, concerned the pension rights of a MtF post-operative man. UK law permitted different pensionable ages for males (65) and females (60).[384] Richards had requested pension rights in 2002, upon turning 60, and had of course been refused. In the appeal the Secretary of State for Work and Pension had correctly noted that this was not a case of unlawful sex discrimination, as the correct comparator for a male with the protected characteristic of gender reassignment is a man without the protected characteristic of gender reassignment, who equally would have been refused a pension at the age of 60. In 2004, the GRA changed the legal situation, allowing pension rights to be granted at 60 for MtF men with a GRC. Richards had undergone surgery but not applied for a GRC when possible to do so.[385] The Court in its judgment stated that Art 4(1) of Council Directive 79/7/ precludes legislation that discriminates against a person on the basis of gender reassignment, reversing the comparator issue, so that the comparator for Richards is not a male without the characteristic of gender reassigment but a female without the

---

enough from the social norm." This is an invitation to allow any claim to be considered acceptable, because no criteria can be imposed upon the recognition of a definition of gender identity as the applicable one.

[383] *Sarah Margaret Richards v Secretary of State for Work and Pensions*, Judgment of 27 April 2006, C-423/04 https://eur-lex.europa.eu/legal-content/EN/TXT/?uri=CELEX%3A62004CJ0423.

[384] Schedule 4, Part 1, paragraph 1 of the Pensions Act 1995 established the pensionable age for men at 65 and for women at 60, as allowed by Article 7(1) of Directive 79//7, which creates an exception to the duty of non-discrimination based on sex of Article 4(1) of the Directive.

[385] Doing so would have allowed Richards to collect the pension from the time the GRC was granted, as per Schedule 5, Part 2, paragraph 7(3) of the GRA 2004.

characteristic of gender reassignment,[386] effectively modifying the domestic law requirement for recognising a change of "gender" (from obtaining a GRC to undergoing surgery and identifying as the opposite sex). It is the sort of faulty reasoning one is forced to follow to make the law accommodate a fiction without admitting it is a fiction, affecting inevitably the issue of the comparator:[387]

> [...] in accordance with settled case-law, the right not to be discriminated against on grounds of sex is one of the fundamental human rights the observance of which the Court has a duty to ensure. The scope of Directive 79/7 cannot thus be confined simply to discrimination based on the fact that a person is of one or other sex. In view of its purpose and the nature of the rights which it seeks to safeguard, the scope of that directive is also such as to apply to discrimination arising from the gender reassignment of the person concerned.

More than 10 years separate the previous case from *M.B. v Secretary of State for Work and Pension*,[388] from 2018[389] but the facts of the case are similar, concerning a MtF transsexual and pension rights, still governed by Council Directive 79/7/EC. "M.B.," a MtF transsexual, applied for a pension at the age of 60 though not in possession of a GRC (requesting one would have forced an annulment as the Same Sex Marriage Act had not come into force yet and "MB" did not want to divorce for religious reasons). The marriage issue became the main point of contention, with the Court arguing that the requirement to divorce constituted unfair sex discrimination rather than, as argued by the UK government, simply one of the criteria obtaining at the time for granting a GRC, since same sex marriage was not legal. The Court does not seem to accept that the GRA is the applicable law at the time and it is the mechanism allowing transsexuals to change their sex for such legal purposes as pension and

---

[386] Stating at paragraph 29: "Unlike women whose gender is not the result of gender reassignment surgery and who may receive a retirement pension at the age of 60, Ms Richards is not able to fulfil one of the conditions of eligibility for that pension, in this case that relating to retirement age."

[387] Paras 23-24 of the Judgment.

[388] *M.B. v Secretary of State for Work and Pensions*, Judgment of 26 June 2018, C-451/16,
https://curia.europa.eu/juris/document/document.jsf?docid=197431&doclang=EN.

[389] Significantly, in his Opinion the Advocate General Bobek refers to transgender and cisgender persons as if they were significant legal categories recognised in the law he is tasked with analysing: Opinion of the Advocate General Bobek of 5 December 2017, C-451/16,
https://eur-lex.europa.eu/legal-content/en/TXT/?uri=CELEX:62016CC0451.

marriage rights. The Court in effect substitutes its own standards (that changing physical, social and psychological criteria should suffice for changing gender) to the one obtaining under the GRA for individuals who are married with a person of the opposite sex and would find themselves in an illegal same sex marriage upon conferral of a GRC. In order to sustain this argument, the Court applies the comparator issue incorrectly. The UK had rightly argued that

> those situations [a person who changed gender after marrying and a person who has not] are not comparable on the ground that the marital statuses of the persons in question are different. A person who has changed gender after marrying finds himself or herself married to a person of the gender that he or she has acquired, in contrast to a person who has retained his or her birth gender and is married to a person of the opposite sex. According to the United Kingdom Government, having regard to the purpose of the marriage annulment condition at issue in the main proceedings—which is to avoid the existence of marriages between persons of the same sex—such a difference means that the situations of those persons are not comparable.

In response the Court argues that in order to be comparable it is sufficient for the two situations to be similar and not identical. But the two situations not only are not identical, but they are not even similar because a different legal framework applies. Heterosexual marriage and same sex marriage were treated differently in UK law at the time, so the two situations are *ipso facto* not comparable.

In the same year the CJEU issued a judgment in an asylum case, *F. v Bevándorlási és Állampolgársági Hivatal*,[390] where "F." was a Nigerian national who applied for asylum in Hungary because of persecution on the basis of his sexual orientation. The question was what assessment could be legitimately carried out at an immigration and asylum interview for assessing a claim of persecution on the basis of sexual orientation. The Court not only refers Hungary to such standards as contained in the Charter of Fundamental Rights, but also to the Yogyakarta Principles, as introduced in the proceedings by the French and Dutch governments, effectively transforming them into the applicable law:[391]

---

[390] *F. v Bevándorlási és Állampolgársági Hivatal*, Judgment of 25 January 2018, C-473/16, https://curia.europa.eu/juris/document/document.jsf?text=&docid=198766&doclang=EN.

[391] An argument for the advancement of trans rights ("beyond the medicalised binary") by Stefano Osella, "The Court of Justice and Gender Recognition: A

The jurisprudence of the Court has been criticised for relying too closely on the gender binary and for focusing too strictly on "gender reassignment."[392] Gender identity theorists who conceptualise identities as being included under a "trans umbrella"[393] will never be satisfied by any reduction of the concept to legal definitions capable of being applied by courts. At the same time as they clamour for the strictly binary medicalisation of gender incongruence in minors, they reject any attempt at categorisation of gender identities, which have to be left entirely to the individual. Gender identity theorists' criticism of the jurisprudence of the Court goes beyond criticising the cautious attitude of the Court (which is not restricted by any means to the area of transgender rights) and puts in question the very idea that sex is a legally relevant category.[394] Severing

---

Possibility for an Expansive Interpretation?," Women's Studies International Forum (2021): 87 doi: https://doi.org/10.1016/j.wsif.2021.102493. The writer starts with a disclaimer to the effect that he will abandon the distinction between sex and gender, and simply refer to gender "in order to underscore its physical as well as its behavioural components." Sex does not have behavioural components per se. The essentialist nature of gender identity theory could not be starker.

[392] Ibidem; see also Mark Bell, "Gender Identity and Sexual Orientation: Alternative Pathways to EU's Equality Law?," The American Journal of Comparative Law, 60 (2012): 127-147, 137; Marjolein van den Brink and Peter Dunn, Transsex and Intersex Equality Rigths in Europe–A Comparative Analysis, European Commission (2018), 11. https://op.europa.eu/en/publication-detail/-/publication/f63460ca-ebac-11e8-b690-01aa75ed71a1/language-en.

[393] Stephen Whittle, "Gender Identity Discrimination," Paper presented at the European Commission conference, Legal seminar on the Implementation of EU law on Equal Opportunities and Anti-Discrimination, Brussels, 6 October 2009; the term has now been adopted by all trans rights organisations and international organisations.The van den Brink-Dunn report for the European Commission adopts the following definition of trans: "The term trans includes those people who have a gender identity and/or a gender expression that is different from the sex they were assigned at birth. "Trans" is an umbrella term that includes, but is not limited to, men and women with trans pasts and people who identify as transsexual, trans, transvestite/cross-dressing, androgyne, polygender, genderqueer, agender, non-binary, gender variant or with any other gender identity and gender expression which is not standard male or female, and who express their gender through presentation (e.g. self-referring language, clothing, etc.) or body modifications, including (but not necessitating) the undergoing of multiple surgical procedures." In its glossary, Stonewall has 11 such umbrella terms, including ace, aro/ace and grey, https://www.stonewall.org.uk/list-lgbtq-terms.

[394] Paul Skidmore, in his "Can transsexuals suffer sex discrimination?" Journal of Social Welfare and Family Law,19 (1997):105 -110, 109, argues that: [T]he legal imagination continues to be limited in its thinking about sex and gender,

the link between sex and sex discrimination based on gender stereotypes, which are resurrected as an identity, makes it impossible for women to argue sex based discrimination, and for courts to have a reliable comparator in order to adjudicate the claim. There is a reason why women can suffer pregnancy discrimination even if they are infertile. It is because assumptions are made about their reproductive capability on the basis of their sex. A man will never suffer from pregnancy discrimination even if he has five children. Because pregnancy does not affect him and no employer will think, we better not hire him, he may become pregnant and require pregnancy leave. No amount of legal imagination can wish away reality and the law needs to keep in place protections that take into account reality. Non-discrimination and equality law are not about espousing the latest academic fashions, but about remembering, in the words of Wisława Szymborska, that "the body is, and is and is."[395] Bell is right to recognise that the "comparator test implodes in the transgender cases." Of course it has the potential of doing so, if a MtF man is compared to a female who is not transgender. The correct comparator is a male who is not transgender, not least because transgender status is not necessarily a sign that one has obtained an official recognition of gender reassignment. To take the UK's Gender Recognition Act, s9 provides that:[396]

> Where a full gender recognition certificate is issued to a person, the person's gender becomes for all purposes the acquired gender (so that, if the acquired gender is the male gender, the person's sex becomes that of a man and, if it is the female gender, the person's sex becomes that of a woman).

Clearly, *e contrario*, an individual who identifies as trans, whatever this umbrella term means, without having obtained a gender recognition certificate is, for all purposes, of the sex indicated on their birth certificate, and the most that the law can guarantee, through the Equality Act, is that the person will not be discriminated against with respect to someone without the protected characteristic of gender reassignment. Any other interpretation would lead to the absurd result that people should be treated not as the sex they are, when this is legally relevant, but as the sex they claim to be even when this is against the information contained on their

---

reinforcing the idea that sex can and should be categorized. It does not yet open up the space for a continuum of sex and a spectrum of genders."

[395] "Torture" in Wisława Szymborska, People on the Bridge, Transl. Adam Czerniaswski, (London: Forest Books 1996).

[396] Gender Recognition Act 2004, https://www.legislation.gov.uk/ukpga/2004/7/section/9.

birth certificate. In effect, it would make obtaining a GRC legally irrelevant, as one could obtain the same advantages even without one. In fact Bell gets close to understanding that transgender status is not necessarily the ground for discrimination and that the correct comparator is essential, especially when gender identity and sexual orientation intersect, when he discusses the *K.B. v NHS* case. In it, as we remember, the claim was about the pension rights of "R.," the FtM female partner of "K.B.," a female. Since according to the law "R." was a female, and same sex marriage was not allowed, "R." could not be granted pension rights as a partner of "K.B.."Bell notes that:[397]

> [I]f KB had married a man and later completed gender reassignment to be recognized as a woman, they could have remained married because British law (at that time) would have continued to regard the couple as being of the opposite sex.

That is because the ground of discrimination is sexual orientation, not gender identity, given that the reason "R." could not get pension rights was because same sex marriage was not allowed. If the partner of "K.B." had been a MtF man, pension rights would not have been affected because a marriage between them would have been possible. Of course "K.B." as a woman would have remained the partner of a male who transitioned as a woman. But it is also the cases that the GRA, which was passed into law the year of the *KB* case, has a special provision for this, because, if a man is allowed to become legally a woman, surely his wife has the right to decide if she wants to remain in what is what, for legal purposes, a form of same sex marriage, though an unusual one.

If the Court is avoiding a strict application of the comparator test, as it already did in the *Richards* case, is because gender identity theory makes it impossible to apply the comparator test properly, to the point of rejecting the very idea of a comparator. When the law ends up claiming that a man is a certain kind of woman (transwoman) and a woman is a certain kind of man (transman), it is too much to ask for courts to keep the proper distinctions in place, so we see them rely instead on some vaguely applied fundamental human right to "self-determination" and "privacy."

An upcoming case at the CJEU will raise a novel and interesting case, i.e. how freedom of movement rights of transgender individuals are affected if

[397] Mark Bell, "Gender Identity and Sexual Orientation: Alternative Pathways to EU's Equality Law?," The American Journal of Comparative Law, 60 (2012): 127-147, 142.

they have a birth certificate with one sex marker in their country of birth and have undergone a legal change of gender in another country, where that is allowed, that may not be recognised in their country of birth. The case involves Arian Mirzarafie-Ahi,[398] a Romanian national who acquired UK citizenship and a GRC.[399] This is the first case where transgender rights are not considered in a matter concerning pension rights or employment rights, but go to the heart of the four freedoms guaranteed by EU law, and whether mutual recognition affects such matters as the legal change of gender, on which EU countries still maintain different procedural requirements.[400]

---

[398] Case C4/23 [Mirin], Opinion of Advocate General Richard de la Tour, 7 May 2004, CURIA - Documents (europa.eu). The AG found a violation of Article 21(1) TFEU. It remains to be seen whether the CJEU will accept the Opinion.

[399] The case bears some similarities with the case of *X. in X. and Y. v Romania*, discussed in the ECHR section.

[400] "Trans Man's Legal Gender Recognition Case in Romania is Referred to the CJEU," tgeu, March 3 2003, https://tgeu.org/trans-mans-lgr-case-in-romania-is-referred-to-cjeu/.

CHAPTER 6

THE INTER-AMERICAN SYSTEM

Without any scientific basis, it is being claimed that "gender identity"–a feeling that can change even from one day to the next–substitutes and erases the sex with which a person was born. There will be no further mention of women and men with their inherent characteristics, but rather of "persons"–neutral, undefined.
—Judge Elizabeth Odio Benito, *Hernández v Honduras*, Partially Dissenting Opinion

The Inter-American Convention on the Prevention, Punishment and Eradication of Violence against Women[401] (Convention of Belém do Pará) of 1994, is a treaty of the Organisaton of American States to address violence against women. The treaty talks about gender based violence in Article 1, and it is clear that gender is used to refer to the social structuring of oppression and discrimination affecting women, and woman is intended to define a human female.

However, in 2017 the Inter-American Court of Human Rights issued advisory opinion OC-24/17, in which it recognised that the Convention of Belém do Pará applied to "transwomen" on the basis of self-identification.[402] The Advisory Opinion was requested by Costa Rica.[403]

[401]Convention on the Prevention, Punishment and Eradication of Violence against Women, 5 March 1995, 33 I.L.M. 1534 (1994).
[402] Inter-American Court of Human Rights, Advisory Opinion of 24 November 2017, OC-24/17. The Opinion garnered the usual positive reception by trans activists and gender theorists. See for example https://www.escr-net.org/caselaw/2018/advisory-opinion-gender-identity-equality-and-non-discrimination-same-sex-couples-2017, https://www.hrlc.org.au/human-rights-case-summaries/2018/5/14/the-inter-american-court-of-human-rights-calls-for-the-recognition-and-protection-of-lgbti-rights, Nicólas Carrillo Santarelli, "Gender Equality and Non-discrimination of Same Sex Couples," American Journal of International Law, 112(3) (July 2018): 479-485, doi: http://doi.org/10.1017/ajil.2018.51.
[403]1. "Taking into account that gender identity is a category protected by Articles 1 and 24 of the ACHR [American Convention on Human Rights], as well as the provisions of Articles 11(2) and 18 of the Convention: does this protection and the

The request is complex and multifaceted (part of it having to do with the procedure for changing one's name) and the Advisory Opinion runs for 130 pages. At paragraphs 145-6 the Court does say this:

> As already mentioned (supra para. 32.h), gender identity creates space for self-identification, in other words, the experience that a person has of his or her own gender and, in some cases, this may eventually involve the modification of the appearance or bodily functions by medical, surgical or other means. However, it is important to stress that gender identity is not a concept that should be systematically associated with physical transformations. This should be understood even in situations in which a person's gender identity or expression is different from the one assigned at birth, or that is typically associated with the sex assigned at birth, because transgender persons construct their identity regardless of medical treatment or surgery (supra para. 32.h).
>
> Consequently, the procedure for name change, change of the photograph and rectification of the reference to sex or gender in records and on identity documents cannot require supporting evidence of total or partial surgery, hormonal therapy, sterilisation, or bodily changes in order to grant the request or to prove the gender identity in question, because this could be contrary to the right to personal integrity recognized in Article 5(1) and 5(2) of the American Convention. Indeed, subjecting the recognition of a transgender person's gender identity to an undesired surgical intervention or sterilisation would mean conditioning the full exercise of several rights,

---

ACHR imply that the State must recognize and facilitate the name change of an individual in accordance with his or her gender identity?"
2. "If the answer to the preceding question is affirmative, could it be considered contrary to the ACHR that those interested in changing their given name may only do so through a judicial procedure, in the absence of a pertinent administrative procedure?"
3. "Could it be understood that, in accordance with the ACHR, Article 54 of the Civil Code of Costa Rica should be interpreted as to imply that those who wish to change their given name based on their gender identity are not obliged to submit to the judicial procedure established therein, but rather that the State must provide them with a free, prompt and accessible administrative procedure to exercise that human right?"
4. "Taking into account that non-discrimination based on sexual orientation is a category protected by Articles 1 and 24 of the ACHR, in addition to the provisions of Article 11(2) of the Convention: does this protection and the ACHR imply that the State should recognize all the patrimonial rights derived from a relationship between persons of the same sex?" and
5. "If the answer to the preceding question is affirmative, must there be a legal institution that regulates relationships between persons of the same sex for the State to recognize all the patrimonial rights that derive from that relationship.

> including the rights to privacy (Article 11(2) of the Convention) and to choose freely the options and circumstances that give a meaning to his or her existence (Article 7 of the Convention), and would lead to the refusal of the full and effective enjoyment of the right to personal integrity. It should be recalled that, in the case of I.V. v. Bolivia, this Court indicated that health, as an integral part of the right to personal integrity, also includes the liberty of everyone to control their health and their body, and the right not to suffer from interferences, such as to be subjected to torture or to non-consensual medical treatments and experiments. The foregoing could also constitute a violation of the principle of equality and non-discrimination contained in Articles 24 and 1(1) of the Convention because cisgender persons would not need to submit to such obstacles and harm to their personal integrity in order to enforce their right to identity.

By now this reasoning is familiar from international legal materials and the case law of the ECHR. There is no original, post-colonial approach to gender identity. Just the wholesale adoption of the concepts developed in Western academia and international trans rights organisations.[404]

A more recent Advisory Opinion by the IACHR, delivered in 2022, concerns the treatment of persons deprived of liberty and has a dedicated section on LGBTI people.[405] The placement of transgender prisoners (usually MtF men) has been an issue of concern in many countries and has generated an immense amout of literature and legal materials.[406] It is no surprise that the Court comes to the conclusion that MtF prisoners should be consulted on placement:

---

404 Who intervened in the proceedings. On top of the OHCHR, there are ADF International, The Australian Human Rights Centre, UNSW Faculty of Law; Avocats sans frontières Canada; UQAM Clinique Internationale de défance des droits humains; Parlamentarians for Global Action; The Impact Litigation Project of the Center for Human Rights and Humanitarian Law at American University Washington College of Law; The John Marshall Law School International Human Rights Clinic. There was also one foreign intervener arguing against, the Center for Family and Human Rights.

405 Inter-American Court of Human Rights, Advisory Opinion of 30 May 2022, OC-29/22 Requested by the Inter-American Commission on Human Rights, Differentiated Approaches with Respect to Certain Groups of Persons Deprived of Liberty, https://www.corteidh.or.cr/docs/opiniones/seriea_29_eng.pdf.

406 Including by the author: see Alessandra Asteriti, "Canaries in the Coalmine," Centre for Crime and Justice Studies, January 30, 2023, https://www.crimeandjustice.org.uk/resources/canaries-coalmine.

> It thus recommends: (a) taking into account the concerns and views of the prisoner; (b) never placing LGBTI prisoners in dormitories or cells together with prisoners who may pose a risk to their safety; (c) never assuming that it is appropriate to house transgender prisoners according to the sex assigned at birth, but rather it be done in consultation with the prisoner concerned and considering the different needs of housing, and (d) ensuring that there is no discrimination in the quality of accommodation provided for LGBTI prisoners.

When the Court deals with the rights of women deprived of liberty,[407] it starts from the international perspective, i.e. the application of the Mandela Rules[408] and especially the Bangkok rules[409] for the conditions of detention of women. Neither set of rules mentions transgender women.[410] Although these rules are soft law, the Geneva Conventions impose sex separations for prisoners of war[411] and this constitutes an appropriate functional analogy for the treatment to be reserved to all persons deprived of liberty. Individual countries may take the Geneva Conventions approach and mandate separation of the sexes in prison, or the UN Rules approach, and simply have prison regulations. In the UK, for example, Rule 12 of the 1999 Prison Rules requires "women prisoners" to be separated from "male prisoners."[412]

When interpreting laws and treaties, judges can look to their "object and purpose." Clearly, in the case of the Geneva Conventions, the purpose of detaining women separately from men is to guarantee the safety, dignity and privacy of women, all irremediably compromised if male and female

---

[407] 43 ff.

[408] The United Nations Standard Minimum Rules for the Treatment of Prisoners, especially Rule 11 https://www.unodc.org/documents/justice-and-prison-reform/Nelson_Mandela_Rules-E-ebook.pdf.

[409] United Nations Rules for the Treatment of Women Prisoners and Non-custodial Measures for Women Offenders with their Commentary, https://www.unodc.org/documents/justice-and-prison-reform/Bangkok_Rules_ENG_22032015.pdf. The word gender in these rules is clearly used as a synonym of sex.

[410] Though Rule 7 of the Mandela Rules provides that prisoners' identity should be recorded in compliance with their "self-perceived" gender this does not seem to affect separation by categories, which is based on sex (Rule 11).

[411] Geneva Convention Relative to the Treatment of Prisoners of War, 75 UNTS 972 of 12 August 1949, Article 14, https://treaties.un.org/doc/Publication/UNTS/Volume%2075/v75.pdf.

[412] The Prisons Rules 1999, https://www.legislation.gov.uk/uksi/1999/728/contents/made.

prisoners are housed together. A similar purpose animates the Mandela Rules and the Bangkok Rules. It does not take much imagination to foresee what would happen to women if prisons had no sex separation and sex offenders were housed in the same quarters as women, sharing facilities such as toilets and cells. If this were to happen to prisoners of war it would be considered a violation of international humanitarian law.

In order for gender identity theory to advocate housing transgender prisoners according to their preferred gender identity, rather than their birth sex, the shift between sex and gender identity must be accepted, to the effect that gender identity does not necessarily match sex at birth but it is left to the individual to decide which sex identity they decide to inhabit (even only temporarily) for the purpose of the application of the law, when the law applies differently to the sexes. Therefore even when the law clearly dictates a separation on the basis of sex, or on the basis of the male/female distinction, gender identity theorists either argue that sex includes gender identity, or that males include females and females include males on the basis of self identification. This is what the Court effectively is doing. From a theoretical perspective, enforcing a binary separation on the basis of gender identity instead of sex, goes against the main tenets of gender theory itself, especially in its newest production, which eschewes any binarism and insists that gender identites are potentially limitless in number.[413] Additionally, if, again on the basis of the most recent gender scholarship, gender identity is fluid and changeable, sometimes on a daily or even hourly basis, and if people can have a gender identity with no specific male or female aspect,[414] how is the law supposed to take these criteria into account in allocation decisions in prisons? The ethical need for the law to be predictable and non arbitrary would seem to require the existence of stable categories. Self-determination stops when the rights of others start. These basic principles seem to be lost to the Court. The safety of female prisoners who have to share accommodations

---

[413] See for example Adams, Felicity and Emmerich, Fabienne,"Mapping the Manifestations of Exclusion: Challenging the Incarceration of Queer People." In The Queer Outside the Law, eds. Senthorun Raj and Peter Dunne (London: Palgrave MacMillan, 2021): 107-142.

[414] Of course one needs to start from Judith Butler's work; see Judith Butler, Gender Trouble: Feminism and the Subversion of Identity (New York: Routledge 1990), but it is the epigones that really show where this theory will take you; see for example Yolanda Flores, "Science, Context, and Gender Fluidity in Public Policy," Public Integrity, 23(6) (2021): 595-609, doi: doi.org/10.1080/10999922.2020.1825181.

with prisoners with a male body and possibly a conviction for sex offences against women is not a concern of the Court, even if female prisoners are known generally to have suffered a higher incidence of rape, sex offences and domestic violence than the general female population,[415] and may have an automatic trauma response to being exposed to male-bodied individuals in close quarters, where they have no chance to escape or isolate. The only concern of the Court seems to be the risk of violence that transgender prisoners may be exposed to (which is never from women prisoners or staff). The Court is equally oblivious to the right of female prison staff not to be forced to conduct body searches on MtF male prisoners (who are likely not to have undergone any SRS), determining that it is a right of transgender prisoners to select the gender (sex) of the staff conducting the body search (para 257).[416]

The Inter-American Commission on Human Rights had already created a unit on the rights of LGBTI persons in 2011. In 2014 a special mechanism by means of the institution of a Rapporteurship on the Rights of Lesbian, Gay, Bisexual, Trans and Intersex (LGBTI) Persons was also created.[417] The last published report from the Commission, detailing the work of its rapporteurs, including the one on LGBTI rights is from 2022.[418] The

---

[415] There is a considerable amount of data on this. To restrict myself to the UK, for ease of accessibility, see Prison Reform Trust, "Majority of women in prison have been victims of domestic abuse," December 4, 2017, https://prisonreformtrust.org.uk/majority-of-women-in-prison-have-been-victims-of-domestic-abuse/, and Madeline Petrillo, "I've the body of a woman but inside I feel like a child," Centre for Crime and Justice Studies, November 25, 2015, https://www.crimeandjustice.org.uk/resources/ive-body-woman-inside-i-feel-child.

[416] It is very difficult to come by data on sexual assaults committed by transgender prisoners in female prisons, not least because once they are registered as females it is impossible to keep statistics. This case in Argentina made the news, about a transgender prisoner impregnating a female prisoner. The facts happened in 2019, when abortion in Argentina was still illegal (it was legalised in December 2020), so we can assume the woman was forced to give birth. Diana Shaw, "Transgender detainee who impregnated fellow inmate is released from prison," Women Are Human, November 28, 2019, https://www.womenarehuman.com/transgender-detainee-who-impregnated-fellow-inmate-is-released-from-prison-to-prevent-further-incident/.

[417] Rapporteurship on the Rights of Lesbian, Gay, Bisexual, Trans and Intersex (LGBTI) Persons, https://www.oas.org/en/iachr/jsForm/?File=/en/iachr/r/DLGBTI/default.asp.

[418] Inter-American Commission on Human Rights, "Annual Report 2022" https://www.oas.org/en/iachr/reports/ia.asp?Year=2022.

Report includes the work done by all 11 special rapporteurs. This is what it says about the work in LGBTI mandate:

> 43.With regards to the Rights of Lesbian, Gay, Bisexual, Trans and Intersex Persons, the IACHR followed up on the situation through nine press releases. On one hand, the Commission welcomed the decision that declares as unconstitutional the criminalization of consensual sexual activity between LGBTI persons in Saint Kitts and Nevis; it also celebrated the life, achievements, and resilience of trans, non-binary, and gender-diverse persons in the framework of the International Transgender Day of Visibility; and welcomed the ruling that declared as unconstitutional those sections in the Sexual Offences Act of Antigua and Barbuda, in force since the colonial era, that criminalized consensual acts between same-sex persons. In addition, it welcomed the announcement of the presidential veto to the "Protection of Life and Family" draft bill in Guatemala. Furthermore, it called on the States to adopt comprehensive measures to prevent violence based on prejudice against lesbians; and in a joint statement with UN Human Rights, the Commission expressed its concern for the increase of stigmatizing narratives that incite hatred, legitimize discrimination, or even incite violence based on prejudice against LGBTIQ+ persons.

The statement is meaningless as worded. No law prohibits relationships between intersex persons (that is what the "I" stands for). It also adds, beyond the scope of the mandate, queer and + identities, which are not defined anywhere in any legal instrument.[419] There is absolutely no legal basis for, and no political agreement around, ideas such as queerness and self defined, open-ended identities such as the "+" community.

An important part of embedding gender identity theory into the work of the Organisation of American States is the work conducted by the Commission and the Court in individual cases, as evidenced in the cases of *T.B. and S.H. v Jamaica*[420] and *Henry & Edwards v Jamaica* for what concerns the Commission[421] and *Vicky Hernández et al v Honduras* for the Court.[422]

---

[419]The Report also mentions a Joint Message from UN Human Rights in the Americas and IACHR on LGBTIQ+ Pride Day from 28/6/2022 https://www.oas.org/en/iachr/jsForm/?File=/en/iachr/media_center/preleases/2022/147.asp.

[420] Report No 401/20, Case 13.095, *T.B. and S.H. v Jamaica*, OEA/Ser.L/V/II Doc 419 December 31, 2020, https://www.oas.org/en/iachr/decisions/2020/jm_13.095_en.pdf.

[421] Report No. 400/20, Case 13.637, *Gareth Henry and Simone Carline Edwards v Jamaica*, OEA/Ser.L/V/II Doc.418 December 31, 2020,

The *T.B. and S.H.* report, from 2020, concerns two gay men."T.B." describes himself as a gay man in his statement about the abuse but is presented as a transwoman by the Petitioner, the organisation Aids-Free World[423] and the Commission uses female pronouns to refer to him. The Offences Against the Person Act in Jamaica criminalises sodomy, defined as anal sex between two males. The application is based both on the abuse suffered unjustly by these two males on the basis of their sexual orientation, and in the case of "T.B." the alleged trans status, and a law violating the principle of non-discrimination and equality before the law and other rights, such as the right to privacy, protected by the Convention. The text of the Act makes it clear that the offence involves only same sex male intercourse or bestiality:

> 76. (Unnatural Crime): Whosoever shall be convicted of the abominable crime of buggery, committed either with mankind or with any animal, shall be liable to be imprisoned and kept to hard labour for a term not exceeding ten years.
>
> 77. (Attempt): Whosoever shall attempt to commit the said abominable crime, or shall be guilty of any assault with intent to commit the same, or of any indecent assault upon any male person, shall be guilty of a misdemeanor, and being convicted thereof, shall be liable to be imprisoned for a term not exceeding seven years, with or without hard labour.
>
> 79 (Outrages on Decency): Any male person who, in public or private, commits or is a party to the commission of, or procures or attempts to procure the commission by any male person of, any act of gross indecency with another male person, shall be guilty of a misdemeanor, and being convicted thereof shall be liable at the discretion of the court to be imprisoned for a term not exceeding two years, with or without hard labour

The statement by "T.B." clearly attributes the discrimination and abuse he suffered to his sexual orientation though one can see a shift in his perception of his own identity, from gay to LGBT. The use of female

---

https://www.oas.org/en/iachr/decisions/2020/JM_13.637_EN.PDF.

[422] *Vicky Hernández et al v Honduras*, Judgment of March 26, 2021 https://www.corteidh.or.cr/docs/casos/articulos/seriec_422_ing.pdf..

[423] https://aidsfreeworld.org/. The organisation is based in New York, though its work seems to be mostly international. Here is how they reported on the Jamaica cases: "Inter-American Commission on Human Rights Censures Jamaica for Violating the Rights of LGBTI Citizens," Aids-free World, December 1, 2020, https://aidsfreeworld.org/statements/2020/12/1.

pronouns by the Commission to refer to "T.B." is absurd given his recollection of the facts:

> On Saturday March 12, 2011 [...] I went up into the town to Kentucky Fried Chicken (KFC) to get something to eat. I was sitting at the table with a friend [...] who has a very feminine appearance and was staring at some guys. The man came and said "Weh yuh a look pan mi fa batty-boy, stop look pan mi" (What are you looking at me for, battyboy, stop looking at me). I feared a confrontation, so I got up and left [...] the guys came after us while ranting and raving, saying to anyone who would listen "Yuh nuh see a two batty boy? Yuh nuh si dem a gay? Wi nuh wan no fish roun yah! (You don't see they are two batty-boys? You don't see they are gay? We don't want any fish (gays) around here. The men were mimicking sound of gunshots [...]. I crossed the street to get away.

Later he adds:

> In Jamaica it is very difficult to access stigma-free public health care as a gay man, especially one who looks like me and is very effeminate [...]. In 2009 when I was 17, I went for my first and only HIV test at a public health clinic in Jamaica [...] however, the treatment that I received caused me to leave the clinic before I took the test and I refused to return to another public health care facility in Jamaica for any other medical care. [...] the nurse handed me a questionnaire to complete. Among other things it had questions about my previous sexual partners. I was afraid to fill it out truthfully because I had only ever had sex with men, which is a crime in Jamaica. Completing the questionnaire would be admitting that I broke the law and could spend up to 10 years in prison. I also did not want to expose myself to further ridicule by admitting that I was gay. So, when the nurse was not looking, I quickly gathered my belongings and left. In 2011 a friend in Trinidad heard about my situation and paid for me to visit him. He promised to let me stay with him and take care of me. However, when I arrived, and he saw how effeminate I was he refused to take me to his home. He said that he was concerned about what the neighbors would say. I ended up sleeping on the streets in Trinidad for eight months. During that time, I met some Trans women who were also homeless, and they helped me to get hormones to start transitioning. [...] When I left Jamaica for Holland in 2012, I sent a message via email to my mother and told her where I was, but she only responded to ask for money and nothing else. She did not ask how I was doing or how I was surviving [...] I miss my family, my home and my country but I know that I cannot return safely until Jamaica gets rid of the anti-buggery law and becomes more accepting of LGBT people like me.

The second report is also from 2020 and also challenges Jamaica's Offences Against the Person Act. Gareth Henry was a gay man who suffered abuse and discrimination becauses of his sexual orientation; Simone Edwards was a lesbian woman who also suffered abuse and discrimination because of her sexual orientation. This case is even clearer that the issue is homophobic discrimination and laws criminalising homosexuality. To describe these two individuals as LGBTI persons is an attempt to erase the nature of their abuse. And yet this is what the Commission does. It is clear that Jamaican law criminalises same sex intercourse, not gender identity. And none of the individuals concerned in the two reports identified as transgender, regardless of the attempt of the Commission and the LGBTI organisations to describe "T.B." as such, while he mostly expresses a male gay identity.

Reframing the narrative of the events as LGBTI discrimination and transforming the anti-sodomy law into a law against LGBT people on the basis of sexual orientation and gender identity is incorrect. No single lesbian is affected by the law and the law has nothing to say about the right of people to express a gender identity incongruent with their sex (considering also that a considerable percentage of males expressing a feminine gender identity are not homosexuals). This is just an attempt to retrofit gender identity into sex orientation as the scope of protection and the extent of the right being protected. These cases, and others, evidence the attempt to retrofit gender identity into historical facts about LGB rights up to and including presenting a gay male as a woman because he is effeminate.

As for the Court, the *Hernández* case is from 2021, so immediately after the two cited reports.[424] The case was referred to the Court by the Commission in 2019 and concerns a MtF man who was involved in prostitution.[425] Hernández had died a violent death while being pursued by the police for escaping arrest for breaking the curfew rules, but Honduras accepted responsibility for the death (though the involvement of the police in the killing was not established, the State has a responsibility to investigate the circumstances of the death, which they failed to do), therefore the Court is assessing the events leading up to the death and the investigation of the death,[426] shifting the case from one of violation of Articles 8 and 25

---

[424] *Vicky Hernández et al v Honduras*, Judgment of March 26, 2021 https://www.corteidh.or.cr/docs/casos/articulos/seriec_422_ing.pdf.

[425] The Court received 18 *amicus curiae* submissions, including by the OHCHR, evidencing the importance of the case in the context of the OAS.

[426] The circumstances of Hernández death are horrendous, though there is no hard evidence that the death is motivated by anti-trans prejudice and prostitutes (the

of the IA Convention of Human Rights to a violation of Article 7(b) of the Belém do Pará Convention (discrimination against women), upon request by the Commission, which asked the Court to apply the Convention to a transgender MtF man. The case rested on the claim that the death of Hernández and the subsequent inaction by the State evidenced a pattern of discrimination against transgender individuals and specifically MtF men. The Court cited this as evidence of this pattern:

> The Commission considered that certain elements analyzed jointly are indicative of whether or not a crime is committed due to prejudice, It indicated that the record of the removal of the corpse mentioned the discovery of a condom that had apparently been used next to the body and understood that this fact could be indicative of sexual violence. It added that Vicky Hernández was murdered with a firearm and that her body was found in a public place. It considered that those elements were consistent with the manner in which most prejudice-based crimes against trans women are committed, quite often in situations connected with sex work. In addition, it recalled that the facts took place in a context of violence and discrimination against LGBT persons in Honduras. In that context, around the time of Vicky Hernández's death, the records began to show an alarming increase in murders connected to the victims' gender identity and expression, together with a recurring pattern of police violence.[427]

None of the elements evidences a specific anti-trans motive, as this treatment could have been meted out to a male or a female prostitute (sexist attitudes towards female prostitutes and homophobic attitudes towards gay prostitutes, combined with a general social condemnation of prostitution would have resulted in an identical outcome). The Court expounds at length on what the right to gender identity requires:

Court calls them sex workers though I prefer not to use this term, which implies that sexual exploitation is a job like any other) are exposed to a much higher level of violence than the general population on the basis of their occupation rather than their identity. For example, witness Claudia Spellmant Sosa admits that the Colectivo Unitad Rosa collected data on police abuse because the police refused to do so because they considered sex work unlawful, without mentioning a specific anti-trans animus (para. 95). The death of female prostitutes usually goes quite unnoticed in the news and there is no Court case on the circumstances and State responsibility on the matter of their death, though the Commisson has expressed its concern, https://www.oas.org/en/iachr/media_center/preleases/2017/036.asp. For some numbers, see for example, Eben Levey, "Honduras: Sex workers targeted," Maryknoll Office for Global Concerns, March-April 2014, https://maryknollogc.org/article/honduras-sex-workers-targeted.

[427] *Vicky Hernández et al v Honduras*, Judgment of March 26, 2021: para 72, note 113, https://www.corteidh.or.cr/docs/casos/articulos/seriec_422_ing.pdf:

> Regarding the relationship between the rights to liberty in the broadest sense, gender expression, gender identity, and privacy, the Court has indicated in other cases that recognition of the affirmation of a person's sexual and gender identity is protected by the American Convention under Articles 7 and 11(2). Accordingly, gender and sexual identity are linked to the concept of liberty, the right to privacy and the possibility of self-determination of all human beings and to freely choose the options and circumstances that give a meaning to their existence in keeping with their personal convictions. Therefore, the State's recognition of gender identity is of crucial importance to ensure that trans persons may fully enjoy their human rights, including protection against violence, torture and ill-treatment.[428]

The Court criticises the State for having recorded Hernández as a male, though the law at the time did not allow a change of sex in official documents, so the State could not do otherwise, and this fact does not show a particular animus against Hernández but simply the application of the law as it was. Whether the law can be construed as being against the right of self-determination of trangender people (which was not a recognised right in 2009) is a separate matter to the one under consideration of the Court, i.e. whether the "specific" circumstances evidence anti-trans behaviour by the State against the "specific" individual because of their transgender status.

The Court's explanation of the extent of protections granted to the right of gender expression[429] incurs in a legal obstacle. The Court claims that transgender individuals should have the "legitimate ability to establish the exteriorization of their persona according to their innermost convictions." No matter how important and valued those convictions are to an individual, their exteriorisation has to respect the rights of others, and international courts' jurisprudence on the right to expression, including religious expression, is extremely clear on this legitimate limitation of freedom of expression, or as the Court puts it, of exteriorisation of belief.[430] No matter how convinced a male is of being a woman,[431] the right of others to apprehend reality on the basis of their own visual and

[428] Ibidem, para. 116.

[429] Ibidem, para. 117.

[430] European Court of Human Rights, "Guide on Article 10 of the European Convention on Human Rights," August 31, 2017, https://www.echr.coe.int/documents/d/echr/guide_art_10_eng.

[431] Usually on the basis of some profoundly regressive stereotypes of how women are supposed to move, talk, dress etc (the dress, speech and mannerisms of the Yogyakarta definition of gender identity is revealing in this regard).

intellectual perception cannot be affected. If a woman sees a man and he says he is a woman and to treat him as a woman, there is neither a legal basis nor a moral imperative for her to obey, not least because women rely on their own instinct to keep safe from male violence, and an essential element of that instinct is to recognise males; it is the *conditio sine qua non* for the functioning of their instinct as a risk assessment strategy. Only social mores can recommend a different reaction, and an acknowledgement of someone's gender identity instead of their sex, but those should be left to the choice of the individual and the legitimacy of those social mores, to the extent that they have legal consequences, needs to be tested in court in compliance with the relevant equality and human rights legislation.

The Court found that Honduras had breached Article 7 of the Belém do Pará Convention, which protects women from gender based discrimination, where gender is intended as "social construct of the identities, attributes and roles that society assigns to women and men."[432] Transgender MtF men are men, and sometimes do not transition until they are middle aged, so the identities, attributes and roles that society assigns to them are those restricted to males. There is no understanding and no explanation of how gender roles that are imposed on the basis of sex, become positive identities that are embraced on the basis of self-identification and need legal protection. The *Hernández* case stands out also because of the amount and nature of remedies, of which of particular interest is the requirement that Honduras pass legislation allowing change of sex by simple self-identification, with no qualifying criterias and with no record kept of the birth sex.[433]

> The adoption of this procedure for the recognition of gender identity must conform to the provisions of Advisory Opinion OC-24/17 of November 24, 2017. In particular, it must ensure that anyone interested in rectifying the annotation of gender or, if applicable, the mention of sex or change of name, and substituting their photograph in the records and/or on their identity document to conform to their self-perceive gender identity, may have access to a procedure: (a) addressed at the complete rectification of the self-perceived gender identity; (b) based solely on the free and informed consent of the applicant without involving requirements such as medical and/or psychological or other certifications that could be unreasonable or pathologizing; (c) that should be confidential, and the changes, corrections or amendments to the records and on the identity

[432] *Vicky Hernández et al v Honduras*, Judgment of March 26, 2021: para 128, https://www.corteidh.or.cr/docs/casos/articulos/seriec_422_ing.pdf.
[433] Ibidem, paras. 170-171.

> documents should not reflect the changes made based on the gender identity; (d) that should be rapid and, insofar as possible, costfree; (e) that should not require evidence of surgery and/or hormonal therapy, and (f) that should not necessarily be regulated by a law. Lastly, the State must present a report every six months from notification of this judgment, indicating in detail the steps taken to comply with this measure. If it considers this helpful, the State may approach organisations such as the OAS Universal Civil Identity Program in the Americas (PUICA) for any advice or assistance that may be useful to comply with the measure ordered.

The partially dissenting opinion of Judge Elizabeth Odio Benito is a welcome injection of legal logic in the proceedings. She notes that it will be impossible for the State to abide at the same time by the requirement to allow a change of sex in public records with no record kept of previous sex and to compile statistics on violence against transgender individuals.[434] Judge Odio Benito also disagrees on the applicability of the Convention of Belém do Pará to the facts as she outlines clearly in these statement:[435]

> (i) the necessary distinction between sex (biological) and gender (hierarchical social construct), and the serious confusion that the erroneous equalizing of "gender identity" with sex has introduced into the academic and political debate; (ii) I will then address the dynamics of the historic and permanent violence against women because they are women (which gave rise to the Convention of Belém do Pará) and the violence suffered by other groups (transvestites, and intersexual and trans persons, for example) protected by the Pact of San José; I

---

[434] This is so obvious, as I have noted already, one wonders how the other judges did not consider it. I should note that this issue has repercussions beyond record-keeping of violence against transgender people. If MtF men's sex offences are recorded as being committed by women, there is no way of proving that self-identification affects women, unless there are some other pieces of information that may give a clue to the sex of the perpetrator. Data collected by the Office of National Statistic in the UK shows that between 2012 and 2018 436 individuals recorded by the Crown Prosecution Service as women were prosecuted for rape, an offence that in English law requires the use of a penis. See Alice Sullivan, "Submission of 27 August 2021," Scottish Parliament' Citizen Participation and Public Petitions Committee, https://www.parliament.scot/chamber-and-committees/committees/current-and-previous-committees/session-6-citizen-participation-and-public-petitions-committee/correspondence/2021/pe1876_h-professor-alice-sullivan-submission-of-27-august-2021.

[435]Odio Benito admits she had not predicted the consequences of the Advisory Opinion of 2017, nor the latest developments in gender identity theory.

> will continue by referring to (iii) the development and historical and practical importance of the Convention of Belém do Pará and why it is not applicable to this case.

With extreme clarity, she outlines the consequences of replacing sex with gender identity as the significant legal category and asks what would happen to women's rights, and feminism, in those changed circumstances. It is the same set of questions that are at the basis of this work, a plea to consider the consequences of legal changes, because legal changes are never without consequences and gender identity theory, like a stone thrown in a pond, creates a series of ripples, that dislodge rights that women have just gotten, fragile conquests that have cost women lives and economic security, and reputations.[436]

[436] Predictably this case comment fails to engage with the merits of Odio Benito's Opinion: Carlos J. Zelada, "Vicky Hernández et al. Honduras: A Landmark Victory with a Bitter Aftertaste," EJIL: Talk!, 27 August, 2021, https://www.ejiltalk.org/vicky-hernandez-et-al-v-honduras-a-landmark-victory-with-a-bitter-aftertaste/.

CHAPTER 7

THE AFRICAN UNION

The evidence strongly suggests that, before colonization, many peoples of the African continent did not have a binary approach to gender or correlate anatomy with gender identity
—Victor Madrigal-Borloz, UN IE on SOGI

The African Charter on Human and People's Rights does not contain any specific reference to gender, gender identity, or LGBT Rights.[437] Article 2 is the non-discrimination provision and lists "other status," under which it is possible to read other categories not included in the original list. To this extent it has been argued for the African Charter as for other human rights instruments, that gender identity is a ground of protection against discrimination. However, it still bears arguing what gender identity means for the purpose of protection. It can either be intended to mean a belief in an immaterial identity, akin to a religious belief in the immortal soul, or a material reality, akin to age or sex. This book argues that gender identity should be properly categorised as a belief, and subjected to the legal criteria that human rights law applies to beliefs and expression of beliefs. Gender identity theorists argue that gender identity is both innate, so akin to a material reality, and self-selected and, crucially, changeable on the basis of self-selection.

In human rights law protected categories are either fixed and independent from one's choice (age, sex and race respond to these criteria, though race is more flexible in the sense that one can have a diverse racial, ethnic and national backgrounds); mutable at will (religions and beliefs, although social constraints may make choice practically impossible); mutable but not at will (disability may be temporary or permanent, for example, but one does not have a choice, or only one restricted by circumstances, such as availability of treatment). Gender identity theorists argue that gender identity belongs to the category of the "mutable at will" characteristics, but

[437] African Charter on Human and People's Rights, 27 June 1981, 1520 UNTS 26363.

that it ought to be treated as a "fixed and independent frrom one's choice" characteristic.

The category selection is an independent regime from the one of the applicability of human rights protections. What I mean is that although religion or political belief are mutable at will, one can be discriminated against on their basis even if one does not abide by those religious precepts or political beliefs. However, what matters is not whether one ought to be protected against discrimination on the basis of any of these categories (of course they should) but what sort of protection one ought to be granted in law. It is banal to state that human rights law distinguishes between absolute and relative rights and that equality law distinguishes between fixed and mutable characteristics. In short, freedom of belief and freedom of expression are relative rights in human rights law, and "belief" is a category subject to specific criteria in equality law (not any belief is deserving of protection, and probably the most important criterion to be met is whether the belief respects the rights of others, a criterion that is derived from the human rights standard as incorporated, for example, in Articles 9 and 10 of the ECHR).[438] Therefore, a proper categorisation of gender identity as a belief would require the application of the proper standard, including the respect of the rights of others, which are not applicable in the case of "fixed and independent from individual choice" characteristics. Being a woman does not affect the rights of others. But a male declaring a female identity and requesting access to services and rights that are allocated to women on the basis of sex has an effect on the women who use those services or avail themselves of those rights. Additionally, gender identity theory requires others to modify their language and channel their reactions in response to a demand they may not recognise as legitimate, precisely because infringing on their own right of belief and expression, and limiting their right to autonomy and security of the person. So when the IE on SOGI says:[439]

> The provisions of the African Charter on Human and Peoples' Rights support the conclusion that every person enjoys the Charter rights irrespective of gender identity.

---

[438] In other words, while a court has no role in establishing someone's age or sex, it is only through a judicial determination that a belief will be accorded protected status.

[439] Human Rights Council, Report of the Working Group on Arbitrary Detention, 30 June 2014, A/HRC/27/47, para 22, https://ap.ohchr.org/documents/dpage_e.aspx?si=A/HRC/27/47.

The statement is too ambiguous to be legally relevant and applicable. Of course the Charter contains the usual prohibition against discrimination on the basis of "other status." Already within the European context this has been interpreted to include discrimination on the basis of sexual orientation and gender identity. This is acceptable provided it is intended to mean discrimination on the basis of homosexuality or gender non-conformity. It is beyond the scope of the Charter, as well as the other instruments, to incorporate a right to self-identify one's gender/sex without any grounding in material reality. It is in fact true that the non-discrimination provision in the Charter is an open list, incorporating "any other status" as a ground for discrimination. But that does not transform a belief, such as the belief that people have a changeable gender identity which trumps their sex, into a status grounded in material reality.

We see here the construction of a narrative that words mean not what they have always meant but what a theory developed in Western academia has decided they mean, and how this interpretation is imposed, in an exercise of cultural colonialism, to non-Western cultures, as part of the usual "human rights and development" package that accompanies economic support and trade deals.[440]

---

[440] The last report by Victor Madrigal-Borloz before he left his role as UN IE on SOGI focuses on colonialism and SOGI issues; Report of the Independent Expert on protection against violence and discrimination based on sexual orientation and gender identity, 25 July 2023, A/78/227, https://documents.un.org/doc/undoc/gen/n23/218/47/pdf/n2321847.pdf?token=kRQUOfUUFU1xgEC5y2&fe=true. The Report is a classic example of imposing one's cultural framework on other cultures; at para. 11, Madrigal-Borloz writes: "Tribes situated in present-day Nigeria did not have a gender-binary and typically did not assign gender at birth, waiting instead until later in the person's life. " This is the language of gender identity theory. More absurdly, Madrigal-Borloz provides an example from the Oromo people in Ethiopia, who, "before colonization," "switched to male and female gender and roles for a period of eight years during their lifetime. " Ethiopia was never colonised, a matter of pride for the country. In any event, his is a very biased reading of the system of "Gada Classes" that only affected "boys." In the first stage, *dabballe*, when the boys are treated as girls and female pronouns are used for them, they have no sisters, *because the sisters are either abandoned to die after birth or given for adoption* [emphasis added]. The family will be able to raise sisters only when the boy passes to the next stage (Asmaron Legesse, Gada: Three Approaches to the Study of African Society, 53–this is the study quoted by Madrigal-Borloz as the source). That Madrigal-Borloz ignores the fact female infanticide was practised to focus on the

Dutifully, the African Commission on Human and People's Rights, in 2014 issued a resolution on the protection against discrimination on the basis of sexual orientation and gender identity:[441] This is the operative text:

> [The African Union] [c]ondemns the increasing incidence of violence and other human rights violations, including murder, rape, assault, arbitrary imprisonment and other forms of persecution of persons on the basis of their imputed or real sexual orientation or gender identity;
>
> Specifically condemns the situation of systematic attacks by State and non-state actors against persons on the basis of their imputed or real sexual orientation or gender identity;
>
> Calls on State Parties to ensure that human rights defenders work in an enabling environment that is free of stigma, reprisals or criminal prosecution as a result of their human rights protection activities, including the rights of sexual minorities; and
>
> Strongly urges States to end all acts of violence and abuse, whether committed by State or non-state actors, including by enacting and effectively applying appropriate laws prohibiting and punishing all forms of violence including those targeting persons on the basis of their imputed or real sexual orientation or gender identities, ensuring proper investigation and diligent prosecution of perpetrators, and establishing judicial procedures responsive to the needs of victims.

Of course there should be no ground for the discrimination and abuse. But being abused because people assume you are trans does not validate the theory that people have a changeable gender identity replacing sex as a legal category. It is just indicative of a society where gender roles are very rigidly enforced and where a man who desires to follow the gender roles assigned to women (or vice-versa) is not acceptable. This does not mean that the gender roles in themselves need any sort of protection or legal endorsement and *a fortiori* that inhabiting a stereotypical feminine gender role transforms a man into any kind of woman.

---

fact they used female pronouns for the boys tells us all we need to know about this theory.

[441] African Commission on Human and Peoples' Rights, Resolution on Protection against Violence and other Human Rights Violations against Persons on the basis of their real or imputed Sexual Orientation or Gender Identity, 12 May 2014, ACHPR/Res.275 (LV) 2014, https://achpr.au.int/en/adopted-resolutions/275-resolution-protection-against-violence-and-other-human-rights-violations.

The construction of the narrative is continued with the Advisory Opinion by the African Court on Human and People's Rights No. 01/2018 of 4 December 2020.[442] The Advisory Opinion is on the compatibility of vagrancy laws with the African Charter. The Court finds them not to be compatible with the Charter on several grounds and explains, at para. 70:

> the Court notes that vagrancy laws, effectively, punish the poor and underprivileged, including but not limited to the homeless, the disabled, the gender-nonconforming, sex workers, hawkers, street vendors, and individuals who otherwise use public spaces to earn a living. Notably, however, individuals under such difficult circumstances are already challenged in enjoying their other rights including more specifically their socio-economic rights. Vagrancy laws, therefore, serve to exacerbate their situation by further depriving them of their right to be treated equally before the law.

The Independent Expert Report takes this as confirmation that this applies to gender identity, confirming its existence.[443] Why should not conforming to stereotypes reify stereotypes into an identity worth of protection? Gender non-conforming does not equal transgender. If gender is a norm enforced in a specific place at a particular time, then, for example, a woman who refuses to abide by the Taliban's ruling on face covering is gender non-conforming. A woman in the UK who does not take her husband's name upon marriage is gender non-conforming. Most people in democratic, progressive societies are gender non-conforming, only in the sense that gender norms are not that strictly enforced, so conforming to them is a matter of choice. Statistically, since almost the totality of the world population is not transgender, gender non-conformity is a behaviour associated with the human condition in general. It is also offensive to assume that anyone who is not transgender is conforming to gender norms. On the contrary, if it is true that "transwomen are women," then most of them are women who conform to stereotypes of femininity. So they are not gender non-conforming at all. Only if one acknowledges that they are in fact males, then one can describe them as gender non-conforming.

---

[442] *Compatibility of Vagrancy Laws with the African Charter on Human and Peoples' Rights and Other Human Rights Instruments Applicable in Africa*, African Court on Human and Peoples' Rights, 40 December 2020, No. 001/2018, https://www.legal-tools.org/doc/91d2p6/pdf.

[443] Human Rights Council, "The Law of Inclusion," 3 June 2021, A/HRC/47/27: para 22, https://documents.un.org/doc/undoc/gen/g21/123/16/pdf/g2112316.pdf?token=qMoUbo07MN5bGqVA3n&fe=true.

The pressure on countries to embed gender identity theory into local laws and policy is especially evident in vulnerable countries that depend more heavily on the assistance of the United Nations and are subjected to a heightened level of scrutiny. The International Service for Human Rights (ISHR)[444] and the International Gay and Lesbian Association (ILGA) now renamed ILGA World to refer to International Lesbian, Gay, Bisexual, Trans and Intersex Association,[445] are two organisation invested in embedding gender identity theory in the work of organisations such as the UN, where ILGA has consultative status at ECOSOC[446] and where the ISHR lobbies to get other NGO to obtain consultative status, as they report on their website (with a focus on NGOs dealing with gender identity). ILGA and ISHR collected all the information relating to LGBTI rights between 2011 and 2021 (with a strong emphasis on the T, of course) by all Special Rapporteurs at the UN and any other Special Procedures work, finding that in 2021, there were 52 communications, 8 reports on country visits and 54 thematic reports in relation to LGBTI topics under the umbrella of Special Procedures.[447]

> The mandates that made the most regular references to SOGIESC issues were the Independent Expert on SOGI and the Special Rapporteur on freedom of expression. In welcome advances some mandates made their first communications covering LGBTI topics (the Special Rapporteur on truth, justice and reparation and the Special Rapporteur on Belarus), and the Special Rapporteur on the right to privacy included SOGIESC issues in their report of country visit for the first time.While slightly less than 50% of all thematic reports mentioned some LGBTI related topics, the level of detail and analysis, as well as which mandates regularly reference SOGIESC issues, indicate that opportunities remain for LGBTI defenders to strengthen this work, including in relation to specific populations within LGBTI communities, such as LBQ women, trans or intersex persons,

---

[444] International Service for Human Rights, https://ishr.ch/.

[445] ILGA World–The International Lesbian, Gay, Bisexual, Trans and Intersex Association, https://ilga.org/.

[446] The history of ILGA's consultative status at ECOSOC is controversial. ILGA was granted the status in 1993, but in 1994, upon discovery that at least three of its affiliates were pro-paedophilia organisations, including the North American Man/Boy Love Association, it lost its status (by Resolution E/1994/L.48). It applied for being granted it again in 1999, 2005 and 2009 but its application was accepted only in 2011 (E/2011/L.36). ILGA Europe was granted consultative status in 2006.

[447] International Service for Human Rights, LGBTI Rights/Updated factsheets on UN Special Procedures, https://ishr.ch/defenders-toolbox/resources/lgbti-rights-updated-factsheets-on-un-special-procedures/.

> BIPOC people with diverse SOGIESC, LGBTI migrants and refugees and LGBTI persons with disabilities.

As the work of the UN tends to have a heavier footprint in poor countries, where there is a greater need for the sort of the economic assistance that the UN can provide directly or foster indirectly, clearly there is more scope for these Special Procedures to initiate the desired legislative change. Richer countries are free to ignore or reject the work of Special Rapporteurs, as the UK did recently in the case of the work of the Special Rapporteur on Extreme Poverty Philip Alston.[448]

Poorer and weaker countries do not have that luxury, so they are targeted by gender identity theory organisations such as ILGA and ISHR. They are the soft underbelly of the international community for the spread of gender identity theory, which is presented for all intents and purposes as a conditionality, much as the World Bank and the IMF did conditioning the realise of funding to the privatisation of services.[449] Effectively, these factsheets increase the pressure on Special Rapporteurs to focus on LGBTI rights in all their work, especially in poorer countries, as evident in this list:[450]

> One important development in the update this year was the inclusion of country mandates to the scope of analysis, covering the 10 mandates that were active in 2021. This includes the Special Rapporteurs and Independent Experts on the situation of human rights in Belarus, Somalia, Mali, Eritrea, Iran, Cambodia, Central African Republic, Myanmar, Democratic People's Republic of Korea and Palestine.

These are the kind of countries where Special Rapporteurs have a country mandate, as opposed to a thematic mandate (disability, poverty etc) to assess the human rights situation. These are countries with some of the most urgent and serious human rights issues in the world, four of them in

---

448 Robert Booth, "UN poverty expert hits back over UK ministers' 'denial of facts'," The Guardian, May 24, 2019, https://www.theguardian.com/society/2019/may/24/un-poverty-expert-hits-back-over-uk-ministers-denial-of-facts-philip-alston.

449 Andy Baker, Shaping the Developing World. The West, the South and the Natural World (Los Angeles: Sage Publications, 2021); Joseph Stiglitz, Globalization and Its Discontents (New York: W.W. Norton & Company, 2002).

450 International Service for Human Rights, LGBTI Rights: UN Special Procedures have increased their engagement with SOGIESC, April 5 2022, https://ishr.ch/latest-updates/lgbti-rights-un-special-procedures-have-increased-their-engagement-with-sogiesc/.

the African continent. Although there is already a Independent Expert for SOGI, these pressure groups are still insisting precious time and resources are taken away from issues such as extreme poverty, war situations and grave violations of human rights to consider whether transgender people can change their birth certificate at will.

"Transcolonialism" also uses cases originating in the domestic courts of these countries as props for embedding gender identity theory, as we shall see in this next chapter. This is not easily done as many of these courts still consider the cases from an LGB lens and we have alreedy seen how cases are misrepresented to give them a gender identity focus instead (the Jamaican reports at the Inter-American Commission for Human Rights are an example).

There is not as of yet a case in the African Court of Human Rights on transgender rights or LGBT (or even LGB) rights, reflecting a certain reluctance of the court to engage in this issue, which in the African continent has been left to domestic courts. In the next chapter there will be an analysis of some cases from domestic courts in African jurisdictions facing transgender issues.

CHAPTER 8

SELECTED CASES IN DOMESTIC COURTS

I am male but I only have female feelings. I used to help my mother in all the housework like cooking, washing and cleaning.
—*NALSA* case, Supreme Court of India

The work of domestic courts, applying domestic law and international law when necessary, is crucial to the development of international law, in the process of accretion that forms the structure of customary international law.[451] Domestic cases can be studied on their own terms, and this chapter will consider some domestic jurisprudence around gender identity and transgender rights issues, rather than look at the comparative work that international court often conduct (we have seen some examples of that in the work of the ECHR, as in the *Goodwin* case).

International law and domestic law are engaged in a continuous dialogue involving mainly the legislature and the judiciary. Countries legislate on matters with international repercussions; domestic courts interpret and apply those laws, often making reference to international customary and conventional law. International courts look at domestic laws as examples of State practice for the development of customary law and analyse the work of domestic courts to ascertain whether they are interpreting international law properly.

The chapter is focusing on courts located in the south of the world, outside the academic circuit of gender identity theorists. The case law from US, Canadian, UK, Australian courts is numerous and growing, but it is case law produced in the centre of gender identity theory. The chapter focuses on the periphery, to assess how gender identity theory spreads and if anything is lost (or gained) in the translation of these rules from one

[451] Though the pronouncement of domestic courts are not per se evidence of State practice, they are proof of State practice as proven by the submissions of States in court proceedings. They also help clarify and crystallise customary law.

jurisdiction to another.[452] I was also interested in looking at cases coming from jurisdictions without a regional human rights to court "to set the tone" (Asia) or where the human rights court still has not engaged with the issue (Africa) to see whether this meant that courts decided the cases on the basis of their constitution or looking at the jurisprudence originating from other domestic courts or other regional human rights courts. In general, the overview of domestic cases seems to indicate that those courts tend to look at domestic courts in other countries more than regional human rights courts or UN semi-judicial bodies.

Domestic courts in developing countries have also been grappling with issues arising from the rising influence of gender identity theory in international human rights law as applied by domestic courts. A 2007 case from the Supreme Court in Nepal, *Sunil Babu Pant and Others v Nepal Government*,[453] concerns the rights of third gender individuals. The first petitioner in the case, Sunil Babu Pant, was a Nepali legislator, the first openly gay one, and one of the drafters of the Yogyakarta Principles of 2006 and of 2017.[454] The second petitioner was also a director of a LGBT Rights organisation, MITINI Nepal, founded in 2002;[455] the third petitioner was the chairman of Cruise AIDS Nepal,[456] finally the fourth petitioner was the executive director of Parichaya Nepal, an organisation that seems now defunct, without seemingly any information available, at least not in English. The writ petition takes issue not only with the legal provisions around recognition of LGBT rights, but also with "social structures and norms" about which one fears the Court can do little in a direct manner. The petition, on the basis of Article 32 of the Constitution

---

[452] For the dangers and pitfalls inherent in legal transmigration see Alessandra Asteriti, "Three Grades of Evil': Nabokov, Wittgenstein and the Perils of Treaty Interpretation," European Society of International Law, 10th Anniversary Conference, 4-6 September 2014, Conference Paper No. 1/2014. https://papers.ssrn.com/sol3/papers.cfm?abstract_id=2545469.

[453] *Sunil Babu Pant and Others v Nepal Government*, Writ Petition No. 917 of 2007 https://translaw.clpr.org.in/wp-content/uploads/2018/12/PantvNepal.pdf. The English translation of the judgment does not seem to be of a good standard, which probably does not help the analysis of the case.

[454] https://yogyakartaprinciples.org/annex/. Here is listed as Sunil Pant, president of the Blue Diamond Society, a LGBT rights organisation in Nepal founded in 2001 https://web.archive.org/web/20060527190617/http://www.bds.org.np/.

[455] MITINI Nepal, https://mitininepal.org.np/.

[456] Their website does not seem active anymore https://cruise-aids-nepal.business.site/.

of Nepal, which gives citizens *locus standi* for petitioning the Supreme Court in an action against an infringement of fundamental rights, asked for an order of *mandamus* to compel the State to protect and guarantee the rights of LGBT people; an order for granting citizenship certificates in the third gender; an order to demand that anti-discrimination and equality legislation for LGBT people; and finally an ad hoc order until the relevant legislation was passed.

The petitioners in the case argued for the option of a third sex to be offered in all documents. At page 7 of the judgment, one can see exactly the danger of gender identity theory to the rights of women. Let us remember this is a judgment of the Supreme Court in Nepal and Nepal came in at 101 in the World Economic Forum's Gender Gap Index in 2020, to look at just one international indicator on women's rights.[457] At page 7 the court states:

> Since our traditional society has recognized only two types of sexes i.e. male and female. A dominant role has been provided to these two sexes "male" and "female" in the society. [sic]

The Court ignores that males and females do not have an equal dominant role in society, and that women suffer discrimination, oppression and exploitation in a way that men do not.[458] When it comes to the language adopted in the discussion on the merites, much of it would now be considered transphobic amongst gender theorists and trans rights activists. It is practically impossible to keep up with the continuous tightening of language requirements of this theory and there is no hope that a peripheral court such as the Nepali one can keep up with the academic debate raging in Western academia about the appropriate language to be adopted when talking about gender related issues. Sometimes the Court simply fails to provide a coherent explanation of the terminology adopted, as in the following passage, where it seems to affirm that one can only determine the gender (or sex?) of intersex individuals on the basis of their sexual orientation:

---

[457] World Economic Forum, Global Gender Gap Report 2020, https://www3.weforum.org/docs/WEF_GGGR_2020.pdf.

[458] The practice of banishing girls and women in "menstrual huts" still persists in Nepal, although it has been outlawed. Rojita Adhikari, "Bringing an end to deadly 'menstrual huts' is proving difficult in Nepal," BMJ (February 2020): 368, doi: https://doi.org/10.1136/bmj.m536.

> The other category of sexual minority are intersexuals who are born naturally with the both genetic organs of male and female. The number of such people is very few. Their gender is determined on the basis of their sexual orientation when they become adult.

The Court, although it claims to rely on the Yogyakarta Principles,[459] adopts definitions that differ considerably from the definitions contained in the Principles, sometimes with no source for them at all, such as the definition of transsexual as "a person, especially a man who feels that he should have been opposite sex, and therefore behaves and dresses like a member of that sex," which seems more appropriate as a definition of a cross-dresser. The definition of sexual orientation is taken from the Cambridge Advanced Learner's Dictionary, which does not match the definitions provided in the Yogyakarta Principles (sexual orientation in the YP refers to attraction to a gender, in their definition to the same or opposite sex). The definitions of transgender and intersexuality are taken from Wikipedia. What one is to make of this, apart from the fact that the Court is clearly completely confused by the whole affair, is not clear.

The court goes on to quote *Corbett v Corbett* (presumably, as it is not cited) claiming that its Court determined gender identity on the basis of genital, chromosomal and gonadal sex. This is an anachronysm, as gender identity was not used in that judgment, and it would not be used in a legal context for many years to come. It is quite clear that the court focus is on so-called "third genders" and therefore not at all useful in a more general approach to gender identity theory. The continuous oscillation between an international jurispruence and production of soft law materials focused on gender identity and transgender individuals and the Nepali focus on third gender individuals diminishes the effect of the comparative exercise by the Court. The very characterisation of the *Goodwin* case as one concerning the rights of third gender individuals illustrates the lack of clarity in the judgment, as well as the confusion between gender and sexual orientation.

One wonders how much is lost in translation but the impression remains of a court grappling with a theory with which it has no familiarity at all (in one paragraph the court talks of people with "various cross dresses"). But the most damaging element is in the presumption that men and women are enjoying their fundamental rights in an equal manner, a condition that is not granted to homosexuals and third genders, as the Court calls them.[460]

---

[459] Possibly the first court to do so.

[460]A case summary is provided by the International Commission of Jurists, *Suni Babu Pant and Others/ v Nepal Government and Others*, Supreme Court of Nepal

And yet these are the judgments that gender identity theorists present as progressive advancements in the recognition of fundamental human rights and proof that gender identity theory is embedded in domestic case law and reflects universal values.[461]

Another early case is a Malaysian one from 2005, *J.G. v Pengarah Jabatan Pendaftaran Negara*.[462] The plaintiff, a MtF man, requested to be declared female and to get a female ID card, after having undergone sex reassignment surgery in Thailand and bringing as proof medical certificates from the doctor who performed the surgery that testified "she is now FEMALE:" The judge wrote a very considered judgment, recognising the possibility of following the *Corbett* route, and not recognising the "psychological element of sex," or at least not letting it prevail over the biological element, and of such cases as *A.G. v Kevin and Others* in the Australian courts, privileging the psychological element, hence self-identification, over the biological criteria. The judge defined these different approaches as the traditional and the progressive. It is difficult not to take issue with this characterisation, when the "progressive" approach can be summed up in this description of the Plaintiff:

> She feels like a woman, lives like one, behaves as one, has her physical body attuned to one, and most important of all, her psychological thinking is that of a woman.

How can attributing to women fixed behaviours and psychological profiles be considered progressive? The Court does not explain what the evidence of this psychological female profile is, leaving the impression that saying

---

(21 December 2007), Summary based on translation published in National Judicial Academy Law Journal, 2 NJA Law Journal 2008, pp. 261-286, https://www.icj.org/sogicasebook/sunil-babu-pant-and-others-v-nepal-government-and-others-supreme-court-of-nepal-21-december-2007/. As a consequence of the case the government of Nepal approved the inclusion of "third gender" in citizenship certificates. The right of "eunuchs" to their own identity certificates is also guaranteed in Pakistan; see *Dr. Mohammad Aslam Khaki and Others v S.S.P. (Operations) Rawalpindi and Others*, Constitutional Petition 43 of 2009, PLD 2013 S.C. 88, https://translaw.clpr.org.in/wp-content/uploads/2018/10/Khaki-v-Rawalpindi.pdf. These cases seem to reflect a toxic mix of sexist assumptions made about women and traditional attitudes towards effeminate males as reflected in culture and religion (to which extensive reference is made).

[461] See the Report of the SOGI IE "The Law of Inclusion," A/HRC/47/27, 21 ff.

[462] *J.G. v Pengarah Jabatan Pendaftaran Negara*, CLJ Bulletin 41/2005, https://icj2.wpenginepowered.com/wp-content/uploads/2012/07/JG-v.-Pengarah-Jabatan-Pendaftaran-Negara-High-Court-of-Kuala-Lumpur-Malaysia.pdf.

one is a woman is sufficient for the purpose of determining sex. Alternatively, as the *NALSA* case shows, evidencing a love for cleaning the house, wearing make-up, and rejecting outside work.

The judge determined that a non better specified liberty right, based on Article 5(1) of the Federal Constitution of Malasyia, dictates that people be able to select their sex for the purpose of ID documentation.

The *NALSA* case from India is probably the most influential case on transgender rights issued by a non-Western court;[463] the case concerned the recognition of transgender individuals as having a specific identity, neither male nor female. In effect the case was concerned both with recognising the existence of a "third gender," on the basis of religious and cultural traditions in the Indian Sub-Continent, and the validation of transsexual/transgender identities, a more recent Western import into Indian law and culture. The uneasy teaming of these two strands makes for an at times confusing argument from the judge. It is worth reporting a quote that the Court cites approvingly as allowing "hijras" to speak of their identity in their own terms:

> My name is Sachin and I am 23 years old. As a child I always enjoyed putting make-up like "vibhuti" or "kum kum" and my parents always saw me as a girl. I am male but I only have female feelings. I used to help my mother in all the housework like cooking, washing and cleaning. Over the years, I started assuming more of the domestic responsibilities at home. The neighbours starting teasing me. They would call out to me and ask: "Why don't you go out and work like a man?" or "Why are you staying at home like a girl?" But I liked being a girl. I felt shy about going out and working.

Gender identity theorists are demanding that international law reifies this interpretation of a woman's role in society and grants womanhood to males on the basis of their compliance with these regressive and sexist gender roles.[464] After all, a male who wants to stay in the kitchen, wash

---

[463] *National Legal Services Authority v Union of India and Others*, Civil Original Jurisdiction Writ Petition (Civil) No. 400 of 2012; Writ Petition (Civil) No. 604 of 2013) https://indiankanoon.org/doc/193543132/.

[464] This post refers to the case as a "monumental step in the right direction." Ashta Khanna and Divesh Sawnhey, "NALSA Judgment: Critique of the Indian Perspective beyond the Adams-and-Eves Worldview," Georgetown University Undergraduate Law Review, Blog, August 25, 2020, https://guulr.com/2020/08/25/nalsa-judgment-critique-of-the-indian-perspective-beyond-the-adams-and-eves-worldview/; though this is just an undegraduate blog,

and clean and refuses outside work, *must* be a female or at least not a *real* male, so some sort of "third gender." Besides being a profoundly anti-feminist and anti-woman move, there is no legitimate legal basis for protecting these stereotypes as criteria of womanhood. On the contrary, Article 5(a) of CEDAW enjoins States:

> To modify the social and cultural patterns of conduct of men and women, with a view to achieving the elimination of prejudices and customary and all other practices which are based on the idea of the inferiority or the superiority of either of the sexes or *on stereotyped roles for men and women* [emphasis added];

A Court that is alive to States' obligations under this Article should note that wanting to work in the house and liking make-up are not exclusive attributes and practices of women, and that men and boys should be free to pursue these occupations just as much as women and girls should not be forced to do so or be limited in their aspirations. Just as a girl should be allowed to work outside the house and be outgoing or assertive, a boy should be allowed to work at home and be shy, without being told that he is not a real boy or a real man for wanting to do so. And the Court should remind India of its obligation under CEDAW not to reify and reinforce these gender stereotypes by legalising the practice of recognising sex on the basis of compliance with gender roles.

The Yogyakarta Principles are mentioned ten times in the judgment, and the judge relies heavily on them, quoting them extensively and even including them, together with international conventions, amongst the applicable law by Indian courts.[465] The Court also relies extensively on jurisprudence from the centre and not the periphery (US, Australia, New Zealand, UK), evidencing a certain level of deference to this jurisprudence,

---

it is quoted by the Global Freedom of Expression Initiative by Columbia University, https://globalfreedomofexpression.columbia.edu/publications/nalsa-judgment-critique-of-the-indian-perspective-beyond-the-adams-and-eves-worldview/. For the effect of the *NALSA* decision on subsequent litigation affecting the transgender community in India, see Akshat Argawal, "Trends in the Legal Uptake of India's Landmark Trans Rights Decision," Oxford Human Rights Hub, April 20, 2022, https://ohrh.law.ox.ac.uk/trends-in-the-legal-uptake-of-indias-landmark-trans-rights-decision/.

[465] (At para. 53). The Court also quotes para. 21 of the CAT of 2008 [sic] as obliging States to refrain from torture "regardless of sexual orientation or transgender identity." The quote is puzzling as the CAT is not from 2008, it is not divided in paragraphs, and does not mention sexual orientation or transgender identity.

consistent with an uncritical application of gender identity theory and its somewhat forced teaming with traditional Indian categories such as hejiras. It is noteworthy that all the categories of transgender or third gender people the Court mentions are males. As already noted, the supposed gender diversity and acceptance of "gender fluidity" in traditional societies is always restricted to effeminate homosexuals,[466] never women who are gender non-conforming. If a girl survives to adulthood, she can hardly dare not to perform a traditional female role. Abuse or death meet the women who dare to rebel. No sacred group for them, and no name to define them. The judgment recognises not only transgender people, but third gender people, i.e. people that do not accept categorisation either as males or females, what would be more often called non binary people, on the basis of a very expansive interpretation of the right to life, interpreted as to allow to live life with dignity; the right to equality and non discrimination (of course a legitimate ground to prohibit discrimination, but not the basis to compel belief in gender identity theory); the right of freedom of expression and finally the right to privacy. We have already considered the counter-arguments to conceptualising gender identity as a material condition, and one covered by privacy at the same time (somewhat counter-intuitively) and the necessity to interpret freedom of expression in the context of its status as a qualified right.

In 2013 the High Court of Kenya faced a claim concerning a transgender individual;[467] the case, *Republic v Kenya National Examination Council & Another Ex Parte Audrey Mbugua Ithibu* concerned a request to change name and removal of gender marker from the graduation certificate by a MtF man who had been under treatment for gender identity disorder for several years. The request could have been accepted for the simple reason that Kenyan law does not require graduation certificates to report the sex of the student. One does not need to prove transgender status, and in fact a result of the judicial review may well have been an order to remove the sex marker from the certificate as irrelevant information. Instead, the judge motivated the decision to accede the request on the basis of a "human right" to self-determine one's gender identity, bolstered by citation of jurisprudence from India and Nepal[468] and explaining that, in lay terms, the

---

[466] Hijras, Eunuchs, Aravanis, Thirunangi, Kothi, Jogtas, Shiv-Shakthis (para 44).

[467] *Republic v Kenya National Examination Council & Another Ex Parte Audrey Mbugua Ithibu,* High Court, Judicial Review Division, [2014] eKLR, http://kenyalaw.org/caselaw/cases/view/101979/.

[468] *National Legal Services Authority v Union of India and Others*, Civil Original Jurisdiction Writ Petition (Civil) No. 400 of 2012; Writ Petition (Civil) No. 604 of

applicant had a female brain in a male body (this sexist remark was considered worth quoting by the High Court of Botswana in the cases presented).

A case in the High Court of Botswana[469] in 2019, *Letsweletse Motshidiemang v Attorney General,* provides an interesting example of the retrofitting of gender identity theory in what are classic LGB discrimination cases. The claimant in the case was a homosexual man challenging the constitutionality of s164 of the Botswana Penal Code (which criminalises sodomy) and was supported by an LGB rights organisation. Additionally, the claimant argued that s164 indirectly discriminated against men, as even if the section is "gender neutral" it affects gay men disproportionately. The Court started its judgment by referring to the Penal Code of Botswana in a manner that seems suspiciously imprecise. The Court paraphrased the relevant section of the Penal Code at paragraph three of the Judgment: "Sections 164 (a) and (c) and 165 of the Penal Code proscribe and criminalise sexual intercourse and/or attempt thereof between persons of the same sex and/or gender."[470]

It seems unlikely that the Penal Code of Botswana, enacted in 1964, prohibited sexual intercourse between people of the same "gender." The relevant section of the Penal Code (164) recites in its entirety:

> 164. Unnatural offences Any person who
>
> (a) has carnal knowledge of any person against the order of nature;
> (b) has carnal knowledge of an animal; or
> (c) permits any other person to have carnal knowledge of him or her against the order of nature, is guilty of an offence and is liable to imprisonment for a term not exceeding seven years.

2013) https://indiankanoon.org/doc/193543132/; *Sunil Babu Pant and Others v Nepal Government,* Writ Petition No. 917 of 2007 https://translaw.clpr.org.in/wp-content/uploads/2018/12/PantvNepal.pdf. The website South Asian Translaw Database https://translaw.clpr.org.in/, collects all case law from South Asia on transgender issues. There are 57 cases in the database as of November 2023, mostly from India (50).

[469] *Letsweletse Motshidiemang v Attorney General*, First Instance Court, 28 June 2019, MAHGB-000591-16, https://www.southernafricalitigationcentre.org/wp-content/uploads/2019/06/Botswana-decrim-judgment.pdf .

[470] It seems bad practice from a Court not quote the article of the Penal Code, on which the entire case rests and the constitutionality of which is being challenged, *verbatim*, deciding instead to summarise it in one line.

This is a pretty standard clause against sodomy involving two men or a men and a woman. Sexual relationships between two women are not contemplated, as is often the case with sodomy laws. No reference to gender at all. The Court inserted a whole section on gender identity (paras. 150 ff) to illustrate what human dignity means in a human rights context, and then equated gender identity with sexual orientation. The claimant is making a claim that would not be sustainable unless one accepted that one's sex is immutable so that one cannot identify out of one's same sex orientation. For the Court to introduce gender identity, and reinterpret s164 as prohibiting sexual relations between same gender couples is quite extraordinary.

It is also noteworthy that the claimant argued s164 was unconstitutional because it was not clearly worded. At para. 197 the Court dismissed this part of the claim on the basis that s164 is clearly worded and refers to anal intercourse. So it is all the more extraordinary that they introduced the provision at the beginning of the judgment as prohibiting sexual intercourse between people of the same sex or the same gender.

The Court cited the Yogyakarta Principles in a manner that appears to be completely unnecessary, as there is considerable evidence from international bodies and domestic courts that sex includes sexual orientation. Where there is clear evidence from international and domestic case law, principles without any legal basis are not necessary to support an argument. It seems the Court introduced them in the judgment only to prop up their status as "authoritative" pronouncements. Finally, the Court itself quoted an unreported judgment from 2017 (which is in fact available,[471] a case that concerned "a transgender"–the case is about FtM woman), in which the State was ordered to change the identity documents of "N.D.," the concerned individual, with the following motivation:

> [...] the State has a duty to uphold the fundamental human rights of every person and to promote tolerance, acceptance and diversity within our constitutional democracy. This includes taking all necessary legislative, administrative and other measures to ensure that procedures exist whereby all State-issued identity documents which indicate a person's gender/sex reflect the person's self-defined gender identity.

[471] *N.D. v Attorney General of Botwswana and Registrar of National Registration*, High Court, 29 September 2017, MAHGB-000449-15, https://www.escr-net.org/sites/default/files/caselaw/nd_judgment.pdf.

> […] the recognition of the Applicant's gender identity lies at the heart of his fundamental right to dignity. Gender identity constitutes the core of one's sense of being and is an integral part of a person's identity. Legal recognition of the Applicant's gender identity is therefore part of his right to dignity and freedom to express himself in a manner he feels psychologically comfortable with.

The *N.D. v Attorney General of Botwswana and Registrar of National Registration* case is in fact more relevant in the embedding of gender identity in law than the 2019 one, where gender identity is retrofitted in a case clearly concerning sexual orientation only. *N.D. v Attorney General* also relied on the Yogyakarta Principles as if they were a source of law, and on judgments of foreign courts, because of the lack of precedent in Botswana's courts. This even if the application was one of breach of "N.D."'s constitutional rights, a matter for which foreign judgments are inevitably of little support. The section of the judgment on the difference between sex and gender is revealing of the extremely regressive nature of gender identity theory and actually goes some way to explain why lobby groups are so keen to spread it in countries with regressive attitudes towards women and gender roles. This excerpt from the judgment is quite illustrative:

> […] It is quite evident that in our daily activities there is no formal distinction between sex and gender and being female and male is generally attributed to having a masculine or feminine outward appearance and demeanour.
>
> [….]
>
> The notion that sex includes societal preconceptions of the role of female or male or how a man or a woman should behave is particularly highlighted by the remarks of the Applicant [….]:
>
> "As my identity documents say I am a woman, society expects me to act in a feminine manner and express myself as a woman. For instance, when I am required to produce my Omang [ID document] at my local supermarket the cashier associates my masculine gender expression as that of a man and I am addressed as 'Sir' but the moment I produce my Omang and it says female, it creates alarm."

Camminga, in his review of the case[472] explains the legal strategy adopted in *N.D.* to convince the judge.

> In summary the litigation strategy for ND's case was to show him as a normal man experiencing abnormal circumstances. The first step to doing this was, perhaps surprisingly, given that this was a court case, "not being too legalistic" [...]
>
> The second strand to this approach was to show the judge how documents related to daily inconveniences: incongruent documents frustrated ND's ability to go about daily tasks, situations that the judge might himself find quite mundane or unremarkable until disrupted. Crucially, tasks also linked to being a man, in this case, *being a provider* [emphasis added], and as such, having an accessible bank account [...] the [...] judge was not progressive; he was a just a man who had come up through the legal system. He had never been a practising lawyer or activist. Due to this, they needed him to see the case as personal, regardless of the support from SALC; it was important for the judge not to think this was an assault on the system but rather the needs of one person. To this end, it was necessary to "you know let him look at one person because it's a person for starters [...] It's an individual having their own individual problems, personal problems" (Rantao, 2018). ND was in court with his partner every day. Rantao notes that because arguments are presented from papers in order to ensure the Judge could put a face to a name, to humanise ND, he made sure to speak to ND in view of the Judge. The Judge never asked who ND was or who Rantao was talking to in the gallery. Yet, in doing so, the image of ND as a just a man with his girlfriend by his side, a *very normal, wholesome and heteronormative image* [emphasis added] was created. [...] We see the outcome of this normalisation strategy in the judge's eyes through his acknowledging that ND is "indeed a man" (para. 62). The Judge placed considerable weight on the fact that ND presented and fit what could be perceived as the stereotypical male appearance: "beard", "broad shoulders", "deep masculine voice".

This quote is sufficient to appreciate how much gender identity theory depends on entrenched gender roles, and cannot be validated without them. It comes as no surprise that a male judge in a conservative society is happy to rely on the premise that women should behave in a feminine manner and that surely they must be some sort of man if they do not. While in Western countries gender identity theorists are keen to burnish

---

[472] B. Camminga, "One for One and One for All? Human Rights and Transgender Access to Legal Gender Recognition in Botswana," International Journal of Gender, Sexuality & Law, 1(1) (2020): 241- 267, doi: https://doi.org/10.19164/ijgsl.v1i1.993

their reputation as the most progressive sector of society, in developing countries with weaker governance and judicial structures they are happy to muscle their way in by exploiting regressive stereotypes of gender roles.

CHAPTER 9

THE BACKLASH AGAINST GENDER IDENTITY

Just realized I only get to yeet 4 teets next week
[emojis sad face and laughing face]
—Dr. Sidhbh Gallagher on TikTok[473]

The Effects of Gender Identity Theory

In order to understand why gender identity theory has generated a backlash and what this consists of, a few variables need to be kept in mind. The first one is that gender identity finds application mostly at the national level, as there is not yet an international treaty on SOGI rights. However this does not mean that gender identity theory has no effect internationally, and this book has analysed its place in international law. One considerable part of this, and one not tackled so far, is the embedding of gender identity theory in standard settings bodies in two international legal regimes: the sport law regime and the health law regime. Both regimes have been greatly influenced by this theory, and in this chapter we will see how and where the backlash has affected the health law regime, and the domestic repercussions in such countries as Sweden, France and the UK. The second one is the more marked effects that this backlash is having at the domestic level, and how this is presented internationally (we have seen how the "gender critical" movement in the UK is misrepresented as a right wing anti-trans movement).[474] And finally the third variable is the

[473] A plastic surgeon in Florida specialising in SRS surgery and other "gender affirming" surgery, including on minors. The phrase refers to mastectomies. She also calles herself Dr. Teetus Deletus. Mark Tighe, "Irish gender affirmation surgeon based in Florida is reported over 'false promotions' in TikToks," Irish Independent, October 9, 2022, https://www.independent.ie/irish-news/health/irish-gender-affirmation-surgeon-based-in-florida-is-reported-over-false-promotion-in-tiktoks/42051361.html.

[474] Kerry O'Halloran, Sexual Orientation, Gender Identity and International Human Rights Law (London: Routledge, 2020), 19, refers to feminists as TERFs and notes their "transphobic tendencies." The acronym TERF (trans excluding radical feminist) is often associated in social media with death and rape threats and

assessment on the ground of the effects of gender identity theory on such vulnerable groups as women, and especially the most vulnerable women, such as prisoners and victims of rape and domestic violence, and children. Collecting data on these effects is not an easy task, for two main reasons: a more practical one is that, if MtF men are simply recorded as female it is impossible to collect robust data on the effects of allowing males to identify as women for all legal and social purposes.[475] The second, more "ideological" point is that any attempt to study the consequences of gender identity theory is immediately labelled as transphobic, with the consequence, for example, that is very difficult to find funding to conduct a project on any gender identity-related field unless one accepts the premises of the theory as part of the project,[476] though this censorious effect is lessening, not a moment too soon.

---

has been recognised as a pejorative term; see *The Queen on the Application of Harry Miller and the College of Policing*, [2020] EWHC 225 (Admin). Nonetheless the term is used by academics, policy makers and politicians.

[475] As Judge Odio Benito noted in her Partially Dissenting Opinion in *Vicky Hernández v Honduras*, at para 3 of the Opinion: "I also disagree with the decision taken concerning the State's obligation, on the one hand, to enact a 'gender identity' law that permits a person to change their sex in the public records without noting this change and, on the other hand, that the State should compile statistics on violence against trans persons. It would be impossible for the State to comply with both obligations simultaneously."
https://www.corteidh.or.cr/docs/casos/articulos/seriec_422_ing.pdf

[476] James Caspian was prevented from conducting a study on "detransitioning youth," see "Bath Spa University 'blocks transgender reserch'," BBC News, September 25, 2017, https://www.bbc.com/news/uk-41384473. Laura Favaro, a Ph.D. student at City University London was not allowed to complete her research on gender critical feminism and is taking her university to an Employment Tribunal, see Umut Özkırıml, "Cancel Culture in Academia, " The Critic, 9 September 2023, https://thecritic.co.uk/cancel-culture-in-academia/. There are many more stories of academics silenced or too afraid to debate this issue, for fear of being labelled transphobic. Some anonymous stories are collected here https://www.gcacademianetwork.org/. The IE on SOGI's report "Practices of Exclusion," 15 July 2021, A/76/152: para. 7, presents all criticism of gender identity as motivated by bigotry.
https://documents.un.org/doc/undoc/gen/n21/192/14/pdf/n2119214.pdf?token=mM2gd1Fi4FRkKwHXah&fe=true.

In speaking of a backlash, I am adopting the language of the former IE on SOGI, Victor Madrigal-Borloz. In his 2022 Report, "Practices of Exclusion,"[477] the IE summaries the content of the Report as follows:

> In the present report, the Independent Expert on protection against violence and discrimination based on sexual orientation and gender identity, Victor Madrigal-Borloz, analyses backlash against the incorporation of gender frameworks in international human rights law.

The first part of this chapter constitutes a sort of "shadow report," providing context and data to the conclusions reached in the official report. To assess the backlash and situate it historically, legally and politically, one has to consider the effects that gender identity theory has had on the ground, and a good starting point is to consider what happened post-*Goodwin*, i.e. after the "trans turn" in human rights law. Many of these effects are extra-legal, some no more than internet fashions. If the effects had been limited to what young people said on social media, I would never have taken an interest.[478] If I did, it is because what young people said was reflected in UN, EU and CoE policies.

Throughout this book I have investigated the effect this theory has on international bodies. Now it is time to go back to the "real world" and consider the effects of this theory on the ground, and how they fed back into the legal world so that they started affecting people who were not aware of the theory at all to begin with. Incidentally, this evidences a vicious social policy loop, as opposed to a virtuous one. A virtuous social policy loop includes citizens' demands being fed to policy makers and legislators and cascading back as laws and policies that are recognised and acknowledged as responding to a general need felt by the citizens. A vicious social policy loop is created when very small interest groups lobby policy makers and legislators to obtain policies and laws that match their demands.[479] When these policies are implemented, the majority of citizerns is unprepared for the consequences and is potentially hostile to them (no

---

[477] Ibidem, Summary.

[478] As someone with a background in international law; sociologists may take a different view.

[479] Kath Murray, Lucy Hunter Blackburn and Lisa Mackenzie of MurrayBlackburnMackenzie, an independent policy analysis group, have done a lot of work on the consequences of gender identity theory for women's rights and on policy capture, see for example "Reform 'Under the Radar'? Lessons for Scotland from the Development of Gender Self-Declaration Laws in Europe," Edinburgh Law Review, 24(2) (2020): 281-289.

woman likes to be told her rapist is a woman when she knows it was a man who raped her), there is a double reaction: on the one hand, a no debate policy: these changes and these laws cannot be questioned, just accepted, and the public needs to be educated about what it really wants; and second, the proliferation of gender identity-friendly "astro-turf" organisations that claim to represent the general interest (often this is accompanied by a heavy corporate campaign in support of those "grass roots demands").[480] In the "Practices of Exclusion" Report, there is a reference to funding of "anti-gender" organisations.[481] Significantly these include only religious or conservative organisations, and no feminist or LGB organisations. It may well be because these organisations are not well founded, relying on individual support by sympathetic individuals. But it also allows the Independent Expert to make the highly policitised, and therefore inappropriate in a UN Report, argument that religious organisations or conservative organisations are *ipso facto* in violation of human rights or that arguing against gender identity theory is in itself a negative thing. Only one narrative is allowed.

The first and most basic consequence of gender identity theory in society is that it has become more difficult for women to use the word woman to define themselves, without complying with the basic tenet of gender identity theory, that womanhood is not a material state but a self-defined feeling that any male can inhabit, even on a part-time[482] or on a temporary

---

[480] LGBT orgaisations such as Stonewall pursue corporate fundig very keenly (https://stonewallhousing.org/corporate-support/) and corporate branding of LGBT issues and especially transgender issues has created its own backlash within the LGBT community.

[481] "Practices of Exclusion," 15 July 2021, A/76/152: para. 37 quotes a report on funding by the Global Philantropy Project, "Meet the Moment: A Call for Progressive Philantropic Response to the Anti-Gender Movement, 2020, https://globalphilanthropyproject.org/wp-content/uploads/2021/02/Meet-the-Moment-2020-English.pdf. There is no mention of feminists and LGB campaigners against gender identity theory, with any criticism of it presented as motivated by "conservative political and religious groups in furtherance of ongoing strategies to attack human rights and self-determination, deny climate science, and promote authoritarianism" (page 5 of the GPP Report).

[482]Gender fluid Pips Bunce, a father of two working at Credit Suisse and going to work sometimes in a wig and stereotypical female clothing, was listed on the 2018 Financial Times Top 100 Women in Business; see Micha Theiner, "Anger over women's business hnour for cross-dressing banker," The Times, 22 September 2018, https://www.thetimes.co.uk/article/anger-over-women-s-business-honour-

basis.[483] Instead of being called simply women, women have been referred to as menstruators,[484] uterus or cervix havers (language that may confuse non native language speakers or disabled women who need medical care provided in easy and accessible language),[485] bleeders.[486] A local youth section of the UK Green Party even referred to women as non-men.[487] There remains, it seems, no legitimate space to assert one's lack of belief in gender identity, and the very statement that sex is immutable is met with accusations of transphobia and hatred.[488] The Report "Practices of Exclusion" asserts that both sex and gender are protected categories in international law.[489] Hopefully it means gender identity, as gender is nothing to be protected, but to be fought and dismantled. This statement is not supported by any evidence, when throughout his work, the

---

for-cross-dressing-banker-h0gv3l7nw#:~:text=A%20male%20Credit%20Suisse%20director,his%20female%20alter%20ego%2C%20Pippa.

483 There is evidence of MtF male prisoners switching again to a male identity upon being freed from female prisons, see https://www.thetimes.co.uk/article/trans-prisoners-switch-gender-again-once-freed-from-womens-units-qjjsd0nlx.

484 Rydström, Klara, "Degendering Menstruation: Making Trans Menstruators Matter," in Bobel C., Winkler I.T., Fahs B., et al., eds, The Palgrove Handbook of Critical Menstruation Studies (Singapore: Palgrave MacMillan, 2020): Chapter 68. To be fair, she calls transmen menstruators too, but then again they are females; Jane Wilbour, Chloe Morrison, Judith Iakavai and Others, "The Weather is not Good: Exploring the Menstrual Health Experiences of Menstruators with and without Disabilities in Vanuatu," The Lancet, 18 (January 2022). In this article the word woman is not mentioned once.

485 Prof. Jenny Gamble and Dr. Karleen Gribble, "'Inclusive' language on maternity care risks excluding many women," The Guardian, May 6, 2022, https://www.theguardian.com/lifeandstyle/2022/may/06/inclusive-language-on-maternity-care-risks-excluding-many-women.

486 Andrew Mark Miller, "Feminine product company slammed for referring to customers as 'bleeders'," Fox Business, March 16, 2022, https://www.foxbusiness.com/politics/feminine-product-company-slammed-referring-customers-bleeders.

487 Charlotte Beale, "Feminists mock Green Party young women's group for invite to 'non-men'," The Independent, April 17, 2016, https://www.independent.co.uk/news/uk/feminists-mock-green-party-young-women-s-invite-to-nonmen-a6987061.html.

488 Council of Europe Parliamentary Assembly, Committee on Equality and Non-Discrimination, "Combating Rising Hate against LGBTI People in Europe," Doc. 15121 Ref. 4524 (September 2020) 20210921-RisingHateLGBTI-EN.pdf (coe.int)

489 IE on SOGI Report "Practices of Exclusion," 15 July 2021, A/76/152: paras. 59-64.

Independent Expert used these words interchangeably and argued against the biological evidence of sexual binarism.

The mistake made by gender identity theorists, as already noted in this volume, is to equate the recognition of sexual binarism with the acceptance of traditional gender roles.[490] This may very well be the case for conservative or religious groups, but for feminists, the acceptance of the reality of sex (without which sexism could not be explained, let alone fought) is accompanied by a rejection of gender roles of femininity and masculinity. It is extremely frustrating to face, after more than 100 years of feminism, people who still are not conversant with the difference between female and feminine. Only someone displaying such a lack of awareness of feminism and the status of women can think, as Madrigal-Borloz does, that what needs challenging is the male/female sex binarism, rather than the feminine/masculine gender roles. One may as well challenge gravity, or molecules. What needs challenging is not the material fact of sex, but the social construct of gender/sexism. Protestations of understanding that sex is a dominant reality are vitiated by the mistaken assumption that binarism is *per se* a form of violence. To the contrary, true emancipation of women cannot be divorced from a deep understanding that women are different, but this difference should not establish a hierarchy of value and therefore of power. Additionally, rejecting the reality of sex does not create an alternative reality, where sex does not matter but gender identity does. It only demonstrates the existence of a belief in gender identity, a belief that sex is "assigned,"[491] which can be recognised in human rights law to the extent that it does not affect the rights of others. The further step undertaken by gender identity theory is to

---

[490] Ibidem, para. 13: "Anti-gender narratives defend a world of absolutes that must be challenged if human rights are to be enjoyed universally. The preconceptions upon which that order is built are that human nature is to be classified with reference to a male/female binary system on the basis of the sex assigned at birth; that people fall neatly and exclusively into that system on the same basis; and that it is a legitimate societal objective that, as a result, people adopt roles, feelings, forms of expression and behaviours that are considered inherently 'masculine' or 'feminine.'"

[491] This belief conveniently ignores that sex can currently be ascertained well before birth with extremely accurate testing, and conversely, that for most of history no medical staff attended births in order to 'assign' sex. Women can birth children without the help of male medical professionals, contrary to what Madrigal-Borloz seems to believe.

downgrade sex to "sex characteristics;"[492] these are several, and do not have to map seamlessly on the two sexes, depriving the sex classification of any real significance.

A less than clear definition of the sex class of women and of the distinction with the sex class of men makes reliable data collection, essential for statistics, for policy making, for academic research and so on, much more difficult and less effective.[493] In the UK, the switch from sex to gender identity in the collection of census data, following a policy decision by the Office of National Statistics (ONS) was reversed thanks to a legal challenge brought by Fair Play for Women.[494] The census in Scotland allowed to collect data on the basis of gender identity, as do Canada and New Zealand. Although it is useful to collect data on the population that defines itself as transgender, allowing people to self-identify in the sex category of their choice on the basis of their gender identity not only affects the reliability of data on sex, but also makes it impossible to collect reliable data on transgender individuals, therefore making it more difficult to track such things as discrimination and health needs specific to the transgender population.

Gender theorists usually ignore this effect and also counter that the number of transgender individuals is too tiny to have a statistical effect. But let's take the example of the Athena Swan Charter, which was established in 2005 to champion female academics, especially in the

---

[492] IE on SOGI Report "Practices of Exclusion," 15 July 2021, A/76/152: para. 16: "The biological reality of sex characteristics must not be conflated with the social construct of gender." While the Yogyakarta Principles still refer simply to sex, in 2017 the Yogyakarta Principles+10 refer to sex characteristics 131 times. By comparison, the word cis or cisgender never appears, and the word transgender only three times (only in the list of organisations). Is anyone still in doubt about the real target of this theory? https://yogyakartaprinciples.org/wp-content/uploads/2017/11/A5_yogyakartaWEB-2.pdf.

[493] Sullivan, Alice, Murray, Kath, and Mackenzie, Lisa, "Why Do We Need Data on Sex?." In Sex and Gender. A Contemporary Reader, Alice Sullivan and Selina Todd, eds, (London: Routledge, 2024): 104-124.

[494] Fair Play for Women Wins High Court Challenge and Judge Orders Sex Must not Be Self-Identified in the Census, 17 March 2021, https://fairplayforwomen.com/fair-play-for-women-wins-high-court-challenge-against-ons-census/. See also Alice Sullivan, "Sex and the Office of National Statistics: A Case Study in Policy Capture," The Political Quarterly 92(4) (June 2021): 638-651, https://doi.org/10.1111/1467-923X.13029.

STEMM subjects.[495] Since 2016, the Athena Swan Charter recommends that data is collected on the basis of the self-declared gender identity of academics, and not their sex. In a small department where there is only one female professor, it is sufficient for one male professor to declare a female gender identity to increase female representation by 100%. In the judiciary, when Victoria McCloud was selected as a Master in the High Court of England and Wales in 2006, the event was described as the second woman ever to be appointed. McCloud is a MtF man who transitioned well into adulthood and never had to face any of the challenges that women in the judiciary or in the professions in general have to face. From this interview it is not clear whether McCloud has a GRC.[496] In short, at a close enough level of granularity of data, even single experiences such as these can affect the statistics and the policy decisions regarding equality duties and gender pay gap. The Report "Practices of Exclusion" claims that:

> […] arguments about data collection must not be used to undermine the rights and recognition of individuals whose gender identity does not align with their biological sex as assigned at birth. In "The law of inclusion" the mandate holder stated that "some of these positions appear to build on the notion, persuasively refuted by an intersectional analysis, that non-trans women are a monolithic interest group that is not significantly traversed by race, age, nationality, and socioeconomic, migratory and other status, and also that they disregard the lived realities of trans men and other gender-diverse persons, and their health, employment, housing and education determinants.[497]

The fact is that sex and self-defined gender identity are two independent variables, generating two separate data sets, and confused references to intersectionality and "lived experiences" are completely irrelevant to the hard fact that in statistics you cannot confuse two data sets without losing clarity and statistical value for the collected data.

---

[495] Advance HE, Athena Swan Charter, https://www.advance-he.ac.uk/equality-charters/athena-swan-charter.

[496] LGBTQI+ History Month 2020: Interview with the Master Victoria McCloud, https://www.youtube.com/watch?v=-kLA28tiVEE.In February 2024, McCloud quit the judiciary citing risk of "politicising the judiciary:" David Barrett, "UK's only trans judge quits over risk of 'politicising the judiciary'," The Times, February 22, 2024, https://www.thetimes.co.uk/article/uks-only-trans-judge-quits-over-risk-of-politicising-the-judiciary-lpsqjtghv.

[497] IE on SOGI Report "Practices of Exclusion," 15 July 2021, A/76/152: para. 61.

Evidently the area where self-identification into the sex class of one's choice can have more problematic consequences is crime data. If a male is allowed to be recorded as a female, crime data risks becoming less reliable. Because women commit a very low number of violent crimes, especially sex offences,[498] even small variations can have statistically significant effects. This statistical anomaly has already been noticed in three jurisdictions, all of which have recently introduced self-identification for the purpose of crime statistics. The first is the United Kingdom, where the sex offences against children committed by female offenders increased 84% between 2015 and 2019, from 1,249 to 2,297.[499]Since, as noted in this chapter, police forces in the UK currently record sex as self-identified gender, it is impossible to know if the spike in numbers is due to more women being reported, women committing more sex offences, or males declaring a female identity. In 2016, Norway introduced self-ID legislation.[500] Statistical data shows that the number of rapes committed by women rose from 12 in 2015 to 44 in 2017.[501] Again, allowing males to identify as females means the real significance of this statistical spike is lost. Finally, in Canada gender identity was included in the Human Rights Act in 2017.[502] The Correctional Service Canada introduced an interim policy allowing prisoners to select prison accommodation in conformity with their gender identity.[503] This was finalised with a permanent policy from 2022.[504] A 2022 study from Correctional Services Canada shows that 82% of gender diverse sex offenders were transwomen.[505] Again, self-

---

[498] According to 2023 UK Governmenent data, 98% of sex offences are committed by males. https://www.gov.uk/government/statistics/offender-management-statistics-quarterly-january-to-march-2023/offender-management-statistics-quarterly-january-to-march-2023#population.

[499] "Female child sex abuse 'remains taboo' while victims struggle," BBC News, January 19, 2021, https://www.bbc.com/news/uk-55338745.

[500] The 2016 Gender Change Act.
https://www.stortinget.no/no/Saker-og-publikasjoner/Saker/Sak/?p=64488.

[501] Politiet, Voldtektssituasjonen I Norge 2017, para 4.1.
https://www.politiet.no/globalassets/tall-og-fakta/voldtekt-og-seksuallovbrudd/voldtektssituasjonen-i-norge-2017.

[502] Canadian Human Rights Act (R.S.C., 1985, c. H-6),
https://laws-lois.justice.gc.ca/eng/acts/h-6/.

[503] Interim Policy Bulletin 584 Bill C-16 (Gender Identity or Expression)
https://www.csc-scc.gc.ca/lois-et-reglements/584-pb-en.shtml.

[504] Commissioner's Directive 100: Gender Diverse Offenders *(CD100)*,
https://www.csc-scc.gc.ca/politiques-et-lois/005006-100-cd-en.shtml.

[505] Correctional Service Canada, Gender Diverse Offenders with a History of Sex Offending, https://www.csc-scc.gc.ca/research/005008-r442_O-en.shtml.

identification risks affecting the quality of this data (how many more are simply recorded as females?), and affects of course the accommodation policy.[506]

If we focus more closely on what happens in criminal trials and sentencing, if a MtF man rapes a woman, the court, and the media,[507] will adopt female pronouns for the rapist, forcing the victim to hear her rapist described as a woman, when she experienced on her own body, as one of the gravest violations of bodily integrity, the act of rape, an act only males can commit.[508] If the rapist is convicted, gender identity theorists will

---

[506] Jo Phoenix, "Rights and Wrongs. How Gender Self-Identication Policy Places Women At Risk in Prisons," MacDonald-Lauriel Institute, 2023. https://macdonaldlaurier.ca/wp-content/uploads/2023/02/20230117_Rights_and_wrongs_Phoenix_PAPER_FWeb.pdf;

[507] Emine Sinmaz, "Trans woman Isla Bryson jailed for eight years for raping two women," The Guardian, February 28, 2023, https://www.theguardian.com/uk-news/2023/feb/28/trans-woman-isla-bryson-jailed-raping-two-women. The case of Isla Bryson provoked such a backlash that Nicola Sturgeon was forced to issue the decision to move Bryson to a male prison almost immediately. Initially Bryson had been placed in a female prison; Libby Brooks, "Trans woman found guilty of rape moved to men's prison," The Guardian, January 26, 2023, https://www.theguardian.com/uk-news/2023/jan/26/trans-woman-isla-bryson-found-guilty-rape-not-be-held-in-womens-prison-sturgeon#:~:text=Isla%20Bryson%2C%20a%20transgender%20woman,an%20intervention%20by%20Nicola%20Sturgeon.

[508] The Equal Treatment Bench Book is a guidance published by the Judicial College in the UK for the conduct of judicial proceedings by judges. In the April 2023 version, the protected characteristic of sex was renamed gender; in the chapter on Trans People [sic] the ETBB recommends the following: "It should be possible to respect a person's gender identity and their present name for nearly all court and tribunal purposes, regardless of whether they have obtained legal recognition of their gender by way of a Gender Recognition Certificate." So alleged rapists will be referred to with female pronouns in front of the victim. This even if the rapist is not in possession of a GRC and therefore is legally male. In effect, all court participants are asked to accept a misrepresentation of reality, in violation of the duty to report the truth. The ETBB adds that: "There may be situations where the rights of a witness to refer to a trans person by pronouns matching their gender assigned at birth, or to otherwise reveal a person's trans status, clash with the trans person's right to privacy. It is important to identify such potential difficulties in advance, preferably at a case management stage." Effectively there could be cases when the witness uses a male pronoun to refer to her rapist and everyone else, including the judge, uses a female pronoun. How can this not affect the credibility of the witness and the proper conduct of the trial? Or will the witness be under pressure to 'respect the privacy' of the rapist and use

insist the rapist is housed in a female prison,[509] in a clear violation of the rights of female prisoners not to be exposed to inhuman and degrading treatment, an absolute right that cannot be balanced against the right of the rapist not to go to a male prison.[510] It is true that some transgender prisoners are at risk in male prisons. So are young gay men, and sex offenders. Not a reason to house them in the female estate.

In a 2021 case in the Queen's Bench Division,[511] a female inmate challenged the policy of housing transgender prisoners with a conviction for sex offences in the female estate;[512] she had been sexually assaulted by a trans prisoner with a GRC (these are normally recorded as female and held in the female estate unless extraordinary circumestances apply). In this case the prisoner was held in the E Wing, a section of the female

---

female pronouns? Is anyone in any doubt that a rapist is a male, taking into account the definition of rape in English law? https://www.judiciary.uk/wp-content/uploads/2023/06/Equal-Treatment-Bench-Book-April-2023-revision.pdf.

[509] The issue of housing MtF male prisoners in female prisons is one of the most contentious. Although it is difficult to obtain reliable data, as many MtF male prisoners are simply recorded as female, newspaper reports can show when these placements create problems. Many of the stories collected in this website concern prison placement stories: https://www.womenarehuman.com/category/crime/. The organisation Keep Prisons Single Sex campaigns for the rights of female prisoners and produces high quality research on the issue, https://kpssinfo.org/. In the UK, stories such as Karen White's (a MtF convicted rapist who was housed in a female prison where four female prisoners were subsequently assaulted) have resulted in considerable commentary, including from gender theorists, see for example Alex Sharpe, "Foxes in the Henhouse: Putting the Trans Women Prison Debate in Perspective," September 11, 2018, https://inherentlyhuman.wordpress.com/2018/09/11/foxes-in-the-henhouse-putting-the-trans-women-prison-debate-in-perspective/.

[510] Phoenix, Jo, "Sex, Gender Identity and Criminology" In Sex and Gender. A Contemporary Reader, eds. Alice Sullivan and Selina Todd (London: Routledge, 2024): 259-277.

[511] *The Queen on the Application of FDJ and Secretary of State for Justice* [2021] EWHC 1764 (Admn).

[512] The policy has since been amended, so that sex offenders who declare a trans identity will be held in a special unit; Public Defender Service, "Specialist prison units for violent or sexual 'Trans women' offenders," March 17, 2023, https://publicdefenderservice.org.uk/news/specialist-prison-units-for-violent-or-sexual-trans-women-offenders/#:~:text=Transgender%20women%20convicted%20of%20violent,housed%20in%20a%20men's%20prison.&text=If%20you%20are%20affected%20by,of%20our%20lawyers%20in%20confidence.

prison for high risk trans prisoners, but the complainant argued they were left unsupervised and free to mingle with the rest of the prison population. The case is a classic example of a judge wrongly applying the proportionality test to an issue that does not permit proportionality, i.e. the issue of a potential breach of Article 3 ECHR:

> [….] I readily accept that a substantial proportion of women prisoners have been the victims of sexual assaults and/or domestic violence. I also readily accept the proposition that some, and perhaps many, women prisoners may suffer fear and acute anxiety if required to share prison accommodation and facilities with a transgender woman who has male genitalia, and that their fear and anxiety may be increased if that transgender woman has been convicted of sexual or violent offences against women. Sexual assault is capable of attaining the level of gravity contemplated by art.3 (though not every sexual assault will necessarily do so). I accept Ms Monaghan's submission that the taking by the Defendant of steps which increase the risk of art.3 mistreatment of women prisoners is within the ambit of art.3. […] In principle, therefore, I accept that arts. 3, 8 and 14 are engaged on the facts alleged in this case. However, the subjective concerns of women prisoners are not the only concerns which the Defendant had to consider in developing the policies: he also had to take into account the rights of transgender women in the prison system.

In defining the Article 3 rights of female prisoners as "subjective concerns" the judge gravely mischaracterises what the case is about, and allows the "rights" of trans male prisoners to prevail over the simple "concerns" of female prisoners. It is a good thing that the recent change in policy vindicates the woman whose safety and dignity were so easily dismissed by the judge.[513]

There is a comparative law element to this issue and one that evidences the problem of unchecked legal transmigration, i.e., the migration of laws from one jurisdiction to another.[514] Specifically, the prison policy for

---

[513] Ministry of Justice, "The Care and Management of Individuals who are Transgender," 31 March 2023, https://kpssinfo.org/the-care-and-management-of-individuals-who-are-transgender-pdf/.

[514] Alessandra Asteriti, "Three Grades of Evil: Nabokov, Wittgenstein and the Perils of Treaty Interpretation," European Society of International Law, 10th Anniversary Conference, Vienna 4-6 September 2014, Paper 1/2014, https://papers.ssrn.com/sol3/papers.cfm?abstract_id=2545469, for an example of legal transmigration of US constitutional law into treaty law via the Bilateral Investment Treaty Model of the US.

transgender prisoners developed by Scotland in 2014,[515] allows prisoners to self-identify in the prison of their choice, with few security checks. This is the language adopted in the guidance:

> A male-to-female person in custody living permanently as a woman without genital surgery should be allocated to a female establishment. She should not be automatically regarded as posing a high sexual offence risk to other people in custody and should not be subject to any automatic restrictions of her association with other people in custody. However, if there is clear evidence that she, as an individual, may pose a sexual offence risk, then this should be dealt with as for any other person in custody posing a risk. Only where a risk assessment determines it is justified, should she be subject to increased staff supervision or restrictions of her association with other people in custody.

In 2016, Malta introduced its own policy on transgender prisoners.[516] The policy allows transgender prisoners to select the accommodation of their choice, with minimal checks. This is the language of the policy:

> A male-to-female inmate living as a woman should be allocated to a female establishment as per gender marker. She should not be automatically regarded as posing a high sexual offence risk to other inmates and should not be subject to any automatic restrictions of her association with other inmates. The Director reserves the right to assign a different allocation if there is clear evidence that the inmate may pose a risk of abuse or be subjected to abuse.

Almost identical language to the Scottish policy. This is no surprise, as the Malta policy quotes as its source the Scotland policy.[517] In itself, this is not so unusual. Both Scotland and Malta pride themselves on their very "progressive" transgender policies, and in fact Malta is first in Europe for transgender rights, according to ILGA Europe.[518] However, Scotland and

---

515 Scottish Prison Service, Gender Identity and Gender Reassignment Policy Review, http://www.sps.gov.uk/Corporate/News/News-8219.aspx-

516 Correctional Services, "Trans, Gender Variant & Intersex Prison Policy," August 2016, https://meae.gov.mt/en/Documents/TRANS%20GENDER%20VARIANT%20and%20INTERSEX%20INMATES%20POLICY/Trans%20Gender%20Variant%20and%20Intersex%20Inmates%20Policy.pdf.

517 "References: Scottish Prison Service Gender Identity and Gender Reassignment Policy for those in our Custody (2014)."

518 Stephen Emms. "Malta: The tiny European island of tolerance," BBC Travel, January 31, 2024, https://www.bbc.com/travel/article/20240130-malta-the-tiny-european-island-of-tolerance. A more critical assessment of Malta's rainbow-

Malta do not have the same "progressive" approach to women's rights. While women in Scotland have reproductive rights, women in Malta do not have access to a pregnancy termination even if their pregnancy is the consequence of a rape. Until 2022 the law did not allow abortions even if the life of the mother was at risk, but even after the change in the law, Malta remains the European country with the most restrictive abortion legislation.[519] These are the dangers of legal transmigration. The Scottish policy, which does not take into proper consideration the risk to women from MtF sex offenders, becomes especially problematic in Malta where, if a female inmate were to be raped (or even have consensual sex) and become pregnant, she would not have access to an abortion. The fact that this of course includes FtM prisoners, so female prisoners, raises the question whether the reproductive rights of FtM women form part of the assessment by ILGA for their Rainbow Map.

The issues raised by self-identification in prisons receive possibly the weakest response by the former IE on SOGI. The charge is that women in prison, who are particularly vulnerable, are affected by MtF male prisoners (many of whom are sex offenders) being allocated to female prisons. This is how the Report deals with the charge:

> Some submissions presented the claim that segregated spaces, particularly prisons, changing rooms and bathrooms, are threatened by the granting of access to trans women. The Independent Expert notes that submissions repeated (often verbatim) the same set of seven alleged incidents of trans women (or persons purporting to be trans women) causing harm to cisgender women in safe spaces. Even among the small set of cited cases,

---

washing in Tiffany Cowen, "Exposed: The Murky Maltese Connections of the Author of the European Resolution on Gender Self-ID," Women Are Human, January 30, 2020, https://www.womenarehuman.com/exposed-the-murky-maltese-connections-of-the-author-of-european-resolution-on-gender-self-id/.

[519] The law before the amendment, https://policehumanrightsresources.org/content/uploads/2016/08/Criminal-Code-Malta-1854.pdf?x49094 (Sub-title VII, Arts 241-244). In 2022, an American tourist experienced severe bleeding in the 16th week of her pregnancy but the doctors refused to intervene because of the strict criminal provisions in the law. The incident was the object of a parliamentary question in the European Parliament (E-002522/2022).https://www.europarl.europa.eu/doceo/document/E-9-2022-002522_EN.html. Almost a year later Malta amended its abortion law to create an exception for the life of the mother. "Malta votes to ease total abortion ban but pro-choice groups brand the new law 'a betrayal'," EuroNews.Health, June 28, 2023, https://www.euronews.com/next/2023/06/28/malta-votes-to-ease-total-abortion-ban-but-pro-choice-groups-brand-the-new-law-a-betrayal.

> several of the incidents recounted in these submissions are factually contested. These evidentiary shortcomings notwithstanding, the mandate holder has previously voiced the view that "the claim that legal recognition of trans women per se threatens safe spaces [...] appears to draw on stigma about predatory determinism" and has suggested a risk management approach that should include all objectively identified risks for safe spaces for all women (including lesbian, bisexual and trans women), which cannot promote, replicate or condone stigma or stereotypes.

The two incidents that the IE refers to are from the US and concern school toilets and changing rooms. In one incident, the school was found to have violated Title IX.[520] The IE does not engage at all with the issue of women in prison. The group "Women are Human,"[521] collects news reports from around the world, including on issues surrounding the presence of MtF men in female prisons, such as policy or legal changes, statistics, and events occurring in prisons and affecting women. From 2018 to 2022 the group collected 432 news reports of crimes committed by transgender individuals. Of these, 39 concern adverse events in female prisons, 9% of the total. 13 in Canada, ten in the US, two in Latin America, ten in the UK, two in the rest of Europe (Ireland) and two in Australia/New Zealand. Numerous other news items concern demands by transgender prisoners to be moved to female prisons, sentencing of transgender prisoners with an order to move them to female prisons, etc. Of the 39 news items, two specifically concern safety and dignity issues of female staff, one a chocking incident of a female inmate, two impregnating a female inmate, six incidents of violence, nine rapes or sexual assaults, and one grooming of a vulnerable mentally disabled female inmate for sex.[522] The very first news item, from 2018, concerns an incident in a UK prison involving an individual by the names Martin Ponting/Jessica Winfield. Ponting had been convicted and sentenced in 1995 of having raped two little girls. In 2017 Ponting declared a female gender identity, changed name to Jessica Winfield and was moved to a female prison (Ponting had not undergone genital surgery). Following the transfer, several women were sexually

---

[520] Dan Whisenhunt, "Department of Education can't substantiate assault in Oakhurst bathroom, finds Title IX violations," decaturish.com, 23 June, 2020, https://decaturish.com/2020/06/department-of-education-cant-substantiate-assault-in-oakhurst-bathroom-finds-title-ix-violations/. Title IX of the Education Amendments of 1972 protects people from sex based discrimination in any education programme or activity receiving federal financial assistance.

[521] Women Are Human, https://www.womenarehuman.com/about-us/.

[522] https://www.womenarehuman.com/category/crime/.

assaulted.[523] These are the very well documented events that the IE is refusing to acknowledge, instead accusing women of "stigmatising" MtF men as sexual predators. In effect, data from different jurisdictions confirms that the highest percentage of sex offenders in any prison population is amongst MtF men.[524]

Males who identify as females are being given access to female sports, competing all the way from school and university sports to the Olympics.[525] If female athletes find the courage to complain[526] that this is neither fair[527] nor safe[528] they are told that transwomen have no athletic

---

[523] Diana Shaw, "Transgender Inmate in Prison for Rape of Young Girls is Accused of Sexual Assaults on Female Inmates," Women Are Human, June 1, 2018, https://www.womenarehuman.com/transgender-man-who-raped-young-girls-housed-in-womens-prison-jessica-winfield-nee-martin-ponting/.

[524] Following a Freedom of Information request by Fair Play for Women it was revealed that in 2018, out of 125 transgender offenders, 60 were sex offenders. The number could be an underestimation, as MtF men with a GRC are counted amongst the female offenders. https://fairplayforwomen.com/transgender-prisoners/. It is very difficult to assess how many male sex offenders show up under the female category. Another FoI request by Fair Play for Women revealed that 16 police forces in the UK record sex as self-identified gender. https://fairplayforwomen.com/police_record_males_as_female/. It is possible to ascertain the true sex of the offender if the offence is recorded as rape, as in the Sexual Offences Act 2003 rape is defined as the non consensual penetration of the vagina, anus or mouth by a penis.

[525] Devine, Cathy, "Sex, Gender Identity and Sport." In Sex and Gender. A Contemporary Reader, Alice Sullivan and Selina Todd, eds., (London: Routledge, 2024): 232-258. This topic cannot be understood properly without considering that in sport not only there was discrimination, but outright exclusion. Women and girls were simply not allowed to compete at all or female sport received insufficient funding and State and/or corporate support.

[526] Aaron Katersky, "Female athletes ask to sue over policy allowing transgender athletes to compete in sports," ABC News, June 7, 2023, https://abcnews.go.com/US/female-athletes-sue-policy-allowing-transgender-athletes-compete/story?id=99878569. It is not very often that female athletes complain as this can result in death threats and abuse, as happened to young athlete Riley Gaines, Natasha Chen, and Cheri Mossburg, "Riley Gaines, outspoken critic of transgender athletes, says she was attacked during event at SFSU," ABC News, April 8, 2023, https://abc7news.com/riley-gaines-attacked-san-francisco-state-assaulted-ambushed/13099865/.

[527] Arguments about fairness are interwoven with arguments about safety but tend to underscore that the physical advantage retained by MtF male athletes even after lowering their testosterone levels (rules vary depending on sport) makes the competition inherently unfair. This advantage is denied by gender identity theorist

advantage and that maybe female athletes should just train a little harder[529] and that sport is not about winning and it is not fair anyway.[530] Considerable data shows that MtF male athletes retain puberty advantage even if they lower their testosterone. Only MtF males are affected, because only they have a male advantage. Male sport has always been a technically open category, but it is impossible for females to qualify and compete,

---

and trans rights activists, see for example Giulia Castagnaro, "New Report Confirms Trans Women Do Not Have Any Biomedical Advantage in Elite Sport," Gender GP, March 28, 2023, https://www.gendergp.com/new-report-confirms-trans-athletes-do-not-have-biomedical-advantage-in-elite-sport/. Legitimate peer reviewed reaserch proves that the biological advantage conferred by puberty cannot be eliminated by artificially lowering testosteron levels; see Emma Hilton and Tommy Lundberg, "Transgender Women in the Female Category of Sport: Perspectives on Testosterone Suppression and Performance Advantage," Sports Medicine, 51(2) (February 2021): 199-214, doi: 10.1007/s40279-020-01389-3.

[528] Incidents involving transgender athletes (always MtF males) have been increasing as the number of these athletes in female sports has been also increasing. See for example Chris Brooke, "Transgender woman footballer quits and threatens to sue for discrimination because rivals refuse to compete against her after she left opponents 'terrified' and broke knee of a player 'blocking her shot'," Mail Online, November 20, 2023, https://www.dailymail.co.uk/news/article-12771191/Transgender-woman-footballer-left-opponents-terrified-broke-knee-player-blocking-shot-quits-team-threatens-sue-discrimination-rivals-refused-compete-against-her.html. Contact sports are of course more dangerous for female athletes; Kevin Harrish, "Transgender woman rugby player injures female opponents," Next Impulse Sports, August 25, 2023, https://nextimpulsesports.com/2023/08/25/transgender-rugby-injure-opponents-ash-davis/. Sometimes these injuries result in a change of the rules, see Sean Ingle, "World Rugby bans trans women from elite women's game due to injury risks," The Guardian. October 10, 2020, https://www.theguardian.com/sport/2020/oct/09/world-rugby-bans-trans-women-from-elite-womens-game-due-to-injury-risks#:~:text=World%20Rugby%20bans%20trans%20women%20from%20elite%20women's%20game%20due%20to%20injury%20risks,-This%20article%20is&text=Trans%20women%20will%20not%20be,new%20guidelines%20for%20transgender%20players.

[529] https://x.com/Riley_Gaines_/status/1710360068154151053?s=20.

[530] Jonathan Liew, "Why the arguments against trans, intersex and DSD athletes are based on prejudice and ignorance" The Independent, February 22, 2019 https://www.independent.co.uk/sport/general/athletics/caster-semenya-news-gender-martina-navratilova-trans-cas-jonathan-liew-column-a8792861.html. This argument clearly confuses procedural fairness and inherent material conditions.

because of the male advantage.[531]Additionally, rules on female sports do not prevent MtF male athletes from competing, they only allow them to compete in the correct sex category, as sport is not divided by gender identity. How could it be, when there are potentially hundreds of them, we are told?

In his report "Practices of Exclusion" Madrigal Borloz ignores the scientific data on the advantage conferred by male puberty, and any issue of privacy and dignity affecting especially young girl athletes, claiming that preventing "transgirls" from competing affects their mental and physical wellbeing, coveniently ignoring that no-one is arguing that they should not compete, but only that they should do so in their sex class. "Transboys," being females, are, as usual, ignored.[532]

One of the most seriously affected categories is disabled women losing the right to select a female carer for intimate care.[533] Any person can self-identify as a female, even in the absence of any medical or surgical intervention, and be assigned for the intimate care of a vulnerable, maybe non verbal woman. Sexual assaults of disabled women are at epidemic levels, as these are probably the most vulnerable women there are, sometimes being incapable to report any sexual assault against them.[534] And as everybody knows, the only way to lower to negligible levels the risk of sexual assault is to provide a female carer. Women in hospitals and other medical settings are losing the right to female wards or female doctors and nurses.[535] In at least one well publicised example, a woman who was raped by a transwoman in a hospital ward initially had her claim

---

[531] John Armstrong, Alice Sullivan and George M Perry, "Performance of Non-Binary Athletes in Mass-Participation Running Events," BMJ Open Sport & Exercise Medicine (2023) doi:10.1136/ bmjsem-2023-001662.

[532] IE on SOGI Report "Practices of Exclusion," 15 July 2021, A/76/152: paras. 65-70.

[533] "Helen: a severely learning-disabled girl: sex-based rights under threat," Transgender Trend, July 10, 2022, https://www.transgendertrend.com/severely-learning-disabled-girl-sex-based-rights-under-threat/.

[534] UN Fact Sheet: Violence Against Women and Girls with Disabilities, https://www.un.org/womenwatch/daw/csw/csw57/side_events/Fact%20sheet%20%20VAWG%20with%20disabilities%20FINAL%20.pdf.

[535] "My body, my choice: privacy, consent and compulsion in personal care," Legal Feminist, July 25, 2020, https://www.legalfeminist.org.uk/2020/07/25/my-body-my-choice-privacy-and-consent-in-personal-care/.

dismissed by the hospital with the motivation that "there were no men in the ward" so she could not have been raped.[536]

Women are losing the right to female only rape shelters and domestic violence shelters.[537] Some of the most traumatised women, who have a panic response to any male bodied individual, are forced to share facilities with male bodied individuals who claim a female gender identity. Women who complain are accused of transphobia or simply ignored. In England a woman sued a rape shelter for not having any female only services available to women who have been raped.[538] In Scotland a MtF man without a GRC, Mridul Wadhwa, was selected as the chief executive of Edinburgh Rape Crisis Centre; Wadhwa declared that women, who have been raped and request female only services, are bigoted and need to be re-educated about trans rights.[539]

Gender identity theorists are insisting children as young as two can already be transgender[540] and that affirming their gender identity through puberty

---

[536] Hayley Dixon, "Hospital told police patient was not raped because alleged attacker was transgender," The Telegraph, March 17, 2022, https://www.telegraph.co.uk/news/2022/03/17/hospital-told-police-patient-not-raped-alleged-attacker-transgender/. NHS Kent and Medway, Ref. FOI.22.KAM017, March 2022, https://www.kentandmedway.icb.nhs.uk/application/files/6616/5537/7359/FOI.22.KAM017_-_Single_sex_accommodation_policy.pdf.

[537] Katie Dangerfield, "Canada's oldest rape crisis centre faces backlash over excluding trans women," Global News, March 19, 2019, https://globalnews.ca/news/5071122/vancouver-rape-relief-and-womens-shelter-funding-trans-women/. Even when there are shelters that accept transwomen, shelters who restrict access based on sex, to cater to traumatised women are attacked or defunded if they refuse to accept males who identify as women.

[538] June Kelly, "Woman suing rape charity over transgender row," BBC News, June 28, 2022, https://www.bbc.com/news/uk-61958346.

[539] Tom Gordon, "Outcry over plan to educate 'bigoted' rape survivors about trans rights," The Herald, August 12, 2021, https://www.heraldscotland.com/politics/19509343.outcry-plan-educate-bigoted-rape-survivors-trans-rights/. Former employee Roz Adams won an Employment Tribunal case for constructive dismissal and belief discrimination against the Edinburgh Rape Crisis Centre, Case No 4102236/2023, 4102236 - Judgment - 14.05.2024 (redacted).pdf - Google Drive.

[540] "Gender-affirmative therapist: Baby who hates barrettes=trans boy; questioning sterilizazion of 11-year olds same as denying cancer treatment," 4thWaveNow, September 29, 2016, https://4thwavenow.com/2016/09/29/gender-affirmative-

blockers,[541] cross-sex hormones and surgery is life saving. In the UK, the number of girls declaring a trans identity has gone up 5,337% in ten years, but it is not possible to investigate this medical issue, as it is transphobic to do so.[542] In some countries girls as young as 12 are getting double mastectomies[543] and go through the menopause in their early 20s.[544] Girls and women seem particularly targeted by the medicalisation of gender identity. This topic will be analysed in more detail in the second part of the chapter, to consider its comparative and international dimension.

Young lesbian girls are told that "translesbians are lesbians"[545] and led to believe that sex is not relevant for sexual orientation, but gender is.[546] The right to same sex orientation is being presented as transphobic,[547] and

---

therapist-baby-who-hates-barrettes-trans-boy-questioning-sterilization-of-11-year-olds-same-as-denying-cancer-treatment/.

541 Michael Biggs, "The Technology of Puberty Suppression," in Alice Sullivan and Selina Todd, Sex and Gender. A Coontemporary Reader (London: Routledge, 2024): 175-193.

542 Transgender Trend, "The Surge in Referral Rates of Girls to the Tavistock Continues to Rise," July 1, 2019, https://www.transgendertrend.com/surge-referral-rates-girls-tavistock-continues-rise/.

543 Annie Tang and others, "Gender-Affirming Mastectomy Trends and Surgical Outcomes in Adolescents," Annals of Plastic Surgery, 88 (May 2022): 325-331 doi: 10.1097/SAP.0000000000003135.

544 With the associated health problems. Puberty blockers can also have a severe effect on children's bodies. A girl who started on puberty blockers at age 11 by 14 had developed crippling osteoporosis. Michael Cook, "Trans narrative under fire in Sweden," BioEdge, May 7, 2022, https://bioedge.org/featured/trans-narrative-under-fire-in-sweden/. Sweden's Karolinska Institute decided to suspend the use of puberty blockers: "Sweden's Karolinska Ends All Use of Puberty Blockers and Cros-Sex Hormones for Minors Outside of Clinical Studies," Society for Evidence Based Gender Medicine, May 5, 2021,
https://segm.org/Sweden_ends_use_of_Dutch_protocol.

545 Already in 1983, Peggy Cohen-Kettenis argued that MtF males who are attracted to women have a lesbian sexual orientation. Peggy Cohen-Kettenis and A.J. Kuiper, "Gender Identity, Gender Roles and Sexual Orientation in Transsexuals," Paper presented at the 8th International Symposium on Gender Dysphoria, Bordeaux 1983.

546 LGBT Youth Scotland, "Good Sex Is (Trans People),"
https://lgbtyouth.org.uk/good-sex-is-trans-people/; Imani Rupert-Gordon, "Honoring Trans Lesbians During Lesbian Visibility Week," National Center for Lesbian Rights, April 29, 2022, https://transequality.org/blog/honoring-trans-lesbians-during-lesbian-visibility-week.

547 James Esses, "Thank you, Nancy Kelley!," The Critic, July 13, 2023,
https://thecritic.co.uk/thank-you-nancy-kelley/.

lesbian women are losing the right to meet and organise on the basis of their sexual orientation.[548] As for almost any element of gender identity theory, the pressure on women to conform is much higher than on men. The concern is glibly dismissed in the Report "Practices of Exclusion," where it is reduced to a matter of consent, as the only frame of reference.[549] The fact that lesbian girls may be under pressure to accept sexual relationships with older males who claim a female and lesbian identity does not seem to raise any concerns of possible coercion, given the unbalance of power inherent in a female-male relationship. If a lesbian sets a date on a dating app and is then confronted by a male claiming to be a lesbian there are issues of safety to be addressed as well. Lesbian are afraid of being accused of transphobia or "sexual racism," if they express a preference for females.[550] The very idea of same sex sexual orientation is contested, once it is defined as attraction towards the same "gender."[551]

Pressure is brought to bear on female academics and professionals who express even the mildest form of criticism towards gender identity theory. It is probably an effect of their professional and intellectual background that these women have been at the forefront of the pushback against the theory, through court cases, especially in the UK, reaffirming their right of freedom of speech. Of the growing number of court cases probably the most consequential one for equality rights in an employment context has

---

[548] In October 2023 the Australian Human Rights Commission denied the Lesbian Action Group the right to have female only events, by denying the application of an exemption from the application of the Sex Discrimination Act 1984. Australian Human Rights Commission, "Summary of the decision on the exemption's application made by the Lesbian Action Group," October 12, 2023, https://humanrights.gov.au/sites/default/files/lesbian_action_group_summary_of_decision_1_0.pdf. See also "Equality Australia welcomes decision to deny exemption to exclude trans women from lesbian event," Equality, October 17, 2023, https://equalityaustralia.org.au/equality-australia-welcomes-decision-to-deny-exemption-to-exclude-trans-women-from-lesbian-even/.

[549] IE on SOGI Report "Practices of Exclusion," 15 July 2021, A/76/152: para. 62.

[550] Sonia Sodha, "If a Lesbian Only Desires Same-Sex Dates, That's Not Bigotry, It's Her Right," The Guardian, May 29, 2022, https://www.theguardian.com/commentisfree/2022/may/29/if-lesbian-prefers-same-sex-dates-thats-not-bigotry-desire-personal-thing.

[551] As in the definition of homosexual on the Stonewall website. https://www.stonewall.org.uk/list-lgbtq-terms.

been *Forstater v CGD*;[552] for freedom of speech, while for hate speech, *Scottow v CPS*.[553]

More recently, the case of *Joanna Phoenix v The Open University*[554] helped reinstate the importance of academic freedom, with the Tribunal Judge finding for the Claimant in a case of discrimination and victimisation as a consequence of her protected gender critical beliefs, resulting in her constructive dismissal. Specifically, at paragraph 22 the Tribunal lamented that the Respondent, in the person of the academics of The Open University found responsible of a campaign of discrimination and victimisation of the Claimant because of her beliefs, lacked the intellectual rigour one associates with academics, a point that is also made on different occasions in this work:

> We had in mind that the majority of the witnesses we heard from were academics. These were professionals who had been trained in the methodology of research and presentation of fact and analysis producing argument. We expected a certain basic level of rigour in presenting the evidence before the Employment Tribunal. There were some witnesses who we address below in our findings who did not meet this standard.

Although these cases, and others, were eventually won, it is clear that the process is the punishment for women who do not espouse gender identity theory. Prevailing after months or years of judicial process is too high a price to pay for expressing one's opinion, even in a shocking and offensive manner.[555] Trying to avoid censure, in a movement that presents as offensive even pronouns, is a fool's errand. The insistence, by the former IE on SOGI, in his "Practices of Exclusion" Report, that gender identity is a "lived experience of every human being" evidences an ideological incapacity to acknowledge that most human beings around the world are not even aware of such a concept, and, of those who are, many reject it as

---

552 *Maya Forstater v CGD Europe, Center for Global Development and Masood Ahmed*, UKEAT/0105/20/JOJ, 10 June 2021, https://assets.publishing.service.gov.uk/media/60c1cce1d3bf7f4bd9814e39/Maya_Forstater_v_CGD_Europe_and_others_UKEAT0105_20_JOJ.pdf.

553 *Katherine Elizabeth Scottow v Crown Prosecution Service*, [2020] EWHC 3421 (Admin), 16 December 2020, https://www.judiciary.uk/wp-content/uploads/2020/12/Scottow-v-CPS-judgment-161220.pdf.

554 *Joanna Phoenix v The Open University*, Employment Tribunal, Case No.: 3322700/2021 & 3323841/2021, Judgment of 22 January 2024, https://www.judiciary.uk/wp-content/uploads/2024/01/Joanna-Phoenix-v-The-Open-University-Employment-Tribunal-Reserved-Judgment.pdf .

555 The standard for the protection of opinions set by the ECHR.

facet of their identity.[556] Madrigal-Borloz seems incapable of accepting that some women do not have a concept of "gender" identity, because being aware of one's sex, and its immutable character, is not a gender identity. *A fortiori* feminist women reject the idea of being "cisgender," i.e. identifying with the gender stereotypes of their sex.

The Affirmative Model of Transgender Care: Comparative and International Approach

Though gender identity theory promotes a completely non-medicalised approach to the recognition of transgender identities in law, it also provides the theoretical underpinning for a highly medicalised "affirmative" treatment of children and adults who experience a disconnect between their mind and body, involving puberty blockers to stop naturally occurring puberty, cross-sex hormones to accentuate secondary sex characteristics of the opposite sex, and finally genital surgery and other surgeries, especially on MtF males to further feminise the body.

The beginnings of gender identity theory are inextricably linked with the advancement in medical science and the developments in the treatment of "transsexuals," first in Europe before the war, and then in the US, especially in the 1950s and 1960s. The beginnings can be seen in the foundation, in 1919, of the Institute for Sexual Research in Germany by Magnus Hirschfeld.[557] Homosexuality was illegal at the time, and it was to remain so under Hitler. It was however possible for transsexuals to obtain a "transvestite pass" (Transevestitenschein). Doctor Hirschfeld was instrumental in the development of the pass policy.[558] Nazism saw the destruction of Hirschfeld's Institute. Hirschfeld has been feted as a hero of gay and trans rights, though his story is not as simple as the hagiographic treatment implies.[559] It is his role in developing the surgical transition of

---

[556] IE on SOGI Report "Practices of Exclusion," 15 July 2021, A/76/152: para. 48.

[557] Magnus-Hirschfeld-Gesellschaft e.V. https://magnus-hirschfeld.de/ausstellungen/institute/.

[558] Livia Gershon,"Gender Identity in Weimar Germany," JSTOR Daily, 18 November 2018, https://daily.jstor.org/gender-identity-in-weimar-germany/, See also Thomas Jander, "A Licence to Be Different," Deutsches Historisches Museum Blog, 23 July 2019, https://www.dhm.de/blog/2019/07/23/whats-that-for-a-licence-to-be-different/.

[559] See Malcolm Richard Clark,"Hirschfeld: The Dodgy High Priest of Quackery," 16 March 2023 https://malcolmrichardclark.substack.com/p/hirschfeld-the-dodgy-high-priest?utm_source=%2Fsearch%2Fhirschfeld&utm_medium=reader2.

people whom he termed "sexual intermediaries" that makes him relevant to the history of the medicalisation of people who feel a disconnect between their body and their mind, a disconnect that is clearly located in the mind, but that is treated by drastic, life limiting surgery.[560] Hirschfeld and his colleagues performed sex reassignment surgery, sometimes with disastrous results. One of his patients was Danish transsexual Lili Elbe, who died from cardiac arrest after an alleged failed uterus implant.

The surgical treatment of transsexuality really took off in the United States after the war, promoted by doctors who had worked with Hirschfeld or been his students in pre-war Berlin. Of them surely the most influential was Dr. Harry Benjamin, author of The Transsexual Phenomen[561] and founder of the International Harry Benjamin Gender Dysphoric Association (IHBGDA).[562] The association was influential in establishing standards of care for gender dysphoria, a task that has now been undertaken by its successor association, the World Professional Association for Transgender Health (WPATH).[563] Their latest standards of care version, Version 8, was released in 2022.[564] There are dedicated chapters for children, adolescents and eunuchs. The publication reveals that there is "limited data on the effect of gender-affirming intervention on the physical, psychological and neurodevelopmental outcomes in youth."[565] Cross-sex hormones for adolescents (called "gender-affirming hormones") are misleadingly described as "inducing female puberty" in boys and "inducing male puberty" in girls.[566] Puberty refers to the maturation of sexual organs and the development of secondary sex characteristics. The artificial inducement of

---

560 Brandy Schillace, "The Forgotten History of the World's First Trans Clinic," Scientific American, May 10, 2021, https://www.scientificamerican.com/article/the-forgotten-history-of-the-worlds-first-trans-clinic/.

561 Harry Benjamin, The Transsexual Phenomenon; a Scientific Report on Transsexualism and Sex Conversion in the Human Male and Female (New York: Ace Pub Co, 1966).

562 Established by Harry Benjamin in 1978, https://webapp1.dlib.indiana.edu/findingaids/view?doc.view=entire_text&docId=VAC9109.

563 World Professional Association for Transgender Health, https://www.wpath.org/.

564 Standards of Care for the Health of Transgender and Gender Diverse People, Version 8, International Journal of Transgender Health, 23 (2022): 1:258. https://doi.org/10.1080/26895269.2022.2100644.

565 Ibidem, 65.

566 Ibidem, 254.

some secondary sex characteristics in the absence of internal and external sexual organs cannot be defined puberty in medical terms. In the children's chapter, it is made clear that these include pre-schoolers, therefore children who are younger than five. One wonders what "symptoms" would make a parent take their child to a doctor to check whether they are "gender diverse" and the standards of care do not explain why gender diverse children need medical care. The publication suggests that children (no age threshold given) may undergo social transition, including, change of name, pronouns, use of toilets and changing rooms of their choice, and "personal expression" (i.e. clothing, hair styles etc).[567] It is suggested that children undergo social transition only at home, or only at school, or both. These are young children still developing an understanding of themselves and the world that surrounds them. It must be very confusing for them to have two different sexed identities. The standards of care admit that "[…] there is a dearth of empirical literature regarding best practices related to the social transition process […].[568] The chapter on "Eunuchs" is a new addition in Version 8. Eunuchs are described as:

> assigned male at birth (AMAB) and wish to eliminate masculine physical features, masculine genitals, or genital functioning.They also include those whose testicles have been surgically removed or rendered nonfunctional by chemical or physical means and who identify as eunuch.[569]

Clearly the standards serve to legitimise the surgical removal of male sexual organs as an elective procedure with no medical need. The WPATH Standards of Care support a highly medicalised approach to gender affirmation, with puberty blockers, hormonal treatment to stop menstruation, cross-sex hormones, surgical intervention and continued hormonal treatment post-surgery. It is revealing that the Standards of Care support the "de-psychopatologisation" of transgender care, not simply the depathologisation of it.[570] Welcoming the move of gender incongruence from the chapter on mental health to the chapter on sexual health by the International Classification of Diseases, Version 11 (ICD-11),[571] signifies legitimising the affirmative medical care of "gender incongruence" while abandoning an approach based on mental health therapeutic support.

---

[567] Ibidem, 76.
[568] Ibidem, 76.
[569] Ibidem, 88.
[570] Ibidem, 17.
[571] World Health Organization, International Classification of Diseases 11th Revision, https://icd.who.int/en.

Importantly, this also includes children, whose sexual health is said to be affected by their gender incongruence.

On 18 December 2023, the WHO announced that it is working on its own guidelines for transgender care.[572] A Guideline Development Group commenced its work in Geneva in February 2024, leaving a very short timeframe for the public to enter comments, and a very short time frame for the work of the Group as well. Concerns have been raised about the composition of the Group[573] and possible conflicts of interest given that several are already involved in affirmative gender care and/or are trans rights activists.

The work of the WPATH, as well as the similar Dutch Protocol developed for the medical care of gender incongruence in Europe is to be seen in the context of the global health law regime, i.e. the development of standards and soft law instruments, on the back of the framework of the WHO classifications, for cross-border and international medical issues, of which transgender care is one of the most successful examples.[574] The treatment of gender identity issues in the Diagnostic and Statistical Manual of Mental Disorders (DSM) by the American Psychiatric Association, which has influence beyond the United States, and in the WHO's International Classification of Diseases (ICD) is especially relevant. The DSM was first published in 1952 and did not contain any reference to gender identity disorder or dysphoria.[575] Clearly the classification of conditions related to

---

[572] "The WHO announces the development of a guideline on the health of trans and gender diverse people," WHO News, December 18, 2023, https://www.who.int/news/item/18-12-2023-who-announces-the-development-of-a-guideline-on-the-health-of-trans-and-gender-diverse-people.

[573] Society for Evidence Based Gender Medicine, "The World Health Organization Announces Transgender Guidelines Plan," December 26, 2023, https://segm.org/world-health-organization-transgender-guidelines.

[574] Jennifer Prah Ruger, "Normative Foundations of Global Health Law," Georgetown Law Journal, 96(2) (2008): 423-443. The border between hard and soft law rules is blurring, with the WHO developing guidelines for the health of trans and gender diverse people: https://www.who.int/news/item/28-06-2023-who-announces-the-development-of-the-guideline-on-the-health-of-trans-and-gender-diverse-people. See also "In Transition: Gender [Identity], Law & Global Health," a USC Law and Global Health discussion that took place in 2016, https://globalhealth.usc.edu/2016/09/02/091316-globalhealthlaw-in-transition-gender-identity/.

[575] For a history of gender in the DSM, see Sarah R Kamens, "On the Proposed Sexual and Gender Identity Diagnoses for DSM-5: History and Controversies," The Humanistic Psychologist, 39(1) (2011), 37-59,

sex and gender identity is quite controversial, given the insistence on depathologisation of gender disorders (and the shameful history of the DSM in classifying homosexuality as a paraphilic disorder), so it is not surprising that it took until 1980 for a classification. In the DSM-III (APA, 1980) gender identity disorder was listed, as well as transsexualism, and transvestic fethishism. Transsexualism, which was given most attention, was defined as follows:

> The essential features of this disorder are a persistent discomfort and sense of inappropriateness about one's assigned sex in a person who has reached puberty. In addition, there is persistent preoccupation, for at least two years, with getting rid of one's primary and secondary sex characteristics and acquiring the sex characteristics of the other sex. Therefore, the diagnosis is not made if the disturbance is limited to brief periods of stress. Invariably there is the wish to live as a member of the other sex.

The DSSM-III defines gender identity disorder as follows:

> The essential features of this disorder are a persistent or recurrent discomfort and sense of inappropriateness about one's assigned sex, and persistent or recurrent cross-dressing in the role of the other sex, either in fantasy or in actuality, in a person who has reached puberty. This disorder differs from Transvestic Fetishism in that the cross-dressing is not for the purpose of sexual excitement; it differs from Transsexualism in that there is no persistent preoccupation (for at least two years) with getting rid of one's primary and secondary sex characteristics and acquiring the sex characteristics of the other sex.

And finally transvestic fetishism is described as follows:

> The essential feature of this disorder is recurrent, intense, sexual urges and sexually arousing fantasies, of at least six months' duration, involving cross-dressing. The person has acted on these urges, or is markedly distressed by them. Usually the person keeps a collection of women's clothes that he intermittently uses to cross-dress when alone. While cross-dressed, he usually masturbates and imagines other males being attracted to him as a woman in his female attire.

In DSM-IV (APA, 1994) transsexualism does not appear anymore and gender identity disorder is defined as follows:

---

doi:10.1080/08873267.2011.539935.

> A. A strong and persistent cross-gender identification (not merely a desire for any perceived cultural advantages of being the other sex). In children, the disturbance is manifested by four (or more) of the following:
>
> 1. repeatedly stated desire to be, or insistence that he or she is, the other sex;
> 2. in boys, preference for cross-dressing or simulating female attire; in girls, insistence on wearing only stereotypical masculine clothing;
> 3. strong and persistent preferences for cross-sex roles in make-believe play or persistent fantasies of being the other sex;
> 4. intense desire to participate in the stereotypical games and pastimes of the other sex;
> 5. strong preference for playmates of the other sex.
>
> B. Persistent discomfort with his or her sex or sense of inappropriateness in the gender role of that sex.
>
> C. The disturbance is not concurrent with a physical intersex condition.
>
> D. The disturbance causes clinically significant distress or impairment in social, occupational, or other important areas of functioning.

It is noticeable that the "disturbance" manifests with perfectly normal behaviour in children who are still developing an understanding of their body and expressing their preferences. Only someone who thinks boys ought not to play with dolls can think that it is a symptom of any disturbance, as opposed to innocent child play. The description seems simply to pathologise non-conformity in children and adults. How much of the distress is due to social stereotypes about appropriate behaviour? DSM-5 (APA, 2013) is the current one (DSM-6 is not expected until 2025). In DSM-5 gender identity disorder was renamed gender dysphoria. The drafting of the section of the DSM-5 on sexual and gender identity disorders was particularly controversial, with trans rights groups contesting the individuals appointed to the working group and the very inclusion of gender identity disorder in the DSM. The initial proposal of the Working Group tasked with the drafting proposed to rename gender identity disorder as gender incongruence, the name under which it is currently described in the WHO's ICD.[576] The debates on the drafting of the definition reveal the inherently political nature of the whole endeavour, with different LGBT, trans and intersex lobbying groups fighting for attention and for their preferred wording to prevail. In the end, the

---

[576] Ibidem, 45.

definition dropped the term incongruence, which is preserved in the description:

> marked incongruence between one's experienced/expressed gender and natal gender of at least 6 months in duration, as manifested by at least two of the following:
>
> A. A marked incongruence between one's experienced/expressed gender and primary and/or secondary sex characteristics (or in young adolescents, the anticipated secondary sex characteristics)
>
> B. A strong desire to be rid of one's primary and/or secondary sex characteristics because of a marked incongruence with one's experienced/expressed gender (or in young adolescents, a desire to prevent the development of the anticipated secondary sex characteristics)
>
> C. A strong desire for the primary and/or secondary sex characteristics of the other gender
>
> D. A strong desire to be of the other gender (or some alternative gender different from one's designated gender)
>
> E. A strong desire to be treated as the other gender (or some alternative gender different from one's designated gender)
>
> F. A strong conviction that one has the typical feelings and reactions of the other gender (or some alternative gender different from one's designated gender)

Although it is defined as dysphoria and needs to be accompanied by distress or social impairment, the diagnostic criteria are greatly depathologised and this is especially evident for the diagnostic criteria in children:

> In children, gender dysphoria diagnosis involves at least six of the following and an associated significant distress or impairment in function, lasting at least six months:
>
> 1. A strong desire to be of the other gender or an insistence that one is the other gender
>
> 2. A strong preference for wearing clothes typical of the other gender
>
> 3. A strong preference for cross-gender roles in make-believe play or fantasy play

4. A strong preference for toys, games or activities stereotypically used or engaged in by the other gender

5. A strong preference for playmates of the other gender

6. A strong rejection of toys, games and activities typical of one's assigned gender

7. A strong dislike of one's sexual anatomy

8. A strong desire for the physical sex characteristics that match one's experienced gender.

In other words, a child can be diagnosed as having gender dysphoria even if he or she does not manifest a strong dislike for his or her body or a desire to modify his or her body, mainly on the basis of his/her play and friendship preferences accompanied by "distress," which seems inconsistent with the decoupling of the condition from body dysmorphia or dysphoria. It is important to remember that one of the main uses of the DSM manual is to provide a guide to medical insurance companies as to which conditions are to be included in their insurance coverage. This definition serves to facilitate the prescription of puberty suppressants in children even younger than ten.[577]

The International Classification of Diseases has a much longer history, with ICD-1 being issued in 1893.[578] ICD-11 was finalised in 2019 and came into force in 2022. As we shall see in chapter 10, the momentous reclassification of gender dysphoria as gender incongruence (one wonders whether this is just a consequence of the debates within the APA in the run-up to the DSM-5 drafting, and whether DSM-6 is going to see a similar shift)[579] is not as consequential as its move from the section on mental and behavioural disorders to the section on conditions related to sexual health. The current categories are "gender incongruence of adolescence and adulthood" and "gender incongruence in childhood." This

---

577 Puberty blockers for transgender and gender-diverse youth, Mayo Clinic, https://www.mayoclinic.org/diseases-conditions/gender-dysphoria/in-depth/pubertal-blockers/art-20459075.

578 The first International List of Causes of Death was compiled by French statistician Jacques Bertillon: J.A. Hirsch and Others, "ICD-10: History and Context," American Journal of Neuroradiology, 37(4) (April 2016): 596-599, doi: 10.3174/ajnr.A4696.

579 In ICD-10, the listed conditions were transsexualism and gender identity disorder in children.

move is openly described as functional, to permit better access to "gender affirmative care," including, evidently, puberty suppressants for children. Gender incongruence in adolescence and adulthood is defined as follows:

> Gender incongruence of adolescence and adulthood is characterized by a marked and persistent incongruence between an individual's experienced gender and the assigned sex, which often leads to a desire to 'transition', in order to live and be accepted as a person of the experienced gender, through hormonal treatment, surgery or other health care services to make the individual's body align, as much as desired and to the extent possible, with the experienced gender. The diagnosis cannot be assigned prior the onset of puberty. Gender variant behaviour and preferences alone are not a basis for assigning the diagnosis.

Gender incongruence in children is defined as follows:

> Gender incongruence of childhood is characterized by a marked incongruence between an individual's experienced/expressed gender and the assigned sex in pre-pubertal children. It includes a strong desire to be a different gender than the assigned sex; a strong dislike on the child's part of his or her sexual anatomy or anticipated secondary sex characteristics and/or a strong desire for the primary and/or anticipated secondary sex characteristics that match the experienced gender; and make-believe or fantasy play, toys, games, or activities and playmates that are typical of the experienced gender rather than the assigned sex. The incongruence must have persisted for about 2 years, and cannot be diagnosed before age 5. Gender variant behaviour and preferences alone are not a basis for assigning the diagnosis.

The Council of Europe welcomed the depathologisation of gender incongruence,[580] which is ironic, as the reclassification as a sexual health disorder makes its medicalisation easier and more profitable. In fact it is not clear why it is necessary to treat with medication and surgery a healthy state of the body and mind. If one were to follow gender identity theory to its logical conclusions, neither the DSM nor the ICD should contain any reference at all to gender identity, just as they do not contain any reference to homosexuality, being just a facet of the universal human condition. However, contrary to sexual orientation, there remains a need, promoted by the pharmaceutical industry, to medicalise gender identity and maintain

---

[580] Council of Europe Commissioner for Human Rights, "ICD11 is a Stride toward Depathologisation of Trans People, but more is needed," May 27, 2019, https://www.coe.int/it/web/commissioner/-/icd11-is-a-stride-toward-depathologisation-of-trans-people-but-more-is-needed.

an industry of puberty suppressants, synthetic hormones and plastic surgery.

The history of the depathologisation of gender dysphoria[581] maps quite well onto the legal attempts to decouple gender reassignment from any medical and surgical intervention, though it seems the real goal for the law is to drop any reference to diagnostic criteria, while in the medical world, ever more sophisticated pharmaceutical and surgical protocols are developed for ever younger individuals. In fact, while in law the significant moment is the conceptualisation of self-identification and of gender identity as a universal characteristics, in the medical realm the crucial moment is the move from cross-sex hormones and surgical modification of adult transsexuals[582] to the suppression of puberty in children. This turn, which expanded exponentially the potential for profitable pharmaceutical intervention in gender confused children,[583] is attributed to Dutch doctor

---

[581] From the OSM III del 1980 (APA) which listed Gender Identity Disorder and Transsexualism, to Gender Dysphoria in the DSM-5 (APA) of 2003, to the Gender Incongruence of ICD-11 of the WHO in 2019.

[582] The first standards of care developed by the IHBGDA restricted surgical intervention to adults, noting its irreversibility. IHBGDA, "Standards of Care: The Hormonal and Surgical Sex Reassignment of Gender Dysphoric Persons," Archives of Sexual Behavior 14(1985): 79-90, doi:10.1007/BF01541354.

[583] Gender reassignment surgery is estimated to be a 5 billion $ market by 2030: PR Newswire, "United States Sex Reassignment Surgery Market Analysis Report 2023: A $5 Billion Market by 2030 - Increasing Prevalence of Gender Dysphoria & Increasing Novel Hormonal Therapies with Better Efficacy," September 15, 2023, https://finance.yahoo.com/news/united-states-sex-reassignment-surgery-231500423.html. Puberty suppression is the first step in the process culminating with SRS. In the US the drug most commonly used as a puberty suppressant is Lupron. The maker of Lupron, Tap Pharmaceutical Products Inc., had to pay $875 million in fraud charges in 2001: Deaprtment of Justice, Tap Pharmaceutical Products Inc. and seven others charge with health care crimes; company agrees to pay $875 million to settle charges, October 3, 2001, https://www.justice.gov/archive/opa/pr/2001/October/513civ.htm. In 2018 another scandal affected Lupron, for serious side effects in women who were prescribed it for the treatment of endometriosis: "Georgia woman says controversial drug led to series of health problems," WSB-TV, October 29, 2018, https://www.wsbtv.com/news/local/georgia-woman-says-drug-used-to-treat-endometriosis-led-to-series-of-health-problems/859263892/.
The current manufacturer of Lupron is AbbVie Inc.; in 2022, Lupron brought it $752 million in revenue, for all its uses (https://www.investopedia.com/articles/markets/040115/how-abbvie-makes-its-money-abbv.asp). The product most used in Europe, Triptorelin, had a revenue of

Peggy Cohen-Kettenis, who, in the 1990s, worked as professor of psychology in the Department of Child and Adolescent Psychiatry at University Medical Centre in Utrecht.[584] In 1987, the HBIGDA and the Academisch Ziekenhuis Vrije Universiteit co-sponsored the Tenth International Symposium on Gender Dysphoria in Amsterdam.[585] Cohen-Kettenis moderated the panel on Developmental and Childhood Issues in Gender Identity. Cohen-Kettenis was also in the Board of Directors of the HBIGDA in the 1990s, providing the link between the developments in Europe and the established medical framework on gender dysphoria in the United States. She also, as noted in her university profile, "contributed to the development of new diagnostic criteria for gender dysphoria, both for the DSM-5 of the American Psychiatric Association (as chair of the working group), and for the ICD-11 of the World Health Organization. These are the two most commonly used systems for classifying psychiatric disorders."

It was Cohen-Kettenis who started a protocol for the treatment of children with gender dysphoria in the mid-1990s,[586] eventually developing treatment with puberty blockers, thanks to her collaboration with two endocrinologists, Louis Gooren and Henriette Delemarre-van den Waal.[587] Children are given gonadotropin-releasing hormone agonists (GnRHa),[588]

$955 million in 2023 and is projected to reach $ 1.5 billion by 2030, "Triptorelin Market Outlook,"Future Market Insights, April 2023, https://www.futuremarketinsights.com/reports/triptorelin-market. There are clearly huge financial interests in promoting puberty suppression, cross-sex hormones and gender affirming surgeries. Mental health intervention are as low cost an alternative as one can imagine in comparison.

[584] Universiteit Utrecht, Prof. Dr. Peggy Cohen-Kettenis, https://www.sg.uu.nl/sprekers/peggy-cohen-kettenis.

[585] The programme is published on Metamorphosis Magazine, 6(1-2) (January-April 1987): 7-8, https://www.digitaltransgenderarchive.net/files/zp38wc69f.

[586] Peggy Cohen-Kettenis, "Die Behandlung von Kindern und Jugendlichen mit Geschlechtsidentitätsstörungen an der Universtät Utrecht," Zeitschrift für Sexualforschung 7 (1994): 231-239.

[587] Biggs, Michael, "The Technology of Puberty Suppression." In Sex and Gender. A Contemporary Reader, eds. Alice Sullivan and Selina Todd, (London: Routledge, 2024): 175-193, 178. Bigg's chapter reconstructs the development of the Dutch Protocol with a wealth of details, especially on the patients and their experience of puberty suppression.

[588] Peggy Cohen-Kettenis and S.H.M. van Goozen, "Pubertal Delay as an Aid in the Diagnosis and Treatment of a Transsexual Adolescent," European Child & Adolescent Psychiatry, 7 (1998): 246-248, doi:10.1007/s007870050073 (the protocol is based on a study involving a single individual); Louis Gooren and Henriette

normally used for treating precocious puberty (that is, to delay puberty that occurs too early in a child), some gynecological conditions in women and prostate cancer in men. Because of their effect, they are also used to treat sexual deviancy in men and are given to sex offenders in some countries.[589] They have never been licensed in any country for their use on children who reached Tanner Stage 2 physiologically (i.e. who do not suffer from precocious puberty) and for being used in conjunction with cross-sex hormones, meaning that the child will never experience puberty at all.[590] Cohen-Kettenis, who developed the Protocol, admitted that gender dysphoria usually resolves itself post-puberty, and this is the reason why treatment of gender dysphoria was always restricted to adults.[591] In other words, puberty is often *the cure* for gender dysphoria, not an aggravating element pushing towards suicide.[592] Cohen-Kettenis argued however that "passing" is easier if medical intervention is started before puberty fully develops the secondary sex characteristics.[593] It is ironic that medical intervention in children was initially justified with the psychological need to "pass" as their desired sex, while gender identity theorists and trans rights activists insist passing is irrelevant and even

Delemarre-van de Waal, "The Feasibility of Endocrine Interventions in Juvenile Transsexuals," Journal of Peychology and Human Sexuality, 8 (1996): 69-74, doi:10.1300/J056v08n04_05.

[589] Alessandra Gallo, Jeffrey Abracen, Jan Looman and others, "The Use of Leuprolide Acetate in the Management of High-Risk Sex Offenders." Sex Abuse 31(8) (December 2019): 930-951, doi:10.1177/1079063218791176.

[590] Mickey Emmanuel and Brooke R. Bokor, "Tanner Stages," National Library of Medicine, 2022, https://www.ncbi.nlm.nih.gov/books/NBK470280/.

[591] Peggy Cohen-Kettenis and S.H.M. van Goozen, "Pubertal Delay as an Aid in the Diagnosis and Treatment of a Transsexual Adolescent," European Child & Adolescent Psychiatry, 7 (1998): 246-248, 246.

[592] A study from Finland concludes that gender dysphoria is not predictive of suicide once co-morbidies are accounted for: Sami-Matti Ruska and others, "All-cause and suicide mortalities among adolescents and young adults who contacted specialised gender identity services in Finland in 1996–2019: a register study," BMJ Mental Health 27(1) (2024): 3009-3040, https://mentalhealth.bmj.com/content/27/1/e300940.info.

[593] Ibidem, 248: "The case of B is the first we know of to show that pubertal delay and subsequent hormonal and surgical intervention in a consistently cross-sex identified person has resulted in a positive outcome." Though she then adds: "The most important advantage of pubertal delay over cross-sex hormone treatment is that no irreversible steps are taken."

transphobic.[594] The disconnect between theory and [medical] practice could not be starker. Cohen-Kettenis' article also makes it clear that puberty delay is functional to surgical treatment, and not the "pause button" that its supporters claim it is, and does not provide any clear diagnostic tool to select the children whose gender dysphoria will resolve with puberty.[595] It is in effect impossible to know which children will overcome their gender dysphoria with puberty before prescribing puberty blockers, as the only way to know this is to allow children to experience puberty, precisely what puberty blockers will not allow to happen. We know that at least 80% of gender dysphoria in children who are not prescribed puberty blockers will resolve with puberty,[596] but if puberty blockers are given, the physiologic process of puberty will be interrupted, making it highly unlikely that it will ever be possible to know which children would have seen their gender dysphoria resolved. In other words, puberty blockers "freeze" dysphoria, and almost all children who are given puberty blockers then choose to take cross-sex hormones as well.[597] The

---

[594] The Gay & Lesbian Alliance Against Defamation (GLAAD) Media Reference Guide suggests to journalists to avoid the term passing as inappropriate and problematic.

[595] Even the Mayo Clinic, one of the most reputable health institutions in the US, claims puberty blockers simply pause puberty and are reversible. https://www.mayoclinic.org/diseases-conditions/gender-dysphoria/in-depth/pubertal-blockers/art-20459075.

[596] Riittakerttu Kaltiala-Heino, Hannah Bergman, Marja Työläjrvi and Louise Frisén,"Gender Dysphoria in Adolescence: Current Perspectives," Adolescent Health Medical Therapy, 9 (2018): 31-41, doi:10.2147/AHMT.S135432. See also Thomas Steensma and Peggy Cohen-Kettenis, "Gender Transitioning Before Puberty?," Archives of Sexual Behaviour, 40 (2011): 649-650, doi:10.1007/s10508-011-9752-2. Even Cohen Kettenis admits the persistence rate in one study is only 15.8% and that the most likely outcome of gender dysphoria in pre-pubertal children is homosexuality, not transgenderism and therefore suggests caution.

[597] Polly Carmichael and Others,"Short Term Outcomes of Pubertal Suppression in a Selected Cohort of 12 to 15 Year Old Young People with Persistent Gender Dysphoria in the UK,"PLoS ONE 16(2) (2021),

Dutch Protocol was soon adopted in other countries, often as a consequence of public pressure and parental lobbying.[598] The European Union Agency for Fundamental Rights provides a map of availability of transgender hormone therapy in Europe; while it is not perfectly clear whether this includes puberty suppression, the reference to young children seems to indicate that.[599]

The spread of the Protocol and the rise of adverse medical effects engendered a backlash both in the courts and in the medical authorities in several European countries and some States of the United States. This will be examined in the final part of this chapter. Before moving on to this phenomenon, which played out mostly on the basis of medical evidence, a legal argument against the suppression of puberty is presented. It should not be necessary to wait either on court cases by regretful adults who were ravaged by unnecessary pharmaceutical and surgical interventions, or longitudinal studies on the effects of puberty suppression on children, which will take years, when there is a legal justification for suspending the use of puberty blockers on children.

The Convention on the Rights of the Child protects, at Article 6, the right to life and development of all children.[600] Beyond the usual obligations, positive and negative, with respect to the right to life, which extends to

---

doi:org/10.1371/journal.pone.0243894 (43 out of 44 children went from puberty blockers to cross-sex hormones); Chantal Wiepjes and Others, "The Amsterdam Cohort of Gender Dysphoria Study (1972-2015): Trends in Prevalence, Treatment, and Regrets," Journal of Sexual Medicine, 15(4) (April 2018): 582-590, doi: 10.1016/j.jsxm.2018.01.016 (only 1.9% of children did not go from puberty blockers to cross-sex hormones); Annelou de Vries and Others, "Puberty Suppression in Adolescents with Gender Identity Disorder: a Perspective Follow-up Study," Journal of Sexual Medicine, 8(8) (August 2011): 2276-2283, doi: 10.1111/j.1743-6109.2010.01943.x. (all children went from puberty blockers to cross-sex hormones).

[598] A good outline of the international spread of the Dutch Protocol in Biggs, Michael, "The Technology of Puberty Suppression." In Sex and Gender. A Contemporary Reader, eds. Alice Sullivan and Selina Todd, (London: Routledge, 2024): 175-193, 181 ff.

[599] European Union Agency for Fundamental Rights, Access to Transgender Hormone Therapy, October 19, 2018, https://fra.europa.eu/en/publication/2017/mapping-minimum-age-requirements-concerning-rights-child-eu/access-transgender-hormone-therapy

[600] 1. States Parties recognize that every child has the inherent right to life.
2. States Parties shall ensure to the maximum extent possible the survival and development of the child.

children, I argue that in the context of childhood, which is defined as reaching to age 18, the right to "development" for a child includes the physical, psychological, educational, mental, spiritual and moral development.[601] The physical development of a child is the process of maturation from child to adult, defined as puberty in medical terms. The literature on Article 6 does not clarify what is intended by development in physical terms, but it is clear puberty is the only way by which a child develops into an adult. The Committee on the Rights of the Child, in its 2016 General Comment,[602] talks about the rights of adolescents. When defining the term, the Committee has this to say:

> The Committee recognizes that adolescence is not easily defined, and that individual children reach maturity at different ages. Puberty occurs at different ages for boys and girls, and different brain functions mature at different times. The process of transitioning from childhood to adulthood is influenced by context and environment, as reflected in the wide variation in cultural expectations of adolescents in national legislations, which afford different thresholds for entry into adult activities, and across international bodies, which employ a variety of age ranges to define adolescence. The present general comment does not seek, therefore, to define adolescence, but instead focuses on the period of childhood from 10 years until the 18th birthday to facilitate consistency in data collection.

The WHO similarly defines adolescence as the period of time between the ages of 10 and 19, in which a child matures physically and intellectually until adulthood is reached.[603] Again, in medical terms this process is called puberty. In fact, together with birth and death, puberty is the only universal human experience. All human beings become adults through the process of puberty, and it is medically known that only through puberty physical and mental maturity is reached. In other words, preventing puberty affects a child's physical and intellectual development. This is essential to understand, because suppressing puberty does not give a child the space to reflect on their gender dysphoria. A child who has had their puberty

---

[601] Vaghri, Ziba, "Article 6: The Right to Life, Survival and Development." In Monitoring State Compliance with the UN Convention on the Rights of the Child. Children's Well-Being: Indicators and Research, eds. Ziba Vaghri, Jean Zermatten, Gerison Lansdown, Roberta Ruggiero (New York: Springer, 2022): 31-40.

[602] Committee on the Rights of the Child, General Comment No. 20 (2016) on the Implementation of the Rights of the Child during Adolescence, CRC/C/GC/20, https://tbinternet.ohchr.org/_layouts/15/TreatyBodyExternal/Download.aspx?symbolno=CRC%2FC%2FGC%2F20&Lang=en.

[603] World Health Organization, Adolescent Health, https://www.who.int/health-topics/adolescent-health#tab=tab_1.

suppressed, will not undergo the intellectual development necessary to make a more mature and considered decision. Their brain development is interfered with in ways that are not even well understood, as there is not sufficient data.[604] The precautionary principle, or the medical "first do not harm" principle would seem to advise not to give medication to children, whose full effects are not known. But this does not seem to be the case for puberty suppression.

International law guarantees the right of children to develop and reach adulthood, enjoying States to put in place programmes to guarantee health rights and education, to protect children against unlawful deaths, for example in the practice of the use of child soldiers, to protect them against exploitation, including child labour, prostitution, trafficking and the marriage of girls. Interfering medically with the physical and intellectual development of children on the basis of a diagnosis that is very likely to resolve itself through puberty is an unlawful interference with their Article 6 rights. Physiological processes such as puberty cannot be 'paused' without effects that are still not well understood. Accompanying the poorly known physical effects are the social effects of preventing a child to mature in line with their chronological age, affecting socialisation, friendships and romantic attachments. The issue of consent is equally fraught, both consent to puberty suppression and to further treatment such as cross-sex hormones and even surgical intervention, since girls as young as 12 are undergoing mastectomy.[605]

In the field of health law, with particular reference to the protocols on puberty suppression and surgical intervention on minors and young adults, we see three specific kinds of backlash. First, the suspension of medical protocols on puberty suppression or the tightening of the standards of care; second, legislative intervention, to outlaw certain procedures or pharmaceutical interventions, especially in US States; and third, litigation in courts, especially in the UK and in the US. The three approaches can

[604] Guido Giovanardi, "Buying Time or Arresting Development? The Dilemma of Administering Hormone Blockers in Trans Children and Adolescents," Porto Biomedical Journal, 2(5) (September-October 20179: 153-156, doi: https://doi.org/10.1016/j.pbj.2017.06.001. As Giovanardi acknowledges: "The primary risks of pubertal suppression include adverse effects on *bone mineralisation* (which can theoretically be reversed with cross-sex hormone treatment) and compromised fertility; *data on the effects on brain development are still limited."*[emphasis added].

[605] Anthony Latham, "Puberty Blockers for Children: Can They Consent?," The New Bioethics, 28(3) (2022): 268-291, doi: 10.1080/20502877.2022.2088048.

affect each other, with litigation bringing about a tightening of the standards, for example. The focus here will be on events taking place in Europe, as the US political environment makes the treatment of this topic highly dependent on the extreme polarisation in US politics, on this as in other issues.

In several European countries, prescribing puberty suppressants has been halted or limited following reports of adverse side effects. In 2021, the Karolinska Institute in Sweden decided to stop prescribing puberty blockers on minors except in clinical studies.[606] In 2022 the Swedish National Board of Health and Welfare reached the same conclusion on the basis of the low quality of the evidence on the effects of puberty suppressants, concluding that:[607]

> As a result of this determination, the eligibility for pediatric gender transition with puberty blockers and cross-sex hormones in Sweden will be sharply curtailed. Only a minority of gender dysphoric youth—those with the "classic" childhood onset of cross-sex identification and distress, which persist and cause clear suffering in adolescence—will be considered as potentially eligible for hormonal interventions, pending additional, extensive multidisciplinary evaluation.

Finland also amended its guidelines in 2020, with the Council for Choices in Healthcare issuing a recommendation tightening the requirements for the pharmaceutical and surgical treatment of gender dysphoria in minors.[608] In 2023, Denmark followed suit, restricting dramatically the provision of puberty suppressants to children, noting many of the adverse effects and problematic co-morbidities and social pressure mechanisms on children, with the incidence of referrals for gender dysphoria at the Pediatric Gender Service growing an incredible 8700% between 2014 and

---

[606] Society for Evidence Based Gender Medicine, "Sweden's Karolinska Ends All Use of Puberty Blockers and Cross-Sex Hormones for Minors Outside of Clinical Studies," May 5, 2021, https://segm.org/Sweden_ends_use_of_Dutch_protocol.
[607] Society for Evidence Based Gender Medicine, Summary of Key Recommendations from the Swedish National Board of Health and Welfare, February 27, 2022, https://segm.org/segm-summary-sweden-prioritizes-therapy-curbs-hormones-for-gender-dysphoric-youth.
[608] Council for Choices in Health Care in Finland, "Medical treatment methods for dysphoria associated with variations in gender identity in minors–recommendation," June 16, 2020,
https://palveluvalikoima.fi/documents/1237350/22895008/Summary_minors_en+(1).pdf/fa2054c5-8c35-8492-59d6-b3de1c00de49/Summary_minors_en+(1).pdf?t=1631773838474.

2022. The policy change in Denmark is especially remarkable as the 2018 guidelines were extremely liberal in allowing gender transition on minors.[609] In 2022 the National Academy of Medicine in France also invited doctors to limit the use of puberty suppressants in children, citing the decision by the Karolinska Institute in Sweden and noting the irreversible nature of the treatments and the serious side effects, including "impact on growth, bone fragility, risk of sterility, emotional and intellectual consequences and, for girls, symptoms reminiscent of menopause."[610]

Finally, we are starting to see policy changes outside of Europe as well. In December 2023, the Royal Australian and New Zealand College of Psychiatrists issued a position statement, inviting caution in the treatment of children experiencing dysphoria and pointing to the lack of high quality evidence for many of the treatments, and quoting the experience of several European countries. What is also noteworthy is that there seems to be a return to reality-based language (sex is registered, not assigned, at birth, for example).[611]

England constitutes the best case study for the backlash against the medicalisation of gender dysphoria in children. Before considering the cases of judicial review of the puberty suppression protocol, a summary of the situation for gender care. The only clinic for the treatment of dysphoric children is located in London and was opened in 1989 as the Gender Identity Development Service at the Tavistock Centre.[612] Under the direction of Polly Carmichael, who became its director in the early 2010s, the clinic lowered the age at which puberty suppressants could be

---

[609] Society for Evidence Based Gender Medicine, "Denmark Joins the List of Countries That Have Sharply Restricted Youth Gender Transitions," August 17, 2023, https://segm.org/Denmark-sharply-restricts-youth-gender-transitions.

[610] Académie Nationale de Médecine, Medicine and Gender Transidentity in Children and Adolescents, 25 February 2022, https://www.academie-medecine.fr/la-medecine-face-a-la-transidentite-de-genre-chez-les-enfants-et-les-adolescents/?lang=en.

[611] Royal Australian and New Zealand College of Psychiatrists, "The role of psychiatrists in working with Trans and Gender Diverse People," December 2023, https://www.ranzcp.org/clinical-guidelines-publications/clinical-guidelines-publications-library/role-of-psychiatrists-working-with-trans-gender-diverse-people.

[612] Gender Identity Development Service, https://gids.nhs.uk/.

prescribed, down to 12 years old and then to 10.[613] Working together with the Gender Identity Research and Education Society (GIRES)[614] and Mermaids UK,[615] it promoted the use of puberty suppressants on children. Their clinical practices and their questionable use of data were part of the proceedings in the judicial review against the GIDS/Tavistock.

However, the judicial review happened in the context of heightened scrutiny about the work of the GIDS. In October 2020, the National Institute for Clinical Excellence (NICE) published two reviews, the Evidence Review: Gender-Affirming Hormones for Children and Adolescents with Gender Dysphoria and Evidence Review: Gonadotrophin Releasing Hormone Analogues for Children and Adolescents with Gender Dysphoria.[616] Both reviews evidenced the very low quality of the collected data and studies, describing them as "poor quality," "biased" and "non reliable." This is especially noteworthy as the drafters of the reports adopt all the language that signals compliance with gender identity theory, from "sex assigned at birth" to "transfemales" and "gender affirming hormones" (instead of cross-sex hormones).

In the Autumn of 2020, NHS England and NHS Improvement commissioned a review of the GIDS with the view of issuing recommendations on the services provided to children affected by gender dysphoria and appointed Dr Hilary Cass, former President of the Royal College of Paediatrics and Child Health to chair the review and issue its reports. The review is motivated by the increase in referrals to the GIDS and the move from a psychotherapeutic approach to treatment to the prescription of puberty suppressants. The Cass review does not cover issues of consent, which were at the time a matter of live judicial proceedings.[617] The Chair produced an interim report in February 2022, after the judicial review decision of December 2020 and the Appeal of September 2021, and a

[613] Biggs Michael, "Britain's Experiment with Puberty Blockers." In Inventing Transgender Children and Young People, eds. Michael Moore and Heather Brunskell-Evans (Newcastle: Cambridge Scholars Publishing): 40-55.

[614] GIRES is a charity for trans and gender diverse people, https://www.gires.org.uk/.

[615] Mermaids is a charity for transgender, gender diverse and non-binary children and their parents, https://mermaidsuk.org.uk/.

[616] The Cass Review, NICE Evidence Reviews, https://cass.independent-review.uk/nice-evidence-reviews/.

[617]https://cass.independent-review.uk/.

Final Report in April 2024,[618] which will be considered after the analysis of the two cases.

Keira Bell is a young woman who, following a problematic childhood and mental health issues developed in adolescence was referred to the GIDS in 2013. She was prescribed puberty blockers at 16, cross-sex hormones at 17 (testosterone) and she underwent a double mastectomy at 20. By the age of 22 she had desisted. At 23 she joined the judicial review against the GIDS/Tavistock. The case was brough to the High Court, sitting as Divisional Court, as a judicial review originally started by Mrs A, the mother of a 15 year old girl with ASD, and nurse Sue Evans, who later dropped away and was replaced by Keira (Quincy in the proceedings) Bell.[619] The judicial review concerned the policy of prescribing puberty suppressing drugs to children and specifically whether children can give informed consent to them, given their effects.The claimants' position was that children are not competent to give consent to puberty suppressants; that information on puberty suppressants provided by GIDS was misleading and insufficient; and, that there was an absence of procedural safeguards. All in all, the GIDS was breaching the Article 8 ECHR rights of its young patients. The Court, from the beginning of its discussion (para. 23) and several times throughout the judgment notes the poor quality of the evidence provided by the Defendant (for example, it took nine years for GIDS to publish a research study on outcomes for referred patients, and this only during the proceedings).[620] The Court reviews the evidence which shows a lack of care for the clinical outcomes of the interventions, and a negligent approach to collecting statistics, especially troubling since the cohort of children grew exponentially in less than a decade (from 97 in 2009 to 2519 in 2018) and their profile changed substantially (a considerable rise in the number of girls and children with other conditions such as autism, or with mental health conditions or a

---

[618] Hillary Cass, Independent Review of Gender Identity Services for Children and Young People: Final Report, April 2024, Final Report – Cass Review.

[619] *Quincy Bell and Mrs A v The Tavistock and Portman NHS Foundation Trust* [2020] EWHC 3274 (Admin), https://www.judiciary.uk/wp-content/uploads/2020/12/Bell-v-Tavistock-Judgment.pdf.

[620] At para. 28 the Court notes that data was not collected on the ages at which children were prescribed puberty suppressants; at para. 35 the Courts notes with surprise that no data was collected on how many children had co-morbidities such as autism; at para. 44 the Court notes GIDS collected no statistics on children assessed as not being Gillick competent; at para. 56 the Court notes GIDS collected no statistics on how many children who were prescribed puberty suppressants progressed to cross-sex hormones.

history of sexual abuse). The Court notes too that the evidence does not seem to indicate that children younger than 16 can be Gillick competent.[621] The Court examines the issue of Gillick competence in detail, especially for what concerns the standard for declaring a child competent for consenting to medical procedures. There are two important considerations: the first, that normally Gillick competence is relevant when approval of medical treatment such as contraception is lacking from the parents, the natural guardians of minors for health decisions (unless a court is called to decide in their place), so the doctor needs to establish whether the advice or care should be given without informing the parents.[622] In the case of the Gillick competence of GIDS patients, GIDS accepted that no treatment would be prescribed against the wishes of the children, even if the parents consented to it, and this clearly could cover cases in which children would never be considered Gillick competent, such as 10-12 years old. In fact, 10-12 years old have been prescribed puberty suppressants. Data reported in the judgment for the years 2019-2020 reports three 10-11 years old; 13 12 years old; and ten 13 years old. More recently disclosed data shows that 70 three- and four-year-old children were referred to the Tavistock in the last decade.[623] Second, that Gillick competence was relevant in the Gillick case in order to prevent girls from falling pregnant at too young an age. In other words, to avoid irremediable consequences such as a pregnacy. In the GIDS case, it is the puberty suppressants that set in motion irrimediable consequences, as almost all the children who are given them then progress on to cross-sex hormones and often surgery,[624] becoming sterile and suffering other permanent changes to their bodies. Therefore, competence must be assessed by a more searching standard, because medical intervention in this case is serious and not reversible. It is not as difficult to explain to a girl who is already having sexual intercourse that

[621] House of Lords, *Gillick v West Norfolk and Wisbeck Health Authority* [1985] 3 All ER 402. The case was a judicial review of the SoS policy to provide contraceptive advice to minors.

[622] Ibidem, 413.

[623] Max Stephens, "More than 70 Children Aged Three and Four Were Sent to the Tavistock Transgender Clinic," The Telegraph, December 26, 2023, https://www.telegraph.co.uk/news/2023/12/26/tavistock-transgender-clinic-children-aged-three-nhs/.

[624] For the Court this was a crucial element in the decision, the link between puberty suppressants and cross-sex hormones, so that in effect consenting to the first meant consenting to the second. Although I agree in principle, the causal link is probably too tenuous legally, and in fact it would have been sufficient to argue that children cannot be Gillick competent for treatment whose long term consequences are untested.

contraception will help her not to get pregnant as it is to explain to a 10 year old what puberty suppressants will do to his or her body, especially as not even doctors are reasonably informed on the effects of puberty suppressants on bone density or intellectual capacity.[625]

The Court comes to two different decisions, for children younger than 16 and for 16-18 years old. For the younger cohort, the Court says:

> Gillick makes clear that any decision is treatment and person specific. However, for the reasons that we have set out above, we think that it is appropriate in this case to give clear guidance as to the application of the Gillick tests to the treatment and cohort of children in question. The conclusion we have reached is that it is highly unlikely that a child aged 13 or under would ever be Gillick competent to give consent to being treated with PBs [puberty blockers]. In respect of children aged 14 and 15, we are also very doubtful that a child of this age could understand the long-term risks and consequences of treatment in such a way as to have sufficient understanding to give consent. However, plainly the increased maturity of the child means that there is more possibility of achieving competence at the older age.

For the 16-18 years old:

> In respect of a young person aged 16 or over, the legal position is different. There is a presumption of capacity under section 8 of the Family Law Reform Act 1969. […] We do however recognise that in the light of the evidence that has emerged, and the terms of this judgment, clinicians may well consider that it is not appropriate to move to treatment, such as PBs or CSH [cross-sex hormones], without the involvement of the court.

The Court of Appeal reversed the judgment of the Divisional Court in 2021.[626] As the Divisional Court before them, the Court of Appeal is keen to point out, at para 3, that its task is not to decide on the merits of the use of puberty suppressants on children, but only whether it is for courts to decide to whom they can be prescribed and how. It also notices, and this is important to the reasoning of the Court, as I shall point out later, that technically it is not the Tavistock that prescribes puberty suppressants. They only refer children to the University College London Hospitals NHS

---

[625] As the Court notes at para. 67, the amended NHS website on puberty suppressants added this disclaimer in June 2020: "Little is known about the long-term side effects of hormone or puberty blockers in children with gender dysphoria."

[626] *Quincy Bell and Mrs. A. v The Tavistock and Portman NHS Foundation Trust*, 17 September 2021, [2021] EWCA Civ 1363.

Foundation Trust or the Leeds Teaching Hospital NHS Foundation, and that it is these two institutions who ultimately seek consent for administering puberty suppressants and, after further consent, cross-sex hormones and ultimately surgery. Each step requires the consent of the child and of the parents and, of course, the positive assessment by the clinician.

At para. 8, the Court sums up the eight grounds of appeal: one and two, that the Divisional Court misapplied Gillick; three, that the Court's conclusions are inconsistent with the Family Law Reform Act 1969;[627] four and five, a challenge to the definition of puberty blockers (the Court always calls them as such) as experimental and their effects as life-changing; six and seven, a challenge to the reliance on expert witnesses presented by the Claimants without permission; eight, a claim that the Court discriminated against gender dysphoric children in breach of Article 14 ECHR.[628] The most important grounds of appeal, and those that determined the success of the appeal, are the Gillick consent one, and the fact that the Divisional Court made findings of fact outside the remit of the judicial review (paras. 37ff), specifically, the fact that puberty blockers lead to cross-sex hormones; the fact that the Tavistock had no collected any data on Gillick competence; and the fact that puberty blockers can be considered "experimental."

I will deal with the issue of competence last. For what concerns the findings of fact, the Court of Appeal contests the way in which the expert evidence was presented by the Claimants and accepted by the Divisional Court (para. 38). Although it is not appropriate to reopen issues of fact in judicial review proceedings, including when analysing the conclusions reached by the Court of Appeal, it is proper to contextualise the criticism of the findings of the Divisional Court. Considering the grounds four, five, six and seven together, the Court of Appeal takes issue with the assessment of puberty blockers by the Divisional Court as experimental and irreversible. Instead the Court accepts the characterisation of them as safe and reversible, which is repeated several times throughout the

627 S8: "[…] consent of a minor over 16 to any surgical [or] medical treatment […] shall be as effective as it would be as if he were of full age." For this reason in the analysis I will focus on issues of consent of under 16s.

628 This claim was not discussed by the Court for reasons of judicial economy. In any event, free standing claims of violations of Article 14 tend not to be successful.

judgment: at para. 25, the Court quotes Dr. Carmichael (head of GIDS) to the effect that puberty blockers have the primary purpose to give the patient time to think about gender identity (this does not seem to chime with the claim that they are actually life saving medication); at para. 29 the Court quotes Prof. Butler (consultant of paediatric endocrinology at UCL) and Dr. Alvi, who had the same role at Leeds, to the effect that puberty blockers are "safe, reversible treatment;" at para. 75, the Court sums up the evidence from the Tavistock and the Trusts to the effect that "the treatment [is] safe, internationally endorsed, reversible […]." Clearly the Court accepts the claim that puberty blockers do not have permanent effects on chilren, being nothing more than a pause button. The Court is also at pains to remind us that the Tavistock does not even prescribe puberty blockers, let alone cross-sex hormones, which can have the effect to sterilise children. It is puzzling then that the Court also accepts as a fact that the Tavistock counsels children on the sterilising effect that can result from puberty blockers, and even suggests that the children preserve their eggs or sperm in case they wish to have children when they reach adulthood. At para. 22, the Court quotes "Dr. Carmichael and Professor Butler provided evidence about the way in which the risks of loss of fertility, sexual function and the effect of puberty blockers on relationships were explained to patients within the consent process." The Court also refers to the study published by GIDS in February 2021.[629] In the study, the claim is made that:

> The implications of treatment for fertility were discussed at the first and second medical visits and all young people were urged to consider storing gametes before starting GnRHa. Access to storage depended on regional availability within the NHS. Note that counselling on fertility continued across the study, and clinicians periodically checked with young people who had decided against storage whether they wished to revisit their decision.

The paragraph refers to the first and second medical visits at the Tavistock, in which the clinicians determine if the child should be referred to the Trusts for the prescription of puberty blockers *only*: if puberty blockers have no sterilising effect, why do children who may be younger than ten at that point, need to be told about the sterilising effect of [puberty blockers] treatment? Because it is medically obvious that, if puberty is suppressed very early, there will be no chance to preserve eggs or sperm in

---

[629] Polly Carmichael and Others, "Short-term outcomes of pubertal suppression in a selected cohort of 12 to 15 year old young people with persistent gender dysphoria in the UK," PloSOne 16(2) (2021), doi: 10.1371/journal.pone.0243894.

case cross-sex hormones are given, so actually, the younger the children are before starting blockers, the more relevant the need to inform them about potential infertility issues. Clearly, if children start blockers after their gonades have matured sufficiently, sperm and eggs can be taken "before" the treatment starts. If the children are very young, they need to be reminded that, if they intend to preserve their sperm or egg they will need to stop their treatment for a sufficiently long time to allow their natural puberty to resume or they will have to wait maybe even a year or more before treatment can start.[630]

Certainly it is correct to uphold the view that courts in judicial reviews should not make their own findings of fact, but not that the Court should accept facts that are inconsistent with each other without questioning them. Clearly, if consent needs to be given also on understanding the possibility that treatment may affect fertility and sexual activity in adullthood, the finding by the Divisional Court that childern at that age could not possibly understand the implications of puberty blockers and consent to them becomes more acceptable. And this brings us to the issue of consent and Gillick competence. Both Courts deal with the issue in detail, coming to opposite conclusions. The Court of Appeal concludes, after a long analysis of Gillick competence, that the Divisional Court has imposed an improper restriction on the Gillick test of competence, and that it is for clinicians and not courts to decide on competence. The Court cites Burke and Gillick approvingly, to the effect that the Court should "confine itself to deciding whether the proposition of law is erroneous and avoid either expressing ex cathedra opinions in areas of social and ethical controversy in which it has no claim to speak with authority or proffering answers to hypothetical questions of law which do not strictly arise for decision" (paras. 76-77). This is certainly a principle that the Courts would be wise to follow, but is the treatment of the Gillick competence test

[630] This is in fact reported in *A.B. and C.D.*, [2021] EWHC 741 (Fam): "XY could decide at any point before she starts on cross-sex hormones ("CSH"), assuming that she does so, to stop taking PBs for a period of at least 6 months and then preserve sperm. However, this course would entail developing male secondary sexual characteristics which she says she would find devastating." The female pronouns will obscure the fact we are talking here about a boy, so sperm preservation, and not eggs. This is important medically, because puberty happens on average at different ages for males and females, and because the process of harvesting and preserving eggs is a lot more invasive and requires, arguably, a higher level of Gillick competence (tthere are side effects that simply do no apply to sperm preservation).This is the perfect illustration of inaccurate language affecting medical clarity.

conducted appropriately? I have already noted that the Divisional Court's analysis of the Gillick competence issue, and the causal test was the weakest part of its judgment. Both the Divisional Court and the Court of Appeal discuss the competence test by reference to a very wide ranging jurisprudence, which goes beyond what I will term the Gillick *strictu sensu* test.

Competence arises in three sets of circumstances in legal proceedings with a medical element: life and death cases, mental capacity cases, and Gillick competence *strictu sensu*.[631] This categorisation is somewhat artificial as cases may present cross-cutting issues, but it is useful to properly categorise the Tavistock case. Although *prima facie* the Tavistock case only raises issues of competence *strictu sensu* there is a reason why it is necessary to look at the other circumstances in which issues of competence are relevant. For the purpose of this analysis I will consider a minor in a Gillick competence *strictu sensu* case as a child below the age of 16, to avoid any conflict with s8 of the Family Law Reform Act 1969.[632] As noted, the first circumstance is life and death cases. As in all medical cases, three parties are relevant: the patient, the parents, or legal guardians, (depending if the patient is a minor or an adult and if the adult is competent to make decisions or is, for example, in a coma), and the doctors. In these cases, often the patient is not in the position to consent to treatment (patients in a coma at the end of life, or very young children

[631] I am not considering the cases where competence was assessed not in a medical case, and that are cited by the Divisional Court or the Appeals Court, such as *Re S. (A Child) (Child Parent: Adoption Consent)* [2019] 2 Fam 177; *L.B.L. v R.Y.J. and V.J.* [2011] 1 FLR 1279; *H. v A Local Authority* [2011] EWHC 1704; *Masterman-Lister v Brutton & Co (Nos. 1 and 2)* [2003] 1 WLR 1511; *In re A. (Adoption: Agreement:Procedure)* [2001] 2 FLR 455; *Sheffield City Council v E.* [2005] Fam 326; *C.C. v K.K. and S.T.C.C.* [2012] COPLR 627.

[632] The issue arose in *Re W. (A Minor) Medical Treatment Courts Jurisdiction)* [1993] Fam 64, conceerning a 16 year old girl in which Lord Donaldson, building on what he had said in *Re R.*, said that consent could be given by parents and children concurrently and each would be valid and protect the doctor against a claim of negligence. As stated by Lord Donaldson in *Re W.*, at para 26: "[…] There can be concurrent powers to consent. If more than one body or person has a power to consent, only a failure to, or refusal of, consent by all having that power will create a veto. […]" A "Gillick competent" child or one over the age of 16 will have a power to consent, but this will be concurrent with that of a parent or guardian. Clearly this is not the same position in Gillick, where the competence in the child to make a decision excluded the parents' right to determine and/or consent to treatment.

with life-threatening conditions). If in a medical decision concerning an adult there is a disagreement between the patient and their family, the patient's will prevails to the extent it is possible to obtain it. If there is a disagreement between the doctor and the patient, the decision is deferred to the courts,[633] as is the case if the parents and the doctor disagree on treatment.[634] Often the issues of consent arise in the context of religious beliefs or mental health issues, the first being exemplified by treatment for Jehovah's Witnesses, who do not accept blood transfusions,[635] and the second by girls affected by anorexia nervosa and refusing treatment.[636] If the objection to treatment is based on religious beliefs, the court will be deciding and usually will give the doctors the last word, against the wishes of the parents and the minor patient if necessary. If the parents and the child do not share a religious belief (a child who refuses treatment on religious reasons and parents who do not share those religious beliefs), the parents will override a child's will even if the child is Gillick competent otherwise, by analogy to cases of mentally ill children (as in the case of anorexia) refusing life-saving treatment, whose lack of consent is overridden by parents' will, with no need for the intervention of a court.[637]

The next set of circumstances is when issues of mental capacity of the patient are at issue, not in a life and death situation and when there is a presumption of capacity.[638] There are several cases in this category

---

[633] If there is no disagreement between the relatives and the doctors but the patient's will cannot be ascertained, there is no need to ask the Court to intervene, see *NHS Trust v Y. (Intensive Care Society Intervening)* [2019] AC 978.

[634] The case of Charlie Gard is probably the most famous. The case reached the UKSC (https://www.supremecourt.uk/cases/docs/charlie-gard-190617.pdf) and the ECHR (*Charlie Gard and Others v UK*, Application No. 39793/17, https://hudoc.echr.coe.int/eng#{%22itemid%22:[%22001-175359%22]}).

[635] *L. (Medical Treatment: Gillick Competency)* [1998] 2 F.L.R. 810. In this case the 14 years old girl who refused a life-saving blood transfusion was judged not to be Gillick competent though "mature for her age."

[636] *Re W. (a Minor) (Medical Treatment: Court's Jurisdiction)* [1993] Fam. 64.

[637] In *Re R. (A Minor) (Wardship Consent to Treatment)* [1992] Fam 11 the Judge determined that the consent of a mentally ill child can be overriden by the court; the case concerned a 15 years old girl who refused anti-psychotic drugs that had been given to her while she was incapable of consenting: the local authority who was her legal guardian had stopped administring the drugs.

[638] This area of law is now regulated by the Mental Capacity Act https://www.legislation.gov.uk/ukpga/2005/9/contents. The case law cited precedes the Act, however is useful to distil some principles that may be relevant in the case of puberty suppression where there are no issues of mental capacity capable of being determined in accordance with the Act.

regarding the sterilisation of mentally disabled women, in which recourse to the Court is not unusual. In *Re D.*,[639] a mother had asked for her mentally ill 11 year old daughter to be sterilised. The psychologist referred the case to the Court, which refused the request to sterilise the girl. In *Re B.*,[640] a local authority in charge of a mentally disabled girl of 15 asked permission to the Court for sterilisation. The House of Lords determined that sterilisation was in the girl's best interest (the girl had a mental age of 5-6). In this type of cases, the House of Lords determined, sterilisation can only take place with the leave of a High Court Judge. However, in *Re E.*,[641] it was determined that a Court's involvment was not necessary because it concerned the therapeutic sterilisation of a young mentally disabled girl, and her parents could provide consent to what was effectively medical treatment to cure a menstrual condition. *Re G.F.*[642] was similarly decided, although in *Re S.*,[643] which concerned a 29 years old mentally disabled woman and the request of an hysterectomy by her mother, the Court rejected the request of the mother and restated the need for this sort of cases to come in front of a court. In summary, normally in these cases if they involve a minor there is a presumption that the parents can consent, unless the sterilisation is considered a disproportionate measure. For adult women, where there is not in law a legal right of the parents to make medical decisions, there will be an application to the Court of Protection. These cases can also involve actions for damages because of negligence, and ultimately may involve the issue whether the patient was able to consent to treatment and/or was given all the relevant information about the circumstances.[644]

---

[639] *Re D. (A Minor) (Wardship Sterilisation)* [1976] 1 All ER 326.
[640] *Re B. (A Minor) (Wardship Sterilisation)* [1987] 2 All ER 206.
[641] *Re E. (A Minor) (Medical Treatment)* [1991] 2 FLR 585.
[642] *Re G.F. (Medical Treatment)* [1992] 1 FLR 293.
[643] *Re S. (Sterilisation Patient's Best Interests)* [2000] 2 FLR 389.
[644] The seminal case for this is *Montgomery v Lancashire Health Board* [2015] UKSC 11 which is relevant because of the test of patient's consent expressed by Lord Kerr, at para 87 of the judgment: "An adult person of sound mind is entitled to decide which, if any, of the available forms of treatment to undergo, and her consent must be obtained before treatment interfering with her bodily integrity is undertaken. The doctor is therefore under a duty to take reasonable care to ensure that the patient is aware of any material risks involved in any recommended treatment, and of any reasonable alternative or variant treatments. The test of materiality is whether, in the circumstances of the particular case, a reasonable person in the patient's position would be likely to attach significance to the risk, or

Finally, Gillick test of competence *strictu sensu* cases are those in which issues of life and death or mental capacity for treatment do not arise–because in those circumstances the will of the child can be overriden by the parents and/or the doctor and court together–and there is a disagreement between the parents and the child about the treatment, so that the doctor needs to assess whether the child is capable to consent in such cases as giving contraceptives, as in the Gillick case itself[645] or in vaccination programmes.[646] It is important to remember that in the case of a child younger than 16 who is Gillick competent and refuses treatment, the doctor can seek the consent of the person with parental responsibility over the child. In other words, parents cannot go against the wish of a Gillick competent child, but if the doctor thinks the treatment is necessary and the child objects, the doctor can seek the consent of the parents, which is still existing "in the background." However, Gillick concerned the opposite scenario, i.e. a child being given advice about contraceptives against the wishes of the parent but in agreement with the doctor, where as is usually the case, the necessary condition for Gillick competence is the fact that the parents do not or would not agree to the treatment. In the case of treatment by puberty suppressants, the default case is that the child, the parents and the clinicians all agree to the treatment. In fact the GIDS does not refer children to the Trusts if their parents do not agree to puberty blockers. Therefore, the fact that the child is not Gillick competent should be irrelevant, because the parents are able to give consent. Gillick competence should only be relevant if the parents do not consent to treatment but this instance would never arise, because GIDS by policy will not treat children whose parents do not consent to treatment. Why is this the case? If puberty blockers really were life-saving, as it is claimed, surely parents should be able to override the child's will.[647] If a child were to be so dysphoric as to be suicidal, but refusing treatment as not believing that suppressing puberty would be helpful, or refusing blockers on

---

the doctor is or should reasonably be aware that the particular patient would be likely to attach significance to it."

[645] A part from Gillick, see also *R. (Axon) v Secretary of State for Health (Family Planning Association Intervening)* [2006] QB 539.

[646] Richard Griffith, "What is Gillick Competence?," Human Vaccine Immunotherapy, 12(1) (2016): 244-247, doi: 10.1080/21645515.2015.1091548:

[647] After all, parental consent, which is part of the parental responsability for the child's welfare, is the legal default to which Gillick constitutes the exception. See *In Re Z. (A Minor) (Freedom of Publication)* [1997] Fam 1; *Portsmouth NHS Trust v Wyatt* [2005] 1 FLR 652; *Re Ashya King* [2014] EWHC 2964 (Fam); *In the matter of E. (A Child) (Medical Treatment)* [2016] EWHC 2267.

political grounds (let's say because not trusting "big pharma" to act in his or her interest), in a usual medical competence situation involving life saving treatment, the parents and the doctors should be able to override the will of a child, even a Gillick competent one. The fact that the Tavistock demands both the parents' and the child's consent is an admission that puberty blockers are an elective treatment with no medical, life-saving, element. Demanding the parent and children to consent is simply a way to avoid claims of negligence, in a model we are familiar with since the first consent forms drafted in the United States in the 1980s and 1990s, to exclude responsibility in the case of malpractice suits for sex reassigment surgery, though, importantly, those concerned only adults seeking treatment.[648]

The Court of Appeal certainly does not investigate the relevance of the Gillick test in a situation in which the only necessary condition for the Gillick test to apply, i.e. lack of consent of the parents, does not apply. In a fractal-like pattern, all the courts facing gender identity issues, from employment tribunals to domestic courts all the way to supreme courts, to regional human rights courts to international treaty bodies' committes, fail to ask themselves the questions that would expose the logical fallacies at the heart of gender identity theory. In this case, why does a doctor need to test a child for Gillick competence if the parents agree to the treatment, and, if the treatment really is life saving,[649] why can't the parents agree to it even against the will of the child, as is normally the case in these circumstances? Althought both GIDS clinicians and the court in *A.B. v C.D.*, considered below, determined that puberty blockers do not constitute a special case as far a the law on competence is concerned, they fail to explain why they are treated differently from any other treatment, from contraceptives, to vaccines, to life saving procedures, requiring instead the concurrent agreement of the parents and the child.

The issue whether parents' could consent to puberty suppression for their child or whether an application to the court was either legally necessary or

[648] See the Report of the Health Law Project, Second ICTLEP Proceedings, Principle 4 and Standards 1 and 2, all referring to waiver of liability forms "to insulate the doctors from any tort liability other than negligence" (the presenter is MtF Martine Rothblatt, another millionaire who bankrolled the 'trans rights movement.' https://www.digitaltransgenderarchive.net/files/p8418n292.

[649] As claimed here Jack Turban and Others, "Pubertal Suppression for Transgender Youth and Risk of Suicidal Ideation," Pediatrics, 145 (2) (2020), doi: 10.1542/ peds.2019-1725.

advisable arose in *A.B. v C.D.*[650] The case was decided after the first Bell case, but before the appeal was decided. The case is typical in that the child, the parents and the clinicians all agreed to puberty suppression.[651]

So the issue in the case was whether, following Bell, the courts should be involved through a best interest application. It should be noted too that since puberty blockers are prescribed by the child's GP, and GPs are not bound by the NHS Trusts' service specification, there was a lack of clarity as to what GPs were or were not allowed to do. The Court reviewed cases in which concurrant consent of Gillick competent children was adjudicated,[652] following Gillick in stating that to the extent that a child becomes competent, the parents' consent cannot override the child's; however, if child and parents agree but the child is in no position to consent to treatment (because of Bell for example) the parents retain their default right to make decisions, on behalf of the child. The Court distinguishes, with difficulty in my opinion, between a child who is not Gillick competent but consents to treatment and a child who is Gillick competent and consents to treatment, although in both cases he or she, for whatever reason, is not capable of lawfully expressing their consent and must therefore rely on their parents consenting on their behalf. In practical terms, the Court goes on, this does not make a difference. The difficulty is that, by definition, someone who is not competent cannot consent. So in effect the Court is saying that potentially the parents could consent to puberty blockers against the wishes of the child or, as the Court opines, if the child is too overwhelmed to make the decision by himself or herself. Following the Court of Appeal's decision that in the case of puberty blockers it is not necessary to request leave of a Court, the judge in this case considers that parents can consent to puberty suppression when children are not in the position to do so and that puberty suppression

---

[650] *A.B. v C.D.* [2021] EWHC 741 (Fam).

[651] As an aside, it is dispiriting that in the 2020s a child is still described by reference to outdated gender stereotypes, in this manner:
"XY [born a boy] came out to her parents as transgender when she was 10 years old in Year 5. According to AB, XY had always only been interested in girls' toys and clothes. When at primary school she, for a period, tried to conform to a more "male" stereotype but she was utterly miserable, became very withdrawn, and was shy and unhappy, particularly at school." The Court also recounts that XY "came out to her parents about being transgender after reading a book where one of the main characters was transgender." There is no evidence of childhood body dysphoria. Only a dislike for stereotypical boy toys and clothes. Apparently, our society is still incapable to conceive that a boy may play with dolls.

[652] *Re R.* and *Re W.*

should not be put in a special category of medical treatment where an application to the court should be always sought.

As noted, in Autumn 2020 Dr Hilary Cass was given the task to report on the provision of care to gender dysphoric children. In February 2022 she issued the "Independent Review of Gender Identity Services for Children and Young People: Interim Report."[653]The material collected in the Interim Report confirms the poor quality of the data, to the point that the two NICE Reviews could not be used as a basis for the Cass Report. Similar critical assessment is done by the Multi-Professional Review Group (MPRG) set up by the NHS, reporting that problems at GIDS prevent them from carrying out their work, flagging particularly the fact that 31% of submissions from GIDS lacked safeguarding information. The Care Quality Commission, after conducting an unannounced visit to the GIDS, delivered an "inadequate" assessment of its performance. The Interim Report recommends that the MPRG continue to monitor and review cases referred by the GIDS to the Trusts. The most troubling elements of the Report are on the one side the statistics, on the other the lack of data and follow up of these very vulnerable children. The Report confirms that the cohort of referrals has changed dramatically in the last ten years: while there has been a definite increase in referrals, the number of girls reporting dysphoria at puberty rose 7040%. The number of boys, many of whom were reporting dysphoria since childhood, rose 1675%, so at a much lower rate. It is useful to remember that, according to the Dutch Protocol, only children presenting dysphoria since early childhood should be approved for puberty suppression. Clearly the Tavistock is going well beyond the criteria devised by the Dutch team of experts in the Netherlands. Other characteristics of the cohort of children are equally problematic: 1/3 of the children are on the autism spectrum or have other neurodiversity; more children than the national average are in care (paras. 3.10-3.11). Other issues arise with respect to the process: the Interim Report singles out the lack of a multidisciplinary approach, of clear criteria for referrals, of a coordinated and standardised data collection, of guidance on the assessment process, of the possibility to access a variety of options, of a formal diagnosis before puberty suppression is initiated, of proper recording of consent from the patients, of any research to understand the neurodevelopmental outcome of puberty suppression. Additionally, the Report confirms that staff felt unable to diverge from a pure affirmative approach and that GPs were being pressured to prescribe puberty blockers

---

[653]https://cass.independent-review.uk/publications/interim-report/.

or cross-sex hormones after they had already been initiated by private providers.

The Interim Report recommends closing the GIDS and replacing it with Regional Centres, better integrated with other services, including local GPs. Based on the evidence collected in the Interim Report, it would have seemed advisable to stop the prescription of puberty suppressants in all circumstances, especially on girls with so-called "Rapid Onset Gender Dysphoria.[654] Unfortunately it seems a different approach has been followed. On the one hand, regional hubs are already in the process of being opened, amidst controversy;[655] on the other, and more seriously, the opening of the first private provider of "gender care" for over-16s, including for the prescription of cross-sex hormones.[656] The Final Report does not recommend a complete stop to the provision of puberty blockers, following instead similar recommendations as reached by other countries, to limit the provision of puberty blockers to children in clinical studies.[657]

It is unfortunate that some of these events were happening while the final report by Dr Cass had not been delivered yet, possibly interfering with the application of its recommendations and creating a policy gap in which private providers can exploit the vulnerability of families and children. The registration of private gender care centres prescribing hormones to over-16s is particularly troubling, given the announcement, in January 2024, that the WHO's Guidelines on the health of transgender and gender diverse people are to be restricted to the treatment of adults only.[658] In the

---

[654] On this phenomenon, see Lisa Littman, "Parents Reports of Adolescents and Young Adults Perceived to Show Signs of Rapid Onset Gender Dysphoria," PloSOne (August 2018), doi: 10.1371/journal.pone.0202330.

[655] Amelia Gentleman, "New NHS children's gender clinic hit by disagreements and resignations," The Guardian, January 18, 2024, https://www.theguardian.com/society/2024/jan/18/new-nhs-childrens-gender-clinic-hit-by-disagreements-and-resignations.

[656] GenderPlus, with offices in London, Birmingham and Dublin; https://www.genderplus.com/.

[657] I have several reservations about the language and the content of the Report, see Alessandra Asteriti, "Reviewing the Cass Review," Gender Dissident, 20 April 2024, Reviewing the Cass Review - by Alessandra Asteriti (substack.com).

[658] "Extended deadline for feedback on development of a WHO guideline on the health of trans and gender diverse people," WHO News, 15 January 2024, https://www.who.int/news/item/15-01-2024-extended-deadline-for-feedback-on-who-development-of-a-guideline-on-the-health-of-trans-and-gender-diverse-people.

accompanying FAQ document,[659] released on the same day, the WHO admits that:

> Why will the guideline only cover adults and not also children or adolescents?
>
> • The scope will cover adults only and not address the needs of children and adolescents, because on review, the evidence base for children and adolescents is limited and variable regarding the longer-term outcomes of gender affirming care for children and adolescents.

In other words the Care Quality Commission registered a provider of a service whose long term effects are not considered advisable for children and adolescents by the WHO, in the absence of sufficient evidence.

---

[659] World Health Organization, "Frequently Asked Questions–WHO development of a guideline on the health of trans and gender diverse people," January 15, 2024, https://cdn.who.int/media/docs/default-source/hq-hiv-hepatitis-and-stis-library/tgd_faq_16012024.pdf?sfvrsn=79eaf57f_1.

CHAPTER 10

CONCLUSIONS

I have a colleague who is transgender. There is a video of him as a toddler–he was assigned female at birth–tearing barrettes out of then-her hair. And throwing them on the ground. And sobbing. That's a gender message.

—Dr. Diane Ehrensaft[660]

The review of the role and effect of gender identity theory in international law has evidenced several problems of legal logic. But the review also showed deeper problems with the theory, at the level of first principles. At the meta-level this theory suffers from the deep inconsistency between the rejection of any grand narrative as hegemonic and "colonialist" (or whatever the enemy du jour is in academia), which it shares with much deconstructionism and post-modernism, and the obsessive insistence on the centrality of gender identity as an innate and inevitable element of the human experience, a narrative that crosses time and space in a hegemonic move not seen since the spread of the monotheistic religions and the age of ideologies. No-one eviscerated this deep inconsistency better than Martha Nussbaum in her critique of Judith Butler's scholarship and her influence on US academia and the ultimately regressive soul of gender theory, though even Nussbaum could not predict how far Butler's claim that sex is socially constructed would take us.[661] This is a logical impasse that cannot be solved. In gender identity theory, this logical impasse manifests itself in the disconnect between the theoretical argument that gender is fluid and changeable, and the absolutely rigid rules on speech, enforcing a mostly binary division between cis and trans, for example. The entire theory is built around dogmatic absolutes, such as that transwomen are women, or that we all have a gender identity, even if we do not believe we do. As

[660] Gender-affirmative therapist: Baby who hates barrettes = trans boy; questioning sterilizazion of 11-year olds same as denying cancer treatment," 4thWaveNow, September 29, 2016, https://4thwavenow.com/2016/09/29/gender-affirmative-therapist-baby-who-hates-barrettes-trans-boy-questioning-sterilization-of-11-year-olds-same-as-denying-cancer-treatment/.

[661] Martha C. Nussbaum, "The Professor of Parody," The New Republic, February 22, 1999, https://newrepublic.com/article/150687/professor-parody.

someone who grew up in a Catholic society, I cannot help being reminded of the debates I used to have with priests (we were forced to have religious education in school) about the fact I did not have an immortal soul, and being reminded I had one and God would acknowledge me as one of his children even if I rejected religion. In fact, while the Catholic religion promised me salvation and paradise, for gender identity theorists I can never be anything better than an "ally." The original sin of "cisness" does not allow for redemption. While "trans people are sacred,"[662] we can only play a walk-on part. As I have already noted, what is problematic is not the idea of a gender identity in itself, provided one intends it as the awareness of one's sex and of the gender roles associated with one's sex. Similarly, I have no problem acknowledging that we have something that we may call soul if we are religious or subconscious if we are not. I have an issue with accepting the belief that the soul is immortal and that it prevails over our body. Mortification of the body in Christian religions was causally connected with the belief that only the soul matters.[663]

Equally, I have no problem accepting that we have an awareness of our sexed body and of the gender rules associated with that sexed body, and that some people wish to refer to this as a gender identity, though it is not a language I would use. What I refuse to believe is that this identity is disconnected from the body and more important than the body itself, to the point that even if our awareness of material reality tells us we are looking at a man, we have to believe he is a woman on the basis of a self-declared ineffable quality. The demands imposed by gender identity theory are even stricter than those imposed by religion. There is no need to change one's language in order to recognise the soul. Recognising a gender identity imposes rigid rules of language and behaviour, on pain even of civil or criminal sanctions for dissenters.[664]

---

662 Emma Keith, "The Story Behind Hopeful Billboard at Vacant Detroit Intersection," Detroit Free Press, September 25, 2019, https://eu.freep.com/story/news/local/michigan/detroit/2019/07/25/transgender-billboard-detroit/1810943001/.

663 Anyone who has seen the photos of young girls proudly displaying their mastectomy scars cannot help being reminded of similar religious images about the mortification of the female flesh. See Miryam Clough, Shame, the Church and the Regulation of Female Sexuality (Abingdon: Taylor and Francis, 2017).

664 Molly Dower, "Beyond Offense: Why the First Amendment Does Not Protect Deliberate Misgendering," Cardozo Law Review, 44(5): 2104-2137, https://cardozolawreview.com/wp-content/uploads/2023/10/DOWER.44.5.6.Print_.pdf.

As noted in several instances in the course of this work, I believe that gender identity should be reframed as a belief protected under freedom of belief and expression. Human rights law has robust provisions for the protection of these freedoms,[665] considered necessary in a democratic society,[666] as do all constitutions of democratic countries. How challenging this proposal is is only too evident after considering how this theory has been embedded in international and domestic laws, and how many social practices have been put in place to encourage and even compel individuals to abide by its tenets.

But certainly the most challenging project is to disimbed gender affirmative care from health care provisions, though the first signs that the medical world is becoming more critical in its approach have been developing, as we have seen in the previous chapter. In more litigious countries, such as the United States, it might take litigation, including class action suits, to make clinical changes possible, and we are seeing the beginning of these negligence and malpractice actions being brought in US courts, including against the American Association of Pediatrics.[667] Other countries, where affirmative care is not as developed and as lucrative, may find it easier to reverse course, avoiding subjecting children and young people to irreversible, iatrogenic medical and surgical treatment to "treat" what we are told is a naturally occuring identity. In another logical flaw of this theory, transgender children are both perfect as they are and in need of drastic medical treatment to fundamentally change their development and their anatomy.

---

[665] For its protection in the European context, see Guide on Article 9 of the European Convention on Human Rights, August 2022, https://www.echr.coe.int/documents/d/echr/guide_art_9_eng.

[666] *Handyside v UK*, Application No. 5493/72, Judgment of 7 December 1976.

[667] Several US States have also imposed restrictions or bans on gender affirmative care, see https://www.findlaw.com/lgbtq-law/state-laws-on-gender-affirming-care.html; for the cases, see *Mosley v Emerson and Others*, filed in the Superior Court of North Carolina on 23 July 2023, https://img1.wsimg.com/blobby/go/ae9895b0-a62f-49d6-99d6-180b933bca97/Prisha%20Mosley%20File-Stamped%20Complaint%207.17.23.pdf; *Ayala v American Academy of Pediatrics and Others*, filed in the Superior Court of Rhode Island 23 October 2023, https://dw-wp-production.imgix.net/2023/10/Ayala-v-AAP-Complaint_stamped.pdf. See also "Legal Action May Change Transgender Care in America," The Economist, March 7, 2023, https://www.economist.com/united-states/2023/03/07/legal-action-may-change-transgender-care-in-america.

The ECHR protects, in its Article 9, freedom of thought, conscience and religion.[668] The right is limited in paragraph 2 of the article "only to such limitations as are prescribed by law and are necessary in a democratic society in the interests of public safety, for the protection of public order, health or morals, or for the protection of the rights and freedoms of others." Domestic equality law may provide its own criteria for the recognition of a belief as a protected belief where religion and belief are protected categories, as in the UK Equality Act 2010.[669] The criteria for the recognition of philosophical beliefs in the Equality Act have been spelled out in the Grainger Case:[670]

(i) The belief must be genuinely held.
(ii) It must be a belief and not an opinion or viewpoint based on the present state of information available.
(iii) It must be a belief as to a weighty and substantial aspect of human life and behaviour.
(iv) It must attain a certain level of cogency, seriousness, cohesion and importance.
(v) It must be worthy of respect in a democratic society, be not incompatible with human dignity and not conflict with the fundamental rights of others.

Point V is clearly the most crucial step of the test and the one where equality law and human rights law intersect more closely; in any event, the Equality Act is to be read in conformity with human rights law and more specifically the ECHR.[671] In effect we could say that any belief that is incompatible with human dignity and conflicts with the rights of others will fail the test both under human rights law and equality law, regardless of whether it satisfies any of the other criteria, though it seems that the test under the EA is more stringent than the test for limitation of beliefs in human rights law, such as the ECHR. The EA does require that the philosophical belief in itself be worthy of respect in a democratic society,

---

[668] This right is similarly protected in the Universal Declaration of Human Rights, the ICCPR and the other regional human rights treaties.

[669] Equality Act 2010, https://www.legislation.gov.uk/ukpga/2010/15/contents. S10 defines the protected category of Religion or Belief: (1) Religion means any religion and a reference to religion includes a reference to a lack of religion.
(2) Belief means any religious or philosophical belief and a reference to belief includes a reference to a lack of belief.

[670] *Grainger plc v Nicholson* [2010] RLR4 (EAT).

[671] Section 3 of the Human Rights Act 1988,
https://www.legislation.gov.uk/ukpga/1998/42/section/3.

although this only excludes beliefs that are so extreme as to be unacceptable in a democracy.[672]

The events surrounding the legal case brought by Maya Forstater against her former employer, Center for Global Development,[673] are a cautionary tale of wrongly framing both gender identity and "gender critical" beliefs. The preliminary hearing which dealt with the status of "gender critical" beliefs under the EA was lost, with Judge Tayler declining to recognise protected belief status to Forstater's beliefs.[674] The judgment was appealed and Forstater won on appeal, with the judge recognising the protected status to her beliefs.[675]The steps by which the judge reaches this decision exemplify the problem of having recognised gender identity as a material identity and not as a belief (Gender Reassignment is a protected category in the Equality Act). The Judge describes Forstater's belief as "the belief that sex is immutable and not to be conflated with gender identity." In my opinion, this description evidences a basic misunderstanding of the issue. The English language has two meanings for "to believe" (and the related noun belief). The first is to know something to be true. The second, to hold a belief, not necessarily based in reality. Section 10 of the EA uses the word belief in its second meaning, holding a belief that may or may not be based in reality. The criteria for protecting a belief under s10 do not include the fact that the belief needs to be based in reality. Believing that sex is immutable is not to be interpreted as "holding the belief that sex is immutable," but as "knowing to be true that sex is immutable," therefore, there is no such a thing as a "gender critical belief," at least not according to the definition provided in Forstater. Knowledge is not a belief. What could be said is that a person who is "gender critical" does not believe in gender identity theory. However, gender identity theory has neither been the object of a case in which a person who believes in it was discriminated against on its basis, nor has it been challenged in a case in which a person

---

[672] Beliefs that "shock, offend or disturb" are still considered protected beliefs by the ECHR, see *Vajnai v Hungary* (2010) 50 EHRR 44, para 46.

[673] A summary of the events here, https://www.forstater.com/forstater-v-cgd/.

[674]*Maya Forstater v CGD Europe, Centre for Global Development, and Masood Ahmed*, Case Number: 2200909/2019, https://assets.publishing.service.gov.uk/media/5e15e7f8e5274a06b555b8b0/Maya_Forstater__vs_CGD_Europe__Centre_for_Global_Development_and_Masood_Ahmed_-_Judgment.pdf?ref=forstater.com.

[675]*Maya Forstater v CGD Europe, Centre for Global Development, and Masood Ahmed*, Appeal No. UKEAT/0105/20/JOJ, https://assets.publishing.service.gov.uk/media/60c1cce1d3bf7f4bd9814e39/Maya_Forstater_v_CGD_Europe_and_others_UKEAT0105_20_JOJ.pdf?ref=forstater.com.

exclusively claimed to be discriminated against on the basis of his or her lack of belief in it.[676] Judge Choudhury, since an alternative claim based on lack of belief was advanced by Maya Forstater, stated: "We refer to this as the "gender identity belief." The Claimant accepted that the gender identity belief was a philosophical belief qualifying for protection under s.10, EqA." It is not for a claimant to determine whether a belief qualifies for protection under the Equality Act but for the court to establish. The Judge also did not explore what relationship, if any, there is between gender identity belief and gender reassignment, which is protected under s7 of the Equality Act.

In an indication of the potential issues of characterising being gender critical as a positive belief, and not simply the absence of gender identity belief, Judge Choudhury declared that it is not the role of the Tribunal "to express any view as to the merits of the either side of [the] debate." It is hard to imagine a similar statement being made about the knowledge that the Earth is round and the belief that it is flat. There is nothing offensive in the knowledge that our sex is binary and immutable, as there was nothing offensive in Galileo or Copernicus saying that the Earth circled around the Sun, although both of them went against religious dogma and both were punished by the Catholic Church for their ideas. We now know that these are not competing beliefs in which the State must remain neutral and, for example, air travel needs to take into account that the Earth is round and not flat, just as medicine has to take into account that female and male bodies differ in fundamental ways. This is not equivalent to censorship. Recognising the distinction between facts and beliefs is absolutely necessary to proper law-making and I would venture, to the integrity of the rule of law itself. Having determined that being aware of the scientific fact of the immutability of sex is only a belief puts women in the invidious position of having to prove the reality of their sex to the satisfaction of a Court in a facts-specific set of circumstances where less educated women will be put at a structural disadvantage and therefore be more easily victimised in the workplace.

Judge Choudhury does not maintain the neutrality that he avers is necessary in deciding freedom of expression issues. At para 104 he states that:

---

[676] Although Maya Forstater also put her claim on an alternative basis of lack of belief, at para 107 of the appeal judgment described by the Employment Tribunal as: "everyone has a gender which may be different to their sex at birth and which effectively trumps sex so that trans men are men and transwomen are women".

> That does not mean that in the absence of such a restriction [under Article 10(2) ECHR] the Claimant could go about indiscriminately "misgendering" trans persons with impunity. She cannot. The Claimant is subject to same prohibitions on discrimination, victimisation and harassment under the EqA as the rest of society. Should it be found that her misgendering on a particular occasion, because of its gratuitous nature or otherwise, amounted to harassment of a trans person (or of anyone else for that matter), then she could be liable for such conduct under the EqA. The fact that the act of misgendering was a manifestation of a belief falling with s.10, EqA would not operate automatically to shield her from such liability.

One cannot accept the concept of "misgendering" if one has not accepted already that gender identities exist and prevail over sex. The "correct" pronouns in English are those that match the sex of the persons they refer to, not their gender identity. This limitation of freedom of belief, that affects women more than men, is dependent on the acceptance of gender identity theory and on reframing the demand made by a man to a woman, to ignore the evidence of her own eyes as a "right," and the refusal of women to submit to this abuse as abusive in itself. Only centring the autonomy of women unveils the power relationship in the "pronoun battle." At para 118 the Judge reiterates that the Claimant is subject to the prohibition of discrimination and harassment under the Equality Act. The fact that a woman denied the right to name reality is herself being harassed is not even contemplated by the Judge. In a feasible scenario, a male employee who has sexually assaulted a female colleague in a situation in which she did not feel confident to report him, may switch to a female identity and demand that his female victim use female pronouns to refer to him. If the female colleague refuses she may be dismissed and her only defence in an Employment Tribunal would require her to reveal the real reason for her refusal to comply.

The review of this case indicates how difficult it will be to dislodge gender identity in its conceptualisation as a material reality and reframing it as a belief, subjected in equality law to the Grainger test (or other as appropriate in different jurisdictions). In doing so, one has to perform the same two-stepped test that we have seen performed in the Forstater case:

1. Whether a belief is "worthy of respect in a democratic society;"
2. Beliefs that shock or disturb, as well as beliefs that may affect the rights of others in other ways, may be subjected to legitimate limitations in an employment context.

A belief that completely destroys the rights of others would not pass the first step of the test. If gender identity theory passes this first step, clearly it can be subjected to legitimate limitations since, with its requirement that people modify their language and behaviour to signal compliance with the tenets of the theory, it affects the rigths of others. Additionally, while the requirements of gender identity theory apply equally to all third parties, they affect women disproportionately, because women are more affected by the requirement to refer to men as women, and women have a higher interest in maintaining single sex services, men being a safety risk to women in a way that women simply are not to men.

A way to test the feasibility of this project is to reconsider the backlash against gender identity. One can revisit all the material effects on women, girls and LGB people that have been listed in Chapter 10 and imagine how they would be affected by reframing gender identity as a belief. Clearly the first and most important is that people would not be allowed to modify their birth certificate and their identity documents to replace their sex with their self-defined gender identity. Sex would continue to be recorded correctly at birth (with the allowed modification for the minuscule percentage of people for whom sex is recorded incorrectly at birth, an ever-lowering number, given the advances in medical science in pre-birth sex detection testing) and maintained in all identification documents. Recording gender identity separately in identity documents or birth certificates is unnecessarily cumbersome, given the ever expanding number of gender identities.

Women would not be prevented from using the word woman to define their sex class. Men who have the belief of having a female gender identity can come up with their own new word to define themselves, without using the word woman. As they are fond of saying, language evolves. A new word is needed. As feminists say, "woman is taken."

Data collection would distinguish clearly between sex and gender identity, not allowing people to select sex on the basis of their gender identity. The integrity of data collection would be preserved, and when necessary, data could be collected separately for people who identify as transgender. Since data collection on transgender people can be done properly only if sex and gender identity are kept strictly separate, this rule should find favour amongst trans rights activists and gender identity theorists as well. Accurate data collection is especially important for crime data, as shown in Chapter 10. No more there would be males recorded as female rapists, and the robustness of crime data would be maintained. Recording separately males who identify as women who commit sex offences will allow to study properly the incidence of sex crimes in the different sub-groups of males. As noted, there is already evidence that males who identify as women commit more sex offences than males in general, but these statistics could underestimate the numbers, as, for example, in the UK males with a GRC are automatically counted as women, and self-ID renders some of these statistics hopelessly inaccurate.

Relatedly, the integrity of criminal trials would be maintained. Males could not demand that courts referred to them as women and female victims would not be forced to attend proceedings in which their male rapist is described as a woman or even, be forced to refer to him as a woman. Prisons would be divided by sex, as recommended the Mandela and Bangkok Rules. Women would not be forced to share prison accommodation with males who claim a female identity (sometimes only for the time when they are in detention); those who are vulnerable to violence in the male estate could be accommodated in a separate male wing in the male estate, which should also be open to young gay prisoners, who also are at risk in male prisons.

Women would have their own rape refuges and domestic violence refuges, where they can be sure they would not have to face their male-created trauma every day, forced to share accommodation with males who claim a female identity but have an easily identifiable male body. Trans rights organisations could spend some of the money they collect on dedicated refuges for transgender people, who have distinct needs.

Health care provision would take into account sex differences. Conditions affecting females are often ignored in research and women are rarely included in clinical trials, part of a larger trend of ignoring the specificity of the female body.[677] Introducing an element of ambiguity about sex classification does not serve the interests of women. The safety of patients is and should be the highest priority, above the feelings of patients who reject their sex and especially, above the demands of staff who want to be treated as the opposite sex. Female doctors and nurses should be available, within reason, to women who request them. Female carers should be available to families and patients who request them. No woman should be told a male nurse is a female nurse when she easily perceives him as a

[677] Caroline Criado Pérez, Invisible Women: Data Bias in a World Designed for Men (London: Vintage Books, 2019).

male. The safety and well-being of patients is the overarching consideration, not the feelings of nursing and medical staff.

Given the overwhelming evidence from scientists and clinicians, sport would be segregated by sex. Female sport is for women and girls. Women are not men with low testosterone, and the advantage men gain with puberty is irreversible, as the changes in their voice are. Boys and men who think they are female can play and compete in male sport, which is already an open category. Sex for entry in the female category can easily be ascertained with a mouth swab. No genital testing necessary. Not only girls and women deserve to compete fairly and safely, but they need and deserve changing rooms that are female only.

Lesbian women and girls would not be be forced to accommodate men who claim to be lesbian and pressure them for sex. They would have the right to meet as lesbians without having to include males. They would again have their own meeting places and bars and clubs where they can get together without males if they want to. Young girls who are questioning their sexual orientation would not be taught that some women have a penis, and sex is not about genitals.

Freedom of speech would be guaranteed and people would be able to debate the merits of gender identity theory and to look at data with rigour and objectivity. University staff would be able to conduct research on any aspect of gender identity theory, but most urgently, on the affirmative gender care on ever younger cohorts of children. The precautioary principle would dictate any decision made about the medicalisation of gender care, and puberty suppressants would not be given to children anymore. Reframing gender identity as a belief would also mean taking gender non-conformity at face value, and not use it anymore, as currently done, as a possible symptom of transgender status. Boys would be allowed to play with dolls without being told that may mean they are really girls, and girls would be able to choose to wear only trousers without being told they must be boys. Sex is morally neutral, but gender identity is not. As its very name implies, it is a social construct, an accretion of stereotypes of masculinity and femininity.which should be left to the freedom of belief of the individual, but should not be reified in law.

The law used to recognise sex for the purpose of discriminating on its basis, but there is no necessary connection between the material reality of sex differentiation and the social reality of sex discrimination. It is not necessary to pretend sex is not real, or not binary, or not immutable, in order to eliminate discriminatory laws and to fight sexist social practices. To recognise some men as women or some women as men, as the law currently does in many countries, simply introduces a category mistake in the law, which impedes its proper functioning–we have seen how the comparator in equality law becomes unworkable, for example. Calls for balancing, or nuance, or proportionality in dealing with gender claims are simply misguided. Category errors in law cannot be cured by proportionality and balancing. The correct categorisation needs to be put in place again. Men are men, no matter what clothes they wear, what past-times they prefer or what sexual preferences they have, and the same can be said for women. Reframing gender identity as a belief naturally has an effect on people who believe in gender identities. There will be no special legal accommodation for their philosophical belief, in line with the treatment of any other philosophical belief. Social behaviour will be left to individuals. If friends and family wish to keep the pretence that their friends and relatives are of a different sex because of their stereotypical presentation, they are of course free to do so. Third parties are under no obligation to keep the pretence, especially to their own detriment, as it is often the case for women. The fact a male wears a dress is not a signal he is a woman, but simply that he likes to wear dresses and he should be free to do so. This is the most that the law should do to accommodate this belief.

Reframing gender identity as a belief presents two main difficulties. The first one is the issue of disabling gender dysphoria in adults, and the second one is the issue of the alleged transgender identity in children. In either case, accommodation outside the law is a separate matter that is outside the scope of this work (for example, what kind of medical care should be used for gender dysphoria). The first issue can be disposed of relatively easily as severe gender dysphoria can be considered a disability and therefore individuals suffering from it can receive the protection equality and human rights law grants with people suffering from temporary or permanent disability.

The creation of the "transgender child" will likely be remembered as the great medical scandal of the beginning of the third millennium.[678] In fact the most deleterious effects have been experienced in the medical field, with the medicalisation of ever younger children, and in education, where

[678] Heather Brunskell Evans and Michele Moore, eds., Transgender Children and Young People. Born in Your Own Body (Newcastle: Cambridge Scholars Publishing, 2018).

children are encouraged to "transition socially" (to disassociate from their body in their social interactions) and are indoctrinated in gender identity theory through concepts such as the "Genderbread Person"[679] and the "Barbie-GI Joe Scale" by Mermaids.[680] Implementing safeguarding laws properly should suffice to shield children from the effects of this theory. If a child manifests symptoms of dissociation from her or his body, she or he should be treated in the way other forms of body dysphoria or dismorphia, such as anorexia, bulimia and self-harm, are treated. In no circumstance should children be validated in their belief that there is something wrong with their body or with their personality.

Restoring the difference between sex and gender and framing gender identity as a belief will return international human rights law to its proper function of protecting human beings against discrimination without compelling people to ignore the evidence of their own eyes and give up their own autonomy and dignity.

---

679 The Genderbread Person, https://www.samkillermann.com/work/genderbread-person/.

680 Mermaids even used this in transgender training for adults. The infantilisation of individuals in gender identity theory is a phenomenon I have already noted in this work. From rainbow families, to top and bottom surgeries to the genderbread person and mermaid children, this theory seems to insist on disguising reality through infantilising language. See Transgender Trend, "What Questions Should a School be Asking about Mermaids Training for Families?" September 9, 2019, https://www.transgendertrend.com/questions-school-mermaids-training-teachers/.

Bibliography

Books

American Psychiatric Association. 2013. Diagnostic and Statistical Manual of Mental Disorders, Fifth Edition. Arlington, VA: American Psychiatric Association.

Arendt, Hannah. 1951. The Origins of Totalitarianism. New York: Schocken Books.

Ashford, Chris and Maine, Alexander, eds. 2020. Research Handbook on Gender, Sexuality, and the Law.

Baker, Andy. 2021. Shaping the Developing World: The West, the South and the Natural World. Los Angeles: Sage Publications.

Benjamin, Harry. 1966. The Transsexual Phenomenon: a Scientific Report on Transsexualism and Sex Conversion in the Human Male and Female. New York: Ace Pub Co.

Butler, Judith. Gender Trouble: Feminism and the Subversion of Identity. New York: Routledge.

Cheltenham: Elgar Publishing Ltd, 2020.

Clough, Miryam. 2017. Shame, the Church and the Regulation of Female Sexuality. Abingdon: Taylor and Francis.

Colker, Ruth. 2023. Sexual Orientation, Gender Identity, and the Law in a Nutshell. Eagan: West Academic Publishing.

Cooper, Davina, Emerton, Robyn, Grabham, Emily, Newman, Han, Peel, Elizabeth, Renz, Flora and Smith, Jessica. 2022. Abolishing Legal Sex. Final Report. London: King's College.

De Beauvoir, Simone. 1953. The Second Sex. Transl. H.M. Parshley. London: Jonathan Cape.

DeLaet, Debra and Cramer, Renée Ann eds. 2019. Gender, Sexuality, and the Law. New York: Routledge.

Dworkin, Ronald. 1986. Law's Empire. Cambridge: Cambridge University Press.

Engels, Frederick. 1941. The Origin of the Family, Private Property and the State, Transl. Alick West, Dona Torr. London: Lawrence and Wishart.

Fuller, Lon. 1964. The Morality of Law. New Haven and London: Yale University Press.

Gonzalez-Salzberg, Damian A. 2019. Sexuality and Transsexuality Under the European Convention of Human Rights: A Queer Reading of Human Rights Law. London: Bloomsbury.

Hellum, Anne, ed. 2017. Human Rights, Sexual Orientation and Gender Identity. New York: Routledge.

Hines, Sally. 2018. Is Gender Fluid? London: Thames & Hudson Ltd.

Hobsbawm, Eric J. 1994. Age of Extremes: The Short Twentieth Century 1914-1991. London: Penguin Books.

Jaramillo, Isabel C. and Carlson, Laura. 2021. Trans Rights and Wrongs: A Comparative Study of Legal Reforms Concerning Trans Persons. New York: Springer International.

Jorgensen, Christine. 2000. A Personal Autobiography. Minneapolis: Cleis Press.

Khan Jalalzai, Musa. 2011. Child Sex, Bacha Bazi and Prostitution in Afghanistan. Saarbrücken: Lap Lambert Academic Publishing GmbH.

Krstić, Ivana, Evola, Marco and Ribes Moreno, Maria Isabel eds. 2023. Legal Issues of International Law from a Gender Perspective. New York: Springer, 2023.

Lau, Holning. 2018. Sexual Orientation and Gender Identity Discrimination. Leiden: Brill.

Long Chu, Andrea. 2019. Females. London: Verso Books.

Luhmann, Niklas. 2004. Law as a Social System. Trans. Klaus A Ziegert. Oxford: Oxford University Press.

Martens, Sibrand Karel, Haak, W.E., Corstens, G.J.M. and Veldt, M.I. 2000. Martens Dissenting: The Separate Opinions of a European Human Rights Judge. Deventer: W.E.J. Tjeenk Willink.

O'Halloran, Kerry. 2020. Sexual Orientation, Gender Identity and International Human Rights Law. London: Routledge.

Pace, John P. 2020. The United Nations Commission on Human Rights: A Very Great Enterprise. Oxford: Oxford University Press.

Palazzini, Laura. 2012. Gender in Philosophy and Law. Dordrecht: Springer.

Renz, Flora. 2024. Gender Recognition and the Law: Troubling Transgender Peoples' Engagement with Legal Regulation. New York: Routledge.

Scherpe, Jens ed. 2015. The Legal Status of Transsexual and Transgender Persons. Cambridge: Cambridge University Press.

Sharpe, Alex. 2002. Transgender Jurisprudence: Dysphoric Bodies of Law. London: Cavendish.

Stiglitz, Joseph. 2002. Globalization and Its Discontents. New York: W.W. Norton & Company.

Stryker, Susan and Whittle, Stephen eds. 2013. The Transgender Studies Reader. New York: Routledge.

Sullivan, Alice and Todd, Selina. 2024. Sex and Gender: A Contemporary Reader. London: Routledge.

Szymborska, Wisława. 1996. People on the Bridge. Transl. Adam Czerniaswski. London: Forest Books.

Tuttle Hansen, Elaine. 1967. Mother Without Child: Contemporary Fiction and the Crisis of Motherhood. Berkeley: University of California Press.

von Arnaud, Andreas, von der Decken, Kristen and Susi, Mart eds. 2020. The Cambridge Handbook of New Human Rights: Recognition, Novelty, Rhetoric. Cambridge: Cambridge University Press.

Weiss, Jillian and Cruz, David. 2021. Gender Identity and the Law. Durham: Carolina Academic Press.

Book Chapters

Adams, Felicity and Emmerich, Fabienne. "Mapping the Manifestations of Exclusion: Challenging the Incarceration of Queer People." In The Queer Outside the Law, edited by Senthorun Raj and Peter Dunne, 107-142. (London: Palgrave MacMillan, 2021).

Auchmuty, Rosemary and Freedman, Rosa. "Sex and Gender in Law." In Sex and Gender: A Contemporary Reader, edited by Alice Sullivan and Selina Todd, 125-138. (London: Routledge, 2024).

Beccalossi, Chiara. "The Italian Vice: Male Homosexuality and British Tourism in Southern Italy." In Italian Sexualities Uncovered, edited by Valeria P. Babini, Chiara Beccalossi and Lucy Riall, 185-206. (London: Palgrave MacMillan, 2015).

Biggs Michael. "Britain's Experiment with Puberty Blockers." In Inventing Transgender Children and Young People, edited by Michael Moore and Heather Brunskell-Evans, 40-55. (Newcastle: Cambridge Scholars Publishing).

Biggs, Michael. "The Technology of Puberty Suppression." In Sex and Gender: A Contemporary Reader, edited by Alice Sullivan and Selina Todd, 175-193. (London: Routledge, 2024).

Devine, Cathy. "Sex, Gender Identity and Sport." In Sex and Gender: A Contemporary Reader, edited by Alice Sullivan and Selina Todd, 232-258. (London: Routledge, 2024).

Hilton, Emma and Wright, Colin. "Two Sexes." In Sex and Gender: A Contemporary Reader, edited by Alice Sullivan and Selina Todd, 16-34. (London: Routledge, 2024).

Lalor, Kay. “Queer Legacies of Colonialism.” In The Queer Outside the Law, edited by Senthorun Raj and Peter Dunne, 23-48. (London: Palgrave MacMillan, 2021).

Lugones, Marìa. “The Coloniality of Gender.” In The Palgrave Handbook on Gender and Development, edited by Wendy Harcourt, 13-33. (London: Palgrave Macmillan, 2016).

Otto, Dianne. “International Human Rights Law: Towards Rethinking Sex/Gender Dualism.” In The Ashgate Research Companion to Feminist Legal Theory, edited by Margaret Davies and Vanessa E Munro, 197-215. (Burlington: Ashgate Publishing Company, 2013).

Phoenix, Jo. “Sex, Gender Identity and Criminology.” In Sex and Gender: A Contemporary Reader, edited by Alice Sullivan and Selina Todd, 259-277. (London: Routledge, 2024).

Rydström, Klara, “Degendering Menstruation: Making Trans Menstruators Matter.” In The Palgrave Handbook of Critical Menstruation Studies, edited by C. Bobel, I.T. Winkler, B. Fahs et al., Chapter 68. (Singapore: Palgrave MacMillan, 2020).

Sullivan, Alice, Murray, Kath, and Mackenzie, Lisa. “Why Do We Need Data on Sex?” In Sex and Gender: A Contemporary Reader, edited by Alice Sullivan and Selina Todd, 104-124. (London: Routledge, 2024).

Vaghri, Ziba. “Article 6: The Right to Life, Survival and Development.” In Monitoring State Compliance with the UN Convention on the Rights of the Child. Children’s Well-Being: Indicators and Research, edited by Ziba Vaghri, Jean Zermatten, Gerison Lansdown, Roberta Ruggiero, 31-40. (New York: Springer, 2022).

Journal Articles

Adhikari, Rojita, “Bringing an end to deadly ‘menstrual huts’ is proving difficult in Nepal.” BMJ (February 2020): 368.

Armstrong, John, Sullivan, Alice and Perry, George M. “Performance of Non-Binary Athletes in Mass-Participation Running Events.” BMJ Open Sport & Exercise Medicine, 9 (2023): e001662.

Ashley, Florence. “What is it like to Have a Gender Identity?” Mind, 132 (October 2023):1053-1073.

Bassetti, Matteo. “Human Rights Bodies’ Adjudication of Trans People’s Rights: Shifting the Narrative from the Right to Private Life to Cruel and Inhuman or Degrading Treatment.” European Journal of Legal Studies, 12(2) (2022): 291-325.

Beccalossi, Chiara. "Italian Sexology. Nicola Pende's Biotypology and Hormone Treatment in the 1920s," Médicalisation de la Sexualité, 12 (2017): 73-97.

Bell, Mark. "Gender Identity and Sexual Orientation: Alternative Pathways to EU's Equality Law?" American Journal of Comparative Law, 60 (2012): 127-147.

Berthet, Valentine. "Norm under Fire: Support for and Opposition to the European Union's Ratification of the Istanbul Convention in the European Parliament." International Feminist Journal of Politics, 24(5) (2022): 675-698.

Bettcher, Talia Mae. "Trans Feminism: Recent Philosophical Developments." Philosophy Compass, 12(11) (November 2017): e12438.

Biggs, Michael. "The Dutch Protocol for Juvenile Transsexuals: Origins and Evidence." Journal of Sex and Material Therapy, 49(4) (2023): 348-368.

Brujić, Marija and Krstić, Vladimir. "Sworn Virgins of the Balkan Highlands." Traditiones 50/3 (2021): 113-130.

Camminga, B. "One for One and One for All? Human Rights and Transgender Access to Legal Gender Recognition in Botswana." International Journal of Gender, Sexuality & Law, 1(1) (2020): 241-267.

Carmichael, Polly and Others. "Short-term outcomes of pubertal suppression in a selected cohort of 12 to 15 year old young people with persistent gender dysphoria in the UK." PloSOne, 16(2) (2021): e0243894.

Cellerino, Alessandro, Borghetti, Davide and Sartucci, Ferdinando. "Sex Differences in Face Gender Recognition in Humans." Brain Research Bullettin, 63(6) (July 2004): 443-449.

Cohen-Kettenis, Peggy and van Goozen, S.H.M. "Pubertal Delay as an Aid in the Diagnosis and Treatment of a Transsexual Adolescent." European Child & Adolescent Psychiatry, 7 (1998): 246-248.

Cohen-Kettenis, Peggy. "Die Behandlung von Kindern und Jugendlichen mit Geschlechtsidentitätsstörungen an der Universtät Utrecht." Zeitschrift für Sexualforschung, 7 (1994): 231-239.

Crawford, Lynda. "A Charm School for Transsexuals." TVIC Journal, 6(54) (1977): 2.

Davidson, Caroline. "How to Read International Criminal Law: Strict Construction and the Rome Statute of the International Criminal Court." St John's Law Review, 91(1) (Spring 2017): 37-103.

De Vries, Annelou and Others. "Puberty Suppression in Adolescents with Gender Identity Disorder: a Perspective Follow-up Study." Journal of Sexual Medicine, 8(8) (August 2011): 2276-2283.

Dower, Molly. "Beyond Offense: Why the First Amendment Does Not Protect Deliberate Misgendering," Cardozo Law Review, 44(5) (2023): 2104-2137.

Duffy, Dianne and Otto, Dianne. "Queering Gender [Identity] in International Law." Nordic Journal of Human Rights, 33(4) (2015): 299-318.

Duffy, Dianne. "Contested Subjects of Human Rights: Trans- and Gender-variants Subjects of International Human Rights Law." The Modern Law Review, 84(5) (2021): 1041-1065.

Dunne, Peter. "(Trans)Forming Single-Gender Services and Communal Accommodations." Social & Legal Studies, 26(5) (March 2017): 1-25.

Dunne, Peter. "YY v Turkey: Infertility as a Pre-condition for Gender Confirmation Surgery." Medical Law Review, 23 (4) (2015): 646-658.

Flores, Yolanda. "Science, Context, and Gender Fluidity in Public Policy." Public Integrity, 23(6) (2021): 595-609.

Frye, Phyllis Randolph. "The International Bill of Gender Rights vs. The Cider House Rules: Transgenders Struggle with the Courts Over What Clothing They Are Allowed to Wear on the Job, Which Restroom They are Allowed to Use on the Job, Their Right to Marry, and the Very Definition of Their Sex." William & Mary Journal of Women & Law, 7(1) (2000): 133-212.

Gallo, Alessandra, Abracen, Jeffrey, Looman, Jan and Others. "The Use of Leuprolide Acetate in the Management of High-Risk Sex Offenders." Sex Abuse, 31(8) (December 2019): 930-951.

Gill, Andrèa. "From Binary to Intersectional to Imbricated Approaches: Gender in a Decolonial and Diasporic Perspective." Contexto Internacional, 41(2) (May/August 2019): 275-302.

Giovanardi, Guido. "Buying Time or Arresting Development? The Dilemma of Administering Hormone Blockers in Trans Children and Adolescents." Porto Biomedical Journal, 2(5) (September-October 2017): 153-156.

Gooren, Louis and Delemarre-van de Waal, Henriette. "The Feasibility of Endocrine Interventions in Juvenile Transsexuals," Journal of Psychology and Human Sexuality, 8 (1996): 69-74.

Griffith, Richard. "What is Gillick Competence?" Human Vaccine Immunotherapy, 12(1) (2016): 244-247.

Harry Benjamin International Gender Dysphoria Association. "Standards of Care: The Hormonal and Surgical Sex Reassignment of Gender Dysphoric Persons." Archives of Sexual Behavior, 14 (1985): 79-90.

Hilton, Emma and Lundberg, Tommy. "Transgender Women in the Female Category of Sport: Perspectives on Testosterone Suppression and Performance Advantage." Sports Medicine, 51(2) (February 2021): 199-214.

Hirsch, J.A. and Others. "ICD-10: History and Context." American Journal of Neuroradiology, 37(4) (April 2016): 596-599.

Holtmaat, Rikki and Post, Paul. "Enhancing LGBTI Rights by Changing the Interpretation of the Convention on the Elimination of All Forms of Discrimination Against Women." Nordic Journal of Human Rights, 33(4) (2015): 319-336.

Holzer, Lena. "Legal Gender Recognition in Times of Change at the European Court of Human Rights." ERAForum, 23 (2022): 165-182.

Hunt, David. "The International Criminal Court: High Hopes, 'Creative Ambiguity' and an Unfortunate Mistrust in International Judges." Journal of International Criminal Justice, 2 (2004): 56-70.

Jakobien Liesker, Henriette. "Caught in a Balancing Act. The European Court of Human Rights and the Road to Recognition for Sexual Minorities." Oslo Law Review, 4(3) (2017): 172-194.

Kaltiala-Heino, Riittakerttu, Bergman, Hannah, Työläjrvi, Marja and Frisén, Louise. "Gender Dysphoria in Adolescence: Current Perspectives." Adolescent Health Medical Therapy, 9 (2018): 31-41.

Kamens, Sarah R. "On the Proposed Sexual and Gender Identity Diagnoses for DSM-5: History and Controversies." The Humanistic Psychologist, 39(1) (2011): 37-59.

Kuhlmann, Katrin and Bahri, Amrita, Gender Mainstreaming in Trade Agreements: A Potemkin Façade? Georgetown University Law Center Research Paper No. Forthcoming Making Trade Work for Women: Key Learnings from the World Trade Congress on Gender, Forthcoming (September 2023) Georgetown Law Faculty Publications and Other Works.

Latham, Anthony. "Puberty Blockers for Children: Can They Consent?" The New Bioethics, 28(3) (2022): 268-291.

Lisa Littman, "Parents Reports of Adolescents and Young Adults Perceived to Show Signs of Rapid Onset Gender Dysphoria," PloSOne (August 2018): e0243894.

Loriga, Leandro. "Body Identity Dysphoria and 'Just Amputation:' State of the Art and Beyond." Human Affairs-Postdisciplinary Humanities & Social Sciences Quarterly, 34(1) (2023): 71-93.

Lugones, Marìa. "Heterosexualism and the Colonial/Modern Gender System." Hypatia, 22(1) (Winter 2007): 186-209.

Murray, Kath, Hunter Blackburn, Lucy and Mackenzie, Lisa. "Reform 'Under the Radar'? Lessons for Scotland from the Development of

Gender Self-Declaration Laws in Europe." Edinburgh Law Review, 24(2) (2020): 281-289.

O'Flaherty, Michael. "The Yogyakarta Principles at Ten." Nordic Journal of Human Rights, 33(4) (2015): 280-298.

Oosterveld, Valerie. "The Definition of 'Gender' in the Rome Statute of the International Criminal Court: A Step Forward or Back for International Criminal Justice?" Harvard Human Rights Journal, 18 (2005): 55-84.

Park, Andrew. "Yogyakarta Plus 10: A Demand for Recognition of SOGIESC." North Carolina Journal of International Law, 44 (2019): 223-272.

Prah Ruger, Jennifer. "Normative Foundations of Global Health Law." Georgetown Law Journal, 96(2) (2008): 423-443.

Riggs, Robert E. "Legitimate Expectation and Procedural Fairness in English Law." The American Journal of Comparative Law, 36(3) (Summer 1988): 395-436.

Ruska, Sami-Matti and Others. "All-cause and suicide mortalities among adolescents and young adults who contacted specialised gender identity services in Finland in 1996–2019: a register study." BMJ Mental Health, 27(1) (2024): 3009-3040.

Sandberg, Kirsten. "The Rights of LGBTI Children under the Convention on the Rights of the Child." Nordic Journal of Human Rights, 33(4) (2015): 337-352.

Santarelli, Nicólas Carrillo. "Gender Equality and Non-discrimination of Same Sex Couples." American Journal of International Law, 112(3) (July 2018): 479-485.

Schillace, Brandy. "The Forgotten History of the World's First Trans Clinic." Scientific American, May 10, 2021.

Sigusch, Volkmar."The NeoSexual Revolution." Archives of Sexual Behaviour, 27 (1998): 331-359.

Skidmore, Paul. "Can transsexuals suffer sex discrimination?" Journal of Social Welfare and Family Law, 19 (1997):105 -110.

Smith, Rhona K.M. "Goodwin v. United Kingdom App. No. 28957/95 and I. v. United Kingdom App. No. 25680/94." The American Journal of International Law, 97(3) (July, 2003): 659-664.

Sotos, Charalampos Sotos and Others. "Origins of Gender Affirmation Surgery: The History of the First Gender Identity Clinic in the United States at Johns Hopkins." Annuals of Plastic Surgery, 83(2) (August 2019): 132-136.

Steensma, Thomas and Cohen-Kettenis, Peggy. "Gender Transitioning Before Puberty?" Archives of Sexual Behaviour, 40 (2011): 649-650.

Stoller, Robert J. "The Hermaphrodic Identity of Hermaphrodites." Journal of Nervous and Mental Disease, 139(5) (1964):53-57.

Sullivan, Alice. "Sex and the Office of National Statistics: A Case Study in Policy Capture." The Political Quarterly, 92(4) (June 2021): 638-651.

Symposium "Queering International Law." American Journal of International Law, 116 (2022): 1-37.

Tang, Annie and Others. "Gender-Affirming Mastectomy Trends and Surgical Outcomes in Adolescents." Annals of Plastic Surgery, 88 (May 2022): 325-331.

Turban, Jack and Others. "Pubertal Suppression for Transgender Youth and Risk of Suicidal Ideation." Pediatrics, 145 (2) (2020).

Van der Vleuten, Anna. "Contestations of Transgender Rights and/in the Strasbourg Court." Politics and Governance, 8(3) (2020): 278-289.

Warren, Samuel D. and Brandeis, Louis. "The Right to Privacy." Harvard Law Review, IV(5) (December 1890): 193-220.

Wiepjes, Chantal and Others. "The Amsterdam Cohort of Gender Dysphoria Study (1972-2015): Trends in Prevalence, Treatment, and Regrets." Journal of Sexual Medicine, 15(4) (April 2018): 582-590.

Wilbour, Jane, Morrison, Chloe, Iakavai, Judith and Others. "The Weather is not Good: Exploring the Menstrual Health Experiences of Menstruators with and without Disabilities in Vanuatu." The Lancet, 18 (January 2022).

Wodda, Aimee and Panfil, Vanessa. "Don't Talk to me about Deception: the Necessary Erosion of the Trans* Panic Defense." Albany Law Review, 78(3) (2015): 927-971.

World Professional Association for Transgender Health. Standards of Care for the Health of Transgender and Gender Diverse People, Version 8. International Journal of Transgender Health, 23 (2022): 1:258.

Newspaper, Magazine and News Sites Articles

"Georgia woman says controversial drug led to series of health problems," WSB-TV, October 29, 2018.

"Legal Action May Change Transgender Care in America." The Economist, March 7, 2023.

Barrett, David. "UK's only trans judge quits over risk of 'politicising the judiciary.'" The Times, February 22, 2024.

BBC News. "Bath Spa University 'blocks transgender reserch.'" BBC News, September 25, 2017.

Beale, Charlotte. "Feminists mock Green Party young women's group for invite to 'non-men.'" The Independent, April 17, 2016.

Bindel, Julie and Newman, Melanie. "The trans rights that trump all." The Critic, April 2021.

Booth, Robert. "UN poverty expert hits back over UK ministers' 'denial of facts.'" The Guardian, May 24, 2019.

Brooke, Chris. "Transgender woman footballer quits and threatens to sue for discrimination because rivals refuse to compete against her after she left opponents 'terrified' and broke knee of a player 'blocking her shot'." Mail Online, November 20, 2023.

Brooks, Libby. "Trans woman found guilty of rape moved to men's prison," The Guardian, January 26, 2023.

Chen, Natasha and Mossburg, Cheri. "Riley Gaines, outspoken critic of transgender athletes, says she was attacked during event at SFSU." ABC News, April 8, 2023.

Clark, Malcolm. "All Rise for the 'Female Penis.'" The Critic, February 8, 2023.

Clifton, Helen and Abbott, Melanie. "Female child sex abuse 'remains taboo' while victims struggle." BBC News, January 19, 2021.

Cook, Michael. "Trans narrative under fire in Sweden." BioEdge, May 7, 2022.

Dangerfield, Katie. "Canada's oldest rape crisis centre faces backlash over excluding trans women." Global News, March 19, 2019.

Davey, Melissa. "'Why is it such a scandalous thing?' the women who have to fight for their right to be child-free." The Guardian, June 8, 2021.

Dembroff, Robin and Payton, Dee. "Why We Shouldn't Compare Transracial to Transgender Identity." Boston Review, 18 November 2020.

Dixon, Hayley. "Hospital told police patient was not raped because alleged attacker was transgender." The Telegraph, March 17, 2022.

Emms, Stephen. "Malta: The tiny European island of tolerance." BBC Travel, January 31, 2024.

Esses, James. "Thank you, Nancy Kelley!" The Critic, July 13, 2023.

Forstater, Maya. "Secrets and Lies." The Critic, August 7, 2023.

Fredericks, Siobhan. "Kaleidoscope." Turnabout, Vol 1 No. 2 (October 1963): 28-30.

Gamble, Prof. Jenny and Gribble, Dr. Karleen. "'Inclusive' language on maternity care risks excluding many women." The Guardian, May 6, 2022.

Gannon, Nicola. "I had the wrong soul in the wrong body." The Times, 7 February 1985.

Gentleman, Amelia. "New NHS children's gender clinic hit by disagreements and resignations." The Guardian, January 18, 2024.

Gordon, Tom. "Outcry over plan to educate 'bigoted' rape survivors about trans rights." The Herald, August 12, 2021.

Heuvel, Jon. "Employers must stop asking women whether they plan to have children." The Times, 22 February 2018.

Ingle, Sean. "World Rugby bans trans women from elite women's game due to injury risks." The Guardian. October 10, 2020.

Jackman, Josh. "Pose Star Indya Moore: Trans Women's Penises are Biologically Female." Pink News, February 19, 2019.

Katersky, Aaron. "Female athletes ask to sue over policy allowing transgender athletes to compete in sports." ABC News, June 7, 2023.

Keith, Emma. "The Story Behind Hopeful Billboard at Vacant Detroit Intersection." Detroit Free Press, September 25, 2019.

Kelly, June. "Woman suing rape charity over transgender row." BBC News, June 28, 2022.

Liew, Jonathan. "Why the arguments against trans, intersex and DSD athletes are based on prejudice and ignorance" The Independent, February 22, 2019.

Miller, Andrew Mark. "Feminine product company slammed for referring to customers as 'bleeders.'" Fox Business, March 16, 2022.

Naquian-Wheeler, André. "The first openly trans playboy cover star remembers Hugh Hefner," i.-d.vice.com, October 2, 2017.

Nussbaum, Martha C. "The Professor of Parody." The New Republic, February 22, 1999.

Özkırıml, Umut. "Cancel Culture in Academia." The Critic, 9 September 2023.

PR Newswire. "United States Sex Reassignment Surgery Market Analysis Report 2023: A $5 Billion Market by 2030 - Increasing Prevalence of Gender Dysphoria & Increasing Novel Hormonal Therapies with Better Efficacy." Yahoo/Finance, September 15, 2023.

Shann, Rosalie. "Sex-swap Tula changes her life." News of the World, October 30, 1983.

Sinmaz, Emine. "Trans woman Isla Bryson jailed for eight years for raping two women." The Guardian, February 28, 2023.

Sodha, Sonia. "If a Lesbian Only Desires Same-Sex Dates, That's Not Bigotry, It's Her Right." The Guardian, May 29, 2022.

St. Phélix, Doreen. "The Rachel Divide: A Disturbing Portrait of Dolezal's Racial Fraudulence," The New Yorker, April 26, 2018.

Stephens, Max. "More than 70 Children Aged Three and Four Were Sent to the Tavistock Transgender Clinic." The Telegraph, December 26, 2023.

Theiner, Micha. "Anger over women's business honour for cross-dressing banker." The Times, 22 September 2018.

Tighe, Mark. "Irish gender affirmation surgeon based in Florida is reported over 'false promotions' in TikToks." Irish Independent, October 9, 2022.

Valenti, Jessica. "Transgender people want to exist without having to prove they are 'real.'" The Guardian, June 20, 2014.

Wells, Arnold. "The Fourth Sex!" The National Insider, July 19, 1964.

Website Content

4th Wave Now, "Gender-affirmative therapist: Baby who hates barrettes=trans boy; questioning sterilization of 11-year olds same as denying cancer treatment." 4thwavenow.com, September 29, 2016.

Académie Nationale de Médecine, Medicine and Gender Transidentity in Children and Adolescents, 25 February 2022.

AIDS-Free World, "Inter-American Commission on Human Rights Censures Jamaica for Violating the Rights of LGBTI Citizens," Aids-free World, December 1, 2020.

Amnesty International, "Crimes of hate, conspiracy of silence: Torture and ill-treatment based on sexual identity" (ACT 40/016/2001).

Argawal, Akshat, "Trends in the Legal Uptake of India's Landmark Trans Rights Decision." Oxford Human Rights Hub, April 20, 2022.

Asteriti, Alessandra, "Canaries in the Coalmine." Centre for Crime and Justice Studies, January 30, 2023.

Asteriti, Alessandra, "Three Grades of Evil: Nabokov, Wittgenstein and the Perils of Treaty Interpretation," European Society of International Law, 10th Anniversary Conference, Vienna 4-6 September 2014, Paper 1/2014,

Ausserer, Caroline, "Stephen Whittle: 'The Yogyakarta Principles provide guidance and are a constant reference point.'" Heinrich Böll Stiftung, July 21, 2016.

Australian Human Rights Commission, "Summary of the decision on the exemption's application made by the Lesbian Action Group," October 12, 2023.

Bosenterfer, Rachel, "Haley Cropper–Coronation Street's Trojan Horse." Material Humanism, June 25, 2020.

Çali, Başak and Helfer, Laurence, "The Gender of Treaty Withdrawal: Lessons from the Istanbul Convention." EJIL Talk!, November 28, 2022.

Cass, Hillary, Independent Review of Gender Identity Services for Children and Young People: Final Report, April 2024.

Castagnaro, Giulia, "New Report Confirms Trans Women Do Not Have Any Biomedical Advantage in Elite Sport." Gender GP, March 28, 2023.

Castagnaro, Giulia, "The Office for National Statistics' Sexual Orientation and Gender Identity Census 2021, GenderGP, January 13, 2023.

Clark, Malcolm Richard,"Hirschfeld: The Dodgy High Priest of Quackery." Substack.com, March 16, 2023.

Cohen-Kettenis, Peggy and Kuiper, A.J., "Gender Identity, Gender Roles and Sexual Orientation in Transsexuals," Paper presented at the 8th International Symposium on Gender Dysphoria, Bordeaux 1983.

Council for Choices in Health Care in Finland, "Medical treatment methods for dysphoria associated with variations in gender identity in minors–recommendation," June 16, 2020.

Cunnigham, Naomi, "My body, my choice: privacy, consent and compulsion in personal care," Legal Feminist, July 25, 2020.

Emmanuel, Mickey and Bokor, Brooke R., "Tanner Stages." National Library of Medicine, 2022.

Equality Australia, "Equality Australia welcomes decision to deny exemption to exclude trans women from lesbian event." EqualityAustralia.org.au, October 17, 2023.

Ettelbrick Paula L. and Trabucco Zeràn, Alia, The Impact of the Yogyakarta Principles on International Human Rights Law Development, YogyakartaPrinciples.org, September 10, 2010.

Euronews and AP, "Malta votes to ease total abortion ban but pro-choice groups brand the new law 'a betrayal.'" EuroNews.Health, June 28, 2023.

European Court of Human Rights, "Guide on Article 10 of the European Convention on Human Rights." echr.coe.int., August 31, 2017.

Fair Play for Women, "Fair Play for Women Wins High Court Challenge and Judge Orders Sex Must not Be Self-Identified in the Census." Fairplayforwomen.com, 17 March, 2021.

Gaetano, Phil, "David Reimer and John Money Gender Reassignment Controversy: The John/Joan Case." Embryo Project Encyclopedia, November 15, 2017.

Gershon, Livia,"Gender Identity in Weimar Germany." JSTOR Daily, November 18, 2018.

Ghosh, Sabyasachi. “Triptorelin Market Outlook,”Future Market Insights, April 2023.

Global Philanthropy Project, “Meet the Moment: A Call for Progressive Philanthropic Response to the Anti-Gender Movement, 2020.

Government of Canada, “Trade and Gender in Free Trade Agreements: The Canadian Approach,” June 15, 2023.

Government’s Equalities Office, “Gender Recognition Certificate Fee Reduced,” gov.uk, May 4, 2021.

Harrish, Kevin, “Transgender woman rugby player injures female opponents.” Next Impulse Sports, August 25, 2023.

ILGA Europe, 2023 Annual Review of the Human Rights Situation of Lesbian, Gay, Trans and Intersex People in Europe and Central Asia, February 20, 2023.

ILGA Europe, “O.H. and G.H. against Germany,” ILGA Europe, June 25, 2019.

International Service for Human Rights, “Adrien-Claude Zoller: ISHR Founder,” Ishr.ch, October 30, 2014.

International Service for Human Rights, “LGBTI Rights: UN Special Procedures have increased their engagement with SOGIESC.” ishr.ch., April 5 2022.

Jander, Thomas, “A Licence to Be Different.” Deutsches Historisches Museum Blog, July 23, 2019.

Khalil, Maryam, “Is the testimony of a man equal to that of two women.” Al Islam, January-March 2017.

Khanna, Ashta and Sawnhey, Divesh, “NALSA Judgment: Critique of the Indian Perspective beyond the Adams-and-Eves Worldview.” Georgetown University Undergraduate Law Review Blog, August 25, 2020.

Levey, Eben, “Honduras: Sex workers targeted,” Maryknoll Office for Global Concerns, March-April 2014.

LGBT Youth Scotland, “Good Sex Is (Trans People),” lgbtyouth.org.uk, 2023.

Mykhlalchenko, Olena and Santagostino Recavarren, Isabel, “In 38 countries, women can still be fired for being pregnant.” World Bank Blogs, 31 May 2021.

Petrillo, Madeline, “I’ve the body of a woman but inside I feel like a child.” Centre for Crime and Justice Studies, November 25, 2015.

Phoenix, Jo, “Rights and Wrongs. How Gender Self-Identication Policy Places Women At Risk in Prisons,” MacDonald-Lauriel Institute, 2023.

Prison Reform Trust, "Majority of women in prison have been victims of domestic abuse." prisonreformtrust.org.uk, December 4, 2017.

Proceedings from the Fifth International Conference on Transgender Law and Employment Policy, July 1996.

Public Defender Service, "Specialist prison units for violent or sexual 'Trans women' offenders," March 17, 2023,

Royal Australian and New Zealand College of Psychiatrists, "The role of psychiatrists in working with Trans and Gender Diverse People," December 2023.

Rupert-Gordon, Imani, "Honoring Trans Lesbians During Lesbian Visibility Week." National Center for Lesbian Rights, April 29, 2022.

Second International Congress on Psychiatry, Law and Ethics, "Symposium on Psycholegal Aspects of Sexual Problems" Tel Aviv, 12-16 February 1986.

Sharpe, Alex, "Foxes in the Henhouse: Putting the Trans Women Prison Debate in Perspective." Warwick Research Archive Portal, September 11, 2018.

Shaw, Diana, "Transgender Inmate in Prison for Rape of Young Girls is Accused of Sexual Assaults on Female Inmates." Women Are Human, June 1, 2018.

Society for Evidence Based Gemder Medicine, "Sweden's Karolinska Ends All Use of Puberty Blockers and Cross-Sex Hormones for Minors Outside of Clinical Studies," May 5, 2021,

Society for Evidence Based Gemder Medicine, "Summary of Key Recommendations from the Swedish National Board of Health and Welfare," February 27, 2022.

Society for Evidence Based Gender Medicine, "Denmark Joins the List of Countries That Have Sharply Restricted Youth Gender Transitions," August 17, 2023,

Society for Evidence Based Gender Medicine, "The World Health Organization Announces Transgender Guidelines Plan." December 26, 2023.

TGEU, "Trans Man's Legal Gender Recognition Case in Romania is Referred to the CJEU." tgeu.org, March 3, 2023.

Transgender Trend, "Helen: a severely learning-disabled girl: sex-based rights under threat." transgendertrend.com, July 10, 2022.

Transgender Trend, "The Surge in Referral Rates of Girls to the Tavistock Continues to Rise." transgendertrend.com, July 1, 2019.

Transgender Trend, "What Questions Should a School be Asking about Mermaids Training for Families?" September 9, 2019.

Whisenhunt, Dan, "Department of Education can't substantiate assault in Oakhurst bathroom, finds Title IX violations." decaturish.com, June 23, 2020.

Whittle Stephen, Turner, Lewis and Al-Alami Maryam, "Engendered Penalties: Transgender and Transsexual People's Experiences of Inequality and Discrimination," ILGA Europe (2007).

Women Are Human, Transgender detainee who impregnated fellow inmate is released from prison," womenarehuman.com, November 28, 2019.

World Economic Forum, "Global Gender Gap Report," 2020.

World Health Organization, "Eliminating forced, coercive and otherwise involuntary sterilization," 2014.

World Health Organization, "Every woman, every child: strengthening equity and dignity through health," January 1, 2013.

World Health Organization, "The WHO announces the development of a guideline on the health of trans and gender diverse people." WHO News, December 18, 2023.

World Health Organization, Adolescent Health, 11 October, 2023.

World Health Organization, International Classification of Diseases 11th Revision (2024).

Zagria, "A Gender Variance Who's Who, 'Siobhan Fredericks (193?-?) scientist, activist.'" Zagria's Blogspot, 13 October 2012.

Zelada, Carlos J., "Vicky Hernández et al. Honduras: A Landmark Victory with a Bitter Aftertaste." EJIL: Talk!, 27 August, 2021.

International Court Cases

European Court of Human Rights

A.D. and Others v Georgia, Application Nos. 57864/17, 79087/17 and 55353/19. Judgment of 1 December 2022.

A.P., Garçon and Nicot v France, Application Nos. 79885/12, 52471/12, and 52596/13, Judgment of 6 April 2017.

B. v France, Merits, Application No. 13343/87, A/232-C, Judgment of 25 March 1992.

Charlie Gard and Others v UK, Application No. 39793/17, Judgment of 13 June 2017.

Christine Goodwin v the United Kingdom, Application No. 28957/95, Judgment of 11 July 2002.

Cossey v the United Kingdom, Application No. 10843/84, Judgment of 27 September 1990.

Grant v the United Kingdom, Application No. 32570/03, Judgment of 23 May 2006.

Handyside v United Kingdom, Application No. 5493/72, Judgment of 7 December 1976.

Identoba and Others v Georgia, Application No. 73235/12, Judgment of 12 May 2015.

L. v Lithuania, Application No. 27527/03, Decision on Admissibility of 6 July 2006.

M. v France, Application No. 42821/18, Decision of 26 April 2022.

O.H. and G.H. v Germany, Application Nos. 53568/18 and 54741/18, Judgment of 4 April 2023.

Ratzenböck and Seydl v Austria, Application No. 28475/12, Judgment of 26 October 2017.

Rees v the United Kingdom, Application No. 9532/81, Judgment of 17 October 1986.

S.V. v Italy, Application No. 55216/08, Judgment of 11 October 2018.

Schlumpf v Switzerland, Application No.29002/06, Judgment of 8 January 2009.

Sheffield and Horsham v the United Kingdom, Application Nos. 31–32/1997/815–816/1018–1019, Judgment of 30 July 1998.

Van Kück v Germany, Application No. 35968/97, Judgment of 18 October 2001.

X. and Y. v Romania, Application Nos. 2145/16 and 20607/16, Judgment of 19 January 2021.

X., Y., and Z. v the United Kingdom, Application No. 21830/93, Judgment of 22 April 1997.

Y. v Poland, Application No. 74131/14, Judgment of 17 May, 2022.

Y.Y. v Turkey, Application No. 14793/08, Judgment of 10 March 2015.

European Court of Justice/Court of Justice of the European Union

F. v Bevándorlási és Állampolgársági Hivatal, Judgment of 25 January 2018, C-473/16.

K.B. v National Health Service Pensions Agency and Secretary of State for Health, Judgment of 7 January 2004, C-117/01.

M.B. v Secretary of State for Work and Pensions, Judgment of 26 June 2018, C-451/16.

Mirin, Case C4/23, Opinion of Advocate General Richard de la Tour, 7 May 2004.

P. v S. and Cornwall County Council, Judgment of 30 April 1996, C-13/94.

Sarah Margaret Richards v Secretary of State for Work and Pensions, Judgment of 27 April 2006, C-423/04.

Inter-American Court of Human Rights and Inter-American Commission of Human Rights

Advisory Opinion of 24 November 2017, OC-24/17.

Advisory Opinion of 30 May 2022, OC-29/22.

Case of Atala Riffo and Daughters v Chile, Judgment of 24 February 2012.

Report No 401/20, Case 13.095, *T.B. and S.H. v Jamaica*, OEA/Ser.L/V/II Doc 419 December 31, 2020.

Vicky Hernández et al v Honduras, Judgment of March 26, 2021.

African Court and Commission of Human and People's Rights

Compatibility of Vagrancy Laws with the African Charter on Human and Peoples' Rights and Other Human Rights Instruments Applicable in Africa, African Court on Human and Peoples' Rights, 40 December 2020, No. 001/2018.

Resolution on Protection against Violence and other Human Rights Violations against Persons on the basis of their real or imputed Sexual Orientation or Gender Identity, 12 May 2014, ACHPR/Res.275 (LV) 2014,

International Court of Justice

Application of the International Convention on the Elimination of All Forms of Racial Discrimination (Qatar v United Arab Emirates), Preliminary Objections, Judgment, I.C.J. Reports 2021, p. 71.

North Sea Continental Shelf, Judgment, I.C.J. Reports 1969, p. 3.

International Criminal Court

The Prosecutor v Jean-Pierre Bemba Gombo and Others, ICC-01/05-01/13.

The Prosecutor v Jean-Pierre Bemba Gombo, ICC-01/05-01/08.

UN Treaty Bodies Decisions

A.B. v Finland, CRC/C/86/D/51/2018.
A.S. v Denmark, CEDAW/C/69/D/80/2015.
Alekseev v Russian Fed., CCPR/C/130/D/2757/2016.
C. v Australia, CCPR/C/119/D/221672012.
E.A. v Sweden, CCPR/C/61/D/690/2015.
Fedotova v Russian Fed., CCPR/C/106/D/1932/2010.
Flamer Caldera v Sri Lanka, CEDAW/C/81/D/134/2018.
G. v Australia, CCPR/C/119/D/2172/2012.
G.H. v Hungary, CEDAW/C/76/D/114/2017.
H.G. v Sweden, CCPR/C/132/D/3266/2018.
H.R.E.S v Switzerland, CAT/C/64/D/783/2016.
H.S. v Denmark, CAT/C/71/D/792/2016.
Ivanov v Russian Fed., CCPR/C/131/D/2635/2015.
J.K. v Canada, CCPR/C/56/D/562/2013.
J.R.R, L.A.A. v Denmark, CCPR/C/132/D/2787/2016.
Joyce Nakato Nakawunde v Canada, CCPR/C/64/D/615/2014.
K.K. v Russian Fed., CEDAW/C/721/D/98/2016.
Kirill Nepomnyashchiy v Russian Fed., CCPR/C/123/D/2318/2013.
Lourdes da Silva Pimentel v Brazil, CEDAW/C/49/D/17/2008.
M.B. v Canada, CCPR/C/128/D/2957/2017.
M.I. v Sweden, CCPR/C/108/D/2149/2012.
M.I. v Sweden, CCPR/C/108/D/2149/2012.
M.K.H. v Denmark, CCPR/C/107/D/2462/2014.
M.Z.B.M. v Denmark, CCPR/C/119/D/2593/2015.
Mikhailova et al. v Russian Fed., CCPR/C/134/D/2943/2017.
P.S. v Canada, CATC/72/D/1000/2020.
R.M. and F.M. v Denmark, CCPR/C/126/D/2685/2015.
S.A.O. v Denmark, CEDAW/C/71/D/101/2016.
S.B. and M.B. v North Macedonia, CEDAW/C/77/D/143/2019.
Savolaynen v Russian Fed., CCPR/C/135/D/2830/2016.
Uttam Mondal v Sweden, CAT/C/46/D/338/2008.
X. v Afghanistan, Sweden, CCPR/C/103/D/1833/2008.

Domestic Court Cases

United Kingdom

A.B. and C.D., [2021] EWHC 741 (Fam).
A.B. v C.D. [2021] EWHC 741 (Fam).

Bellinger v Bellinger [2003] UKHL 21.
C.C. v K.K. and S.T.C.C. [2012] COPLR 627;
Corbett v Corbett [1970] 2 All ER 33.
Gillick v West Norfolk and Wisbeck Health Authority [1985] 3 All ER 402.
Grainger plc v Nicholson [2010] RLR4 (EAT).
H. v A Local Authority [2011] EWHC 1704.
In re A. (Adoption: Agreement:Procedure) [2001] 2 FLR 455.
In Re Z. (A Minor) (Freedom of Publication) [1997] Fam 1.
In the matter of E. (A Child) (Medical Treatment) [2016] EWHC 2267.
Joanna Phoenix v The Open University Employment Tribunal, Case No.: 3322700/2021 & 3323841/2021, Judgment of 22 January 2024.
Katherine Elizabeth Scottow v Crown Prosecution Service [2020] EWHC 3421 (Admin), 16 December 2020.
L. (Medical Treatment: Gillick Competency) [1998] 2 F.L.R. 810.
L.B.L. v R.Y.J. and V.J. [2011] 1 FLR 1279.
Masterman-Lister v Brutton & Co (Nos. 1 and 2) [2003] 1 WLR 1511.
Maya Forstater v CGD Europe, Center for Global Development and Masood Ahmed, UKEAT/0105/20/JOJ, 10 June 2021.
Maya Forstater v CGD Europe, Centre for Global Development, and Masood Ahmed, Case Number: 2200909/2019.
Montgomery v Lancashire Health Board [2015] UKSC 11.
NHS Trust v Y. (Intensive Care Society Intervening) [2019] AC 978.
Opinion of Lady Haldane in Petition of For Women Scotland Limited for Judicial Review of the Revised Statutory Guidance Produced by the Scottish Ministers under S7 of the Gender Representation on Public Boards (Scotland) Act 2018, [2022] CSOH 90.
Opinion of Lady Haldane in Petition of For Women Scotland Limited for Judicial Review of the Revised Statutory Guidance Produced by the Scottish Ministers under S7 of the Gender Representation on Public Boards (Scotland) Act 2018 [2023] CSIH 37.
Opinion of the Court delivered by Lady Dorrian, in the Reclaiming Motion by For Women Scotland Limited, against the Lord Advocate, the Scottish Ministers [2022] CSIH 4.
Portsmouth NHS Trust v Wyatt [2005] 1 FLR 652;
Quincy Bell and Mrs. A. v The Tavistock and Portman NHS Foundation Trust [2020] EWHC 3274 (Admin).
Quincy Bell and Mrs. A. v The Tavistock and Portman NHS Foundation Trust [2021] EWCA Civ 1363.
R. (Axon) v Secretary of State for Health (Family Planning Association Intervening) [2006] QB 539.

R. (On the Application of T.T. v The Registrar General for England and Wales and Others [2019] EWHC 2384 (Fam).

Re Ashya King [2014] EWHC 2964 (Fam).

Re B. (A Minor) (Wardship Sterilisation) [1987] 2 All ER 206.

Re D. (A Minor) (Wardship Sterilisation) [1976] 1 All ER 326.

Re E. (A Minor) (Medical Treatment) [1991] 2 FLR 585.

Re G.F. (Medical Treatment) [1992] 1 FLR 293.

Re R. (A Minor) (Wardship Consent to Treatment) [1992] Fam 11.

Re S. (A Child) (Child Parent: Adoption Consent) [2019] 2 Fam 177.

Re S. (Sterilisation Patient's Best Interests) [2000] 2 FLR 389.

Re W. (A Minor) Medical Treatment Courts Jurisdiction) [1993] Fam 64

Shamoon v Chief Constable of the Royal Ulster Constabulary [2003] ICR 337 HL.

Sheffield City Council v E. [2005] Fam 326.

The Queen (on the application of (1) Alfred McConnell, (2) Y.Y. (by his litigation friend Claire Brooks)) and The Registrar General for England and Wales and (1) Secretary of State for Health and Social Care; (2) Minister for Women and Equalities; (3) Secretary of State for the Home Department and The Aire Centre [2020] EWCA Civ 559.

The Queen on the Application of FDJ and Secretary of State for Justice [2021] EWHC 1764 (Admn).

The Queen on the Application of Harry Miller and the College of Policing, [2020] EWHC 225 (Admin).

France

Madame C. v Madame N., Cour d'Appel de Toulouse, 9 February 2022, Case No. 16/04/2022, No. RG 20/03128.

United States/Canada

Ayala v American Academy of Pediatrics and Others, Superior Court of Rhode Island 23 October 2023.

M. v M. (A) (1984) 42 RFL (2d) 267.

M.T. v J.T., Superior Court of New Jersey, Appellate Division, United States (22 March 1976).

Mosley v Emerson and Others, Superior Court of North Carolina on 23 July 2023.

Kenya

Republic v Kenya National Examination Council & Another Ex Parte Audrey Mbugua Ithibu, High Court, Judicial Review Division, [2014] eKLR.

Botswana

Letsweletse Motshidiemang v Attorney General, First Instance Court, 28 June 2019, MAHGB-000591-16

N.D. v Attorney General of Botswana and Registrar of National Registration, High Court, 29 September 2017, MAHGB-000449-15.

National Legal Services Authority v Union of India and Others, Civil Original Jurisdiction Writ Petition (Civil) No. 400 of 2012; Writ Petition (Civil) No. 604 of 2013).

South Africa

W. v W. (1976) (2) SALR 308.

India

National Legal Services Authority v Union of India (NALSA) and Others, Civil Original Jurisdiction Writ Petition (Civil) No. 400 of 2012; Writ Petition (Civil) No. 604 of 2013).

Malasya

J.G. v Pengarah Jabatan Pendaftaran Negara, CLJ Bulletin 41/2005.

Pakistan

Dr. Mohammad Aslam Khaki and Others v S.S.P. (Operations) Rawalpindi and Others, Constitutional Petition 43 of 2009, PLD 2013 S.C. 88.

Nepal

Sunil Babu Pant and Others v Nepal Government, Writ Petition No. 917 of 2007 and *Sunil Babu Pant and Others/ v Nepal Government and Others*, Supreme Court of Nepal (21 December 2007).

Australia/New Zealand

Attorney-General for the Commonwealth v Kevin and Jennifer [2003] FamCA 94 (21 February 2003).

Attorney-General v Otahuhu Family Court [1995] 1 NZLR 603).

Australia Re Kevin (validity of marriage of transsexual) [2001] Fam CA 1074).

UK and Scottish Parliament Reports

Alice Sullivan, "Submission of 27 August 2021," Scottish Parliament' Citizen Participation and Public Petitions Committee.

Gender Recognition Bill HL, Volume 655: debated on Thursday 18 December 2003.

Gender Recognition Bill HL, Volume 655: debated on Thursday 27 November 2003.

Gender Recognition Bill HL, Volume 655: debated on Thursday 8 January 2004.

Gender Recognition Bill, Volume 418: debated on Monday 23 February 2004.

Scottish Parliament, Equalities, Human Rights and Civil Justice Committee, Official Report of Monday 19 December 2022.

UK Parliament, Dr. Nicola Williams, "Written Evidence from Fair Play for Women," PPP0011, December 2017.

UN Reports and Documents

CAT Committee, General Comment No. 2 (24 January 2008) CAT/C/GC/2.

CEDAW Committee, General recommendation No. 28 (16 December 2010) CEDAW/C/GC/28.

CEDAW Committee, General Recommendation No. 37 (13 March 2018) CEDAW/C/GC/37.

CEDAW Committee, General recommendation No. 39 (26 October 2022) CEDAW/C/GC/39.

Commission of Human Rights, Sixtieth Session, List of Attendance (22 April 2004) E/CN.4/2004/INF.1.

CRC Committee, General Comment No. 13 (18 April 2011) CRC/C/GC/13.

CRC Committee, General Comment No. 15 (17 April 2013) CRC/C/GC/15.

CRC Committee, General Comment No. 20 (6 December 2016) CRC/C/GC/20.

CRC Committee, General comment No. 21 (20 June 2017) CRC/C/GC/21.

CRC Committee, General comment No. 25 (2 March 2021) CRC/C/GC/25.

CRC Committee, Joint general comment No. 3 of the Committee on the Protection of the Rights of All Migrant Workers and Members of Their Families and No. 22 of the Committee on the Rights of the Child (16 November 2017) CMW/C/GC/3-CRC/C/GC/22.

CRC Committee, Joint general comment No. 4 of the Committee on the Protection of the Rights of All Migrant Workers and Members of Their Families and No. 23 of the Committee on the Rights of the Child (16 November 2017) CMW/C/GC/4-CRC/C/GC/23.

Department of Economic and Social Affairs, Population and Development. Programme of Action adopted at the International Conference on Population and Development (5-13 September 1994) ST/ESA/SER.A/149.

ECOSOC, Introduction of the United Nations Legal Identity Agenda: a holistic approach to civil registration, vital statistics and identity management: report of the Secretary General (18 December 2019) E/CN.3/2020/15.

Joint written statement submitted by Action Canada for Population and Development (ACPD), Canadian HIV/AIDS Legal Network, Centre for Women's Global Leadership (Global Center, CWGL), Global Rights, International Service for Human Rights (ISHR), International Women's Health Coalition (IWHC) and New Ways: Women for Women's Human Rights [The promise of the Human Rights Council: Marginalised groups, sexual orientation and gender identity], A/HRC/1/NGO/47 of 28 June 2006.

HRC, Concluding observations on the seventh periodic report of the Russian Federation (28 April 2015) CCPR/C/RUS/CO/7.

HRC, Concluding observations on the third periodic report of Kuwait (11 August 2016) CCPR/C/KWT/CO/3.

HRC, Report of the Special Rapporteur on the Right to Privacy (24 March 2020) A/HRC/43/52.

HRC, Report of the Working Group on Arbitrary Detention (30 June 2014) A/HRC/27/47.

HRC, Resolution 32/2 (15 July 2016) A/HRC/RES/32/2

HRC, Resolution 17/19 (14 July 2011) A/HRC/RES/17/19.

HRC, Resolution 27/32 (2 October 2014) A/HRC/RES/27/32.

HRC, Resolution 8/11 (18 June 2011) A/HRC/RES/8/11.
HRC, Third Regular Session, Compilation of Statements by Amnesty International (November-December 2006) IOR/41/034/2006.
ICESCR Committee, General Comment No. 20 (2 July 2009) E/C.12/GC/20.
ICESCR Committee, General Comment No. 22 (2 May 2016) E/C.12/GC/22.
OHCHR, Born Free and Equal (2019) HR/PUB/12/06/Rev.1.
OHCHR, Discriminatory Laws and Practices and Acts of Violence against Individuals Based on their Sexual Orientation and Gender Identity (2011) A/HRC/19/41.
OHCHR, Living Free and Equal (2016) HR/PUB/16/3.
OHCHR, Resolution 17/19 (17 June 2011) A/HRC/RES/17/19.
OHCHR, Update of Report A/HRC/19/41 (4 May 2015) A/HRC/29/23.
OHCHR; Report Discrimination and violence against individuals based on their sexual orientation and gender identity (4 May 2015) A/HRC/29/23.
Permanent Representative of the United States to the United Nations, Letter to the Secretary General of the UN (18 March 2009) A/63/778.
Permanent Representatives of Argentina, Brazil, Croatia, France, Gabon, Japan, the Netherlands and Norway to the United Nations, Letter addressed to the President of the General Assembly (18 December 2008) A/63/635.
Preparatory Committee on the Establishment of an International Criminal Court, Report of the Inter-sessional Meeting from 19 to 30 January 1998 in Zutphen, The Netherlands, A/AC.249/1998/L.13.
Report of the Independent Expert on protection against violence and discrimination based on sexual orientation and gender identity, Protection against Violence and Discrimination Based on Sexual Orientation and Gender Identity (25 July 2023) A/78/227.
Report of the Independent Expert on protection against violence and discrimination based on sexual orientation and gender identity, The Law of Inclusion (3 June 2021) A/HRC/47/27.
Report of the Independent Expert on protection against violence and discrimination based on sexual orientation and gender identity, Visit to Georgia (15 May 2019) A/HRC/41/45/Add 1.
Report of the Independent Expert on protection against violence and discrimination based on sexual orientation and gender identity, Practices of Exclusion (15 July 2021) A/76/152.
Report of the Special Rapporteur on the human right to safe drinking water and sanitation (27 July 2016) A/HRC/33/49.

Report of the Special Rapporteur on the Right of Everyone to the Enjoyment of the Highest Attainable Standard of Physical and Mental Health (27 April 2010) A/HRC/14/20.

Report of the Special Rapporteur on the right of everyone to the enjoyment of the highest attainable standard of physical and mental health Dainius Puras–Addendum–Visit to Malaysia (19 November–2 December 2014, 30 April 2015) A/HRC/29/33/Add.1.

Report of the Special Rapporteur on torture and other cruel, inhuman and degrading treatment or punishment (1 February 2013) A/HRC/22/53.

Report of the United Nations High Commissioner for Human Rights, Discriminatory laws and practices and acts of violence against individuals based on their sexual orientation and gender identity (17 November 2011) A/HRC/19/41.

UN Fact Sheet, Violence Against Women and Girls with Disabilities (February 2013).

UN Women, Beijing Declaration and Platform for Action, United Nations (1995).

UN Women, Strategic Plan 2022-2025 (12 July 2021) UNW/2021/6.

UNGA Resolution 60/251, Human Rights Council (15 March 2006) A/RES/60/251.

UNGA Third Committee, Strengthening the role of the United Nations in the promotion of democratization and enhancing periodic and genuine elections (31 October 2023) A/C.3/78/L.51.

UNGA, Report of the Special Rapporteur on the promotion and protection of human rights and fundamental freedoms while countering terrorism (3 August 2009) A/64/211.

UNGA, Resolution 69/182 Extrajudicial, summary or arbitrary executions (30 January 2015) S/RES/69/182.

UNGA, United Nations Rules for the Treatment of Women Prisoners and Non-custodial Measures for Women Offenders with their Commentary (Bangkok Rules) (21 December 2010).

UNGA, United Nations Standard Minimum Rules for the Treatment of Prisoners (Nelson Mandela Rules) (17 December 2015).

UNHCR and UNICEF, Background Note on Sex Discrimination and Birth Registration (6 July 2021).

UNHCR, UNHCR Guidance Note on Refugee Claims Relating to Sexual Orientation and Gender Identity (21 November 2008).

United Nations, Gender Mainstreaming: An Overview (New York: United Nations Publications, 2002).

World Conference on Human Rights in Vienna, Vienna Declaration and Programme of Action (25 June 1993).

COE Reports and Documents

Ad Hoc Committee on Preventing and Combating Violence against Women and Domestic Violence, Report of the 3rd Meeting (16 April 2010) CAHVIO (2009) 34 Rev.

Commissioner for Human Rights (27 May 2019) ICD11 is a Stride toward Depathologisation of Trans People, but more is needed.

Commissioner for Human Rights, Human Rights and Gender Identity, CommDH/IssuePaper (2009)2.

Commissioner for Human Rights, Proceedings of the Roundtable "Human Rights of LGBTI People in Europe: Current Threats to Equal Rights, Challenges Faced by Defenders, and the Way Forward" (8 December 2021) CommDH(2021)32.

Commissioner of Human Rights, Discrimination on grounds of sexual orientation and gender identity in Europe, Council of Europe Publishing (June 2011).

Council of Europe Newsroom, Ending misconceptions about the Convention on Preventing and Combating Violence against Women and Domestic Violence, News 2018, 22 November 2018.

Council of Europe Newsroom, The Russian Federation is excluded from the Council of Europe, March 16, 2022.

Ministers' Deputies Decisions, 863rd (DH) Meeting 2 and 3 December 2003, CM/Del/Dec (2003)863.

Parliamentary Assembly, Committee on Equality and Non-Discrimination, Combating Rising Hate against LGBTI People in Europe (September 2020) Doc. 15121 Ref. 4524.

Parliamentary Assembly, Condition of Transsexuals (29 September 1989) Recommendation 1117.

Parliamentary Assembly, Discrimination against transgender people in Europe (22 April 2015) Resolution 2048.

Parliamentary Assembly, Discrimination on the basis of sexual orientation and gender identity (29 April 2010) Resolution 1728.

Parliamentary Assembly, Private and family life: achieving equality regardless of sexual orientation (10 October 2018) Resolution 2239.

Parliamentary Assembly, Putting an end to coerced sterilisations and castrations (26 June 2013) Resolution 1945.

Steering Committee for Equality between Men and Women, 18th Meeting, Strasbourg, 21-23 April 1999, CM/99/82.

Steering Committee for Human Rights: Report on the implementation of Recommendation CM/Rec (2010)5 of the Committee of Ministers to member States (21 March 2013) CDDH(2013)R77 Add.VI.

Steering Committee on Anti-Discrimination, Diversity and Inclusion, Thematic Report on Legal Gender Recognition in Europe on the Implementation of CM/Rec(2010)5 (June 2022).

Steering Committee on Anti-discrimination, Diversity and Inclusion, Thematic Report on Legal Gender Recognition CM/Rec (2010) 5

XXXIII Colloquy on European Law on the topic "Transsexualism, Medicine and Law" (Strasbourg: Council of Europe, 1995)

EU Reports and Documents

Communication from the Commission to the European Parliament, the Council, the European Economic and Social Committee and the Committees of the Regions, "Union of Equality: LGBTIQ Equality Strategy 2020-2025," COM 2020/698 final,

Council Directive of 9 February 1976 on the implementation of the principle of equal treatment for men and women as regards access to employment, vocational training and promotion, and working conditions, O.J. 1976 L 39, p. 40.

Directive 2006/54/EC of the European Parliament and of the Council of 5 July 2006 on the implementation of the principle of equal opportunities and equal treatment of men and women in matters of employment and occupation (recast) (26 July 2006) OJ L 204.

Directorate General for Internal Policies, Cristina Castagnoli, "Transgender Persons' Rights in the EU Member States," 2010,

Directorate General for Justice and Consumers, "Legal gender recognition in the EU," (June 2020.

EP Committee on Equality and Non-Discrimination, Combating Rising Hate against LGBTI People in Europe, Doc 15121 Ref 4524 (September 2020).

European Commission, Legal Gender Recognition in the EU: The Journeys of Trans People Towards Full Equality (2020).

European Parliament, Resolution on Discrimination Against Transsexuals, Doc. A 3-16/89, OJ C 256, 9.10.1989.

European Union Agency for Fundamental Rights, "A Long Way to Go for LGBTI Equality," 2020.

European Union Agency for Fundamental Rights, Access to sex reassignment surgery, October 19, 2018,

European Union Agency for Fundamental Rights, Access to Transgender Hormone Therapy, October 19, 2018,

European Union Agency for Fundamental Rights, Homophobia and Discrimination on the Grounds of Sexual Orientation in the EU Member States: Part I – Legal Analysis' (2009).
Marjolein van den Brink and Peter Dunn, Transsex and Intersex Equality Rights in Europe–A Comparative Analysis, European Commission (2018).
Stephen Whittle, "Gender Identity Discrimination," Paper presented at the European Commission conference, Legal seminar on the Implementation of EU law on Equal Opportunities and Anti-Discrimination, Brussels, October 6, 2009.

International Legal Instruments

African Charter on Human and People's Rights, 27 June 1981, 1520 UNTS 26363.
Convention against Torture and Other Cruel, Inhuman or Degrading Treeatment or Punishment, 10 December 1984, 1465 UNTS 85.
Convention on the Elimination of All Forms of Discrimination against Women, 18 December 1979, 1249 UNTS 13.
Convention on the Prevention and Punishment of the Crime of Genocide, 9 December 1948, 78 UNTS 277.
Convention on the Prevention, Punishment and Eradication of Violence against Women, 5 March 1995, 33 I.L.M. 1534 (1994).
Convention on the Rights of Persons with Disabilities, 13 December 2006, 2515 UNTS 3.
Convention on the Rights of the Child, 20 November 1989, 1577 UNTS 3.
Council of Europe Convention on Preventing and Combating Violence against Women and Domestic Violence, 11 May 2011, 3010 UNTS 52313.
European Convention for Human Rights: Convention for the Protection of Human Rights and Fundamental Freedoms, 3 September 1953, 213 UNTS 221.
Geneva Convention Relative to the Treatment of Prisoners of War, 75 UNTS 972 of 12 August 1949.
International Convention for the Protection of All Persons from Enforced Disappearance, 20 December 2006, 2716 UNTS 3.
International Convention on the Elimination of All Forms of Racial Discrimination, 7 March 1966, 660 UNTS 195.
International Convention on the Protection of the Rights of All Migrant Workers and Members of Their Family, 18 December 1990, 2220 UNTS 3.

International Covenant on Civil and Political Rights, 16 December 1966, 999 UNTS 171.
International Covenant on Economic, Social and Cultural Rights, 16 December 1966, 993 UNTS 3.
Rome Statute of the International Criminal Court, 2187 UNTS I-38544.